Security and Privacy Issues for IoT and WSN-based Real-time Applications

This book explores the security and privacy challenges associated with real-time applications of the Internet of Things (IoT) and wireless sensor networks (WSN) technologies. It provides detailed insights into the unique security and privacy concerns, such as malicious attacks, data breaches, insider threats, and privacy breaches, that arise in the context of real-time applications, like in smart homes, smart cities, industrial automation, healthcare, and other time-sensitive domains to offer practical solutions and strategies to mitigate these risks.

- Covers various aspects of security and privacy, including authentication, access control, data integrity, confidentiality, availability, threat detection and mitigation, privacy-preserving techniques.
- Investigates the possibilities of cross-layer approaches to address the specific requirements of real-time applications and develop innovative solutions.
- Gaining insights into fundamental limits through information-theoretic research, new protocol designs are developed to access the medium in an energy-efficient manner to improve the performance and reliability of WSN and IoT networks for real-time applications.
- Discusses the sustainable requirements of emerging real-time applications, such as low energy consumption and high data rates.
- Offers an interdisciplinary approach that encompasses areas of communication, networking, and information theory to guide real-life deployment of IoT/WSN-based monitoring systems.

It is a valuable reference for readers who want to gain a deeper understanding of the challenges and solutions related to the security and privacy of IoT and WSN in the context of real-time applications.

Chapman & Hall/CRC Cyber-Physical Systems

SERIES EDITORS:

Jyotir Moy Chatterjee
Lord Buddha Education Foundation, Kathmandu, Nepal

Vishal Jain
Sharda University, Greater Noida, India

Cyber-Physical Systems: A Comprehensive Guide
By: Nonita Sharma, L K Awasthi, Monika Mangla, K P Sharma, Rohit Kumar

Introduction to the Cyber Ranges
By: Bishwajeet Pandey and Shabeer Ahmad

Security Analytics: A Data Centric Approach to Information Security
By: Mehak Khurana & Shilpa Mahajan

Security and Resilience of Cyber Physical Systems
By: Krishan Kumar, Sunny Behal, Abhinav Bhandari and Sajal Bhatia

Cyber Security Applications for Industry 4.0
By: R Sujatha, G Prakash, Noor Zaman Jhanjhi

Cyber Physical Systems: Concepts and Applications
By: Anupam Baliyan, Kuldeep Singh Kaswan, Naresh Kumar, Kamal Upreti and Ramani Kannan

Intelligent Security Solutions for Cyber-Physical Systems
By: Vandana Mohindru Sood, Yashwant Singh, Bharat Bhargava and Sushil Kumar Narang

Federated Learning for Smart Communications using IoT Application
By: Kaushal Kishor, Parma Nand, Vishal Jain, Neetesh Saxena, Gaurav Agarwal, Rani Astya

Security and Privacy Issues for IoT and WSN-based Real-time Applications
By: Manoj Tolani, Arun Balodi, Ambar Bajpai, Vishal Jain, Piya Kovintave*wat*

For more information on this series please visit: www.routledge.com/Chapman--HallCRC-Cyber-Physical-Systems/book-series/CHCPS?pd=published,forthcoming&pg=1&pp=12&so=pub&view=list?pd=published,forthcoming&pg=1&pp=12&so=pub&view=list

Security and Privacy Issues for IoT and WSN-based Real-time Applications

Edited by
Manoj Tolani, Arun Balodi, Ambar Bajpai,
Vishal Jain and Piya Kovintavewat

CRC Press
Taylor & Francis Group
Boca Raton London New York

CRC Press is an imprint of the
Taylor & Francis Group, an **informa** business

First edition published 2025
by CRC Press
2385 NW Executive Center Drive, Suite 320, Boca Raton FL 33431

and by CRC Press
4 Park Square, Milton Park, Abingdon, Oxon, OX14 4RN

CRC Press is an imprint of Taylor & Francis Group, LLC

ISBN: 9781032776682 (hbk)
ISBN: 9781032794303 (pbk)
ISBN: 9781003491910 (ebk)

DOI: 10.1201/9781003491910

Typeset in Times
by Newgen Publishing UK

Contents

About the Editors

Manoj Tolani earned a B.Tech from IIMT Engineering College, Meerut, India, in 2010, an M.Tech from Madan Mohan Malviya University of Technology, Gorakhpur, India, in 2012 from the Department of Electronics and Communication Engineering. He earned his Ph.D. from the Department of Electronics and Communication Engineering, Indian Institute of Information Technology Allahabad, India. He was an Assistant Professor at PSIT College of Engineering, Kanpur, from 2012 to 2015. He was engaged as a teaching cum research associate (TRA) in the Department of ECE, IIIT-Allahabad, in 2020. Later he was at the Atria Institute of Technology, Bangalore, as Assistant Professor (Research) from 2021 to 2023. Currently, he is an Assistant Professor at Manipal Institute of Technology, Manipal Academy of Higher Educations, Manipal Campus. His research interests include wireless sensor network, Internet of Things, and photonics. He has published 33 journal and conference papers (23 Science Citation Index (SCI) journals, two international conferences).

Arun Balodi Senior Member IEEE, Fellow IETE, Life Member ISTE is currently Professor and Chairman at the Department of Electronics and Communication Engineering, Dayananda Sagar University in Bangalore, India. Dr. Arun completed his Ph.D. from the Department of Electrical Engineering, Indian Institute of Technology, Roorkee, India, 2018, M.Tech in Digital Signal Processing, from Govind Ballabh Pant Engineering College, Pauri, India, 2010, and B.Tech. in Electronics and Communication Engineering from the Uttar Pradesh Technical University, Lucknow, India, 2005. He was awarded the Gold Medal in M. Tech and the Academic Excellence Award in 2010 and 2011. His research interests span biomedical signal and image processing and artificial intelligence. Dr. Arun has more than 15 years of teaching and research experience in various institutions in India. His research areas are Digital signal and image processing, medical image analysis, machine learning, and pattern recognition. He has published over 42 papers in peer-reviewed journals, international conferences, and holds three patents. He is an active researcher and reviewer for various indexed journals and conferences and has given various technical talks. He has actively participated in more than 34 Faculty Development Programs (FDPs) and more than 100 webinars and conducted workshops in the domain of signal and image processing. He has delivered expert talks in more than 21 short term programs (STPs), conferences, and webinars.

Dr. Balodi received a certificate of appreciation and research incentive for his research contribution in publishing journal papers, patents, book chapters, and international conference papers in the years 2020 and 2021 from Atria Institute of Technology, Bengaluru. He also received the research excellence award and incentive for research contribution for publishing journal papers, patents, book chapters, and international conference and editing one international book in the academic year 2022–23.

Ambar Bajpai, is currently an associate professor at GITAM (deemed-to-be) University, Bangalore, India. His alma maters are Chulalongkorn University, Thailand and Birla Institute of Technology and Science, India. Dr. Ambar has more than 16 years of teaching and research experience in various institutions in India and abroad. Dr. Bajpai received various scholarships, mainly prestigious graduate school scholarships, 90th-year research scholarship, GATE, and overseas academic presentation scholarship during his Ph.D. and M.Eng. His areas of interest are iterative channel coding in 5G, Metaverse, and beyond and visible light communication. He has published more than 51 papers in peer-reviewed journals, international conferences, and book chapters and has delivered invited talks in India and abroad related to the broad domain of wireless communication. He has been volunteering in IEEE Bangalore section as an ExeCom Member, Founder Secretary in the Information Theory Society Chapter, treasurer, and ExeCom roles of various technical society chapters including IEEE SIGHT Bangalore Section.

Vishal Jain is a Professor in the Department of Computer Science and Engineering, School of Engineering and Technology, Sharda University, Greater Noida, India. Before that, he worked as an Associate Professor at Bharati Vidyapeeth's Institute of Computer Applications and Management (BVICAM), New Delhi. He has more than 18 years of experience in academics. He has earned degrees: Ph.D (CSE), M.Tech (CSE), MBA (HR), MCA, MCP, and CCNA. He has more than 2200 research citations with Google Scholar (h-index score 24 and i-10 index 55) and has authored more than 150 research papers in professional journals and conferences. He has authored and edited more than 60 books (most of them are indexed at the Scopus) with various reputed publishers, including Elsevier, Springer, IET, Apple Academic Press, CRC, Taylor & Francis Group, Scrivener, Wiley, Emerald, NOVA Science, River Publishers, IGI-Global and Bentham Science. He has more than 200 Scopus publications. His research areas include machine learning, information retrieval, semantic web, ontology engineering, data mining, ad hoc networks, sensor networks and network security. He received a Young Active Member Award for the year 2012–13 from the Computer Society of India, and Best Faculty Award for the year 2017 and Best Researcher Award for the year 2019 from BVICAM, New Delhi.

Piya Kovintavewat earned a B.Eng. degree (summa cum laude) from Thammasat University, Thailand, in 1994, an M.Sc. degree from the Chalmers University of Technology, Sweden, in 1998, and a Ph.D. degree from the Georgia Institute of Technology, USA, in 2004, all in electrical engineering. He is currently working with Nakhon Pathom Rajabhat University (NPRU). Prior to that, he worked as an engineer with Thai Telephone and Telecommunication Company, Thailand, from 1994 to 1997, and a research assistant with the National Electronics and Computer Technology Center, Thailand, in 1999. He also had work experiences with Seagate Technology, Pennsylvania, USA, in the summers of 2001, 2002, and 2004. His research interests include coding and signal processing as applied to digital data storage systems.

Contributors

Nasser S. Albalawi
Northern Border University
Rafha, Saudi Arabia

Sajid Ali
University of Education
Lahore, Pakistan

Ambar Bajpai
GITAM (Deemed to be University)
Bengaluru, India

Arun Balodi
Dayananda Sagar University
Bengaluru, India

Puttamadappa Chaluve Gowda
Dayananda Sagar University
Bengaluru, India

Susanta Das
Ajeenkya DY Patil University
Pune, India

Pooja Dehankar
Ajeenkya DY Patil School of Engineering
Pune, India

Liping Du
University of Science and Technology
Beijing, China

Supraja Eduru
Dayananda Sagar University
Bengaluru, India

Trupti Gangakhedkar
East West Institute of Technology
Bengaluru, India

Amarjeet Ghosh
IES College of Technology
Bhopal, India

Sampada HK
Atria Institute of Technology
Bengaluru, India

Divyashree Habbanakuppe Balachandra
Dayananda Sagar University
Bengaluru, India

Talea Huraysi
Cardiff University
Cardiff, UK

Arpita Kadel
Shri G.S. Institute of Technology and Science
Indore, India

Nandini Prasad Kanakapura Shivaprasad
Dayananda Sagar Academy of Technology and Management
Bengaluru, India

Farhana Kausar
Atria Institute of Technology
Bengaluru, India

Pankaj Kumar
Manipal Institute of Technology
Manipal Academy of Higher Education
Manipal, India

Sathish Kumar Kumaravel
Vel Tech Rangarajan Dr. Sagunthala R&D Institute of Science and Technology
Chennai, India

Bhaskar MK
Atria Institute of Technology
Bengaluru, India

Kala Raja Mohan
Panimalar Engineering College
Chennai, India

Saranga Mohan
GITAM (Deemed to be University)
Bengaluru, India

Regan Murugesan
Vel Tech Rangarajan Dr. Sagunthala R&D
Institute of Science and Technology
Chennai, India

Muhammad Muzamil Aslam
Universiti Brunei Darussalam
Brunei, Pakistan

Ambika N
St. Francis College
Bengaluru, India

Muhammad Nauman Irshad
King Mongkut's University of Technology
Thonburi, Bangkok

Felicia Kikelomo Oluwalola
University of Ilorin
Ilorin, Nigeria

Daniel Oluyemi
Kwara State University
Malete, Nigeria

Akhilesh Panchal
Amity University
Gwalior, India

Sunita Panda
GITAM (Deemed to be University)
Bengaluru, India

Amit Kumar Pandey
Rajkiya Engineering College
Ambedkar Nagar, India

Yogesh Patidar
Government Polytechnic College
Mandsaur, India

R. Narmada Devi
Vel Tech Rangarajan Dr. Sagunthala
R&D Institute of Science and Technology
Bengaluru, India

Stefano Rinaldi
University of Brescia
Italy

Rakhi S
Atria Institute of Technology
Bengaluru, India

Pulkit Singh
SRM Institute of Science and Technology
Chennai, India

Gaurav Suman
Manipal Institute of Technology, Manipal
Academy of Higher Education
Manipal, India

Manoj Tolani
Manipal Institute of Technology
Manipal Academy of Higher Education
Manipal, India

Ali Tufail
Universiti Brunei Darussalam
Brunei, Pakistan

Shipra Upadhyay
M S Ramaiah Institute of Technology
Bangalore, India

N.P. Yadav
Hubei University of Science and Technology
Hubei, CHina

1 Introduction of Security and Privacy Issues for IoT and WSN

Felicia Kikelomo Oluwalola and Daniel Oluyemi

1.1 INTRODUCTION

In recent years, the interaction between individuals and technology has experienced profound changes, primarily driven by the widespread adoption of wireless sensor networks (WSN) and Internet of Things (IoT) devices. These interconnected networks of smart devices have enabled unprecedented advancements in automation, efficiency, and convenience across numerous sectors such as industry, transportation, healthcare, and smart homes. IoT refers to the interconnection of devices via wireless networks, where intelligent nodes are equipped with sensors, software, and other technologies that enable the gathering and sharing of data over the internet. On the other hand, WSNs comprise spatially dispersed autonomous sensors that collaboratively send data to a central system, typically monitoring physical or environmental factors such as humidity, temperature, and pressure.

IoT technology facilitates the remote sensing and control of smart objects ranging from rice cookers and thermostats to vehicles, refrigerators, routers, cameras, and televisions via the internet. These devices create large volumes of data, most of which are sensitive, thereby raising concerns regarding privacy breaches and unauthorized access. A key challenge in this context is the susceptibility of IoT and WSN systems to cyberattacks. Such attacks may vary in complexity, from basic forms like data interception and unauthorized access to more advanced threats such as malware injection and denial-of-service (DoS) attacks. Breaches in these systems can lead to privacy violations, including identity theft, surveillance, and profiling. The interconnectedness of IoT devices amplifies these risks, as the compromise of one device can propagate across the network, causing widespread disruption and jeopardizing confidential data. Furthermore, the integration of data from multiple IoT sources can enable the creation of detailed profiles of individuals and their behaviors, raising ethical concerns about potential misuse by governments and corporations.

While IoT and WSN technologies hold the potential to revolutionize various aspects of daily life, it is important to address the associated security and privacy challenges. Protecting these systems from cyberattacks and ensuring the appropriate handling of sensitive data are critical. By prioritizing security and privacy in the design, implementation, and management of IoT and WSN infrastructures, the benefits of these technologies can be fully realized while minimizing potential risks.

DOI: 10.1201/9781003491910-1

1.1.1 Key Contributions of the Chapter

The major contributions of this chapter are as follows:

1. A review of recent and relevant studies on security and privacy issues in IoT and WSN
2. An examination of the history and evolution of IoT and WSN technologies
3. An overview of the architecture of IoT systems
4. An analysis of the security issues associated with IoT architecture
5. A discussion of the security requirements for IoT systems
6. An exploration of security solutions for the application of IoT technologies

1.2 RELATED WORKS

In recent years, considerable efforts have been dedicated to tackling the security and privacy challenges within the Internet of Things (IoT). A wide range of studies and surveys have been conducted to address the security concerns related to IoT technologies. Yang et al. (2017) provide a comprehensive survey that highlights security and privacy challenges, particularly with low-end systems, offering solutions tailored to such devices. Various authors have discussed security challenges related to IoT networks, devices, and systems. For instance, Gopi and Rao (2018) categorize security issues into four phases: (1) constraints of IoT devices, such as extending battery life; (2) lightweight computational techniques; (3) classification of security threats; and (4) mechanisms for access control and network architecture. Similarly, Weber (2015) emphasizes security and privacy challenges in IoT, proposing a security model for IoT-based devices. Aleisa and Renaud (2017) examine privacy concerns, their associated risks, and potential solutions for addressing these challenges within the IoT ecosystem. Tewari and Gupta (2020) offer a survey that explores vulnerabilities in IoT device security by analyzing their layered architecture, identifying new security risks, and proposing methodologies for mitigating these challenges.

Hassan (2019) compares multiple studies focusing on various aspects such as simulation tools, methods, device security, and privacy concerns within the IoT space. This analysis explores contemporary IoT security techniques, including authentication, encryption, and trust management, while highlighting emerging technologies designed to enhance device protection. Other research delves into personal safety and privacy issues specific to IoT devices, illustrating the uniqueness of these concerns compared to other industries (Bamasag & Youcef-Toumi, 2015). IoT devices, which are typically interconnected, pose significant security risks, with threats varying depending on the attacker's intent. These risks can be categorized as either natural or human-induced. While data can be safeguarded against natural threats, physical damage to equipment may render devices irreparable. On the other hand, human-induced threats, such as cyberattacks, require more sophisticated defenses. Cybersecurity threats targeting IoT devices generally fall into two categories: one where the attacker attempts to disable the device, and the other where unauthorized access to the device is sought through methods like malware, denial-of-service (DoS) attacks, SQL injection, and cybercrime. As technology evolves, so too do the complexity and severity of these attacks, drawing the attention of researchers who aim to address these challenges. The rapid expansion of connected devices further exacerbates these issues, as security and privacy challenges grow at an accelerated rate (Xu et al., 2018; Deshmukh-Bhosale & Sonavane, 2019; Hukkeri & Goudar, 2019).

To address these concerns, a range of emerging technologies has been integrated with IoT, such as fog computing, artificial intelligence (AI), and blockchain. These advanced technologies offer promising solutions to IoT security and privacy challenges. Blockchain technology, in particular, has garnered significant attention due to its potential as a trusted intermediary for securing IoT devices and protecting sensitive data. By integrating blockchain with IoT, researchers have identified an efficient solution for addressing privacy and security issues. Several studies (Guan & Ge, 2017; Gope et al., 2018; Niu et al., 2019; Naqvi et al., 2020) have explored the synergy between various technologies, presenting blockchain as a robust solution for enhancing IoT security. Sengupta et al. (2020) further investigate security and privacy challenges within the industrial IoT sector, advocating for blockchain-based solutions to mitigate potential risks. Wang et al. (2020) examine blockchain's capabilities, such as access control, decentralization, asymmetric encryption, and smart contracts, to safeguard IoT systems. Khan and Salah (2018) explore the layered architecture of networking, management, and communication protocols, while Qian et al. (2018) focus on layer-based security and privacy challenges in IoT. Sultan et al. (2019) propose security solutions that eliminate the need for a third party to secure IoT devices. Further research by Dorri et al. (2017) and Naqvi et al. (2022) examines the security mechanisms afforded by blockchain's decentralized nature in scenarios involving remote clouds, network terminals, and devices.

Blockchain technology, which has gained prominence through applications like Bitcoin (Sarwar et al., 2021; Akram et al., 2022), is increasingly relevant to IoT security. However, IoT devices remain vulnerable to cyberattacks and cannot autonomously ensure their security (Minoli & Occhiogrosso, 2018). Moreover, once blockchain technology is implemented, certain challenges, such as handling after-the-fact interventions, persist (Iqbal, 2021). Nonetheless, blockchain can enhance security by enabling secure communication of sensitive data and information (Fan et al., 2018).

1.3 EVOLUTION OF IOT TECHNOLOGY

Over the past two decades, the growth of IoT applications has rapidly intensified. Although the concept of IoT surfaced more than 20 years ago, the foundational technologies supporting it had been under development for many years beforehand. The term "Internet of Things" was first coined by Kevin Ashton at the Massachusetts Institute of Technology (MIT) in 1999. Since then, IoT has gained substantial momentum across various industries, though its initial adoption faced hurdles due to low network performance (Singh et al., 2015).

The foundation of IoT is built upon the Internet itself, which originated as the Advanced Research Projects Agency Network (ARPANET). Initially, ARPANET served primarily academic and research institutions, facilitating the exchange of information, pioneering new interconnection methods, and linking defense department computer centers with public and private sectors across the United States (Bolt, 1981).

Another pivotal technology for the development of IoT is radio-frequency identification (RFID). Although its origins can be traced back to World War II, significant advancements were made during the 1950s and 1960s. In 1973, Mario W. Cardullo was granted the first US patent for an RFID tag that featured rewritable memory, while in the same year, Charles Walton secured a patent for a passive transponder used for unlocking doors remotely. These innovations laid the groundwork for IoT by facilitating object identification and communication.

The integration of embedded computer systems was another critical step in IoT's evolution. Embedded systems, which are computer systems embedded within larger systems, began utilizing single-board computers and microcontrollers, essential components in IoT technology (Manley, 1974). One notable example of early IoT-like experimentation occurred when a Coca-Cola machine was connected to the internet, allowing it to report the availability and temperature of its contents (Machine, 2014). However, limited network performance restricted the widespread use of such technologies. The concept of ubiquitous computing, introduced by Mark Weiser, became fundamental to IoT by proposing that computing would be embedded seamlessly into everyday objects, often operating invisibly in the background (Weiser, 1999).

The RFID field was further advanced by the establishment of the Auto-ID Center at MIT, which sought to develop affordable chips capable of storing and transmitting information via the Internet. As digitalization expanded, the internet became central to numerous applications, necessitating that businesses and products maintain an online presence and provide real-time information. Despite these advancements, IoT devices in the early stages still required significant human interaction and monitoring through various interfaces and applications.

With the rapid advancement of IoT technologies, industries across numerous verticals have been increasingly incentivized to invest in IoT solutions to streamline business operations, reduce risk, and improve customer experiences. However, IoT extends far beyond merely affixing sensors to objects and branding them as "smart." IoT refers to a comprehensive network of connected devices ranging from mobile phones and smartwatches to automobiles and household appliances enabled by sensors and technologies such as RFID. True IoT solutions require robust infrastructure for data collection, processing, and the ability to trigger actions through applications.

IoT has fundamentally transformed traditional communication models into machine-to-machine (M2M) communication. This shift has had a profound impact on sectors such as business, healthcare, and industry, as well as everyday life. Today's industrial vision of IoT aims to "connect the unconnected," facilitating seamless communication between all types of devices. However, the growing complexity and power of these interconnected devices make them more vulnerable to cyberattacks, making security one of the most pressing concerns facing IoT development (Huang et al., 2016).

Table 1.1 outlines the evolution of IoT. The history of IoT reflects its transformative technological potential. From early networking experiments to the rise of sophisticated digital platforms, IoT has evolved to overcome geographic barriers, expand access to information, and enhance

TABLE 1.1
Evolution of IoT Technology

Period	Key Developments
1970s–1980s	i. Early concepts of networking and interconnected devices emerged. ii. Embedded internet-connected devices began to take shape.
1990s	i. Introduction of radio frequency identification (RFID) for tracking and identification. ii. TCP/IP became the standard communication protocol for the internet.
2000s	i. Development of wireless sensor networks (WSNs). ii. Standardization of the Zigbee protocol for low-power, low-data-rate wireless communication in IoT devices.
Mid-2000s	i. The launch of the Arduino platform enabled easy prototyping of IoT devices. ii. MQTT (message queuing telemetry transport) gained popularity as a communication protocol for IoT devices.
Late 2000s	i. The term "Internet of Things" gained widespread recognition. ii. Expansion of IPv6 to accommodate the growing number of IoT devices.
2010s	i. Introduction of cloud systems, such as AWS IoT and Azure IoT, specifically designed for IoT applications. ii. Smart home technologies like Nest thermostats and Philips Hue lighting systems gained popularity.
Mid 2010s	i. Rapid growth in industrial IoT (IIoT) applications, particularly in manufacturing and logistics. ii. Edge computing became a key method for processing data closer to the source.

TABLE 1.1 (Continued)
Evolution of IoT Technology

Period	Key Developments
Late 2010s	i. Introduction of 5G technology, providing faster and more reliable communication for IoT devices. ii. Exploration of blockchain technology to enhance IoT security and trust mechanisms.
2020s	i. Integration of AI and machine learning with IoT devices for enhanced data analytics and automation. ii. Expansion of smart city projects leveraging IoT for urban infrastructure improvements.
Present day	i. Ongoing advancements in edge computing, artificial intelligence, and connectivity (6G, low-power wide-area networks). ii. Continued focus on interoperability, security, and privacy within IoT ecosystems.

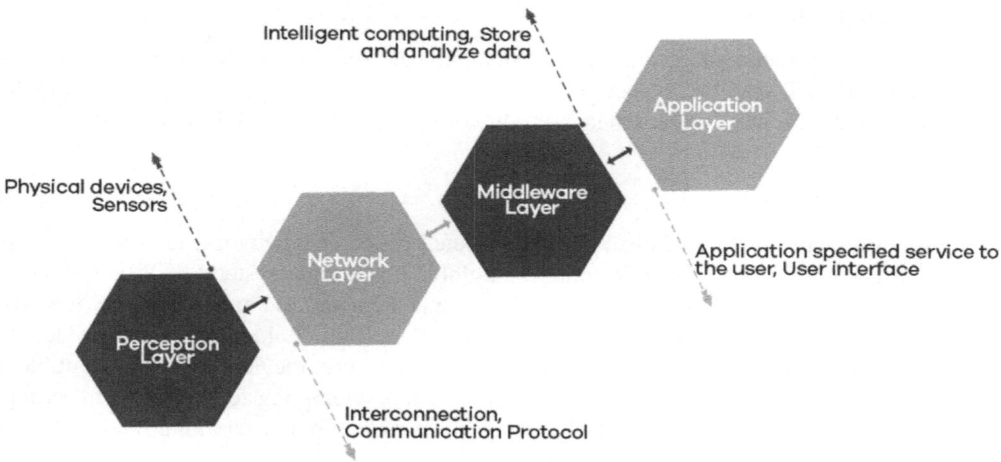

FIGURE 1.1 General IoT architecture.

communication. As technology continues to evolve, IoT is poised to play an increasingly pivotal role in shaping the future.

1.4 ARCHITECTURE OF IOT

IoT enables the seamless integration of various devices, requiring a flexible and layered architecture. Numerous scholars have proposed different architectures for IoT, focusing particularly on the middleware and network layers, which address the unique demands of IoT systems. A widely accepted core IoT architecture, as depicted in Figure 1.1, consists of four main layers: the perception layer, network layer, middleware layer, and application layer (Adat & Gupta, 2018). Each of these layers plays a crucial role in facilitating information transfer within the network and delivering tailored services based on application-specific needs.

The perception layer detects and collects data through sensor nodes and other hardware components (Puthal et al., 2016). It functions as the intermediary between the physical environment and the IoT network by capturing environmental data. The network layer connects these intelligent devices to the internet and other systems, handling the transmission and processing of sensor data (Bello et al., 2017). This layer ensures efficient data flow within the IoT system.

The middleware layer, which operates between the network and application layers, plays a pivotal role in managing data and ensuring efficient service delivery. It processes the sensor data and enables the system to make informed decisions based on these outcomes. This layer ensures scalability, compatibility with other systems, and the ability to meet increasing demands (da Cruz et al., 2018).

The application layer, at the top of the architecture, delivers business services by analyzing the collected data and making data-driven decisions to meet user requirements. It determines the optimal time for executing specific tasks based on the analyzed data. The application layer includes various applications tailored to the specific needs of different businesses. One example is the constrained application protocol (CoAP), which is an alternative to HTTP designed for devices with limited resources (Saadeh et al., 2016).

1.5 SECURITY ISSUES IN LAYERED IOT ARCHITECTURE

IoT has witnessed substantial advancements, but significant security challenges remain. Various vulnerabilities in IoT systems expose them to a range of attacks. This section examines the security concerns associated with each layer of the IoT architecture and outlines potential threats.

1.5.1 Perception Layer

The perception layer consists of all devices connected to the IoT network, including sensors, actuators, Zigbee, RFID systems, QR codes, and global positioning systems (GPS) (Jing et al., 2014). At this level, the security threats primarily occur at the node, and most vulnerabilities arise from external sources like embedded sensors and actuators (Suo et al., 2012). As these devices are typically constrained by low memory and limited battery life, they are highly susceptible to attacks. Consequently, they are often targeted by attackers attempting to exploit them through tactics like denial-of-service (DoS) attacks, tampering, node capture, jamming, and malicious data injection (Singh et al., 2017).

1.5.2 Network Layer

The network layer transmits vast amounts of data, making it especially susceptible to attacks that may lead to network congestion. The primary security issues in this layer focus on ensuring data authentication and integrity during transmission. Despite the stronger security mechanisms in place, the network layer remains susceptible to threats such as counterfeit attacks and man-in-the-middle assaults (Kraijak & Tuwanut, 2015). Common attacks in this layer include:

i. *Replay attacks*: Attackers capture and retransmit a segment of communication between two parties for malicious purposes, such as replicating a transaction (Turkanović et al., 2014).
ii. *Denial of service (DoS) attacks*: These attacks entail inundating the network with excessive traffic, thereby obstructing legitimate users from accessing critical services. (Padmavathi & Shanmugapriya, 2009).

iii. *Man-in-the-middle attacks*: An attacker intercepts communication between two parties to either eavesdrop on the exchange or impersonate one of the parties, potentially altering or stealing information. (Padhy et al., 2011).
iv. *Malicious code injection*: This situation arises when an attacker compromises a node by introducing malicious code, thereby gaining control over the network or causing its disruption. (Fulare & Chavhan, 2011).
v. *Distributed denial of service (DDoS)*: In a Distributed denial of service (DDoS) attack, numerous compromised nodes inundate the network with malicious traffic, thereby disrupting service availability for legitimate users.

1.5.3 Middleware Layer

The middleware layer, positioned above the network layer, is tasked with managing extensive data processing and facilitating intelligent decision-making (Bouloukakis et al., 2019). It benefits from advancements in cloud computing, big data processing, and databases, but the challenge of managing enormous data sets persists. A significant issue in this layer is distinguishing legitimate data from malicious information, as attackers can manipulate or replace legitimate data with fraudulent information. This can result in network disruptions or system failures. Other key concerns include multi-party authentication for resource-constrained devices and the secure storage of data in the cloud (Razouk et al., 2017).

1.5.4 Application Layer

The application layer includes smart devices that provide tailored services to users. These devices are typically lightweight, energy-efficient, and susceptible to security threats (Sethi & Sarangi, 2017). Malicious actors can exploit software vulnerabilities, altering program codes and causing applications to malfunction. This may prevent the software from fulfilling its intended purpose or lead it to perform unauthorized actions. Additionally, the application layer handles data exchange, leading to concerns about access control, data privacy, and potential information leaks (Jolfaei & Kant, 2019). Common risks include spear-phishing attacks, software vulnerabilities, malicious code injection, and hacking of smart meters or grids.

1.6 SECURITY REQUIREMENTS IN IOT

The foremost concern in IoT systems is security and privacy, necessitating a comprehensive understanding of the required security measures. This is especially important given the rise in cyber threats and the frequent occurrence of zero-day attacks. These attacks, which exploit unknown vulnerabilities, allow adversaries to bypass existing security frameworks, leading to network disruptions and inconveniencing legitimate users.

Information assurance involves ensuring that information systems operate as intended while preserving their security. According to the National Institute of Standards and Technology (NIST), it encompasses "measures that safeguard and preserve information and information systems by ensuring their confidentiality, authentication, integrity, availability, and non-repudiation" (Nieles et al., 2017). This discipline also involves the restoration of information systems through the implementation of security measures, as well as detection and response mechanisms. In the context of IoT-based systems, which merge digital and physical environments, information assurance is critical for fulfilling security requirements and addressing potential vulnerabilities (Russell & Van Duren, 2016).

To guarantee the secure operation of IoT networks and devices, comprehensive IoT security standards are essential. Strong authentication and access control mechanisms must be in place to prevent unauthorized access and protect the system from cyberattacks. These mechanisms must facilitate the identification and authentication of both users and devices, manage access to sensitive information, and establish detailed permissions to ensure that only authorized entities have access to the system. Furthermore, data generated by IoT devices must be encrypted to ensure privacy and confidentiality while safeguarding against alterations that could compromise its integrity and authenticity.

In addition to safeguarding data, network and device security are essential components of IoT security. IoT systems need to be protected against network-based attacks, while physical threats, such as theft, damage, and tampering, should be addressed through integrated security features within the devices (Taherdoost, 2023).

1.7 SECURITY SOLUTIONS FOR IOT

The Internet of Things (IoT) introduces distinctive security challenges owing to its extensive network of interconnected devices, which are often engineered for minimal human intervention. Protecting the security and privacy of IoT systems is crucial, as these devices frequently handle sensitive personal data through collection, storage, and analysis. To address these issues, a range of security solutions has been proposed, each focusing on specific aspects of IoT security, including authentication, data encryption, and intrusion detection.

Mutual authentication is a critical aspect of IoT security, especially since most IoT devices operate with minimal human intervention. These devices are typically designed for everyday use, focusing on the collection, storage, and analysis of personal data. As such, they need the capability to be managed remotely and receive automated updates. To safeguard against unauthorized access, authentication and access control mechanisms must be implemented at the perception layer, ensuring the legitimacy of network nodes (Saadeh et al., 2016). Additionally, data encryption and confidentiality measures are vital to protect stored data from tampering and to prevent the injection of malicious code. However, implementing comprehensive encryption systems can be resource-intensive for IoT devices, which often have limited computational power. Therefore, lightweight cryptographic protocols must be employed to mitigate these challenges (Jolfaei & Kant, 2017). Intrusion detection systems are also essential in detecting harmful activities within the network (Bütün et al., 2019).

Li et al. (2019) developed a certificate-less conditional authentication system for vehicles that eliminates the need for certificate storage in traffic announcements. This system utilizes two unique tags associated with the vehicle's secret key, employing cryptographic techniques like the discrete logarithm (DL) problem and computational Diffie–Hellman (CDH) problem. While this approach strengthens security, it remains vulnerable to certain types of attacks.

Al et al. (2021) proposed an enhanced channel allocation system utilizing commutative RSA (CRSA) to improve throughput and reduce communication overhead. This system employs encryption by utilizing random number parameters for both encryption and decryption, which are shared among vehicles. However, the key management overhead and storage requirements make the system prone to key exposure.

Meshram et al. (2021) proposed a secure communication protocol for smart cities that integrates a smart card, password, and chaotic maps. While this lightweight protocol provides improved security, the potential theft of the smart card could expose the city to vulnerabilities from side-channel attacks.

Han et al. (2021) presented a ciphertext-policy attribute-based encryption (CP-ABE) system for securing communication using frequent item sets generated by mining association rules. This system is limited to attributes with similar frequency properties and may be vulnerable if an adversary infiltrates the electronic control unit (ECU).

Wazid et al. (2019) proposed a fog-server-based authentication mechanism employing elliptic curve cryptography (ECC). This mechanism dynamically adds nodes but does not offer strong resistance to denial of service (DoS) attacks.

Pascale et al. (2021) developed an embedded intrusion detection system in vehicles using machine learning techniques. The system identifies potential cyberattacks by analyzing parameters like RPM and speedometer readings, though it does not focus on data transmission security.

Pradeep and Sunitha (2022) proposed a CHAP PPP-based authentication protocol for smart city applications. While the system is simple and effective for preventing replay attacks, it lacks robust verification mechanisms, leaving it vulnerable to physical attacks.

Aman et al. (2020) designed a secure communication system for vehicular networks using physical unclonable functions (PUF). This system reduces authentication overhead but remains susceptible to system exposure during challenge–response pair (CRP) updates.

Xu et al. (2020) introduced an energy-efficient transaction model using blockchain to reduce network load. This model uses an adaptive linear prediction technique, but its security mechanisms are basic and may be inadequate for high-security environments.

Wang et al. (2021) proposed a blockchain-based authentication mechanism for healthcare systems that ensures reliable communication while minimizing costs. However, this approach may incur significant storage costs (Table 1.2).

1.8 CONCLUSION

The integration of IoT devices into modern life is becoming increasingly prevalent, with applications spanning various sectors, including homes, businesses, education, and transportation. These devices offer enhanced connectivity and collaboration, enabling stakeholders to gain deeper insights into business operations and improve overall productivity and efficiency. However, as the potential for IoT grows, so do the risks associated with their use. A significant challenge lies in the absence of unified standards in the IoT sector, leading to vulnerabilities across the network. The lack of a standard IoT architecture continues to be a pressing issue.

In this chapter, we concentrated on the security and privacy challenges inherent to the Internet of Things (IoT). We investigated the overall IoT architecture and critically assessed the security risks associated with various stages of the IoT protocol stack, including the perception, network, and application layers. Additionally, we reviewed some of the necessary security services for IoT and provided a summary of current approaches to safeguard IoT systems. Despite these advancements, a universally accepted method for securing resource-constrained IoT devices remains elusive. Existing network protocols and security measures need enhancement to address the specific security requirements of IoT technology effectively.

In conclusion, while IoT devices offer tremendous opportunities to revolutionize industries, their widespread adoption must be accompanied by robust security measures. This chapter highlights the urgent need for comprehensive security frameworks tailored specifically for IoT systems. As IoT progresses, its security protocols must also advance to ensure that the advantages of this technology are achieved without jeopardizing safety or privacy. Effectively addressing these challenges will be crucial for fostering the development of more sophisticated and secure IoT infrastructures in the future.

TABLE 1.2
A Comparative Analysis of IoT Security Solutions

Reference	Objective	Methodology Employed	Data Type	Pros	Cons
Li et al. (2019)	Eliminate dependency on certificate storage	Public Key Infrastructure (PKI)	Vehicle data	Certificate less	Vulnerable to certain attacks
Meshram et al (2021)	Secure smart city communication	Chaotic map	Smart city	Lightweight	Security enhancements needed
Al et al (2021)	Minimize communication and key management overhead	Cluster-based Resource Scheduling Algorithm (CRSA)	Throughput enhancement	Improved throughput	Risk of key exposure
Han et al. (2021)	Build frequent item sets for communication	Ciphertext-Policy Attribute-Based Encryption (CP-ABE)	Attribute-based data	Enhanced speed	Limited to the same attribute set
Wazid et al. (2019)	Secure wireless communication	Elliptic Curve Cryptography (ECC)	Surrounding data	Dynamic node addition	Vulnerable to DoS attacks
Pascale et al. (2021)	Detect cyberattacks in vehicles	Machine learning	Parameters like RPM	High detection accuracy	Insufficient focus on data transmission aspects
Pradeep & Sunitha (2022)	Secure smart city applications	Challenge-Handshake Authentication Protocol (CHAP PPP)	Operational city data	Simple computational requirements	Lacks system verification
Aman et al. (2020)	Resist physical attacks, secure communication	Physical unclonable functions (PUF)	Network traffic	Low overhead, reduced authentication packets	Vulnerabilities exposed through CRP updates
Xu et al. (2020)	Improve energy efficiency, prevent attacks	Blockchain	Vehicular data	Suitable for large data sets	Basic security mechanisms
Wang et al (2021)	Ensure reliable communication in healthcare	Blockchain, PUF	Health data	Low cost	High storage cost

REFERENCES

Adat, V., & Gupta, B. B. (2018). Security in Internet of Things: issues, challenges, taxonomy, and architecture. *Telecommunication Systems*, *67*, 423–441.

Akram, M., Iqbal, M. W., Ali, S. A., Ashraf, M. U., Alsubhi, K., & Aljahdali, H. M. (2022). Triple key security algorithm against single key attack on multiple rounds. *Computers, Materials & Continua*, *72*(3), 6061–6077.

Al-Absi, M. A., Al-Absi, A. A., Fu, R., Kim, K. H., Lee, Y. S., Lee, B. G., ... & Lee, H. J. (2021). Secure and efficient high throughput medium access control for vehicular ad-hoc network. *Sensors*, *21*(14), 4935.

Aleisa, N., & Renaud K., (2017). Privacy of the Internet of Things: a systematic literature review. *Proceedings of the 50th Hawaii International Conference on System Sciences,* (pp. 1–10), Hilton Waikoloa Village, Hawaii.

Aman, M. N., Javaid, U., & Sikdar, B. (2020). A privacy-preserving and scalable authentication protocol for the internet of vehicles. *IEEE Internet of Things Journal*, *8*(2), 1123–1139.

Bamasag, O. O., & Youcef-Toumi, K. (2015, October). Towards continuous authentication in internet of things based on secret sharing scheme. In *Proceedings of the WESS'15: Workshop on Embedded Systems Security* (pp. 1–8).

Bello, O., Zeadally, S., & Badra, M. (2017). Network layer inter-operation of Device-to-Device communication technologies in Internet of Things (IoT). *Ad Hoc Networks*, *57*, 52–62.

Bolt, B. (1981). *A History of the ARPANET: The First Decade*. Bolt Beranek and Newman.

Bouloukakis, G., Georgantas, N., Ntumba, P., & Issarny, V. (2019). Automated synthesis of mediators for middleware-layer protocol interoperability in the IoT. *Future Generation Computer Systems*, *101*, 1271–1294.

Butun, I., Österberg, P., & Song, H. (2019). Security of the Internet of Things: vulnerabilities, attacks, and countermeasures. *IEEE Communications Surveys & Tutorials*, *22*(1), 616–644.

da Cruz, M. A., Rodrigues, J. J. P., Al-Muhtadi, J., Korotaev, V. V., & de Albuquerque, V. H. C. (2018). A reference model for internet of things middleware. *IEEE Internet of Things Journal*, *5*(2), 871–883.

Deshmukh-Bhosale, S., & Sonavane, S. S. (2019). A real-time intrusion detection system for wormhole attack in the RPL based Internet of Things. *Procedia Manufacturing*, *32*, 840–847.

Dorri, A., Kanhere, S. S., Jurdak, R., & Gauravaram, P. (2017, March). Blockchain for IoT security and privacy: The case study of a smart home. In *2017 IEEE International Conference on Pervasive Computing and Communications Workshops (PerCom Workshops)* (pp. 618–623). IEEE.

Fan, K., Wang, S., Ren, Y., Yang, K., Yan, Z., Li, H., & Yang, Y. (2018). Blockchain-based secure time protection scheme in IoT. *IEEE Internet of Things Journal*, *6*(3), 4671–4679.

Fulare, P. S., & Chavhan, N. (2011). False data detection in wireless sensor network with secure communication. *International Journal of Smart Sensors and AdHoc Networks (IJSSAN)*, *1*(1), 66–71.

Gope, P., Amin, R., Islam, S. H., Kumar, N., & Bhalla, V. K. (2018). Lightweight and privacy-preserving RFID authentication scheme for distributed IoT infrastructure with secure localization services for smart city environment. *Future Generation Computer Systems*, *83*, 629–637.

Gopi, A., & Rao, M. K. (2018). Survey of privacy and security issues in IoT. *International Journal of Engineering & Technology*, *7*(2.7), 293–296.

Guan, Y., & Ge, X. (2017). Distributed attack detection and secure estimation of networked cyber-physical systems against false data injection attacks and jamming attacks. *IEEE Transactions on Signal and Information Processing over Networks*, *4*(1), 48–59.

Han, M., Zhu, M., Cheng, P., Yin, Z., & Qu, H. (2021). Implementing an efficient secure attribute-based encryption system for IoV using association rules. *Symmetry*, *13*(7), 1177.

Hassan, W. H. (2019). Current research on Internet of Things (IoT) security: A survey. *Computer networks*, *148*, 283–294.

Huang, X., Craig, P., Lin, H., & Yan, Z. (2016). SecIoT: a security framework for the Internet of Things. *Security and Communication Networks*, *9*(16), 3083–3094.

Hukkeri, G. S., & Goudar, R. H. (2019). IoT: issues, challenges, tools, security, solutions and best practices. *International Journal of Pure and Applied Mathematics*, *120*(6), 12099–12109.

Ibarra-Esquer, J. E., González-Navarro, F. F., Flores-Rios, B. L., Burtseva, L., & Astorga-Vargas, M. A. (2017). Tracking the evolution of the internet of things concept across different application domains. *Sensors*, *17*(6), 1379.

Iqbal, W. (2021). Business process model for IoT based systems operations. *Lahore Garrison University Research Journal of Computer Science and Information Technology*, *5*(4), 1–10.

Jing, Q., Vasilakos, A. V., Wan, J., Lu, J., & Qiu, D. (2014). Security of the Internet of Things: perspectives and challenges. *Wireless Networks*, *20*, 2481–2501.

Jolfaei, A., & Kant, K. (2017). A lightweight integrity protection scheme for fast communications in smart grid. In *14th International Joint Conference on e-Business and Telecommunications, ICETE 2017* (pp. 31–42). SciTePress.

Jolfaei, A., & Kant, K. (2019, June). Privacy and security of connected vehicles in intelligent transportation system. In *2019 49th Annual IEEE/IFIP International Conference on Dependable Systems and Networks–Supplemental Volume (DSN-S)* (pp. 9–10). IEEE.

Khan, M. A., & Salah, K. (2018). IoT security: Review, blockchain solutions, and open challenges. *Future Generation Computer Systems*, *82*, 395–411.

Khraisat, A., & Alazab, A. (2021). A critical review of intrusion detection systems in the internet of things: techniques, deployment strategy, validation strategy, attacks, public datasets and challenges. *Cybersecurity*, *4*, 1–27.

Kraijak, S., & Tuwanut, P. (2015, October). A survey on internet of things architecture, protocols, possible applications, security, privacy, real-world implementation and future trends. In *2015 IEEE 16th International Conference on Communication Technology (ICCT)* (pp. 26–31). IEEE.

Kumar, S. A., Vealey, T., & Srivastava, H. (2016, January). Security in internet of things: Challenges, solutions and future directions. In *2016 49th Hawaii International Conference on System Sciences (HICSS)* (pp. 5772–5781). IEEE.

Li, J., Ji, Y., Choo, K. K. R., & Hogrefe, D. (2019). CL-CPPA: Certificate-less conditional privacy-preserving authentication protocol for the Internet of Vehicles. *IEEE Internet of Things Journal*, *6*(6), 10332–10343.

Machine, C. (2014). The only coke machine on the internet. www.researchgate.net/publication/368304364_IoT_Botnet_Detection_Using_an_Economic_Deep_Learning_Model

Manley, J. H. (1974, May). Embedded computers: software cost considerations. In *Proceedings of the May 6–10, 1974, National Computer Conference and Exposition* (Pp. 343–347).

Meshram, C., Ibrahim, R. W., Deng, L., Shende, S. W., Meshram, S. G., & Barve, S. K. (2021). A robust smart card and remote user password-based authentication protocol using extended chaotic maps under smart cities environment. *Soft Computing*, *25*(15), 10037–10051.

Minoli, D., & Occhiogrosso, B. (2018). Blockchain mechanisms for IoT security. *Internet of Things*, *1*, 1–13.

Naqvi, M. R., Iqbal, M. W., Ashraf, M. U., Ahmad, S., Soliman, A. T., Khurram, S., ... & Choi, J. G. (2022). Ontology driven testing strategies for IoT applications. *Computers Materials and Continua*, *70*(3), 5855–5869.

Naqvi, M. R., Iqbal, M. W., Shahzad, S. K., Tariq, I., Malik, M., Ehsan, F., ... & Tabassum, N. (2020). A concurrence study on interoperability issues in IoT and decision making based model on data and services being used during inter-operability. *Lahore Garrison University Research Journal of Computer Science and Information Technology*, *4*(4), 73–85.

Nieles, M., Dempsey, K., & Pillitteri, V. Y. (2017). An introduction to information security. *NIST Special Publication*, *800*(12), 101.

Niu, Y., Zhang, J., Wang, A., & Chen, C. (2019). An efficient collision power attack on AES encryption in edge computing. *IEEE Access*, *7*, 18734–18748.

Padhy, R. P., Patra, M. R., & Satapathy, S. C. (2011). Cloud computing: security issues and research challenges. *International Journal of Computer Science and Information Technology & Security (IJCSITS)*, *1*(2), 136–146.

Padmavathi, D. G., & Shanmugapriya, M. (2009). A survey of attacks, security mechanisms and challenges in wireless sensor networks. *arXiv preprint arXiv:0909.0576.*

Panarello, A., Tapas, N., Merlino, G., Longo, F., & Puliafito, A. (2018). Blockchain and iot integration: A systematic survey. *Sensors*, *18*(8), 2575.

Pascale, F., Adinolfi, E. A., Coppola, S., & Santonicola, E. (2021). Cybersecurity in automotive: An intrusion detection system in connected vehicles. *Electronics*, *10*(15), 1765.

Pradeep, R., & Sunitha, N. R. (2022). Formal verification of CHAP PPP authentication protocol for smart city/safe city applications. *Journal of Physics: Conference Series* (Vol. 2161, No. 1, p. 012046). IOP Publishing.

Puthal, D., Nepal, S., Ranjan, R., & Chen, J. (2016). Threats to networking cloud and edge datacenters in the Internet of Things. *IEEE Cloud Computing*, *3*(3), 64–71.

Qian, Y., Jiang, Y., Chen, J., Zhang, Y., Song, J., Zhou, M., & Pustišek, M. (2018). Towards decentralized IoT security enhancement: A blockchain approach. *Computers & Electrical Engineering*, *72*, 266–273.

Razouk, W., Sgandurra, D., & Sakurai, K. (2017, October). A new security middleware architecture based on fog computing and cloud to support IoT constrained devices. In *Proceedings of the 1st International Conference on Internet of Things and Machine Learning* (pp. 1–8).

Russell, B., & Van Duren, D. (2016). *Practical Internet of Things Security*. Packt Publishing Ltd.

Saadeh, M., Sleit, A., Qatawneh, M., & Almobaideen, W. (2016, August). Authentication techniques for the internet of things: A survey. In *2016 Cybersecurity and Cyberforensics Conference (CCC)* (pp. 28–34). IEEE.

Saadeh, M., Sleit, A., Qatawneh, M., & Almobaideen, W. (2016, August). Authentication techniques for the internet of things: A survey. In *2016 Cybersecurity and Cyberforensics Conference (CCC)* (Pp. 28–34). IEEE.

Sarwar, M. I., Iqbal, M. W., Alyas, T., Namoun, A., Alrehaili, A., Tufail, A., & Tabassum, N. (2021). Data vaults for blockchain-empowered accounting information systems. *IEEE Access*, *9*, 117306–117324.

Sengupta, J., Ruj, S., & Bit, S. D. (2020). A comprehensive survey on attacks, security issues and blockchain solutions for IoT and IIoT. *Journal of Network and Computer Applications*, *149*, 102481.

Sethi, P., & Sarangi, S. R. (2017). Internet of things: Architectures, protocols, and applications. *Journal of Electrical & Computer Engineering*, *1*, 9324035.

Singh, J., Pasquier, T., Bacon, J., Ko, H., & Eyers, D. (2015). Twenty security considerations for cloud-supported Internet of Things. *IEEE Internet of Things Journal*, *3*(3), 269–284.

Singh, S., Sharma, P. K., Moon, S. Y., & Park, J. H. (2017). Advanced lightweight encryption algorithms for IoT devices: survey, challenges and solutions. *Journal of Ambient Intelligence and Humanized Computing*, 1–18.

Sultan, A., Mushtaq, M. A., & Abubakar, M. (2019, March). IOT security issues via blockchain: a review paper. In *Proceedings of the 2019 International Conference on Blockchain Technology* (pp. 60–65).

Suo, H., Wan, J., Zou, C., & Liu, J. (2012, March). Security in the internet of things: a review. In *2012 International Conference on Computer Science and Electronics Engineering* (Vol. 3, pp. 648–651). IEEE.

Taherdoost, H. (2023). Security and internet of things: benefits, challenges, and future perspectives. *Electronics*, *12*(8), 1901.

Tewari, A., & Gupta, B. B. (2020). Security, privacy and trust of different layers in Internet-of-Things (IoTs) framework. *Future Generation Computer Systems*, *108*, 909–920.

Turkanović, M., Brumen, B., & Hölbl, M. (2014). A novel user authentication and key agreement scheme for heterogeneous ad hoc wireless sensor networks, based on the Internet of Things notion. *Ad Hoc Networks*, *20*, 96–112.

Wang, Q., Zhu, X., Ni, Y., Gu, L., & Zhu, H. (2020). Blockchain for the IoT and industrial IoT: A review. *Internet of Things*, *10*, 100081.

Wang, W., Chen, Q., Yin, Z., Srivastava, G., Gadekallu, T. R., Alsolami, F., & Su, C. (2021). Blockchain and PUF-based lightweight authentication protocol for wireless medical sensor networks. *IEEE Internet of Things Journal*, *9*(11), 8883–8891.

Wazid, M., Bagga, P., Das, A. K., Shetty, S., Rodrigues, J. J., & Park, Y. (2019). AKM-IoV: Authenticated key management protocol in fog computing-based Internet of vehicles deployment. *IEEE Internet of Things Journal*, *6*(5), 8804–8817.

Weber, R. H. (2015). Internet of things: Privacy issues revisited. *Computer Law & Security Review*, *31*(5), 618–627.

Weiser, M. (1999). The computer for the 21st century. *ACM SIGMOBILE Mobile Computing and Communications Review*, *3*(3), 3–11.

Xu, B., Wang, W., Hao, Q., Zhang, Z., Du, P., Xia, T., ... & Wang, X. (2018). A security design for the detecting of buffer overflow attacks in IoT device. *IEEE Access*, *6*, 72862–72869.

Xu, X., Zhao, H., Yao, H., & Wang, S. (2020). A blockchain-enabled energy-efficient data collection system for UAV-assisted IoT. *IEEE Internet of Things Journal*, *8*(4), 2431–2443.

Yang, Y., Wu, L., Yin, G., Li, L., & Zhao, H. (2017). A survey on security and privacy issues in Internet-of-Things. *IEEE Internet of Things Journal*, *4*(5), 1250–1258.

2 Systematic Literature Review on Security and Privacy Issues on WSN and IoT

Arpita Kadel, Trupti Gangakhedkar, Yogesh Patidar, Amarjeet Ghosh, Akhilesh Panchal, and Nasser S. Albalawi

2.1 INTRODUCTION

The rapid expansion of the Internet of Things (IoT) and wireless sensor networks (WSN) has brought significant advancements across various industries, enabling real-time data collection, monitoring, and decision-making. These technologies are now integral to applications ranging from smart homes and healthcare to industrial automation and smart cities. However, with this widespread adoption comes a growing concern for security and privacy. WSN and IoT devices are often deployed in resource-constrained environments, where limited computational power and energy resources make it challenging to implement robust security measures without compromising performance [1–3]. Additionally, the scalability of IoT networks, with their vast number of interconnected devices, adds complexity to managing security and privacy. Ensuring data integrity, preventing unauthorized access, and protecting sensitive information from breaches are critical issues that must be addressed. Moreover, the heterogeneity of devices and the dynamic nature of IoT environments further complicate the implementation of consistent security policies [2]. As these networks continue to grow and evolve, addressing the security and privacy challenges inherent in WSN and IoT systems is essential to unlocking their full potential across a wide range of applications.

Encryption plays a crucial role in securing the Internet of Things (IoT) by protecting the confidentiality, integrity, and authenticity of data as it is transmitted between devices. In the IoT ecosystem, where vast amounts of sensitive information are exchanged, encryption ensures that this data is inaccessible to unauthorized parties [4–7,9]. By converting data into an unreadable format using cryptographic algorithms, encryption prevents attackers from intercepting and deciphering sensitive information such as personal data, financial transactions, or control commands. Additionally, encryption helps in maintaining the integrity of data by ensuring that any unauthorized alterations are detectable, thereby protecting against tampering. It also plays a vital role in authentication, where encrypted credentials can verify the identities of devices and users, ensuring that only authorized entities can access the network. Given the diversity and scale of IoT devices, implementing strong, efficient encryption methods is essential for safeguarding the entire ecosystem against a wide range of cyber threats [8–11].

Privacy risks in smart homes are increasingly concerning as the adoption of interconnected devices grows. These devices, such as cameras, voice assistants, and sensors, continuously collect vast amounts of data, including personal activities, preferences, and daily routines. The constant

DOI: 10.1201/9781003491910-2

monitoring by these devices raises the risk of unauthorized access or surveillance, where sensitive information could be exposed or misused. Moreover, smart home devices often transmit data to cloud services for processing, which can be vulnerable to breaches if not properly secured [13]. Additionally, many smart devices have varying levels of security, and older or less secure devices might be exploited by attackers, leading to potential privacy violations. The aggregation of data from multiple devices can also create a detailed profile of the occupants, which, if compromised, could lead to identity theft, unauthorized tracking, or other privacy invasions. As smart homes become more prevalent, ensuring robust privacy protections and secure data handling practices is essential to safeguard the privacy of individuals [12–18].

Smart home devices manage encryption by utilizing lightweight encryption algorithms designed to provide a balance between security and performance. These algorithms, such as AES-128, require less computational power and energy, making them suitable for resource-constrained devices. Additionally, smart home devices often implement end-to-end encryption to protect data from the moment it leaves the device until it reaches its destination, ensuring that sensitive information is not exposed during transmission. To further enhance security, many devices use secure key management practices, such as storing encryption keys in hardware security modules or using key exchange protocols like Diffie–Hellman. This helps protect the keys from being intercepted or compromised. By combining these strategies, smart home devices can effectively manage encryption, providing robust security without significantly impacting device performance [19–23].

Security and privacy issues in WSN and IoT are critical concerns as these technologies become increasingly integrated into various aspects of daily life, as shown in Figure 2.1. WSN and IoT consist of a vast array of interconnected devices that collect, process, and transmit data. Given the limited computational power, memory, and energy resources of many IoT and WSN devices, implementing robust security measures can be challenging. Security issues primarily involve protecting these networks from threats such as hacking, unauthorized access, data interception, and tampering. The risk is particularly high in environments where these devices are deployed in large numbers, such as smart homes, healthcare systems, industrial automation, and smart cities, where a breach in security can lead to significant consequences [22–27].

Privacy issues are equally concerning, as WSN and IoT devices often handle large amounts of personal and sensitive data, including health information, location data, and behavioural patterns.

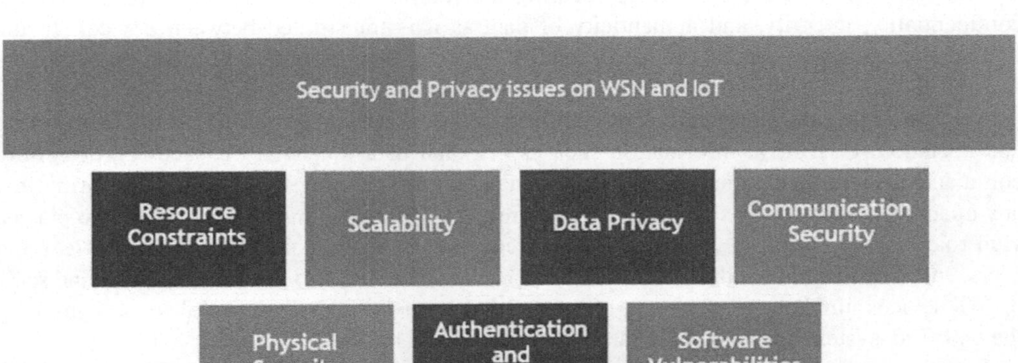

FIGURE 2.1 Security and privacy issues on WSN and IoT.

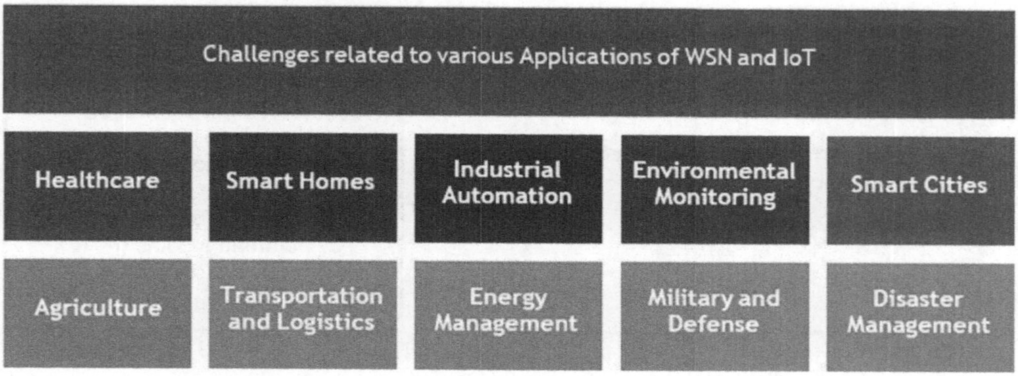

FIGURE 2.2 Challenges related to various applications of WSN and IoT.

Ensuring the privacy of this data is challenging, especially as it is transmitted across networks that may not always be secure. The potential for unauthorized access to this data raises concerns about data breaches, identity theft, and the misuse of personal information. Furthermore, as IoT devices become more pervasive, the aggregation of data from multiple sources can lead to detailed profiles of individuals, making privacy protection even more critical. Addressing these security and privacy issues is essential to fully realize the potential of WSN and IoT technologies while safeguarding users' data and privacy.

Figure 2.2 represents various applications of WSN and IoT, highlighting the specific challenges associated with each domain. WSN and IoT technologies are widely used across sectors such as healthcare, smart homes, industrial automation, environmental monitoring, smart cities, agriculture, transportation and logistics, energy management, military and defence, and disaster management. Each application leverages interconnected devices to gather and analyse data, automate processes, and enhance efficiency. However, deploying these technologies also introduces significant challenges, particularly related to security and privacy.

In healthcare, the challenge lies in safeguarding sensitive patient data to ensure reliable monitoring of health conditions. In smart homes, privacy risks arise from various devices collecting personal data, necessitating robust encryption and access controls. Industrial automation and environmental monitoring face challenges in securing the vast amounts of data sensors generate, ensuring that the systems remain resilient to cyber threats. Similarly, smart cities and military applications require comprehensive strategies to protect critical infrastructure from cyberattacks. The diversity and scale of these applications make it essential to address the specific security and privacy challenges inherent in each domain to ensure the safe and efficient operation of WSN and IoT systems [26–35].

2.2 INCLUSION AND EXCLUSION CRITERIA OF RESEARCH WORKS

To analyse the selection of paper for review, we have followed PRISMA analysis as shown in Figure 2.3. The PRISMA flowchart illustrates a systematic review process where studies are identified, screened, assessed for eligibility, and ultimately included or excluded based on predefined criteria. The flowchart provides statistical insights into how many studies were considered at each stage, which helps in understanding the rigour and selectivity of the review process.

The systematic review began with the identification of 512 records from databases. After initial screening, 52 duplicate records were removed, leaving 460 unique studies to be screened

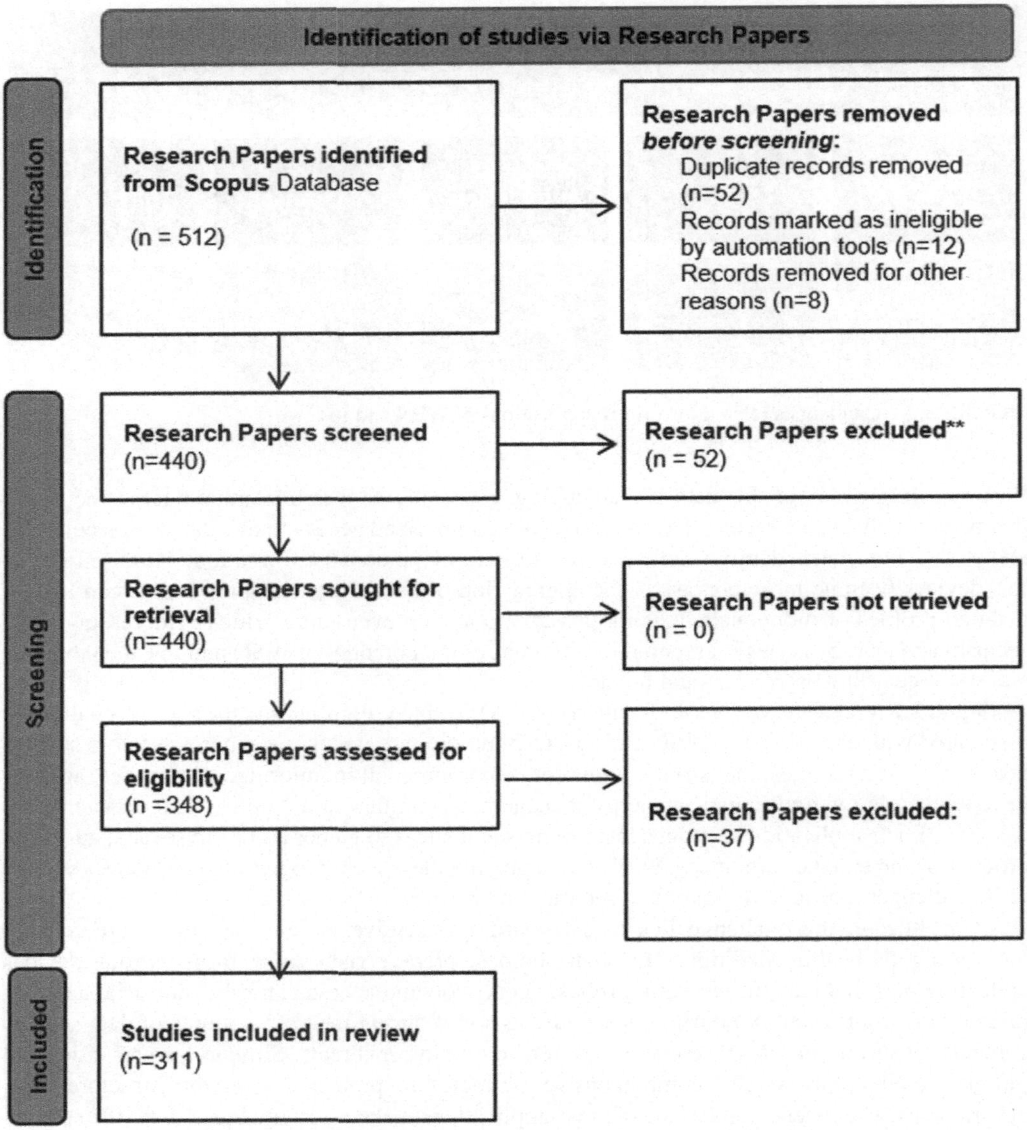

FIGURE 2.3 PRISMA analysis.

further. The inclusion criteria were applied to ensure that only studies directly relevant to the research question, such as those addressing security and privacy issues in WSN and IoT, were considered. This screening process resulted in 440 studies being considered suitable for retrieval [1–57].

Out of these 440 studies, none were excluded at the retrieval stage, demonstrating that the researchers successfully accessed all the studies deemed relevant. However, during the eligibility assessment, where studies were closely examined for methodological rigour, relevance, and other quality indicators, 37 studies were excluded. This exclusion may have been due to factors such as methodological flaws, outdated information, or irrelevance to the specific research focus.

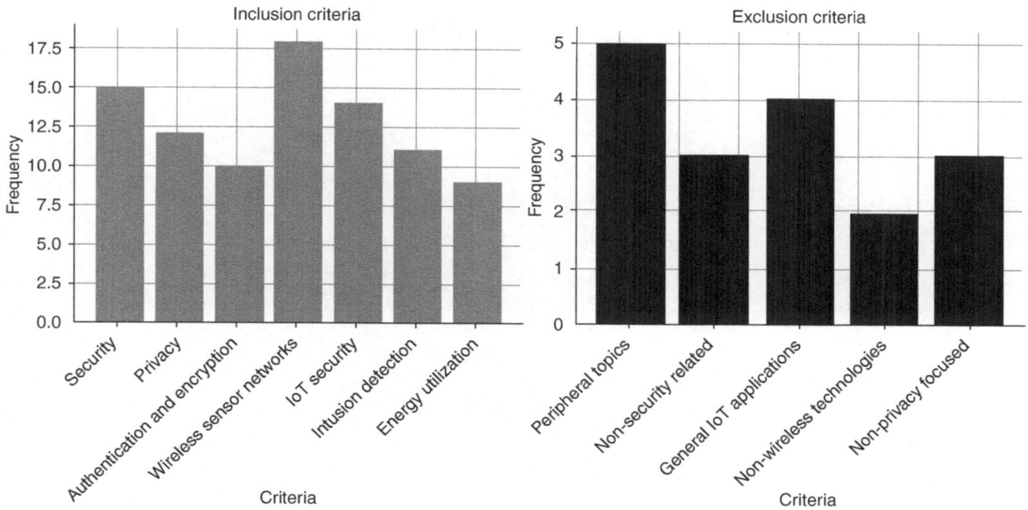

FIGURE 2.4 Inclusion and exclusion criteria of research works.

Ultimately, 311 studies were included in the review, representing about 61 percent of the initially identified records. This statistic highlights the selectivity and rigour of the inclusion criteria, ensuring that the final review was based on the most relevant and high-quality evidence. The exclusion of 201 studies throughout the process (52 duplicates, 52 during screening, and 37 during eligibility assessment) underscores the importance of careful and systematic evaluation to maintain the review's focus and credibility.

Figure 2.4 presents two bar charts, the first figure represents the inclusion criteria, and the other shows the exclusion criteria, both of which were applied during the PRISMA-based systematic review process. The inclusion criteria chart on the left highlights the frequency with which various factors were considered essential for including studies in the review. Key criteria such as "security," "privacy," "wireless sensor networks," and "IoT security" appear frequently, indicating that studies focusing on these areas were prioritized. "Wireless Sensor Networks" and "Security" had the highest frequencies, emphasizing their importance in the context of the review.

On the right, the exclusion criteria chart illustrates the factors that led to the exclusion of studies. "Peripheral Topics" had the highest frequency, suggesting that studies not directly related to the core focus of the review were commonly excluded. Other significant exclusion factors included "Non-Security Related" and "General IoT Applications," indicating that studies that did not address specific security or privacy concerns were also omitted. Together, these charts demonstrate the rigorous and focused approach taken during the review, ensuring that only the most relevant and high-quality studies were included while irrelevant or less pertinent studies were systematically excluded.

2.3 SYSTEMATIC LITERATURE ANALYSIS

For the systematic literature review analysis, the co-occurrence of the keywords and authors is analysed. The analysis is shown in Figure 2.5. Central concepts such as "wireless sensor networks," "security," "sensor nodes," and "authentication" are prominently featured, indicating their critical importance and frequent discussion in the literature. The close connections between

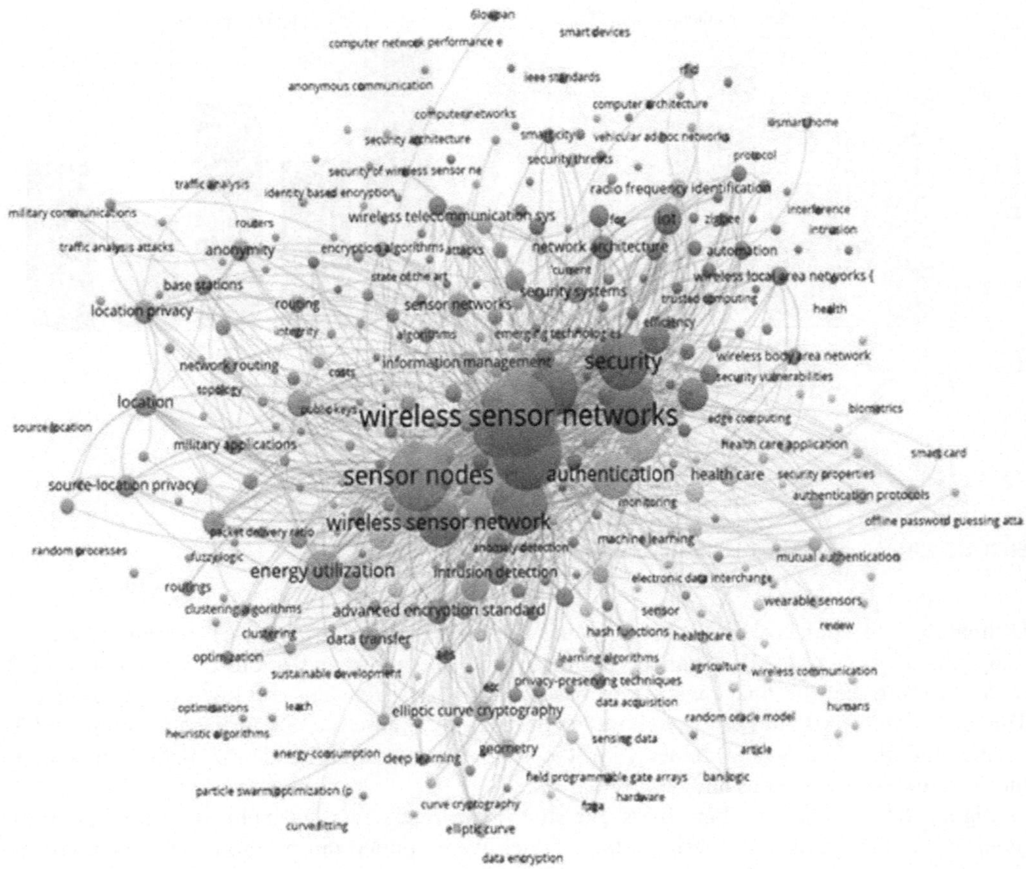

FIGURE 2.5 Network visualization of WSN and IoT security.

these topics suggest that they are often addressed together, highlighting the intertwined nature of security and network management in WSN and IoT. Additionally, the presence of "privacy," "location privacy," and "encryption" as interconnected nodes suggests that privacy concerns are a significant focus, particularly in relation to protecting sensitive data and securing communication channels. The visualization also highlights the diversity of related topics, such as "energy utilization," "intrusion detection," and "machine learning," reflecting the multifaceted challenges of securing WSN and IoT systems. The thematic clusters, distinguished by different colours, point to distinct areas of research, such as healthcare applications, smart cities, and environmental monitoring, each with its own set of security and privacy challenges. The complexity of addressing security and privacy in WSN and IoT, where a broad range of interconnected issues must be managed to ensure the safe and effective deployment of these technologies [32–40].

The network visualization is shown in Figure 2.6, highlights the evolution and interconnections of key topics related to IoT and WSN from 2017 to 2020. Prominent nodes like "IoT," "system," "algorithm," "technology," and "node" suggest that these are central themes in the research during this period. The colour gradient, ranging from blue to yellow, indicates the time frame in which these topics gained prominence, with yellow representing more recent focus areas.

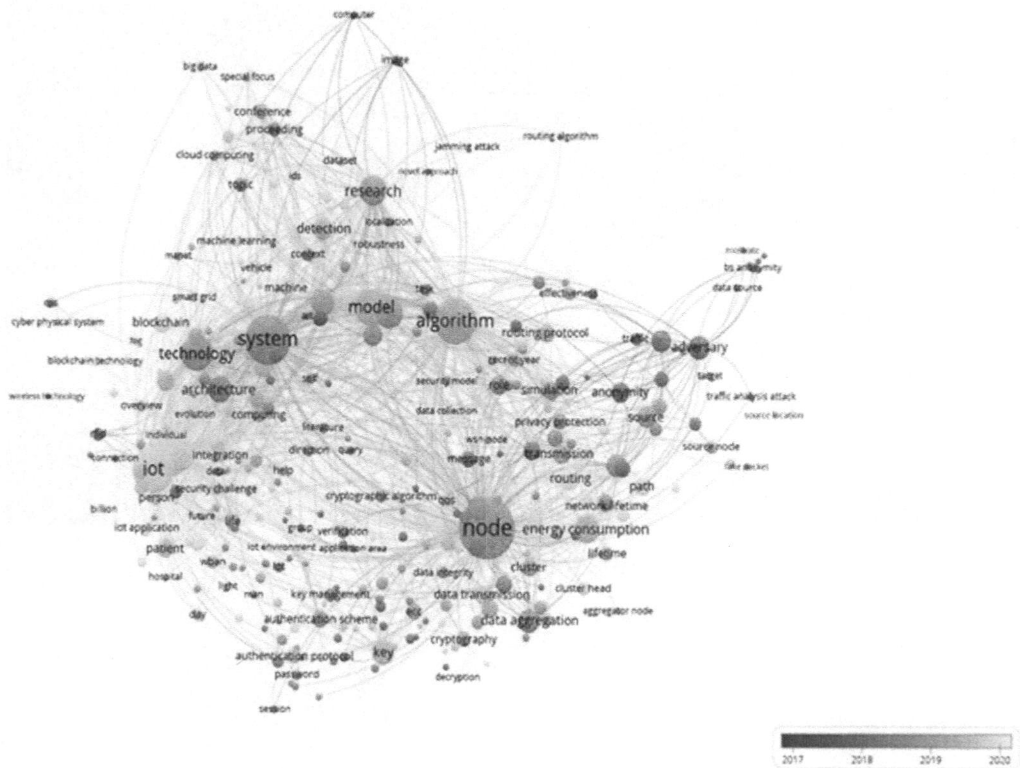

FIGURE 2.6 Evolution of IoT and WSN research topics (2017–2020).

Topics such as "blockchain," "privacy protection," and "energy consumption" are shown to be increasingly relevant, reflecting their growing importance in the context of IoT security and efficiency. The dense connections between nodes such as "algorithm," "energy consumption," and "routing" suggest that these are not only critical areas of study but also highly interrelated, indicating that advancements in one area often impact others. The visualization also shows the emergence of complex challenges like "adversary" and "anonymity," which are tightly linked to privacy and security concerns. The network illustrates a dynamic and evolving field where new technologies and methodologies are continually integrated to address the multifaceted challenges of IoT and WSN systems [39–48].

The heatmap visualization is shown in Figure 2.7, which showcases the prominent researchers contributing to the field of WSN and IoT. The intensity of the yellow regions indicates areas of high concentration, suggesting that these researchers are highly active and influential within the academic community. Names like "Liu, X.," "Zhang, X.," "Wang, J.," and "Chen, Y." appear in the densest clusters, reflecting their significant contributions to the field. The spread of these clusters across different areas of the map may indicate collaboration networks or distinct research focuses among groups of researchers. The presence of multiple clusters suggests that the field is broad, with various sub-domains being explored by different groups of researchers. The heatmap highlights key individuals driving research in WSN and IoT, providing insight into the academic landscape of this rapidly evolving field [49–53].

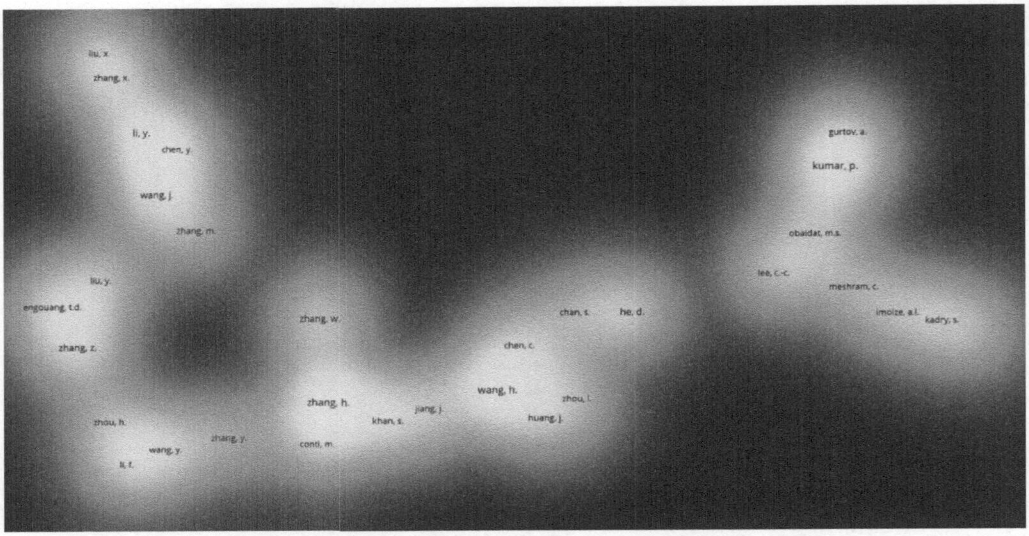

FIGURE 2.7 Heatmap of key researchers in WSN and IoT.

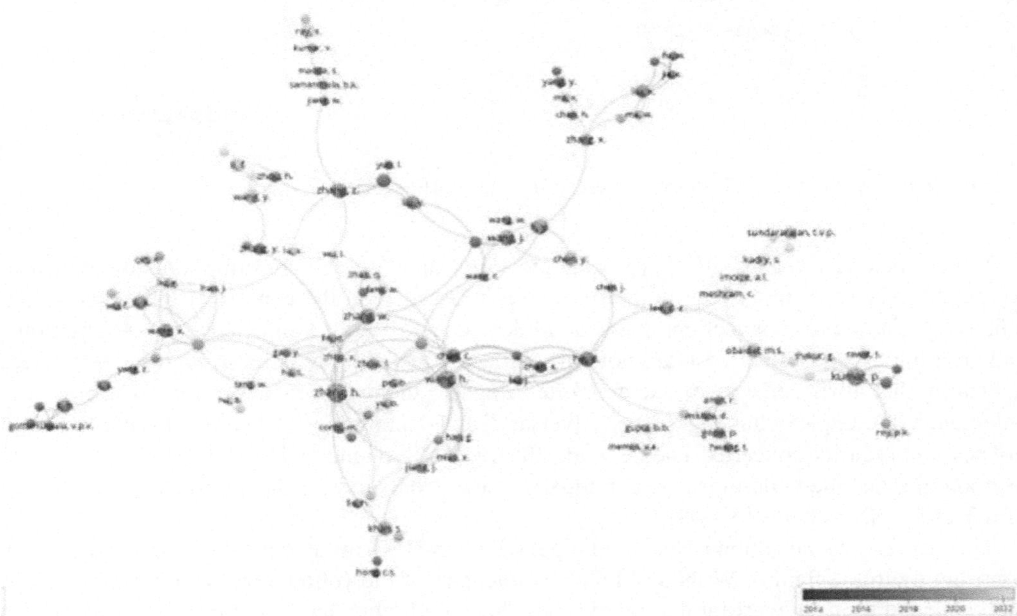

FIGURE 2.8 Evolution of influential researchers in WSN and IoT (2014–2022).

The network visualization is shown in Figure 2.8, which map displays the collaboration patterns and temporal evolution of key researchers in the field of WSN and IoT over the years 2014 to 2022. The nodes represent individual researchers, and the connecting lines indicate collaborations between them. Several prominent clusters can be observed, each representing a group of researchers who have worked closely together. For example, researchers like "Wang H.,"

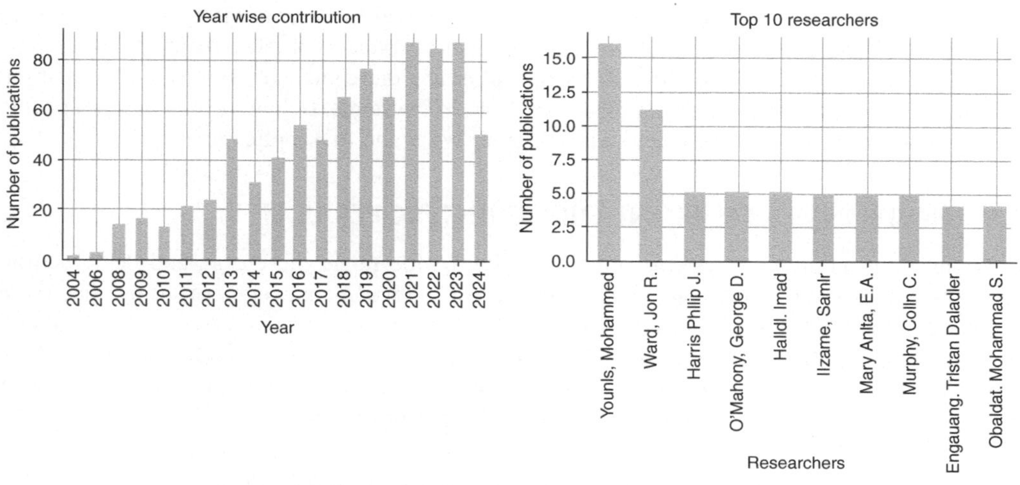

FIGURE 2.9 Year-wise contribution of researchers in the last 20 years.

"Zhang H.," and "Chen C." appear to be central figures within their clusters, suggesting that they are pivotal in fostering collaborations within their networks. The presence of yellow nodes, such as "Kumar P." and "Obaidat M.S.," indicates active and recent research collaborations, showing their continued influence in the field [52–57].

The interconnectedness of the nodes highlights the collaborative nature of research in WSN and IoT, with many researchers working across different groups and contributing to various studies. The visualization also shows that the field is dynamic, with new collaborations forming over time, as indicated by the yellow nodes. This network map provides valuable insights into the key players and collaborative dynamics that have shaped the research landscape in WSN and IoT over the past few years.

The left chart of Figure 2.9 shows the number of publications per year from 2004 to 2024, highlighting the growth and development of research in WSN and IoT over time. The chart shows a steady increase in the number of publications starting around 2010, with significant growth occurring between 2015 and 2021. The peak years, 2020 and 2021, saw the highest number of publications, each exceeding 80. This trend indicates a burgeoning interest in and expansion of research activity in these fields during these years. The slight decline in 2022 and 2023 may reflect a stabilization or shift in research focus. The data for 2024 is understandably lower, as it likely reflects partial data for the year.

The right chart identifies the top 10 researchers based on their publication output in WSN and IoT. "Younis, Mohamed" leads with the highest number of publications, followed by "Ward, Jon R." and "Harris, Philip J." These researchers are recognized as leading contributors to the field, with their work significantly influencing the direction of research. The rest of the top 10, including "O'Mahony, George D." and "Hafidi, Imad," show a steady output, underscoring their continued impact in advancing the field. The relatively even distribution of publications among these top researchers suggests a collaborative and competitive research environment.

2.4 APPLICATION-SPECIFIC SECURITY AND PRIVACY ISSUES

WSN and IoT have become integral to various applications across different sectors, from healthcare and smart cities to agriculture and military operations as shown in Figure 2.10. These technologies offer significant advantages by enabling real-time monitoring, data collection, and automated decision-making. However, they also introduce complex security and privacy challenges unique to each application domain. Addressing these challenges is critical to ensuring the safe, efficient, and reliable operation of WSN and IoT systems. Below, we explore the specific security and privacy issues associated with different WSN and IoT applications.

2.5 ENVIRONMENTAL MONITORING (INTEROPERABILITY)

Environmental monitoring systems often integrate a wide range of sensors and devices from different manufacturers, making interoperability a significant challenge. Ensuring that these diverse devices can communicate and work together securely is crucial to maintaining the integrity and reliability of the collected data. Interoperability issues can lead to vulnerabilities, where insecure communication channels or incompatible devices may expose the system to cyber threats, compromising the accuracy and security of environmental data.

2.6 INDUSTRIAL AUTOMATION (DEVICE HETEROGENEITY)

In industrial automation, a variety of devices, including sensors, actuators, and control systems, are interconnected to streamline manufacturing processes. The heterogeneity of these devices, each with different capabilities and security features, creates challenges in maintaining a unified and secure network. Managing this diversity is critical to prevent security breaches, as weaker devices could become entry points for attackers, potentially disrupting operations and compromising sensitive industrial data.

2.7 SMART HOMES (RELIABLE CONNECTIVITY)

Smart home environments rely heavily on continuous and reliable connectivity between various IoT devices, such as security cameras, smart thermostats, and voice assistants. Disruptions in connectivity can lead to gaps in security, where devices may become vulnerable to attacks or fail to function correctly. Ensuring reliable and secure communication among devices is essential to protect the privacy and safety of the home's occupants, as any breach could expose personal data or allow unauthorized access to the home.

2.8 HEALTHCARE (DATA PRIVACY AND CONFIDENTIALITY)

In healthcare, IoT devices are used to monitor patients' vital signs, manage medical equipment, and store sensitive health records. The privacy and confidentiality of this data are paramount, as breaches could have severe consequences, including identity theft, unauthorized access to medical records, and compromised patient safety. Ensuring robust encryption and access controls in healthcare IoT systems is essential to protect sensitive patient information from cyber threats.

2.9 SMART CITIES (SCALABILITY)

Smart cities integrate a vast array of IoT devices and sensors to manage urban infrastructure, traffic, energy consumption, and public safety. The scalability of these systems poses significant security and privacy challenges as the increasing number of connected devices and data points expands the potential attack surface. Ensuring that the system can scale securely without introducing vulnerabilities is crucial to maintaining the safety and efficiency of smart city operations.

2.10 AGRICULTURE (ENERGY EFFICIENCY)

In agricultural IoT systems, energy efficiency is a critical concern, as many sensors and devices are deployed in remote locations with limited access to power. These devices must operate securely while conserving energy, which often involves trade-offs between security and power consumption. Ensuring that agricultural IoT systems can maintain secure communication and data integrity without compromising energy efficiency is essential for the reliable operation of precision agriculture technologies.

2.11 TRANSPORTATION AND LOGISTICS (PHYSICAL SECURITY)

IoT devices in transportation and logistics are used to track vehicles, monitor cargo conditions, and optimize supply chain operations. The physical security of these devices is paramount, as tampering with or physically accessing these devices could lead to the theft of goods, disruption of logistics operations, or unauthorized tracking of vehicles. Implementing robust physical and cybersecurity measures is necessary to protect the integrity of transportation and logistics networks.

2.12 ENERGY MANAGEMENT (SOFTWARE VULNERABILITIES)

Energy management systems leverage IoT devices to monitor and control energy consumption in buildings, industries, and smart grids. Software vulnerabilities in these systems can lead to severe consequences, including unauthorized control over energy distribution, data breaches, or disruptions in energy supply. Ensuring that the software managing these systems is secure and regularly updated is critical to preventing cyberattacks that could compromise energy infrastructure.

2.13 MILITARY AND DEFENCE (COMMUNICATION SECURITY)

In military and defence applications, IoT devices are used for surveillance, communication, and battlefield management. Communication security is paramount in these environments, as any breach could lead to the interception of sensitive information, disruption of military operations, or exposure of strategic assets. Implementing advanced encryption and secure communication protocols is essential to protect military IoT systems from cyber threats and ensure the confidentiality and integrity of defence operations.

2.14 DISASTER MANAGEMENT (AUTHENTICATION AND AUTHORIZATION)

IoT devices play a crucial role in disaster management by providing real-time data on environmental conditions, coordinating emergency response efforts, and managing resources. Authentication and authorization are critical in these systems to ensure that only authorized personnel can access and control the devices. This is essential to prevent malicious actors from disrupting disaster response operations or accessing sensitive information during emergencies. Implementing robust security measures in disaster management IoT systems is vital to ensuring the effectiveness and safety of emergency response efforts.

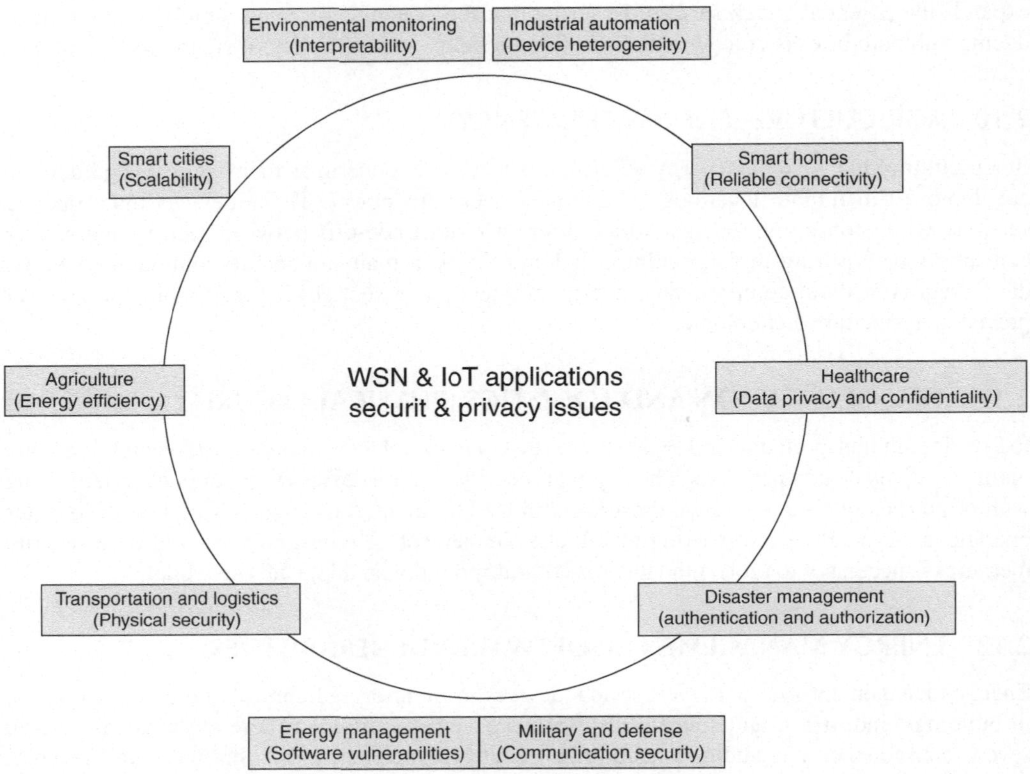

FIGURE 2.10 Security and privacy issues across various WSN and IoT applications.

2.15 DISCUSSION

The analysis of security and privacy issues across various applications of WSN and IoT highlights the intricate and multifaceted challenges faced by these technologies. As WSN and IoT become more pervasive in critical sectors such as healthcare, smart homes, industrial automation, and smart cities, the need for robust security measures becomes increasingly paramount. Each application domain presents unique challenges: for instance, healthcare systems require stringent data privacy and confidentiality measures to protect sensitive patient information, while industrial automation must address the heterogeneity of devices to ensure seamless and secure operations. The analysis shows that these challenges are not only technical but also involve careful consideration of the operational environment and the specific requirements of each application.

The inclusion and exclusion criteria applied in the systematic review emphasize the importance of focusing on the most relevant and high-quality studies to address these complex issues. The visualization of the research landscape, including the identification of key researchers and the evolution of research topics over time, underscores the dynamic nature of the field. It reveals how certain topics, such as energy efficiency in agriculture or communication security in military applications, have gained prominence as the threats and vulnerabilities associated with WSN and IoT have evolved. This evolution is reflective of the broader technological advancements and the growing recognition of the critical role that security and privacy play in the successful deployment of these technologies.

Ultimately, the discussion underscores the need for continued research and innovation to address the security and privacy challenges inherent in WSN and IoT. As these technologies continue to expand into new domains, the development of scalable, interoperable, and energy-efficient solutions will be essential. The findings suggest that a holistic approach, integrating insights from various application areas and focusing on both technical and policy solutions, is necessary to mitigate risks and ensure the resilience of WSN and IoT systems. This comprehensive approach will not only enhance the security and privacy of these technologies but also support their broader adoption and integration into critical infrastructure worldwide.

2.16 CONCLUSION

This study provides a comprehensive analysis of the security and privacy challenges associated with the deployment of wireless sensor networks (WSN) and the Internet of Things (IoT) across various application domains. The findings underscore the diverse and evolving nature of these challenges, driven by the specific operational environments and the critical role that these technologies play in sectors such as healthcare, smart cities, and industrial automation. The application-specific challenges, such as data privacy, device interoperability, and energy efficiency, highlight the need for customized security measures that address the unique vulnerabilities of each domain. The study also demonstrates the value of systematic reviews and data visualization in identifying key research areas and guiding future innovations in the field.

In conclusion, the continued expansion of WSN and IoT into new areas requires an ongoing commitment to developing robust, scalable, and context-aware security solutions. As these technologies become increasingly integral to modern infrastructure, the development of effective security and privacy frameworks will be essential to ensuring their safe and sustainable deployment. The insights gained from this study can guide researchers, policymakers, and industry stakeholders in their efforts to enhance the security and privacy of WSN and IoT systems, ultimately supporting their broader adoption and integration into critical infrastructure worldwide.

REFERENCES

[1] B. Kumara and S. A. Padmanabhan, "A condition-based distributed approach for secured privacy preservation of nodes in wireless sensor networks IoT," *International Journal of Reconfigurable and Embedded Systems*, vol. 13, no. 2, pp. 441–449, 2024. doi: 10.11591/ijres.v13.i2. pp441–449.

[2] S. C. Mary, K. Murugeswari, S. Jyothi Shri, and N. Senthamilarasi, "A secure and effective data aggregation in WSN for improved security and data privacy," *Review of Computer Engineering Research*, vol. 10, no. 3, pp. 83–95, 2023. doi: 10.18488/76.v10i3.3494.

[3] Z. Xu, D. He, P. Vijayakumar, B. B. Gupta, and J. Shen, "Certificateless public auditing scheme with data privacy and dynamics in group user model of cloud-assisted medical WSNs," *IEEE Journal of Biomedical and Health Informatics*, vol. 27, no. 5, pp. 2334–2344, 2023. doi: 10.1109/JBHI.2021.3128775.

[4] P. Anandan, N. Krishnaraj, N. Kumaratharan, and N. Anbuselvan, "Privacy preserving encryption with reliable data transmission for cluster based vehicular networks," in *Blockchain Enabled Secure Big Data Computing for Smart Cities Using Internet of Things*, 2023, pp. 329–351. NOVA Science Publisher.

[5] S. Urooj, S. Lata, S. Ahmad, S. Mehfuz, and S. Kalathil, "Cryptographic data security for reliable wireless sensor network," *Alexandria Engineering Journal*, vol. 72, pp. 37–50, 2023. doi: 10.1016/j.aej.2023.03.061.

[6] Y. Yanti, Y. Away, T. Y. Arif, and N. Nasaruddin, "Routing technique in location source privacy for wireless sensor network: A review," in *AIP Conference Proceedings*, vol. 3082, no. 1, 2024. doi: 10.1063/5.0201634.

[7] A. Elkhalil, J. Zhang, R. Elhabob, and N. Eltayieb, "POOSC: Provably online/offline signcryption scheme for vehicular communication in VANETs," *Computing*, vol. 105, no. 11, pp. 2539–2561, 2023. doi: 10.1007/s00607-023-01196-4.

[8] I. B. Chettri, S. Ray, and P. Das, "SAK-SAE: A secure authentication and key-exchange scheme for smart agricultural environment using fuzzy extractor," in *OCIT 2023–21st International Conference on Information Technology, Proceedings*, 2023, pp. 867–873. doi: 10.1109/OCIT59427.2023.10430994.

[9] A. Ayub Khan, A. Laghari, M. Rashid, H. Li, A. Rehman Javed, and T. R. Gadekallu, "Artificial intelligence and blockchain technology for secure smart grid and power distribution automation: A state-of-the-art review," *Sustainable Energy Technologies and Assessments*, vol. 57, 2023. doi: 10.1016/j.seta.2023.103282.

[10] M. Supriya and T. Adilakshmi, "Security aware cluster-based routing using MTCSA and HEA for wireless sensor networks," *International Journal of Intelligent Systems and Applications in Engineering*, vol. 11, no. 2, pp. 663–669, 2023.

[11] A. N. Anjali, C. B. Sreelakshmi, and T. R. Nair, "Blackhole attack detection in wireless sensor network using backpropagation algorithm," in *2023 14th International Conference on Computing Communication and Networking Technologies, ICCCNT 2023*, 2023. doi: 10.1109/ICCCNT56998.2023.10307586.

[12] H. Moudoud, Z. Abou El Houda, and B. Brik, "Advancing security and trust in WSNs: A federated multi-agent deep reinforcement learning approach," *IEEE Transactions on Consumer Electronics*, 2024. doi: 10.1109/TCE.2024.3440178.

[13] S. K. Erskine, "Secure data aggregation using authentication and authorization for privacy preservation in wireless sensor networks," *Sensors*, vol. 24, no. 7, 2024. doi: 10.3390/s24072090.

[14] S. R. Jena, M. Z. U. Rahman, D. K. Sinha, P. R. Kumar, V. Vrince, K. U. Singh, T. Syamsundararao, J. N. V. R. S. Kumar, and J. Balajee, "An innovative secure and privacy- preserving federated learning based hybrid deep learning model for intrusion detection in internet-enabled wireless sensor networks," *IEEE Transactions on Consumer Electronics*, 2024. doi: 10.1109/TCE.2024.3442015.

[15] M. Al-Zubaidie and R. A. Muhajjar, "Integrating trustworthy mechanisms to support data and information security in health sensors," *Procedia Computer Science*, vol. 237, pp. 43–52, 2024. doi: 10.1016/j.procs.2024.05.078.

[16] S. Bharany and M. Maashi, "A critical investigation into the blockchain technology and its present-day uses," in *2023 3rd International Conference on Computing and Information Technology, ICCIT 2023*, 2023, pp. 69–72. doi: 10.1109/ICCIT58132.2023.10273943.

[17] G. K. Kumar, S. K. Prashanth, E. Padmalatha, M. V. K. Reddy, N. R. Devi, L. Abualigah, P. Chithaluru, and M. Kumar, "An optimized meta-heuristic clustering-based routing scheme for secured wireless sensor networks," *International Journal of Communication Systems*, vol. 37, no. 11, 2024. doi: 10.1002/dac.5791.

[18] S. M. S. Bukhari, M. H. Zafar, M. A. Houran, S. K. R. Moosavi, M. Mansoor, M. Muaaz, and F. Sanfilippo, "Secure and privacy-preserving intrusion detection in wireless sensor networks: Federated learning with SCNN-Bi-LSTM for enhanced reliability," *Ad Hoc Networks*, vol. 155, 2024. doi: 10.1016/j.adhoc.2024.103407.

[19] A. Jonnala, R. Ampani, D. F. Abbasi, A. Alsadoon, and P. W. C. Prasad, "data security risk mitigation in the cloud through virtual machine monitoring," *Lecture Notes in Electrical Engineering*, vol. 1029, pp. 227–238, 2023. doi: 10.1007/978-3-031-29078-7_20.

[20] S. Suryawanshi, N. S. Patankar, Y. S. Deshmukh, and N. L. Shelake, "An investigation on leveraging wireless sensor networks and radio frequency identification to develop internet of things applications," in *14th International Conference on Advances in Computing, Control, and Telecommunication Technologies, ACT 2023*, 2023, pp. 2336–2342.

[21] J. A. I. Syed Masood, M. Jeyaselvi, N. Senthamarai, S. Koteswari, M. Sathya, and N. S. K. Chakravarthy, "Privacy preservation in wireless sensor network using energy efficient multipath routing for healthcare data," *Measurement: Sensors*, vol. 29, pp. 1–11, 2023. doi: 10.1016/j.measen.2023.100867.

[22] B. S. E. Zoraida and G. Indumathi, "A comparative study on software-defined network with traditional networks," *TEM Journal*, vol. 13, no. 1, pp. 167–176, 2024. doi: 10.18421/TEM131-17.

[23] N. Chandnani and C. N. Khairnar, "A reliable protocol for data aggregation and optimized routing in IoT WSNs based on machine learning," *Wireless Personal Communications*, vol. 130, no. 4, pp. 2589–2622, 2023. doi: 10.1007/s11277-023-10393-5.

[24] Akhilesh Panchal and Rajat K. Singh, "EEHCHR: energy efficient hybrid clustering and hierarchical routing for wireless sensor networks," *Ad Hoc Networks (Elsevier),* vol. 123, no. 1, 102692, 2021.

[25] Akhilesh Panchal and Rajat K. Singh, "EOCGS: energy efficient optimum number of cluster head and grid head selection in wireless sensor networks," *Telecommunication Systems (Springer),* vol. 78, no. 1, pp. 1–13, 2021.

[26] R. Paul, S. Rai, S. Banerjee, and P. Meher, "A robust smart card based authentication and key agreement scheme for WSN using fuzzy extractor," *Peer-to-Peer Networking and Applications*, vol. 17, no. 1, pp. 432–450, 2024. doi: 10.1007/s12083-023-01583-w.

[27] S. A. Ettyem, I. Ahmed, W. S. Ahmed, N. A. Hussien, M. G. Majeed, K. Cengiz, and N. Benameur, "Intelligent wireless sensor networks for healthcare: bridging biomedical clothing to the IoT future," *Journal of Intelligent Systems and Internet of Things*, vol. 9, no. 2, pp. 36–50, 2023. doi: 10.54216/JISIoT.090203.

[28] A. Gunasekaran, "Internet of Things-based wireless sensor networks for monitoring access constraint security measures in liable data aggregation," *International Journal of Communication Systems*, vol. 36, no. 17, 2023. doi: 10.1002/dac.5596.

[29] J. Saini and R. Kait, "Exploring machine learning strategies for intrusion detection in wireless sensor networks," in *2024 IEEE Sth International Conference for Convergence in Technology, I2CT 2024*, 2024. doi: 10.1109/I2CT61223.2024.10543320.

[30] Y. Patidar, M. Jain, and A. K. Vyas, "Optimal stable cluster head selection method for maximal throughput and lifetime of homogeneous wireless sensor network," *SN Comput Sci,* vol. 5, no. 218, pp. 1–9, Jan. 2024, doi: 10.1007/s42979-023-02459-9.

[31] A. Panchal and R.t K. Singh, "EADCR: energy aware distance based cluster head selection and routing protocol for wireless sensor networks," *J. of Circuits, Systems, and Computers (World Scientific)* vol. 30, no. 4, pp. 2150063, 2021

[32] A. Alsumayt, M. Alshammari, Z. M. Alfawaer, F. N. Al-Wesabi, N. El-Haggar, S. S. Aljameel, S. Albassam, S. AlGhareeb, N. M. Alghamdi, and N. Aldossary, "Efficient security level in wireless sensor networks (WSNs) using four-factors authentication over the Internet of Things (IoT)," *PeerJ Computer Science*, vol. 10, 2024. doi: 10.7717/peerj-cs.2091.

[33] V. U. Ihekoronye, C. I. Nwakanma, D. S. Kim, and J. M. Lee, "ASR-Fed: agnostic straggler-resilient semi-asynchronous federated learning technique for secured drone network," *International Journal of Machine Learning and Cybernetics*, 2024. doi: 10.1007/s13042-024-02238-9.

[34] C. Vinola, P. Solainayagi, P. G. Kuppusamy, G. Premi, and C. Srinivasan, "Data Privacy and Confidentiality in Healthcare Applications of IoT-Enabled Wireless Sensor Networks," in *2023 2nd International Conference on Smart Technologies for Smart Nation, SmartTechCon2023*, 2023, pp.610–614. doi: 10.1109/SmartTechCon57526.2023.10391743.

[35] V. V. Gijare, S. D. Rajput, S. Ambala, M. S. Aware, W. V. Ashok, Y. Gandhi, and I. Memon, "Designing a decentralized IoT–WSN architecture using blockchain technology," in *WSN and IoT: An Integrated Approach for Smart Applications*, 2024, pp. 291–313. doi: 10.1201/9781003437079-13.

[36] K. Sharma, S. Chhabra, and S. Rani, "Analysis of node security optimization in WSN," in *Artificial Intelligence, Blockchain, Computing and Security: Volume 1*, vol. 1, pp. 504–509, 2023. doi: 10.1201/9781003393580-77.

[37] M. Singh and M. P. Singh, "Congestion avoidance with source location privacy using octopus-based dynamic routing protocol in WSN," *Wireless Networks*, vol. 29, no. 2, pp. 729–748, 2023. doi: 10.1007/s11276-022-03165-9.

[38] A. O. Khadidos, N. Alhebaishi, A. O. Khadidos, M. Altwijri, A. G. Fayoumi, and M. Ragab, "Efficient key distribution for secure and energy-optimized communication in wireless sensor network using bioinspired algorithms," *Alexandria Engineering Journal*, vol. 92, pp. 63–73, 2024. doi: 10.1016/j.aej.2024.02.064.

[39] Y. A. Bangash, W. Iqbal, S. Rubab, A. W. Khan, and W. Aman, "BSLPSDN: Base station location privacy via software-defined networking (SDN) in wireless sensor networks," *International Journal of Communication Systems*, vol. 36, no. 17, 2023. doi: 10.1002/dac.5601.

[40] S. Sharma, A. Kaur, D. Gupta, S. Juneja, and M. Kumar, "Dragon fly algorithm based approach for escalating the security among the nodes in wireless sensor network based system," *SN Applied Sciences*, vol. 5, no. 12, 2023. doi: 10.1007/s42452-023-05614-2.

[41] M. Anoop, L. W. Mary, A. J. Wilson, and W. S. Kiran, "Optimized graph transformer with molecule attention network based multi class attack detection framework for enhancing privacy and security in WSN," *Multimedia Tools and Applications*, 2024. doi: 10.1007/s11042-024-19516-x.

[42] T. Kanwar, G. Gupta, Sonia, and R. Kumar, "A review about privacy and security within WBAN utilizing cryptology," in *2023 3rd International Conference on Advance Computing and Innovative Technologies in Engineering, ICACITE 2023*, 2023, pp. 1838–1843. doi: 10.1109/ICACITE57410.2023.10182916.

[43] L. Al-Qaisi, S. Hassan, and N. H. Zakaria, "Performance evaluation of rank attack impact on routing protocol in low-power and lossy networks," *Indonesian Journal of Electrical Engineering and Computer Science*, vol. 36, no. 1, pp. 242–251, 2024. doi: 10.11591/ijeecs.v36.i1.pp242-251.

[44] M. Garg and Y. Dogra, "ASLPP-RR routing based on improved IDAF-FIT clustering with secure data aggregation in wireless sensor network," in *2023 3rd International Conference on Advance Computing and Innovative Technologies in Engineering, ICACITE 2023*, 2023, pp. 1655–1658. doi: 10.1109/ICACITE57410.2023.10182879.

[45] R. H. C. and G. C. D., "Privacy-aware novel lightweight cryptography mechanism for IoT (Internet of Things) Security," *Multimedia Tools and Applications*, 2024. doi: 10.1007/s11042-024-18517-0.

[46] T. Rajendran, S. V. Shri Bharathi, S. Sridhar, and T. Anitha, "A study on blockchain technologies for security and privacy applications in a network," *SSRG International Journal of Electronics and Communication Engineering*, vol. 10, no. 6, pp. 69–91, 2023. doi: 10.14445/23488549/IJECE-V10I6P107.

[47] R. V. Krishna, G. Balachandran, S. Prasad Ch, and S. Ranjith, "Nature-inspired algorithms to perform localization and security in wireless sensor networks," in *Proceedings of the 2023 International Conference on Innovative Computing, Intelligent Communication and Smart Electrical Systems, ICSES 2023*, 2023. doi: 10.1109/ICSES60034.2023.10465305.

[48] A. C. S. Sheela, B. S. Ahamed, D. Poornima, and A. C. S. Sagayaraj, "Integration of wireless sensor networks with IoT in smart transportation systems and traffic management," in *1st International Conference on Emerging Research in Computational Science, ICERCS 2023 – Proceedings*, 2023. doi: 10.1109/ICERCS57948.2023.10433998.

[49] A. Soni, "A concentrated energy consumption wireless sensor network by symmetric encryption and attribute based encryption technique," *Journal of Cybersecurity and Information Management*, vol. 12, no. 1, pp. 8–18, 2023. doi: 10.54216/JCIM.120101.

[50] G. Thakur, M. S. Obaidat, P. Sharma, S. Prajapat, and P. Kumar, "A provably secure authenticated key agreement protocol for industrial sensor network system," *Concurrency and Computation: Practice and Experience*, 2024. doi: 10.1002/cpe.8250.

[51] N. V. Ravindhar, S. Sasikumar, and N. Bharathiraja, "Integration of cloud-based scheme with industrial wireless sensor network for data publishing in privacy of point source," *International Journal of Cloud Computing*, vol. 13, no. 2, pp. 124–138, 2024. doi: 10.1504/IJCC.2024.137408.

[52] J. Mante-Khurpade, M. Dhotay, P. Patil, S. Kulkarni, S. Budhavale, and S. Ikhar, "Enhancing data privacy in wireless sensor network using homomorphic encryption," *Journal of Discrete Mathematical Sciences and Cryptography*, vol. 27, no. 2, pp. 833–842, 2024. doi: 10.47974/JDMSC-1959.

[53] N. Mathur and S. Sinha, "Security model and access control mechanisms for attack mitigation in IoE," in *Blockchain Technology for IoE: Security and Privacy Perspectives*, 2023, pp. 67–100. doi: 10.1201/9781003366010-6.

[54] A. Rejeb, K. Rejeb, A. Appolloni, S. Jagtap, M. Iranmanesh, S. Alghamdi, Y. Alhasawi, and Y. Kayikci, "Unleashing the power of internet of things and blockchain: A comprehensive analysis and future directions," *Internet of Things and Cyber-Physical Systems*, vol. 4, pp. 1–18, 2024. doi: 10.1016/j.iotcps.2023.06.003.

[55] N. Dhanalakshmi, "QoS based authentication and clustering in WSN with proficient meta-heuristic based fuzzy logic decision module," *Ad-Hoc and Sensor Wireless Networks*, vol. 57, no. 1-2, pp. 35–58, 2023. doi: 10.32908/ahswn.v57.7553.

[56] M. Singh and M. P. Singh, "Awareness based gannet optimization for source location privacy preservation with multiple assets in wireless sensor networks," *Concurrency and Computation: Practice and Experience*, vol. 36, no. 21, 2024. doi: 10.1002/cpe.8191.

[57] K. E. Hemapriya and S. Saraswathi, "An energy efficient, spontaneous, multi-path data routing algorithm with private key creation for heterogeneous network," *Communications in Computer and Information Science*, vol. 1973, pp. 248–263, 2024. doi: 10.1007/978-3-031-50993-3_20.

3 Cyber Security Concerns of IoT for Real-time Applications

A Review

Muhammad Muzamil Aslam, Ali Tufail,
Muhammad Nauman Irshad, Sajid Ali, and Liping Du

3.1 INTRODUCTION

Every gadget with an internet access is susceptible to theft and hacking. Billions of linked devices can be exploited to acquire personal information, disseminate viruses, and even do bodily harm in the era of the IoT (Misailov et al., 2024).

IoT cybersecurity will continue to be a key factor for manufacturers and end users as more government organizations, corporations, and consumers use and rely on IoT apps. Manufacturers must incorporate security measures even though end users bear some of the responsibility for IoT security (Hossain et al., 2024). This is a joint obligation.

Devices with internet access present numerous security risks. IoT connects previously unconnected devices, but general cybersecurity issues are not brand new. Hackers have been a problem for us for as long as we have benefited from the internet.

3.1.1 Overview of IoT and Its Integration in Real-Time Applications

Establishing an internet connection between a physical object and another device is the procedure. Kevin Ashton initially used the phrase "IoT" in 1999. Everything that has embedded sensors and the capacity to gather and send data across a network, including people and cars, is referred to as a "thing" (Lilhore et al., 2024).

Because it's so simple to connect equipment, people, and data, the IoT streamlines, enhances, and automates the process. Utilizing sensors, networks, and artificial intelligence could improve the efficacy of many systems. There is a reduction in costs that was not achievable before.

As per Statista, the IoT market is expected to rise to $483 billion by 2027, having reached $201 billion in 2022 alone. This trend is expected to continue. More studies present a similar picture, indicating that the IoT has a promising future.

IoT largely functions without the need for human interaction. These days, people can save a significant amount of time by having machines handle data collecting and processing chores. Human workers can spend more time on creative ideas and less time gathering data, allowing them to concentrate on applying it (Liang et al., 2024).

DOI: 10.1201/9781003491910-3

Often, IoT is used to increase productivity. One popular example is tracking vehicle miles and trips. Instead of employing personnel to track each vehicle's mileage and activities, large corporations with fleets of vehicles can turn to firms that provide IoT development services to create a platform that can be examined via IoT.

The future of chatbots can also be altered by IoT through its integration with other technologies, such as artificial intelligence. IoT devices have the capability to gather patient data and send it to physicians for examination.

By utilizing sensors, gadgets, and other facilities, IoT integration is transforming how businesses operate. The volume of data handled by IoT devices is enormous due to the annual growth in the number of connected devices.

This trend is unstoppable; according to IDC estimates, by 2025 there will be over 41.6 billion connected devices, possibly producing 79.4 ZB of data (Karthikeyan et al., 2024).

The volume and caliber of data from IoT devices will dictate how much practical data is needed for effective digitization. Businesses that include IoT into their operations can improve data availability and notify staff members of any events happening within the organization, giving them access to real-time insights that can be used immediately.

3.1.2 Importance of Addressing Cyber Security Concerns in IoT for Real-Time Applications

Unauthorized entry can have detrimental effects on the IoT. Imagine a situation in which a medical equipment or critical health data could be compromised by illegal access to a patient monitoring device (Karthikeyan et al., 2024; Liang et al., 2024; Lilhore et al., 2024). In a similar vein, hostile interference or accidents in the transportation sector might result from illegal access to vehicle control systems.

To tackle this issue, IoT cybersecurity employs robust user permission procedures, robust access controls, and robust authentication techniques. Reducing the possibility of illegal interference, it makes sure that only people or devices with the right authorization and credentials can access and use IoT devices (Kane, 2024; Lilhore et al., 2024).

3.1.3 Data Confidentiality

In the case of medical devices or industrial IoT, IoT devices frequently manage sensitive data, such as private medical information. To stop this information from getting into the wrong hands, data confidentiality is essential. To prevent unwanted parties from accessing data, IoT cybersecurity use encryption to protect information both during transmission and storage (Sinche et al., 2020). To make sure that only people with the right authorization and justifications can access this data, access controls further restrict who can view or retrieve it.

3.1.4 Prevention of Data Tampering

IoT data disruption can be quite hazardous. Utilizing encryption technology, data integrity can be confirmed through IoT cybersecurity. In other words, while transmission or storage, the data is examined for any unlawful alterations or changes. The system has the ability to take action in the event that it detects tampering, such as alerting the administrator or not acting on the modified data (Prasad et al., 2024; Senthil kumar & Vijay Anand, 2024). Ensuring the accuracy and reliability of decisions and actions derived from IoT data is ensured by cybersecurity controls.

3.1.5 Network Security

The foundation of IoT cybersecurity is cybersecurity since the IoT ecosystem is heavily reliant on network connectivity. Intrusion detection systems watch out for any dangers and questionable activities, while firewalls prevent unwanted users from accessing the network.

It is also very difficult for thieves to intercept or alter data in transit since secure communication protocols like HTTPS and MQTT-TLS encrypt data as it moves across the network. Cybersecurity measures contribute to ensuring the overall security and dependability of IoT applications by safeguarding IoT network infrastructure (Khan et al., 2024a).

3.1.6 Attacks Mitigation

The IoT industry is frequently targeted by cyberattacks because of the vast number of devices in use and the possible consequences of compromising these devices. The most frequent dangers to IoT devices include ransomware, malware, and distributed denial of service (DDoS) attacks. Cybersecurity breaches or data theft can occur from infected IoT devices (Alwahedi et al., 2024; Rekeraho et al., 2024). The detection and elimination of malware from devices is accomplished by IoT cybersecurity using antivirus and anti-malware solutions.

With backup systems and incident response plans, ransomware—which has the ability to lock down IoT devices and demand a fee to unlock—can be lessened. By using traffic filtering, rate limiting, and network monitoring to identify and stop DDoS assaults, we can ensure system availability without sacrificing performance. DDoS attacks have the potential to overwhelm IoT network traffic.

3.1.7 Update and Patch Management

Cybercriminals may be able to take advantage of weaknesses in the software and firmware that IoT devices usually run on. Regular updates and patch management are crucial for IoT cybersecurity in order to tackle this problem. In order to fix known vulnerabilities, this entails applying routine software and firmware upgrades supplied by device makers (Wu et al., 2024).

Furthermore, vulnerability assessments and vulnerability scans are used to help prioritize updates based on vulnerability severity and detect potential vulnerabilities that may need to be patched.

3.1.8 Regulations

Privacy and data protection laws must be followed since IoT devices frequently gather, send, or process sensitive data. Ensuring that these devices adhere to industry-specific legislation and standards, like General Data Protection Regulation (GDPR), Health Insurance Portability and Accountability Act (HIPAA), or International Organization for Standardization's ISO 27001, is possible through the implementation of IoT cybersecurity.

Encryption of data while it's in transit and at rest, stringent access restrictions, thorough records and audit trails, and quick notification of authorities and impacted parties are a few of the compliance methods used in IoT cybersecurity. Your company will be able to avoid fines for non-compliance if these procedures are followed.

3.1.9 Awareness

The way people behave has a big influence on IoT security. Ensuring user education regarding best practices is a crucial component of the IoT. Creating secure and one-of-a-kind passwords for gadgets and accounts is one aspect of this education. In addition, phishing attempts that target IoT devices or networks should be recognized and avoided, and education should emphasize general security hygiene—not disclosing private information or using default passwords, for example—and the importance of keeping devices updated with the most recent security patches.

3.1.10 Scope of the Chapter

In-depth analysis of cybersecurity concerns pertaining to real-time IoT applications is the aim of this chapter. The purpose of this chapter is to analyze the difficulties and weaknesses that real-time IoT systems encounter and to investigate security solutions, best practices, and measures that may be applied to reduce the risks involved. The goal of this chapter is to increase the reader's comprehension of the significance of resolving security issues in real-time IoT installations by offering a thorough overview of network security issues.

Regarding IoT systems utilized in real-time applications, this chapter primarily addresses cyber security issues. It addresses several subjects, such as the foundations of IoT for real-time applications, typical cyber security issues, security solutions and procedures, intrusion detection and prevention, privacy and data protection, and pertinent case studies. With a focus on the particular security issues that arise in real-time IoT applications, the chapter offers a thorough review of the subject. Additionally, it provides suggestions for future lines of inquiry and advice for practitioners and legislators on how to successfully protect real-time IoT systems.

3.2 FUNDAMENTALS OF IOT FOR REAL-TIME APPLICATIONS

Millions of public, private, academic, business, and government networks are connected via a range of wireless, fiber optic, and electronic networking technologies, spanning from local to worldwide networks. Televisions, air conditioners, smart TVs, vehicle keys, and other devices are all familiar to most people (Al-Ghaili et al., 2023). The term "IoT" refers to the collection of smart devices that are locally connected and then connected to the internet. Connecting any physical object, place, or thing to the internet is the essence of the very basic idea known as the "IoT." The notion is quite wide and can be defined in a variety of ways, which may lead to ambiguity rather than a narrow and precise definition. With so many applications and possibilities available on the IoT, it might be challenging to identify a notion. Figure 3.1 shows the IoT real-time applications.

3.3 FUNDAMENTAL COMPONENTS OF IOT

3.3.1 Explanation of IoT Architecture and Components

With the help of a structural pattern called service-oriented architecture (SOA), individual components can offer services to one another. Several web aspects, including networks, communication, business models, procedures, and secure communication processes, are incorporated into the design of IoT architecture. The growth, scaling, and interoperability of various devices and their models should all be taken into account while constructing an IoT architecture (H. U. Khan et al., 2023). With the help of a set of clearly defined small objects or sub-systems, a complex system, such as SOA, is managed.

3.3.1.1 Sensors or Devices

To detect physical phenomena, an input device called a sensor produces an output signal. The broadest definition of a sensor is a machine, module, sensor, or subsystem that senses events or

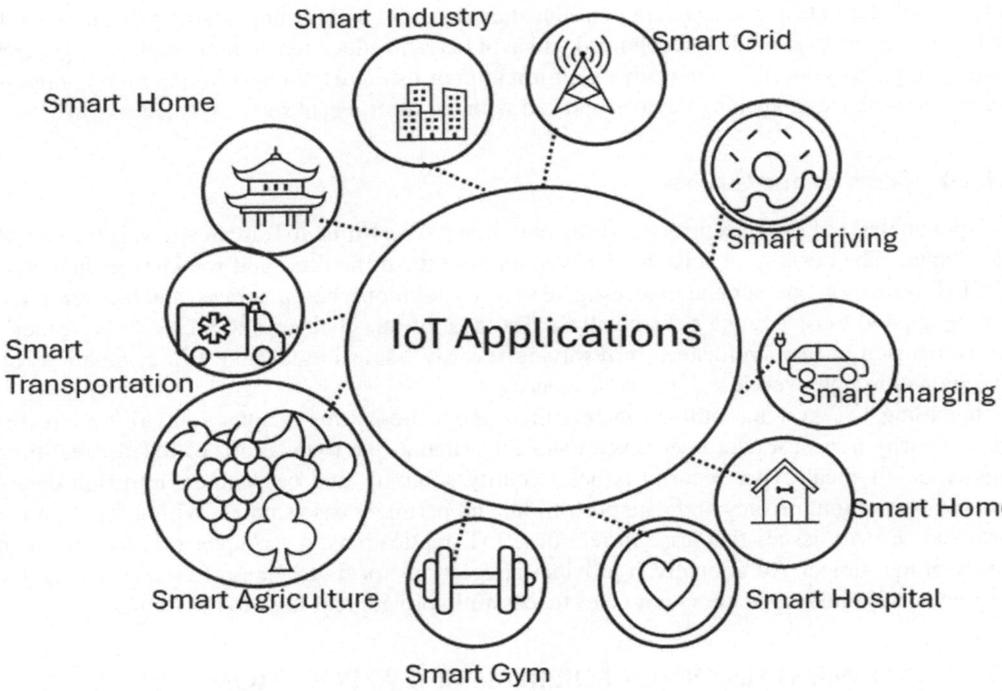

FIGURE 3.1 Real-time applications of IoT.

changes in its environment and sends the information to other electronics, usually a processor or controller. There are various types of sensors like temperature, pressure, humidity, Magnetic, touch, gas, biometric, vibration and many more (Kane, 2024; S. I. Khan et al., 2024; Rekeraho et al., 2024).

3.3.1.2 Connectivity

The cloud infrastructure receives all of the sensor data that has been gathered. Various communication channels should be used to link the sensors to the cloud. It is also possible for the controlling output to employ a separate connectivity. The connectivity mediums are like WiFi, ZigBee, Bluetooth, CAN bus, ethernet LAN, and many more.

3.3.1.3 Data Processing and User Interface

IoT sensors transmit data to the processing unit by acting as input devices. Microcontrollers and microprocessors are the two categories of processing units. These processing units perform both data manipulation and primary logic. IoT's brain is comprised of them. The device that receives sensor data processes it, computes it, and then sends commands to the actuators is called the controller. The commonly used microprocessors and controllers are Raspberry Pi, ESP8266, Arduino UNO, and many more. Figure 3.2 represents the major components used in IoT.

It should be possible for end users to access these IoT input/output devices. Smartphone apps, software, online apps, and voice commands can all be used to create a user interface. Because the cloud serves as the hub for all IoT components, these user interfaces are connected to it. Not all communication is, though, user-based. Users should also be able to automate cascade actions

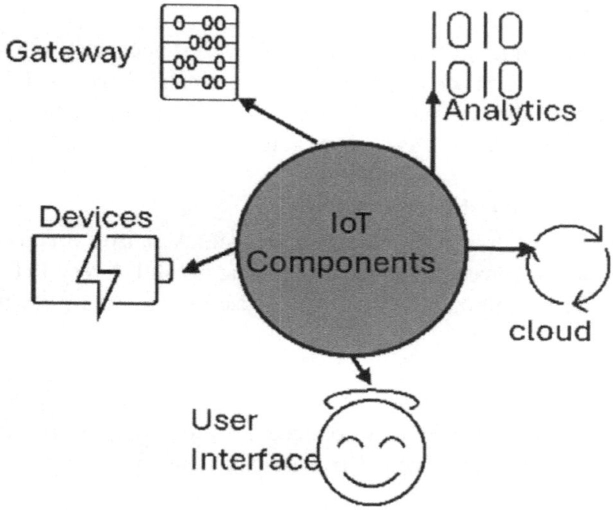

FIGURE 3.2 Major IoT components.

based on the specific IoT application. When motion is detected, lights, for instance, automatically turn on.

3.3.2 Discussion on the Characteristics and Requirements of Real-Time Applications in IoT

Transportation, energy, manufacturing, healthcare, and every other business is being disrupted by the IoT. Numerous data points are produced by IoT devices, and these points can be examined to enhance operations, spur creativity, and open up new business prospects.

Communication networks, gateways, cloud-based data processing and storage systems, and IoT devices are some of the components that make up an IoT system. Sensors and additional technologies are used by IoT devices to gather data, which is subsequently transferred to the cloud for processing and archiving. For administering and regulating IoT networks and devices, the cloud also offers a centralized platform (S. I. Khan et al., 2024; Sinche et al., 2020; Yadav et al., 2024).

Big data analytics, cloud computing, machine learning, wireless communication protocols, and security technologies are just a few of the many technologies used in IoT development.

In general, the IoT is a quickly developing sector with the potential to completely change many different businesses as well as how we live and work. The prospects for innovation and success in this industry will only increase with the increasing prevalence of IoT devices and systems.

IoT is defined as a method of connecting through embedded internet devices that may be used to add functionality in common things by allowing them to transmit and receive data. Data is pervasive in today's world. Therefore, IoT may alternatively be defined as data analysis leading to meaningful action that is initiated following data exchange(S. I. Khan et al., 2024; Rekeraho et al., 2024). Applications for IoT can be developed in the following areas: agricultural, asset monitoring, energy, defense, safety and security, education, waste management, healthcare products, telemedicine, smart city applications, etc. IoT is distinguished by the essential characteristics listed below.

3.3.2.1 Connectivity

An imperative need for IoT infrastructure is connectivity. It is necessary to link IoT objects to the IoT infrastructure. We have to make sure that connections can be made at all times, by anybody, anywhere. For instance, connections made between individuals via mobile phones and between things connected to the internet, such as routers, gateways, and sensors.

3.3.2.2 Intelligence and Identity

It's critical to extract knowledge from the produced data. A sensor, for instance, may produce data, but only if the data is correctly analyzed will it be helpful. Every IoT gadget has an individual identification. The equipment's identifier is useful for tracing it and occasionally for checking on its state.

3.3.2.3 Scalability

Every day, more and more objects are being connected to the IoT. Therefore, an IoT system ought to be able to handle the significant growth. The massive amount of data produced as a result needs to be handled carefully.

3.3.2.4 Complexity

When situations and contexts change, IoT devices should be able to adjust to them quickly. Pretend you have a security camera. It ought to be flexible enough to operate in various lighting conditions and times of day (morning, afternoon, and night).

3.3.2.5 Self-Configuring

Among the key features of the IoT is that it is self-configuring. Without requiring much user input, IoT devices may update their software to meet needs. They are also capable of configuring the network, which makes it possible to integrate new devices into an established network.

3.3.2.6 Architecture

There is no way for IoT architecture to be uniform. To function in the IoT network, it should be hybrid, supporting goods from many manufacturers. Every engineering branch does not own IoT. Interaction across domains makes IoT a reality.

3.3.2.7 Interoperability

To enable communication between them and other systems, IoT devices use standardized protocols and technologies. A fundamental feature of the IoT is interoperability. In spite of the underlying technology or manufacturer, it describes the capacity of various IoT devices and systems to interact and share data with one another.

Since interoperability allows disparate systems and devices to operate together flawlessly and offers a seamless user experience, it is essential to the success of the IoT. It would be impossible to share data and develop new services and applications if IoT systems were restricted to standalone data and device silos in the absence of interoperability.

3.3.2.8 Safety

When an individual uses all of his or her gadgets to access the internet, there is a risk that their private information could be exposed. For the user, this can result in a loss. As such, the main obstacle is data security. In addition, a massive amount of equipment is needed. There could also be a risk to IoT networks. Thus, the safety of the equipment is equally important.

3.3.2.9 Sensors and Actuators

An essential part of the IoT is embedded sensors and actuators. They enable data collection and transmission from IoT devices as well as interaction with their surroundings.

Sensors are gadgets that are able to pick up on changes in the surrounding conditions, such light, sound, temperature, or movement. Devices with sensors integrated into them can gather environmental data in IoT systems (Al-Ghaili et al., 2023; Ansar et al., 2023a).

Actuators are gadgets that can execute tasks like opening and closing doors, adjusting the speed of a motor, and turning on lights. Actuators are incorporated within devices in IoT systems, enabling them to take actions depending on information gathered by sensors.

IoT devices may gather data about their surroundings, interpret that data, and take appropriate action depending on the findings thanks to the combination of actuators and sensors. As a result, many different operations and jobs, including energy management, predictive maintenance, and home automation, can now be automated.

Standards-based communication protocols like as Bluetooth Low Energy (BLE), Zigbee, and Wi-Fi are used by sensors and actuators to guarantee that they can interact with one other as well as with other devices and systems. IoT systems require embedded sensors and actuators in order to gather, process, and communicate with their surroundings in novel and creative ways.

Interacting with the environment and gathering and transmitting data are made possible by IoT devices that are fitted with sensors and actuators (Ansar et al., 2023b; Vangala et al., 2022).

3.4 EXAMPLES OF REAL-TIME APPLICATIONS IN VARIOUS DOMAINS

It is undeniable that IoT may significantly improve our lives, given its constantly rising appeal in both residential and commercial contexts. New sensors, wireless networks, and all that comes with the IoT are being embraced by a growing number of companies across several industries. Figure 3.3 represents the real-time applications of IoT. Some sectors have implemented IoT in practical ways:

3.4.1 Food: Smart Refrigerators

You can monitor food that might soon spoil thanks to sensors and cameras built into smart refrigerators.

Without reaching inside the refrigerator, you can keep an eye on how much food is remaining. You may look up any recipe online and then let the cooking directions come from your refrigerator. Meal lists that are created on the fridge and synced in real-time with your phone are available. To use food at its peak nutritional value, set expiration dates and receive alerts when it is fresh (Mahamat et al., 2023).

One of the best examples of such gadgets is LG Smart Refrigerators, which have an integrated display that lets you use your phone to order groceries and meals, change the thermostat, and check to see if the door is open.

3.4.2 Transportation

In a few years, driverless vehicles will be commonplace. But even without self-driving cars, there are plenty of instances where IoT is employed in everyday driving. Take General Motors' OnStar, for example, as a safety service. In addition to uploading data to the cloud and an on-demand advisor, the car's sensor may detect engine issues and collisions. The TV commercials have been shown to you. The advisor talks directly with the motorist and

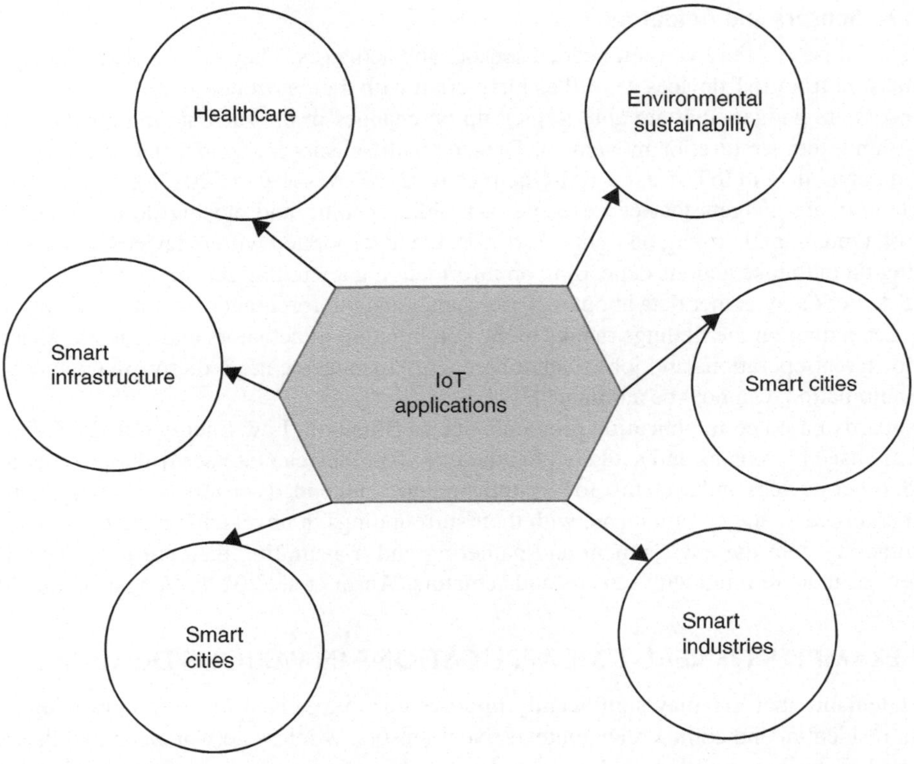

FIGURE 3.3 Real-time applications in IoT.

contacts emergency services as necessary. The GPS helps the advisor pinpoint your car's precise location as well. With the adviser's ability to perform remote diagnostics on the car, the responding technician will be ready if the problem is mechanical (Chaurasia & Kumar, 2023; Jahangeer et al., 2023).

3.4.3 Agriculture

Agriculture stands to benefit greatly from IoT. It is estimated that by 2050, there will be roughly 10 billion people on Earth. The expansion of agricultural systems is consequently a priority for governments. Farmers are using technology in their agricultural methods as a result of this and climate change (Morimoto & Hayashi, 2017; Navulur et al., 2017; Ullah et al., 2017).

The nature of the soil and the amount of fertilizer are disclosed by sensors. Many elements, including CO_2 levels, humidity, moisture content, acidity level, and the quantity of appropriate fertilizers applied, affect how well a harvest performs.

Farmer water management and usage are improved by IoT applications such as smart irrigation. When the soil reaches a certain level of dryness, the IoT gadget initiates the water flow. It also cuts the flow off after a certain level of moisture is reached. Errors caused by humans are reduced as a result.

The same robotic vacuuming experience is available to you with robotic lawnmowers. Designed to cut grass on lawns, this gadget is an independent robotic mower. Rain sensors are just one feature of the increasingly advanced artificial raspberry.

3.4.4 Healthcare

One of the newest uses of the IoT in the healthcare industry is the rise of contemporary wearables. Quite a few insurance companies have been pushing the usage of fitness trackers in recent years. They assert that assisting people in achieving better health is their main objective. It would be preferable, though, to state that their purpose is to enable an insurance company to determine if a policyholder is qualified for coverage (Ahsan & Siddique, 2022; MKS, 2023).

These days, it's simple to purchase a lot of fitness and medical wearables. One branded device that women may use to track their pregnancy is called AVA. It helps women who want to get pregnant and indicates when a pregnancy test might be more reliable. Smart toothbrushes, such as the Philips Sonicare, are another groundbreaking example. Naturally, an electric motor that determines where to brush, how quickly to move it, and how to maintain optimal dental hygiene powers a smart toothbrush. The tips of smart roots have sensors so you can wash your teeth more efficiently.

With its improved sensors, a smart brush collects information about your brushing patterns, missed areas, tension, and other factors. Using your smartphone, you may access this important information and discover potential ways to improve your dental hygiene.

3.4.5 M2M Automation and Industrial Asset Management

With the advent of supervisory control and data acquisition (SCADA) and remote monitoring tools for handling and directing data from manufacturing machinery remotely, machine-to-machine (M2M) solutions gained popularity. Sensor data collection and network distribution are the primary objective of M2M technology (Aslam et al., 2020; Gupta & Gupta, 2016; M. M. Aslam, Liping Du, 2020; F. N. Yang et al., 2019).

Device connectivity, the ideal location for smart sensor placement, is among the most crucial elements. IoT solutions, which do not require human workers, can use sensors to automate sales forecasting, distribution, and communication.

One further practical application of the IoT in manufacturing is industrial asset management. From the raw materials used in manufacturing to the final items kept in a storage, businesses can monitor every asset thanks to IoT devices. Rather than closing the business and manually counting the inventory, you may conveniently manage it in this method.

3.4.6 Energy

Climate, humidity, temperature, and lighting are just a few of the things that may be tracked with IoT sensors. By combining data from IoT sensors, algorithms that control energy use and make the necessary modifications can be developed, doing away with the need for human intervention. Significant energy savings are possible for both private homes and companies with IoT-driven environmental control, which ultimately helps everyone—including the environment!

Larger-scale analysis of variables like consumption can be done with the use of data collected by the IoT to assist in running municipal power networks more effectively. Additionally, by using sensors to identify outages more quickly, repair personnel may respond more quickly and blackout times can be reduced(Kodali & Mahesh, 2017; Qayyum et al., 2015).

3.4.7 Fleet Management

Fleet car IoT sensor installations have significantly improved driving through geolocation, performance analysis, fuel economy, telemetry control, and information gathering.

Between the cars, managers, and drivers, they aid in creating efficient connectivity. They guarantee that all information regarding the condition, functionality, and requirements of the vehicle is known to both drivers and owners. With the advent of real-time maintenance alerts, drivers are no longer required to notice problems.

3.4.8 Smart Grid and Energy Saving

Better network monitoring and control are made possible by IoT technology, which is found in everything from intelligent energy meters to strategically placed sensors at distribution points and production plants.

The implementation of information technology in a smart grid provides a comprehensive approach to minimize waste and increase electrical efficiency, economy, and dependability. It is significantly more beneficial for defect detection, decision-making, and repair when there is bidirectional communication between the service provider and the end user. Additionally, it assists consumers in keeping an eye on their usage habits and implementing the most effective energy-saving strategies (Edmund et al., 2023; Kodali & Mahesh, 2017; Paulson et al., 2017).

3.4.9 Water Supply

An external sensor that is linked to the internet and software is integrated into water meters to facilitate the smooth collecting, processing, and analysis of data. This enhances the ability to identify supply service problems, publish results, and better understand customer trends.

They also provide real-time tracking of consumption information by means of an app or website for end customers. The detection of leaks via automatic warnings that indicate consumption over the usual range record has greatly reduced water usage (Aslam et al., 2023; Guo et al., 2023; Irshad et al., 2019).

3.5 CYBER SECURITY CHALLENGES IN IOT FOR REAL-TIME APPLICATIONS

Figure 3.4 represents the IoT security challenges. The following are the security challenges for IoT real-time applications.

3.5.1 Lack of Industry Foresight

The automotive and healthcare sectors have been quick to embrace IoT devices in an effort to increase efficiency and production. On the other hand, inadequate cybersecurity considerations have frequently been overlooked during this digital transition. The amount of money needed to effectively safeguard IoT devices was something that many businesses in these industries had not budged from (Aslam et al., 2022; Irshad et al., 2019).

As a result of their loss of vision, they are now more vulnerable to cybersecurity attacks. These industries are particularly concerned because, in comparison to their conventional IT infrastructure, IoT devices may have fewer security measures, making them more susceptible to assaults (Radoglou Grammatikis et al., 2019; Williams et al., 2022).

3.5.2 Resource Constraints

IoT devices lack the processing capability to enable advanced security features like firewalls or powerful antivirus programs. Because of their lightweight and power-efficient designs, some

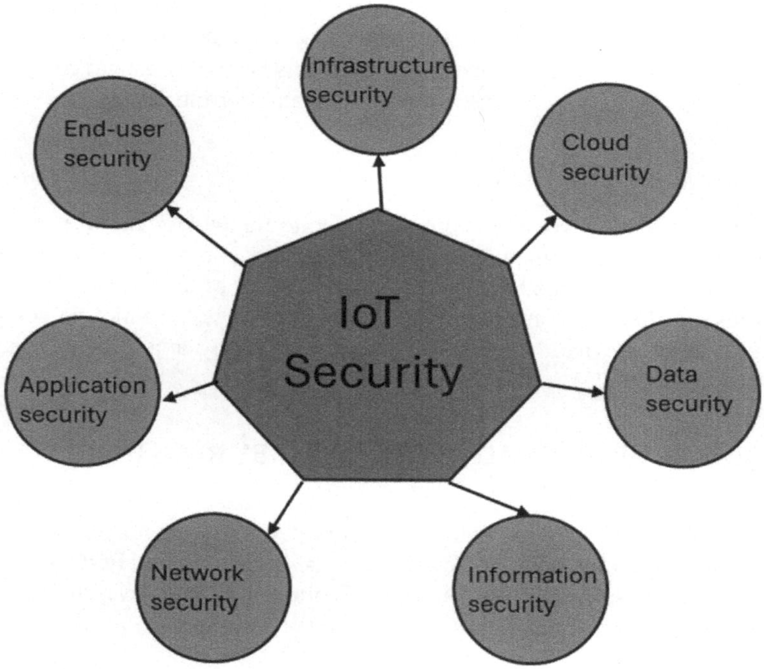

FIGURE 3.4 Cybersecurity in IoT applications.

IoT devices are less equipped to apply robust security safeguards. Devices that use technologies like Bluetooth are especially prone to this problem. These resource limitations have previously resulted in data breaches in a few automobile systems (Hassija et al., 2019).

3.5.3 Weak Default Passwords

Default passwords on many IoT devices are frequently weak and simple to decipher. The significance of replacing these passwords with more secure ones might not be apparent to users. IoT devices are vulnerable to brute-force attacks and other forms of hacking when default passwords are left unfixed. Consequently, it is crucial to reinforce default password restrictions and train users on password management (Mazhar et al., 2023).

3.5.4 Lack of Encryption

An enormous amount of network traffic coming from IoT devices is sent in cleartext. Data breaches and security dangers are more likely when encryption is absent. Unencrypted data is easier for cybercriminals to intercept and manipulate. Therefore, it is essential to make sure that all IoT devices are secure and that data is encrypted while it is being transmitted in order to reduce this danger (Rajmohan et al., 2022).

3.5.5 Remote Exposure

IoT gadgets are by definition frequently online, giving potential attackers a big attack surface. The threat of hackers engaging with equipment remotely exists even though this connectivity improves functionality. Campaigns by hackers, such phishing, may become more successful due to this enhanced accessibility. To prevent unwanted access and data breaches, IoT cybersecurity solutions, like cloud security, need to take into account this larger attack surface by putting strong security measures in place (Amit Kumar Singh and Stefano Berretti, 2023).

3.5.6 Multiple Connected Devices

The majority of firms have several linked devices due to the widespread use of IoT. This connectivity increases the risk even though it makes things more convenient. A single compromised or misconfigured device has the ability to affect the security of all devices linked to the same network. Because of this interconnection, the network as a whole cannot be compromised by weaknesses in a single device, hence it is imperative to apply appropriate management and security policies (MKS, 2023).

3.6 UNIQUE SECURITY CHALLENGES POSED BY REAL-TIME APPLICATIONS IN IOT

There are several common security challenges while developing IoT apps. Resolving vulnerabilities in authentication protocols and device firmware is one of them. Furthermore, it involves making sure that data is sent and stored securely. While not all-inclusive, the list of major IoT security issues is provided below.

3.6.1 Lack of Standardization

The absence of standards in IoT poses a significant security concern. It is challenging to guarantee compatibility and interoperability across them because there are so many distinct devices, protocols, and platforms. This may result in weaknesses that hackers may take advantage of.

3.6.2 Weak or Nonexistent Authentication

Weak or nonexistent authentication is a serious problem for IoT. Because many IoT devices have weak security features, they are open to intrusions.

3.6.3 Inadequate Software Security

Security of IoT devices is challenging because they frequently operate on embedded systems with little power. Vulnerabilities may result from this, which attackers may exploit. Further complicating matters with regard to security is the fact that embedded systems frequently include specialized hardware and software.

3.6.4 Insufficient Network Security

As unprotected networks are frequently used by IoT devices to connect to the internet, they are open to attack. An intruder may be able to obtain sensitive information by intercepting, for instance, conversations between an IoT device and the internet (Thilakarathne et al., 2020).

Furthermore, assaults on other networked devices might be initiated via unprotected networks as well.

3.6.5 Limited Physical Security

Given that IoT devices are frequently small and simple to hide, leaving them open to physical attacks, limited physical security is a major problem for them. Tampering, stealing, or outright destroying an IoT device are examples of physical attacks. Such actions may lead to data loss, system outages, and unwanted access to private data.

3.6.6 Inadequate Data Protection

Due to the fact that IoT devices generate and gather vast amounts of data, which leave them open to attack, inadequate data protection is a serious security risk. Information about finances, personal details, and other sensitive data may be included in this data. Inappropriate protection for sensitive data may allow it to end up in the wrong hands and be misused.

3.6.7 Limited Privacy Protections

Users' privacy must be protected because IoT devices frequently gather and transmit personal data. This can include sensitive data, location information, and other personal information. If this information is not adequately safeguarded, it may be exploited for nefarious activities such as identity theft or targeted advertising.

3.6.8 Inability to Update or Patch Devices

Because it's hard or impossible to repair or upgrade many IoT devices, they're open to assault. Accordingly, a vulnerability cannot be patched once it is found, leaving the device open to intrusions.

It's also not possible to get security updates or patches for some gadgets since their manufacturers no longer support them. Due to their inability to be updated or patched, these devices are vulnerable to cyberattacks since it is impossible to defend them against known flaws.

3.6.9 Growing Threat of IoT Malware and Ransomware

This raises the possibility that ransomware and viruses will attack these gadgets. IoT-connected gadgets are multiplying at a rapid rate, which is why. Their attractiveness as targets for attacks has been recognized by cybercriminals.

We must take IoT botnet malware into consideration while assessing the major risks. A prevalent type of malware that targets IoT devices are these bots. Several devices are compromised by malicious actors who take advantage of weaknesses in IoT platforms. After this, they employ them to execute massive assaults.

A prominent instance concerning a botnet on IoT devices is the Mirai botnet assault. By assuming default passwords, the Mirai malware was able to infect a significant number of low-security IoT devices, such as routers, cameras, and digital video recorders (DVRs).

3.6.10 Limited Regulatory Oversight

Because it might be challenging to guarantee that IoT devices are secure, the lack of governmental control surrounding these devices can be a serious security risk.

3.6.11 Lack of Visibility and Control

Often without the user's awareness or involvement, IoT devices are made to function in the background. Understanding and managing their conduct may become challenging as a result.

Consider the possibility that an IoT gadget, like a smart camera, is inadvertently transmitting data to a cloud server. Identifying and stopping malicious activities may be challenging due to this lack of insight into the behavior of the device.

3.6.12 Rushed App Releases and Insufficient Testing

The lack of attention to testing and development is the root cause of this security issue. Some businesses rush to release IoT goods onto the market at the expense of security. Moreover, the issue is exacerbated once security updates stop coming once the system is implemented. Thankfully, people are becoming more conscious about IoT security these days. The value of device security is becoming more widely acknowledged.

3.6.13 Difficulty in Detecting and Responding to Threats

Cybersecurity cameras, smart appliances, and thermostats are just a few examples of IoT devices that frequently work in the background, gathering and sending data continuously. Security threats can be challenging to identify and address because these devices are often not used frequently and are connected to the internet.

To initiate a cyberattack, for instance, a hacker might be able to access a gadget without the owner's knowledge.

3.7 CASE STUDIES

Some case studies related to breaches in IoT devices are presented below.

3.7.1 Leak of Passwords

Leaked passwords was the biggest hack since the 32 million accounts were impacted by the 2009 attack on the RockYou website.

Technology and data security solutions are always changing, as are the strategies employed by cybercriminals to fool companies and staff into clicking on documents and links in emails. Because of this, our blog post titled "10 Steps to Protect Your Business from Cybercrime" outlines simple strategies to stop cybercrime (Zahedian Nezhad et al., 2024).

3.7.2 Cyberattack with Ransomware

One of the biggest ransomware attacks of all time occurred in 2017, affecting over 200,000 PCs across 150 countries. Finally, the ransomware caused a $6 billion global repair bill and had a major effect on several industries (Nadhan & Jeena Jacob, 2024).

3.7.3 Yahoo Was Hacked Online

The 2014 Yahoo account hack, which affected 500 million users, was one of the biggest cyberattacks of the year. Bank information was not taken during the hack, but passwords and other personal data were (Ponomareva et al., 2023).

3.7.4 Cyberattack on Adobe

The initial assumption was that 2.9 million customers' data had been compromised by the Adobe assault. In addition, the private data of up to 38 million people was stolen! All 35.1 million users lost their user IDs and passwords, according to Adobe, even though only the payment card details and passwords of the first 2.9 million customers were hacked.

3.7.5 Virus Melissa

One of the first and most dangerous cyberthreats was the Melissa Virus, which was developed in 1999 by programmer David Lee Smith. He forwarded a file infected with viruses to Microsoft Word users. Opening the file allowed the malware to go active, seriously harming hundreds of companies, including Microsoft. The impacted systems will likely require repairs totaling $80 million (Y. Yang et al., 2019).

These are a few examples of cyberattacks that significantly affect various markets and companies.

3.8 SECURITY MEASURES AND SOLUTIONS FOR REAL-TIME IOT APPLICATIONS

It takes time to secure IoT apps. Thorough preparation, initiative, and consistent observation are necessary.

3.8.1 Awareness

Determine, evaluate, and rank possible vulnerabilities in IoT applications as part of threat modeling. By incorporating IoT apps into their entire security plan, IT managers can incorporate the recommended security actions. To adequately capture the current state of IoT applications, security models need to be updated (Mishra et al., 2014).

3.8.2 Risk Management

Based on the degree of concern, rank and classify IoT threats and take appropriate action. This is something that many development teams forget to consider when putting risks in the context of actual business scenarios and possible consequences. Even though an IT department may consider an outage or failure of a single IoT application insignificant, a business may suffer a substantial loss of revenue.

3.8.3 Maintenance

In order to guarantee network security overall, administrators should implement updates for IoT applications as quickly as possible. Make sure you only use updates that have been approved and confirmed. If you update apps remotely, make sure all update streams are encrypted using a secure network technique like a virtual private network (VPN). System and device authentication is enabled by a secure public key infrastructure (PKI).

3.8.4 Networking

Controlling communication between services in a network is done by a specific infrastructure layer called a service mesh. An application's service request distribution is managed by a service mesh. A service mesh can be used for disaster recovery, encryption, load balancing, and service discovery, among other things. Connectivity between services can be accelerated, dependable, and secure with the use of a service mesh.

3.8.5 Network Safety and Security

IoT applications can be secured against malicious access with the help of firewalls, encryption, and secure communication protocols. IoT applications should be included in routine application security testing procedures, along with devices, standards, and communication protocols utilized throughout the network, to ensure security.

3.8.6 Authentication

The development of safe password creation and update processes is an essential component of a comprehensive password protection strategy for IoT applications. The default passwords for IoT devices and apps must be changed. When feasible, in addition to passwords, extra authentication elements should be employed. The possibility that authentication data will ever be hacked is decreased by using the encrypted TLS communication protocol.

3.8.7 Security

Encrypt data traveling between IoT devices, applications, and backend systems to keep it safe from hackers. This involves employing the PKI security model to guarantee that the sender and recipient are both verified by the system before transmission, as well as encrypting data while it's in transit and at rest.

3.8.8 Secure Control Apps

IoT applications must be appropriately secured, as must the systems and apps that access them. In addition to keeping the attack from spreading further, this keeps the client—an IoT device or system—uncompromised by an external attack.

3.8.9 Integration

One common way that data is sent and pulled between systems and apps is through application program interfaces (APIs). Attackers can also connect to IoT apps in this manner. Threats are simpler to identify when an API can only be used by authorized devices and apps. API versioning is another tool that IT administrators should use to find and remove redundant or out-of-date versions of an API.

3.8.10 Monitoring

The last step in protecting your IoT application is to monitor it. Organizations may improve incident response and lessen the effect of an attack or breach by monitoring IoT applications and promptly identifying and addressing possible security vulnerabilities. By displaying a dedication to security, it also assists businesses in meeting regulatory obligations and gaining the trust of their clients.

3.9 PRIVACY AND DATA PROTECTION IN REAL-TIME IOT

IoT data security goes one step further with encryption. When sensitive data is sent between devices, encryption is crucial. Imagine an enemy that ambushes a commander who gives the order to launch an attack. This can be achieved by encrypting the data with a cipher like AES, which makes it unreadable by the general public(Qiu et al., 2020; Roman et al., 2013).

Securing data in transit isn't the only aspect of protecting your IoT data, though. Furthermore, the "data at rest" that is kept on your IoT devices needs to be protected as well. These include audit and log files, as well as information regarding the device's identity, configuration, state during use, and programming. Using solutions that offer integrity and confidentiality for these files will help you stop illegal access to your IoT data. Data integrity ensures that unauthorized parties haven't changed the information, while confidentiality—achieved through encryption—guarantees that anyone without the necessary keys cannot access the data (Tawalbeh et al., 2020).

Lastly, possession of a device may alter over time. Countless research works have illustrated the massive amount of data loss that may occur when devices, such as cell phones, are transferred between owners. However, if the data on the IoT device is encrypted, a simple "key wipe" will prevent a new owner from accessing the previous owner's data. In the event that the keys are lost, all encrypted data is irreversibly lost.

3.10 FUTURE RESEARCH DIRECTIONS AND RECOMMENDATIONS

So, considering the aforementioned, what does the IoT hold in store? As many as 20.6 billion gadgets with various forms of connectivity are expected by 2020, according to a Gartner estimate (Stamford, 2024). HP projects that by 2025, this figure may rise to 1 trillion, an astounding figure. Per a report by Cisco (Annual & Report, 2018), over the course of the next ten years, IoT devices will generate $14.4 trillion in value across various businesses.

Stated differently, our lives—both personally and professionally—could soon undergo radical changes due to the IoT. To a greater or lesser extent, many of the technologies listed are already in use. You cannot turn back now, that much is certain. The IoT provides an unparalleled level of efficiency and control that no sector can overlook.

Which way do you interpret that? Career opportunities abound in the profitable field of IoT and its congruence with technologies like ITIL, Blockchain, and Big Data.

3.11 CONCLUSION

In order to help readers better grasp the significance of IoT security, this chapter explained the potential and history of connected devices. It also emphasized the devices' value and possible future expansion. Best practices for security are more crucial than ever as the IoT movement brings millions of new gadgets to the market every year. All connected devices expand the network's attack surface, and each unprotected device serves as a point of entry for malevolent cybercriminals. Devices like smart bulbs are easily unlocked despite their limited usefulness and versatility.

The devices and data that are required for application development are frequently collected, managed, and protected via IoT. The interplay and computation of IoT objects and devices enhances living comfort and security. Real-time item monitoring, inventory automation, and item information and status management are all possible with IoT. Systems for data integrity, secrecy, authentication, and authorization must be developed in order to handle the massive volume of data that is transferred between network devices. Improved authentication of many systems, particularly wireless systems, is the main goal of the project.

In the field of IoT security, significant work remains to be done. The volume of research and challenges in this field require attention from researchers. modern, high-security gadgets, the requirement for appropriate masking techniques and end-to-end encryption algorithms, safe cloud computing, and the improvement of the fog layer using encryption and machine learning techniques. One of the key challenges in IoT is optimization, including deep learning and artificial intelligence. With a huge number of servers, blockchain is severely constrained. In order to overcome this issue, there are several effective techniques that can replace nodes and use a lot of resources. There is a possibility that future research will concentrate on different technologies like blockchain, AI, and machine learning.

REFERENCES

Aakash Yadav. (2022, December 7). *Top 10 IoT Applications in 2024*. https://hackr.io/blog/author/aakash.yadav

Abhiranjan. (n.d.). *IoT From a Beginner's Perspective*. www.aapnainfotech.com/iot-beginners-perspective/

Ahsan, M. M., & Siddique, Z. (2022). Industry 4.0 in healthcare: A systematic review. *International Journal of Information Management Data Insights*, *2*(1), 1–14. https://doi.org/10.1016/j.jjimei.2022.100079

Al-Ghaili, A. M., Gunasekaran, S. S., Jamil, N., Alyasseri, Z. A. A., Al-Hada, N. M., Ibrahim, Z. A. Bin, Bakar, A. A., Kasim, H., Hosseini, E., Omar, R., Kasmani, R. M., & Razali, R. A. (2023). A review on role of image processing techniques to enhancing security of IoT applications. *IEEE Access*, *11*, 101924–101948. https://doi.org/10.1109/ACCESS.2023.3312682

Alwahedi, F., Aldhaheri, A., Ferrag, M. A., Battah, A., & Tihanyi, N. (2024). Machine learning techniques for IoT security: Current research and future vision with generative AI and large language models. *Internet of Things and Cyber-Physical Systems*, *4*, 167–185. https://doi.org/10.1016/j.iotcps.2023.12.003

Annual Report (2018). *White Paper: Cisco Public*. CISCO. www.cisco.com/c/en/us/solutions/collateral/executive-perspectives/annual-internet-report/white-paper-c11-741490.html

Ansar, S. A., Arya, S., Aggrawal, S., Saxena, S., Kushwaha, A., & Pathak, P. C. (2023a). *Security in IoT Layers: Emerging Challenges with Countermeasures*. In: Shukla, P.K., Singh, K.P., Tripathi, A.K., Engelbrecht, A. (eds) Computer Vision and Robotics. Algorithms for Intelligent Systems, (pp. 551–563). Springer, Singapore. https://doi.org/10.1007/978-981-19-7892-0_44

Aslam, M. M., Ahmed, Z., Du, L., Hassan, M. Z., Ali, S., & Nasir, M. (2022). An overview of recent advances of resilient consensus for multiagent systems under attacks. In *Computational Intelligence and Neuroscience* (Vol. 2022). Hindawi Limited. https://onlinelibrary.wiley.com/doi/10.1155/2022/6732343

Aslam, M. M., Irshad, M. N., Azeem, H., & Ikram, M. (2020). Cost effective and energy efficient intelligent smart home system based on IoT. *Afyon Kocatepe University International Journal of Engineering Technology and Applied Sciences*, *3*(1), 10–20.

Aslam, M. M., & Liping Du, Z. A. (2020). An overview of recent advances in resilient consensus control of multiagent systems under cyber physical attacks. *Journal of Electrical Engineering & Technology*. Submitted for publication.

Aslam, M. M., Tufail, A., Kim, K. H., Apong, R. A. A. H. M., & Raza, M. T. (2023). A comprehensive study on cyber attacks in communication networks in water purification and distribution plants: challenges, vulnerabilities, and future prospects. *Sensors*, *23*(18), 7999. https://doi.org/10.3390/S23187999

Chaurasia, N., & Kumar, P. (2023). A comprehensive study on issues and challenges related to privacy and security in IoT. *E-Prime – Advances in Electrical Engineering, Electronics and Energy*, *4*, 100158. https://doi.org/10.1016/J.PRIME.2023.100158

Edmund, A. N., Alabi, C. A., Tooki, O. O., Imoize, A. L., & Salka, T. D. (2023). Artificial intelligence of internet of medical things (AIoMT) in smart cities: A review of cybersecurity for smart healthcare. *Taylor & Francis*, 271–292. www.routledge.com/Handbook-of-Security-and-Privacy-of-AI-Enabled-Healthcare-Systems-and-Internet-of-Medical-Things/Imoize-Balas-Solanki-Lee-Obaidat/p/book/9781032440798?srsltid=AfmBOopqY2sd2g5Q5kZQAGAqxc75RfFmybgGeReCeJ7ZUulYwbUaJ2gO

Guo, Y., Irshad, M. N., Aslam, M. M., Qurban, A., & Raza, A. (2023). IHGWO-Based Optimization of IoT Wireless Sensor Networks. *Proceedings of the 19th ACM International Symposium on QoS and Security for Wireless and Mobile Networks*, 97–104. https://doi.org/10.1145/3616391.3622769

Gupta, S., & Gupta, B. B. (2016). Automated discovery of JavaScript code injection attacks in PHP web applications. *Physics Procedia*, *78*(December 2015), 82–87. https://doi.org/10.1016/j.procs.2016.02.014

Hassan, R., Qamar, F., Hasan, M. K., Aman, A. H. M., & Ahmed, A. S. (2020). Internet of things and its applications: A comprehensive survey. *Symmetry*, *12*(10), 1674. https://doi.org/10.3390/SYM12101674

Hassija, V., Chamola, V., Saxena, V., Jain, D., Goyal, P., & Sikdar, B. (2019). A survey on IoT security: application areas, security threats, and solution architectures. *IEEE Access*, *7*, 82721–82743. https://doi.org/10.1109/ACCESS.2019.2924045

Hossain, M., Kayas, G., Hasan, R., Skjellum, A., Noor, S., & Islam, S. M. R. (2024). A holistic analysis of internet of things (IoT) security: principles, practices, and new perspectives. *Future Internet*, *16*(2), 40. https://doi.org/10.3390/FI16020040

Irshad, M. N., Du, L., Khoso, I. A., Javed, T. Bin, & Aslam, M. M. (2019). A hybrid solution of SDN architecture for 5g mobile communication to improve data rate transmission. *2019 28th Wireless and Optical Communications Conference, WOCC 2019 – Proceedings*, *Wocc*, 1–5. https://doi.org/10.1109/WOCC.2019.8770664

Jahangeer, A., Bazai, S. U., Aslam, S., Marjan, S., Anas, M., & Hashemi, S. H. (2023). A review on the security of IoT networks: from network layer's perspective. *IEEE Access*, *11*, 71073–71087. https://doi.org/10.1109/ACCESS.2023.3246180

Kane, L. (2024). *Architectures for Performance and Security in IoT Smart Grids*. PhD Thesis, Queensland University of Technology. Https://doi.org/10.5204/THESIS.EPRINTS.245555

Karthikeyan, M., Manimegalai, D., & RajaGopal, K. (2024). Firefly algorithm based WSN-IoT security enhancement with machine learning for intrusion detection. *Scientific Reports*, *14*(1), 1–15. https://doi.org/10.1038/s41598-023-50554-x

Khan, H. U., Sohail, M., Ali, F., Nazir, S., Ghadi, Y. Y., & Ullah, I. (2023). Prioritizing the multi-criterial features based on comparative approaches for enhancing security of IoT devices. *Physical Communication*, *59*, 102084. https://doi.org/10.1016/J.PHYCOM.2023.102084

Khan, S. I., Ray, B. R., & Karmakar, N. C. (2024). RFID localization in construction with IoT and security integration. *Automation in Construction*, *159*, 105249. https://doi.org/10.1016/j.autcon.2023.105249

Kodali, R. K., & Mahesh, K. S. (2017). Low cost implementation of smart home automation. *2017 International Conference on Advances in Computing, Communications and Informatics, ICACCI 2017*, *2017-Janua*, 461–466. https://doi.org/10.1109/ICACCI.2017.8125883

Li, Y., & Liu, Q. (2021). A comprehensive review study of cyber-attacks and cyber security; Emerging trends and recent developments. *Energy Reports*, *7*, 8176–8186. https://doi.org/10.1016/J.EGYR.2021.08.126

Liang, P., Yang, L., Xiong, Z., Zhang, X., & Liu, G. (2024). Multi-level intrusion detection based on transformer and wavelet transform for IoT data security. *IEEE Internet of Things Journal*, *11*(15). https://doi.org/10.1109/JIOT.2024.3369034

Lilhore, U. K., Dalal, S., & Simaiya, S. (2024). A cognitive security framework for detecting intrusions in IoT and 5G utilizing deep learning. *Computers & Security*, *136*, 103560. https://doi.org/10.1016/J.COSE.2023.103560

Mahamat, M., Jaber, G., & Bouabdallah, A. (2023). Achieving efficient energy-aware security in IoT networks: a survey of recent solutions and research challenges. *Wireless Networks*, *29*(2), 787–808. https://doi.org/10.1007/s11276-022-03170-y

Mazhar, T., Talpur, D. B., Shloul, T. Al, Ghadi, Y. Y., Haq, I., Ullah, I., Ouahada, K., & Hamam, H. (2023). Analysis of IoT security challenges and its solutions using artificial intelligence. *Brain Sciences*, *13*(4), 1–30. https://doi.org/10.3390/BRAINSCI13040683

Misailov, A. Y., Mishra, N., Lakhanpal, S., Prakash, A., & Sharma, N. (2024). Enhancing home security with IoT devices: A vulnerability analysis using the IoT security test. *BIO Web of Conferences*, *86*, 01084. https://doi.org/10.1051/BIOCONF/20248601084

Mishra, D., Das, A. K., & Mukhopadhyay, S. (2014). A secure user anonymity-preserving biometric-based multi-server authenticated key agreement scheme using smart cards. *Expert Systems with Applications*, *41*(18), 8129–8143. https://doi.org/10.1016/j.eswa.2014.07.004

MKS. (2023, January 12). *Top 8 Applications of IoT in Healthcare*. Website blog. https://Conceptsall.Com/Applications-of-Iot-in-Healthcare/.

Morimoto, E., & Hayashi, K. (2017). Design of smart agriculture Japan model. *advances in Animal Biosciences*, *8*(2), 713–717. https://doi.org/10.1017/s2040470017000371

Nadhan, A. S., & Jeena Jacob, I. (2024). Enhancing healthcare security in the digital era: Safeguarding medical images with lightweight cryptographic techniques in IoT healthcare applications. *Biomedical Signal Processing and Control*, *88*, 105511. https://doi.org/10.1016/j.bspc.2023.105511

Navulur, S., Sastry, A. S. C. S., & Giri Prasad, M. N. (2017). Agricultural management through wireless sensors and internet of things. *International Journal of Electrical and Computer Engineering*, *7*(6), 3492–3499. https://doi.org/10.11591/ijece.v7i6.pp3492-3499

Paulson, E., Kamaludin, M., Kamilah, S., & Dauda, U. (2017). *Cognitive Radio in 5G A Smart City Perspective Cognitive Radio in 5G — A Smart City Perspective —. January*. The 2017 Malaysia-Japan Workshop. The Institute of Electronics, Information and Communication Engineers on Radio Technology. https://ken.ieice.org/ken/paper/0bpP/eng/

Ponomareva, N., Hazimeh, H., Kurakin, A., Xu, Z., Denison, C., McMahan, H. B., Vassilvitskii, S., Chien, S., & Thakurta, A. G. (2023). How to DP-fy ML: A practical guide to machine learning with differential privacy. *Journal of Artificial Intelligence Research*, *77*, 1113–1201. https://doi.org/10.1613/jair.1.14649

Prasad, A., Singh, T. P., & Dwivedi Sharma, S. (Eds.). (2024). *Communication Technologies and Security Challenges in IoT*. Springer. https://link.springer.com/book/10.1007/978-981-97-0052-3

Qayyum, F. A., Naeem, M., Khwaja, A. S., Anpalagan, A., Guan, L., & Venkatesh, B. (2015). Appliance scheduling optimization in smart home networks. *IEEE Access*, *3*, 2176–2190. https://doi.org/10.1109/ACCESS.2015.2496117

Qiu, J., Tian, Z., Du, C., Zuo, Q., Su, S., & Fang, B. (2020). A Survey on Access Control in the Age of Internet of Things. *IEEE Internet of Things Journal*, *7*(6), 4682–4696. https://doi.org/10.1109/JIOT.2020.2969326

Radoglou Grammatikis, P. I., Sarigiannidis, P. G., & Moscholios, I. D. (2019). Securing the *Internet of Things*: Challenges, threats and solutions. Internet of Things, 5, 41–70. https://doi.org/10.1016/J.IOT.2018.11.003

Rajmohan, T., Nguyen, P. H., & Ferry, N. (2022). A decade of research on patterns and architectures for IoT security. *Cybersecurity*, *5*(1), 2. https://doi.org/10.1186/s42400-021-00104-7

Rekeraho, A., Cotfas, D. T., Cotfas, P. A., Tuyishime, E., Balan, T. C., & Acheampong, R. (2024). Enhancing security for IoT-based smart renewable energy remote monitoring systems. *Electronics*, *13*(4), 756. https://doi.org/10.3390/electronics13040756

Roman, R., Zhou, J., & Lopez, J. (2013). On the features and challenges of security and privacy in distributed internet of things. *Computer Networks*, *57*(10), 2266–2279. https://doi.org/10.1016/j.comnet.2012.12.018

Senthil kumar, C., & Vijay Anand, R. (2024). Security in IoT-enabled smart agriculture systems. *Internet of Things, Part F2482*, 279–300. https://link.springer.com/book/10.1007/978-981-97-0052-3

Sinche, S., Raposo, D., Armando, N., Rodrigues, A., Boavida, F., Pereira, V., & Silva, J. S. (2020). A survey of IoT management protocols and frameworks. *IEEE Communications Surveys and Tutorials*, *22*(2), 1168–1190. https://doi.org/10.1109/COMST.2019.2943087

Singh, A.K., & Berretti, S. (2023). Medical Information Security and Privacy Solution for Smart Healthcare Industries. *Journal of Biomedical and Health Informatics (JBHI)*, 1–5.

Stamford. (2024, January 17). *Gartner Forecasts Worldwide IT Spending to Grow 6.8% in 2024*. www.gartner.com/en/newsroom/press-releases/01-17-2024-gartner-forecasts-worldwide-it-spending-to-grow-six-point-eight-percent-in-2024

Tawalbeh, L., Muheidat, F., Tawalbeh, M., & Quwaider, M. (2020). IoT privacy and security: challenges and solutions. *Applied Sciences*, *10*(12), 4102. https://doi.org/10.3390/app10124102

Thilakarathne, N. N., Kagita, M. K., & Gadekallu, Dr. T. R. (2020). The role of the internet of things in health care: A systematic and comprehensive study. *International Journal of Engineering and Management Research*, *10*(4), 145–159. https://doi.org/10.31033/ijemr.10.4.22

Ullah, A., Ahmad, J., Muhammad, K., Lee, M. Y., Kang, B., Soo, O. B., & Baik, S. W. (2017). A survey on precision agriculture: technologies and challenges. *The 3rd International Conference on Next Generation Computing (ICNGC2017b)*, *January 2018*, 1–4.

Vangala, A., Das, A. K., Chamola, V., Korotaev, V., & Rodrigues, J. J. P. C. (2022). Security in IoT-enabled smart agriculture: architecture, security solutions and challenges. *Cluster Computing 2022 26:2*, *26*(2), 879–902. https://doi.org/10.1007/S10586-022-03566-7

Williams, P., Dutta, I. K., Daoud, H., & Bayoumi, M. (2022). A survey on security in internet of things with a focus on the impact of emerging technologies. *Internet of Things*, *19*, 100564. https://doi.org/10.1016/J.IOT.2022.100564

Wu, X., Jing, Z., & Wang, X. (2024). The security of IoT from the perspective of the observability of complex networks. *Heliyon*, *10*(5), e27104. https://doi.org/10.1016/j.heliyon.2024.e27104

Yadav, S., Hashmi, H., Vekariya, D., N, Z. A. K., & J, V. F. (2024). Mitigation of attacks via improved network security in IOT network environment using RNN. *Measurement: Sensors*, *32*, 101046. https://doi.org/10.1016/J.MEASEN.2024.101046

Yang, F. N., Wu, C. Y., & Lin, H. Y. (2019). Design and implementation of CPS-based automated management platform. *Proceedings – 2018 IEEE International Conference on Systems, Man, and Cybernetics, SMC 2018*, *May*, 2293–2298. https://doi.org/10.1109/SMC.2018.00394

Yang, Y., Zheng, X., Guo, W., Liu, X., & Chang, V. (2019). Privacy-preserving smart IoT-based healthcare big data storage and self-adaptive access control system. *Information Sciences*, *479*, 567–592. https://doi.org/10.1016/j.ins.2018.02.005

Zahedian Nezhad, M., Bojnordi, A. J. J., Mehraeen, M., Bagheri, R., & Rezazadeh, J. (2024). Securing the future of IoT-healthcare systems: A meta-synthesis of mandatory security requirements. *International Journal of Medical Informatics*, 105379. https://doi.org/10.1016/j.ijmedinf.2024.105379

4 Security Concerns of IoT/WSN for Real-time Applications

Rakhi S, Sampada HK, Bhaskar MK, Farhana Kausar, and Arun Balodi

4.1 INTRODUCTION

One of the most significant components of every IoT device is sensors. While sensors are not new, its growing significance and associated design, integration, and security challenges have been exacerbated by their integration with wireless technologies and the growing IoT applications that require them. We have a variety of historical sensors at our disposal, including seismometers, auxanometers, crescographs, and galvanometers, to name a few. The advancement of wireless communication and the development of telecommunication technology have led to increased efforts in the integration of sensors with wireless antennas, which can transmit sensing data over long distances. The combination of sensors and wireless communication technology has made it possible for the individuals to obtain important information from remote locations. By 2025, it is predicted that there will be 75 billion IoT devices, which will greatly boost the demand for sensors in the wireless communication space. IoT-enabled WSN has a wide range of applications. Information is gathered by IoT devices is sent to a central data server. The information is processed, compiled, filtered, and subjected to numerous other operations by the central data server. Applications of IoT are beneficial to the government, businesses, and individual consumers. IoT devices include, but are not limited to, laptops, smartphones, Fitbits, smart watches, refrigerators, coffee makers, and Google Home etc. IoT applications can be used with devices that have sensors and an Internet connection. A complete picture is given in Figure.4.1. As IoT devices become more and more popular, a number of challenges will arise in order to meet end user requirements [1]. Security is a main challenge in IoT/WSN networks.

The IoT and its sensors are transforming the way we think about security, from industrial safety measures to national defence systems to home and personal security systems. By gathering and sharing environmental data, these devices make it possible to monitor, identify, and react in real time to viable security threats [2]. WSN is used in military, environmental monitoring, crop monitoring, and health care monitoring and many more. Furthermore, wireless sensor networks are essential for smart cities, smart homes, smart transportation, smart businesses, etc. Human lives are being changed by wireless sensor networks. There are numerous contexts where the information security of WSN is important, including military, healthcare, disaster management and other fields. Without security safeguards, open wireless communication channel technology—which wireless sensor networks use to transfer data—is very vulnerable to attacks. Nevertheless, the computational load derived from the usual cryptographic defence approach is unsuitable for a wireless sensor network. Thus, selecting a suitable encryption technique to guarantee the security

DOI: 10.1201/9781003491910-4

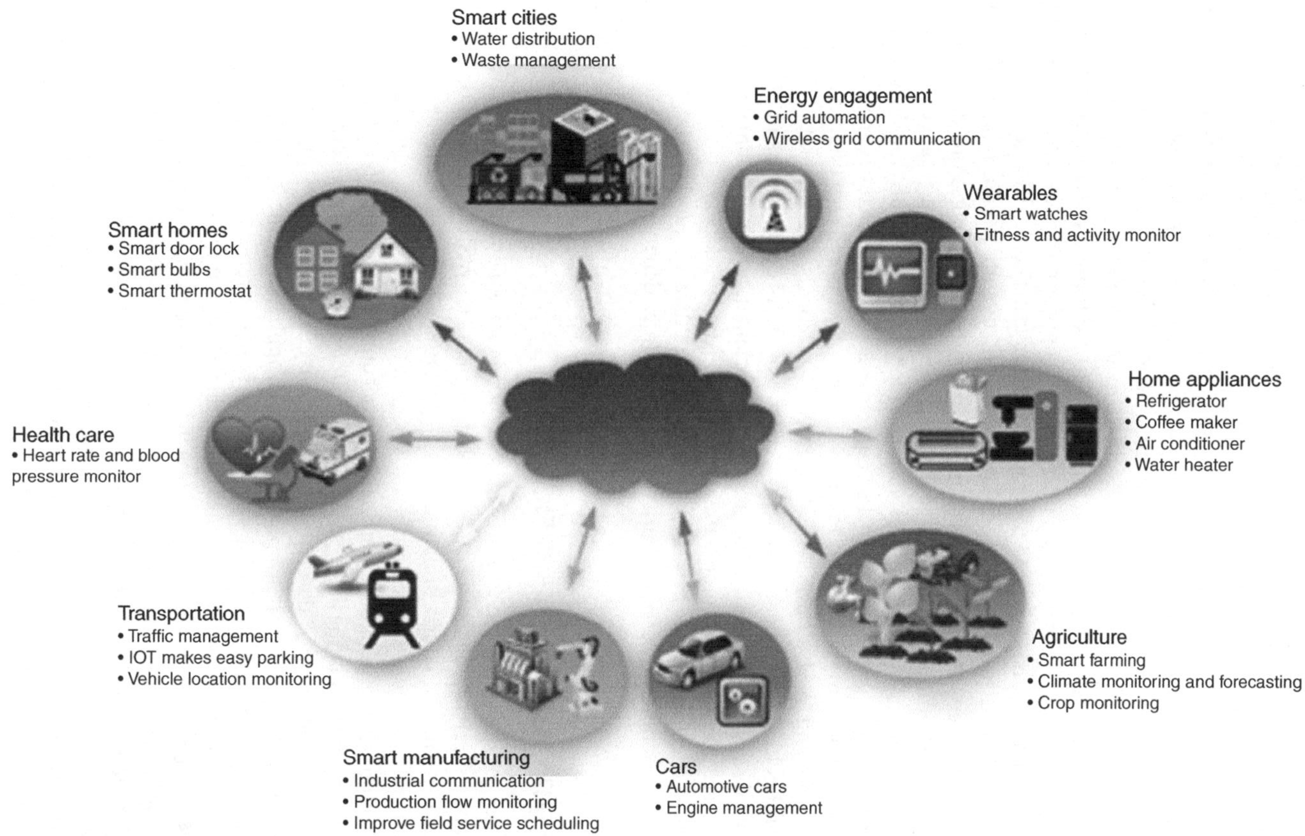

FIGURE 4.1 IoT-enabled WSN applications in real time.

of WSN data is also a major issue. Threats to IoT devices and implementations could jeopardize consumer security and privacy, which could impact how useful its deployment [3,4]. Shouldn't the network security and data protection adhere to fundamental standards and principles of integrity, authentication, availability, authorization, and user privacy? Yes, it should. But because of its inherent vulnerability to threats, users' security and privacy may be jeopardized, which may have an impact on its practical development [5,6].

Several studies and advancements have been made in the field of IoT and its security concerns. But there are still problems and obstacles that must be resolved in order to secure the IoT in the wireless environment. Device diversity, scalability, compatibility and resource constraints are few of them in an unsecured network. As a result, there are security flaws in IoT systems, making them open to numerous attacks. Due to their low power and limited processing and storage capacity, WSNs have security-related problems. A prerequisite for a wireless sensor network is that the information shouldn't be disclosed to unapproved parties. The devices and users on the network should be able to distinguish between authorized and unauthorized users, and that information shouldn't be changed at any point by unauthorized parties. All things considered, the security risks associated with implementing IoT technologies must be carefully taken into account to prevent this promising technology from becoming widely used unethically. Addressing the diversity of security and privacy concerns in its requirements and properties is the most important challenge when integrating WSNs into IoT applications. This is because traditional telecommunication networks and WSNs have a wider variety of protocols and methods, which are more important for this kind of applications [7]. A majority of WSN deployments in the IoT are used to collect sensitive data and information from hostile or unattended environments [8]. A certain amount of security against unauthorized access to this private and sensitive data and information is required because the security and privacy of user data cannot be compromised. These networks are susceptible to various security risks due to their dependence on radio transmission and routing.

4.2 SECURITY ASPECTS: A BIG PICTURE

When it comes to connecting devices, WSN is a crucial component of the IoT infrastructure. In both technologies, privacy and security are crucial topics. The WSN's primary job is to transfer data from devices and send it to a sink node in an appropriate format. On the other hand, the IoT integrates several protocols and technologies to collect, handle, and transmit data over a network for the appropriate use or decision-making procedure. [9,10]. Both technologies—IoT and WSN—place significant emphasis on security and safety. The major concerns are the security, authenticity, and timeliness of data coming from sensor nodes for the proper functioning of every WSN and IoT application. Depending on the application, the security level for WSN varies. In fact, based on their particular applications, wireless sensor networks' (WSN) security requirements can differ greatly. Various use cases, depending on their sensitivity, risk exposure, and the possible repercussions of security breaches, require varying degrees of security. These sensors increase security but come with risks. Every gadget has the potential to be a cyberattack at entry point. It is vital but difficult to ensure data encryption and secure communication protocols due to the devices' limited processing power. It can be difficult to ensure seamless communication with so many devices from various manufacturers. It is difficult to standardize communication protocols without sacrificing functionality or security. As IoT networks grow, managing and integrating thousands or millions of sensors within existing systems without compromising performance is challenging. Figure 4.2 shows the complete picture of IoT challenges and requirements [11].

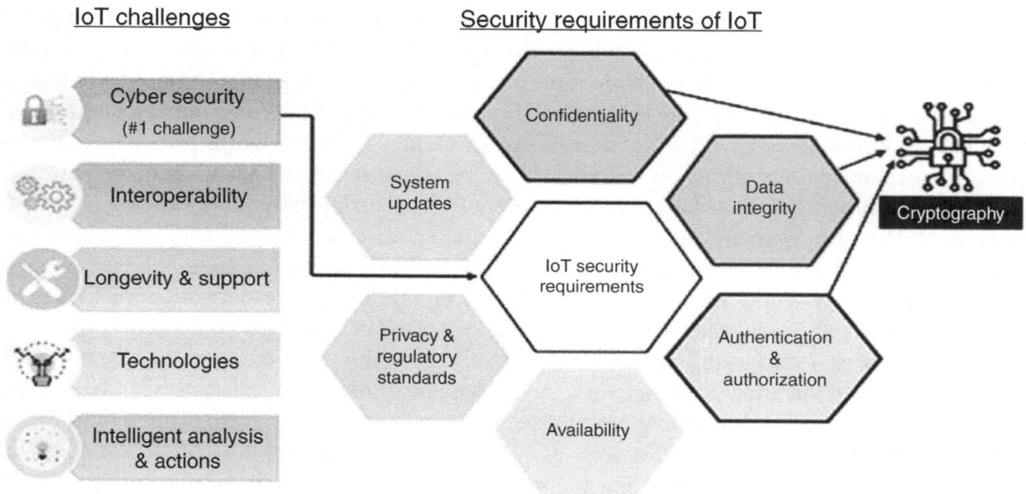

FIGURE 4.2 IoT challenges and requirements.

Security is the main challenge among all other aspects. IoT security is divided into three areas: data security, device security and communication security. Privacy, confidentiality, availability and integrity come under data security. Protecting information from unauthorized access and disclosure is data confidentiality. It ensures that sensitive data is only accessible to those who are authorized, protecting the privacy of the data content. An essential component of information security is data confidentiality. Confidentiality in the context of security refers to the practices and guidelines implemented to prevent unauthorized access and disclosure of data, ensuring that sensitive information is only accessible by those who are authorized. Integrity in security refers to the assurance that information is accurate, complete and unaltered unless by authorized actions. Availability ensures that authorized users can access data and related systems when needed. Availability is important because it guarantees that users, applications and systems can access data and services as expected. This part of security involves ensuring that systems run constantly, without unplanned downtime, and that they bounce back quickly from malfunctions to avoid service or operational interruptions. These three aspects are the fundamental component of the CIA triad—confidentiality, integrity and availability—which outlines the core principles of information security [12].

4.2.1 Security Issues in IoT

Since IoT network frequently link a multitude of devices that gather and transmit data across a variety of environments—from personal and home applications to industrial and urban infrastructures—security of these networks is of utmost importance. IoT networks present particular security issues and challenges because of their unique features, which include their size, diversity and the critical nature of some of their applications etc. IoT has unquestionably had a transformative impact, but it's widespread proliferation has also given rise to serious concerns about security, privacy and trust. These concerns are major roadblocks to the widespread adoption and advancement of IoT technology. The explosive growth of IoT is linked to an increase in security, privacy and trust concerns because of its reliance on the internet infrastructure [13]. In wireless sensor networks, security means preventing unwanted users from accessing, using, disclosing, disrupting, changing or destroying the network or its data. The vast IoT network poses new security challenges and risks, broadening the range of possible attacks and raising the possibility that hackers will be able to obtain more sensitive IoT network data to further their attack.

Security measures guard against threats like eavesdropping, tampering, impersonation, and denial-of-service attacks by utilizing encryption techniques, secure routing protocols, authentication mechanisms and intrusion detection systems. Ensuring that data is gathered, utilized and shared within wireless sensor networks without jeopardizing individual privacy is known as privacy. Because WSNs frequently gather enormous amounts of data, some of which can be extremely sensitive or personal (such as personal activities or health status), hence privacy concerns in these networks are especially important. In wireless sensor networks, trust pertains to the level of confidence placed in the network's operational integrity, data and component parts. Thus, robust security, privacy and trust are critical to the functioning and success of IoT across all IoT tiers, including the network, service-application and physical device layers. The speed at which the IoT is developing has put security experts and cybercriminals in a race. Since there are billions of interconnected objects, they can exchange private information that could be compromised. Consequently, enhancing IoT security and maintaining user privacy is a difficult task. It is not uncommon for an unknown object in a different security domain to communicate with a physical object. For the security and privacy of the two physical objects, building a basic relationship based on trust is essential. How to prevent unauthorized users from accessing physical objects is the cornerstone to ensuring their security, privacy and ownership. Even though it's standard procedure to use biometric information to associate physical objects with their owners, many new security and privacy concerns still need to be addressed.

4.2.2 IoT Challenges in Security

An overview of the main issues pertaining to IoT network security is provided below [14]:

Heterogeneity: IoT networks generally comprise a diverse array of devices with varying operating systems, hardware specifications and communication protocols. It is difficult to implement uniform security measures because of this diversity.

Scalability: Scalable security solutions that can effectively manage and protect massive numbers of devices are necessary due to the sheer volume of devices connected to IoT networks.

Resource Constraints: The complexity of security features that can be directly implemented on IoT devices is limited by the limited computational power, memory, and energy resources of many of these devices.

Network Security: Since wireless networks are frequently used by devices for communication, they are susceptible to cyberattacks such as eavesdropping and interception.

Physical Security: IoT devices' security may be compromised by theft or tampering as a result of unauthorized access. While data processing and transmission security is WSNs' primary focus, physical security is also crucial to maintaining the network's availability and integrity.

Privacy Concerns: The large volume of private information that IoT devices gather raises serious privacy issues that call for strong data protection protocols.

The physical, network and application layers are the specific targets of intentional attacks on IoT systems. The above-mentioned issues affect all these layers. Every IoT layer has different requirements, and standards must always be met in the event when potential threats are detected. By means of sensors that generate, collect and distribute data to users through the network

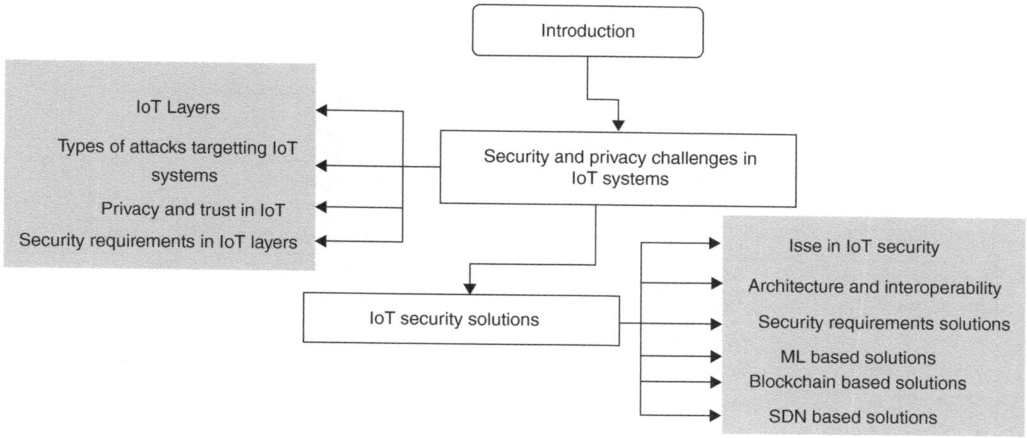

FIGURE 4.3 Security challenges and solutions.

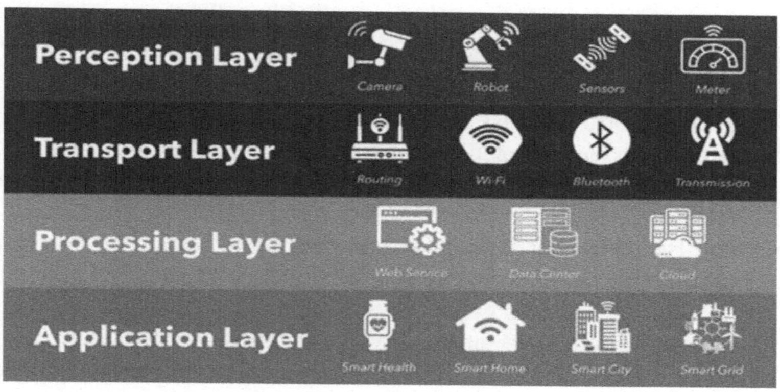

FIGURE 4.4 Layered architecture of IoT.

layer, which subsequently transmits this data to the application layer for user consumption [15]. Through IoT layers, the real world is integrated into computer-based systems. Consequently, the confidentiality and reliability of IoT services—which include sensitive information about individuals, businesses, and governments—become more and more crucial. The flow diagram in Figure 4.3 shows the challenges and solutions of the IoT security and privacy issues.

IoT networks and systems are inherently vulnerable because of the proliferation of IoT devices and their widespread availability, posing a threat to user security and privacy. Numerous critical infrastructures rely on IoT devices, which are susceptible to cyberattacks. This necessitates a thorough examination of IoT security requirements, threats, architectural difficulties and defences against IoT cyberattacks. Much effort has been put into securing IoT systems and enhancing privacy and trust, employing a range of strategies.

Security issues specific to each IoT layer arise because each layer is distinct in the functions and technologies it integrates with. As seen in Figure 4.4, the perception layer, also referred to as the sensors layer, is where IoT device-generated data is located, gathered and prepared for transmission to the network layer. On the other hand, the network layer routes the IoT data generated

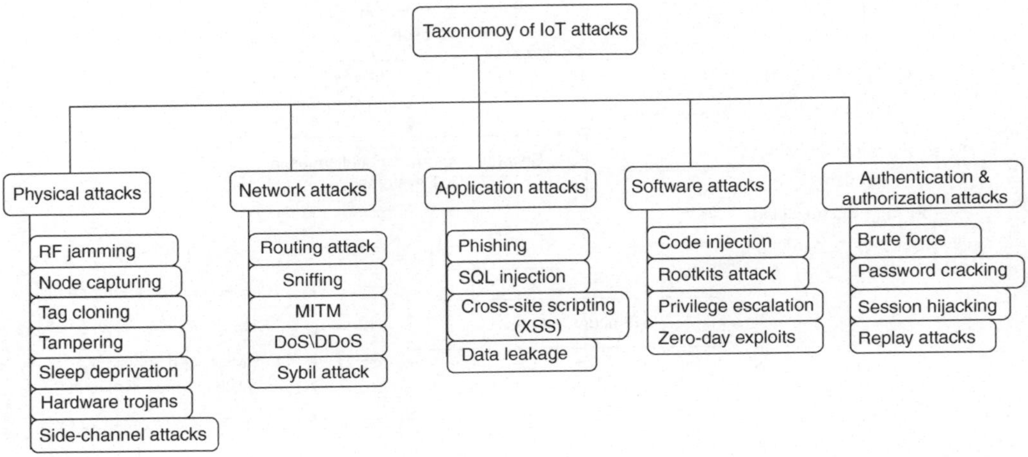

FIGURE 4.5 Security attack types.

at the lower layer to various hubs. It consists of essential parts like Internet gateways, cloud computing platforms, switches and routers. Numerous radio technologies, such as 2G, 3G, LTE, WiFi, Bluetooth and ZigBee, are used at the network layer. Additionally, by gathering, sorting and transmitting data between sensors, gateways at this layer serve as an interface between nodes [16]. Gathering information from the environment and sending it to another layer so that actions can be taken in response to that information is the main responsibility of the perception layer. The transport layer of an IoT system architecture is used to transfer data from different devices to an on-premises or cloud data centre. The middleware layer, also known as the processing layer, contains advanced features like computation, storage, processing and the ability to take action. The application layer manages each step of the application process by using information from the middleware layer.

Figure 4.5 shows the various types of security attack in IoT/WSN in each layer [5]. Few of them are discussed here. Node tampering, which involves replacing the sensor node or some of its hardware, is the act of physically gaining access to confidential information or the provision of services. This is one method of deploying nodes to manipulate the data flow. Replay attacks involve nodes obtaining data from nearby legitimate nodes and retransmitting it in an attempt to gain network trust. In a sinkhole attack, the malicious nodes claim for maximum resources and try to reroute the packets through it. Then it drops all packets without forwarding. The whole systems can be controlled by code injection. Node jamming is a denial-of-service (DoS) attack where the attackers does not allow legitimate nodes to transmit by making channel busy all the time. Sleep deprivation makes the nodes not to enter to sleep mode and that leads to drainage of node's power [17].

4.3 TOOLS AND TECHNIQUES FOR SECURITY

There are many methods and techniques to mitigate security attacks in WSN. Few are discussed in detail.

4.3.1 Public Key-based Security Management Scheme

Neither the conventional pre-distributed key management technique nor the public key-based security can work efficiently in an IoT pervasive computing environment. The Public Key

Infrastructure (PKI), on which this key management system is based, allows nodes to securely communicate over an untrusted network without first needing to share a secret key [20,25]. For the random or dynamic key negotiation, none of the static key management schemes or those based on trusted third-party schemes can satisfy their requirements. Because in sensor networks any two strange physical objects may need to communicate with each other at any time, this further restricts data exchange and raises serious security and privacy issues. The processing, memory and energy capacities of IoT devices, especially sensor nodes, are constrained. The computational burden of public key operations, such as Rivest–Shamir–Adleman (RSA) and elliptic curve cryptography (ECC), is higher than that of symmetric key operations. The topology of wireless sensor networks is subject to dynamic changes. To handle these changes, robust and flexible key management is needed. Nodes may go offline and new nodes may join. Because of its computational requirements, public key cryptography may result in increased latency and decreased throughput, which could have an effect on real-time data processing in WSNs. Public key-based key management schemes are becoming more and more practical for safe and effective operation in IoT wireless sensor networks, despite being more complicated and demanding than symmetric key schemes. These schemes offer clear advantages in terms of security and scalability [18,21]. To overcome the resource limitations common to these networks, however, considerable thought and optimization are needed.

Benefits of public key-based security management scheme:

- *Security*: The private key do not need to be shared or transmitted, so security is increased.
- *Scalability*: The ability to grow without requiring the distribution of new keys to every node as more and more are added.
- *Flexibility*: Accommodates a range of cryptographic methods, such as digital signatures, encryption, and certificate-based authentication.

Because of the special requirements and features of WSN, identity-based cryptography (IBC) can be especially helpful. In WSN, sensor nodes often have limited resources, such as memory, processing power and energy. Because of the overhead involved in managing certificates and key distribution, traditional PKI approaches might not be feasible in these kinds of environments. A centralized Certificate Authority (CA) and certificate management are no longer necessary with IBC. Alternatively, sensor nodes can obtain their public keys directly from their identities, like their distinct network addresses or node IDs. Key management is made simpler, and overhead is decreased.

4.3.2 Cloud and Edge Computing

Cloud and edge computing is crucial to the architecture of IoT and WSN systems because it allows data processing to happen closer to the data source rather than relying on a central data centre [22]. This method has a number of advantages, such as decreased latency, less bandwidth consumption and improved application performance. But incorporating edge computing into WSN and IoT environments also brings unique security issues that need to be resolved. IoT devices based on edge computing are vulnerable to numerous new security and privacy flaws [23,24]. The edge node serves as a link between the perception network and the cloud, putting it in close proximity to both the data source and local data centres. This proximity renders it vulnerable to attack and increases the risk of sensitive data leaking. Because IoT-based ubiquitous computing frequently necessitates data sharing and data use across security domains, the sharing and use of sensitive data must comply with incredibly complex security and privacy regulations. For example, what are the best ways for a data owner to securely outsource their data? Because cloud computing offers infinite processing and storage capacity, it is crucial to the Internet of Things [19].

There are many ways to secure the network in edge computing. To prevent unwanted access to sensitive data, use robust encryption protocols for both data in transit and at idle state. Using robust multi-factor authentication systems to confirm users' and devices' identities is another method. By using sophisticated access control systems, you can ensure that users and devices can only access the information and resources needed to perform their tasks. By updating software and firmware frequently to guard against known vulnerabilities is a better solution. Include automated systems to update edge devices on a regular basis and install intrusion detection at the network edge to keep an eye on suspicious activity and take immediate action. By creating networks with features like failover, redundancy and self-healing mechanisms to make them resistant to attacks and failures is one of the best option against any attacks. Executing energy-efficient security procedures to make sure that the device's limited resources aren't depleted.

The challenges in cloud and edge computing in WSN are given below:

- *Resource Restrictions*: The edge devices usually have low processing and storage capacities; the complexity of security protocols and algorithms that can be used may be limited.
- *Physical Security Risks*: Since edge devices are frequently placed in easily accessible areas, they are susceptible to physical manipulation.
- *Complexity of Management*: Updating and maintaining security protocols on a large number of edge devices can require more time and effort than centralized management.

4.3.3 Machine Learning (ML) Techniques

Security systems in WSN can enhance their detection capabilities, adjust to novel threats and enhance responses more successfully than with conventional approaches by utilizing ML techniques [4]. Because of their distributed architecture and the often limited resources of individual sensors, WSNs are particularly susceptible to a variety of grave security vulnerabilities. After being trained to identify typical network behaviours, machine learning algorithms can be used to identify anomalies or strange patterns that could point to a security breach, such as an attempted intrusion or a malevolent insider. Machine learning can improve signature-based intrusion detection systems (IDS) by allowing the system to automatically learn and update detection patterns in real time without the need for human intervention. This allows the system to identify and stop new and evolving threats.

By examining how code behaves when it runs on sensor nodes, machine learning models are able to detect malicious software by identifying deviations from normal behaviour. In WSNs, where traditional antivirus solutions are too resource-intensive, this is especially helpful. By examining past data and spotting trends or correlations that might indicate an impending attack, machine learning is able to anticipate possible weaknesses and threats. This enables administrators to take proactive preventive action. Maintaining the integrity of the data gathered is essential in a WSN. By comparing data with expected patterns or behaviours, machine learning can assist in identifying data that may have been manipulated. For instance, ML systems may identify abrupt changes in sensor readings of environmental data so that additional research is conducted. However, there are many challenges in incorporating ML algorithms in WSN as discussed below.

- *Restrictions on Resources*:
  The processing power, memory and energy supply of WSN nodes are frequently constrained, which limits the complexity of ML algorithms that can be installed directly on these devices.

- *Capability to Scale*:
  Large-scale WSN deployments may require centralized data processing due to their inherent limitations. Approaches to distributed or federated learning must be developed to manage scalability.
- *Availability and Quality of Data*:
  Effective machine learning requires labelled training data of a high calibre. It can be difficult to gather and classify enough of this kind of data in WSNs.
- *Model Management and Updating*:
  It can be difficult to deploy and update machine learning models over a large network of dispersed sensor nodes, especially when trying to do so without interfering with network functionality.

Organizations can greatly improve their capacity to identify and react to security threats quickly and efficiently by incorporating machine learning into the WSN security infrastructure. Nevertheless, in order to meet the particular difficulties of WSN environments, great thought must be given to the design and implementation of ML systems.

4.3.4 Software Defined Radio (SDR)

With software defined radio in WSNs, software updates can dynamically program and modify the radio properties of the sensors, including frequency range, modulation type and communication protocols. By enabling adaptable responses to different network conditions and threats, this capability enhances the security and resilience of the network. SDR makes it possible to dynamically alter modulation schemes and encryption techniques in response to attacks that are detected or based on the perceived threat level. Even in the face of changing threats, this flexibility can aid in maintaining the security of communications. SDR can be used to keep an eye out for illegal transmissions on the spectrum, which could be signs of eavesdropping attempts or security breaches. Early threat detection and response are facilitated by this monitoring. SDR provides the ability to update the communication protocols as per the latest security standards and practices, thereby maintaining high levels of network security against new vulnerabilities. Security patches and updates can be rolled out across the network swiftly and uniformly, ensuring that all nodes are equally secured and reducing the network's exposure to exploit. With SDR, networks can be designed to ensure continuous availability and operation in the event of an attack by automatically switching to backup systems.

The challenges in SDR in WSN are given below:

Power Consumption: SDRs have the potential to use more power than conventional fixed-function radios, which is important to take into account in WSN environments where power is limited.

Cost and Complexity: Sensor node costs and complexity may rise as a result of SDR implementation.

Security of SDR itself: Since SDR's software acts as a new entry point for potential threats, it needs to be protected from attacks.

4.3.5 Other Technologies

Constrained application protocol (CoAP) is an application layer protocol designed for devices with constrained resources [26]. By merging IPv6 and LoWPAN, IPv6 low power wireless personal

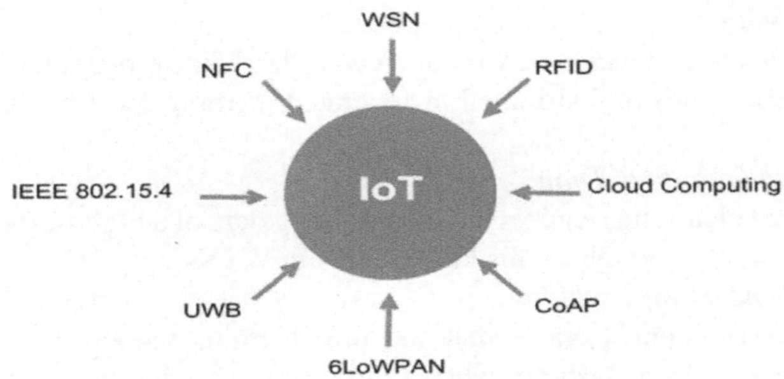

FIGURE 4.6 IoT technologies.

area network (6LoWPAN) makes it easier to send IPv6 packets over IEEE 802.15.4 networks [25]. The 6LoWPAN is suitable for the IoT and offers a number of advantages. However, it is susceptible to various attacks, such as denial-of-service attacks and eavesdropping. Ultra wideband (UWB) is a good technology for a variety of IoT applications because it uses less power and has greater precision and security [14]. IEEE 802.15.4 protocol controls the MAC (medium access control) and physical layers of wireless personal area networks (WPANs). It provides a way to connect low-energy objects in one's living area. Near field communication (NFC) is a short-range technology used in many IoT applications, such as payment and authentication. The NFC simplifies network access and data exchange. However, the device is susceptible to information leakage because an attacker could intercept the wireless signal it produces [27]. The different IoT technologies are displayed in Figure 4.6.

IoT security is a difficult task. All IoT devices, however, are designed to be small and have limited resources (processing, battery, and storage). Conventional security measures are impossible to implement since they need a lot of difficult and intricate process. Creating a lightweight security mechanism for a highly constrained device is the main challenge.

4.4 RESULTS AND DISCUSSIONS

IoT security can be accomplished with a variety of methods and instruments. We discuss the implications of some of these tactics in detail.

The results of the statistical analysis on WSN security implementations on the examined ML algorithms are displayed in Figure 4.7. The analysis reveals the kind of security that WSNs have in place as well as the proportion of ML algorithms that are employed in each type. Figure 4.7 illustrates that 41 percent of the examined studies employed machine learning algorithms to detect intrusions. Eighteen percent follows it closely in error detection, 14 percent of the remaining is for authentication and another 14 percent is for diverse security aspects. This is due to the fact that machine learning algorithms necessitate training processes and are costly to implement on hardware (devices). Moreover, the majority of it was applied to preserve network availability, and applying integrity and confidentiality at the same time was difficult.

Infrastructures for public key cryptography have been suggested, including PKI and identity-based cryptography (IBC) in WSN. Although IBC doesn't have a certificate issue, making it the ideal option for WSNs, but it doesn't scale well for big networks. PKI is therefore required for the IoT's scale.

Cloud computing presents a very promising solution for sensor-cloud infrastructure due to its features such as agility, dependability, portability, real-time, flexibility and others. In structural

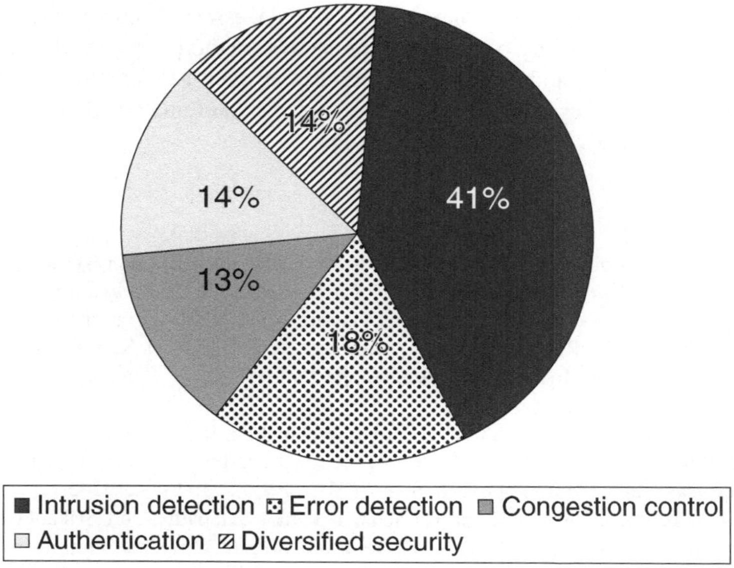

FIGURE 4.7 Statistical analysis.

health and environment-based monitoring, highly sensitive data is used, and standard data tools that are available in terms of data scalability, performance, programmability or accessibility cannot handle these applications. Therefore, in order to handle these extremely sensitive applications, a more robust infrastructure is needed, perhaps with real-time tools installed.

SDR provides the flexibility and adaptability required in the quickly changing technology landscapes, and it offers substantial advantages for IoT and WSNs. However, for its deployment to be effective, it must be balanced against drawbacks like complexity and increased power consumption. To create secure connections and an overall secure network, penetration testing is necessary to find security flaws and solutions to outside intrusions. Penetration testing is a methodical process of modelling attacks from malevolent sources in order to assess the security of the communication systems and protocols.

4.5 CONCLUSION

The particular needs and limitations of the network, such as the sensitivity of the data, node capabilities and environmental factors, determine which security technique is best for WSN. An approach that is layered and integrates multiple techniques, like combining cryptographic methods with intrusion detection and secure data aggregation, can offer a more resilient security solution that tackles various potential vulnerabilities in WSN. The purpose of this chapter is to draw attention to the growing issue of security threats in IoT/WSN and to stress the importance of taking preventative security measures. It is proposed that certain traits and behaviours that could lead to threats have the characteristics that set them apart from the rest of the workforce. The latest tools and technologies that help prevent attacks can easily detect these traits. It is essential to comprehend and represent the actions and motives of the offender and the user. Enhancing this area will unquestionably increase readiness and help avert incidents. Although no system is entirely secure, security cannot be maximized without considering human factors. To be effective in a cyber realm, a certain amount of trust must be placed in it, but ongoing verification using cutting-edge AI and ML tools and technologies is also necessary. Security threat detection is a developing study area with plenty of room for innovative methods and novel techniques. There are several machine learning and modelling techniques, as well as many audit sources, that can be efficiently gathered. However, building efficient and exact automated monitoring and analysis systems for detecting threats in WSN is challenging.

REFERENCES

[1] Adam, M., Hammoudeh, M., Alrawashdeh, R., and Alsulaimy, B. (in press). A survey on security, privacy, trust, and architectural challenges in IoT systems, *IEEE Access*, https://pure.kfupm.edu.sa/en/publications/a-survey-on-security-privacy-trust-and-architectural-challenges-i.

[2] Yao, X., Farha, F., Li, R., Psychoula, I., Chen, L., & Ning, H. (2021). Security and privacy issues of physical objects in the IoT: Challenges and opportunities. *Digital Communications and Networks*, 7(3): 373–384.

[3] Shapla Khanam, Ismail Bin Ahmedy, Mohd Yamani Idna Idris, Mohamed Hisham Jaward, and Aznul Qalid Bin Md Sabri (2020) A survey of security challenges, attacks taxonomy and advanced countermeasures in the internet of things. *IEEE Access*, 8: 219709–219743.

[4] Bhabendu Kumar Mohanta, Debasish Jena, Utkalika Satapathy, and Srikanta Patnaik (2020). Survey on IoT security: Challenges and solution using machine learning, artificial intelligence and blockchain technology. *Internet of Things*, 11: 100227.

[5] Hichem Mrabet, Sana Belguith, Adeeb Alhomoud, and Abderrazak Jemai. (2020). A survey of IoT security based on a layered architecture of sensing and data analysis. *Sensors*, 20(13): 3625.

[6] Arpna Saxena and Sangeeta Mittal (2022). Internet of medical things (IoMT) security and privacy: A survey of recent advances and enabling technologies. In *Proceedings of the 2022 Fourteenth International Conference on Contemporary Computing*, pp. 550–559.

[7] Khan, N.A., Awang, A., and Karim, S. A. A. (2022) Security in Internet of Things: a review, *IEEE Access*, 10: 104649–104670, 2022, doi: 10.1109/ACCESS.2022.3209355.

[8] Kansal, P., Kansal, D., and Balodi, A. (2010). Compression of various routing protocol in wireless sensor network. *International Journal of Computer Applications,* 5(11): 0975–8887.

[9] Tolani, M., Bajpai, A., Balodi, A. et al. (2023). Energy-efficient duty-cycle hybrid medium access control protocol for wireless sensor network. *Wireless Personal Communication* 131: 609–621.

[10] Moni Sree, H., Pavithra, R., Nithyaa Shri R. B. and Shanthi, M. (2021). Review on IoT security and its real-time application. *2021 International Conference on Advancements in Electrical, Electronics, Communication, Computing and Automation (ICAECA)*, Coimbatore, India, 2021, pp. 1–6, doi: 10.1109/ICAECA52838.2021.9675718.

[11] Khan, Naqash Azeem, Azlan Awang, and Samsul Ariffin Abdul Karim. (2022). Security in internet of things: A review. IEEE access 10: 104649–104670.

[12] Harbi, Y., Aliouat, Z., Harous, S., Bentaleb, A., and Refoufi, A. (2019). A review of security in internet of things. *Wireless Personal Communications*, 108: 325–344.

[13] Abiodun, O. I., Abiodun, E. O., Alawida, M., Alkhawaldeh, R. S., and Arshad, H. (2021). A review on the security of the internet of things: challenges and solutions. *Wireless Personal Communications*, 119: 2603–2637.

[14] Jamshed, M. A., Ali, K., Abbasi, Q. H., Imran, M. A., and Ur-Rehman, M. (2022). Challenges, applications, and future of wireless sensors in Internet of Things: A review. *IEEE Sensors Journal*, 22(6): 5482–5494.

[15] Undercoffer, J., Avancha, S., Joshi, A., and Pinkston, J. (2002, October). Security for sensor networks. In *CADIP Research Symposium* (pp. 25–26).

[16] Deep, S., Zheng, X., Jolfaei, A., Yu, D., Ostovari, P., and Kashif Bashir, A. (2022). A survey of security and privacy issues in the Internet of Things from the layered context. *Transactions on Emerging Telecommunications Technologies*, 33(6): e3935.

[17] Choudhary, V., Srivastava, A., Kumar, A., and Taruna, S. (2022). Comparative Analysis of Security Issues and Trends in IoT and WSN. *SAMRIDDHI: A Journal of Physical Sciences, Engineering and Technology*, 14(2): 216–222.

[18] Burhanuddin, M. A., Mohammed, A. A. J., Ismail, R., Hameed, M. E., Kareem, A. N., and Basiron, H. (2018). A review on security challenges and features in wireless sensor networks: IoT perspective. *Journal of Telecommunication, Electronic and Computer Engineering (JTEC)*, 10(1-7): 17–21.

[19] Jabeen, T., Jabeen, I., Ashraf, H., Jhanjhi, N. Z., Yassine, A., and Hossain, M. S. (2023). An intelligent healthcare system using IoT in wireless sensor network. *Sensors*, 23(11): 5055.

[20] Majid, M., Habib, S., Javed, A. R., Rizwan, M., Srivastava, G., Gadekallu, T. R., and Lin, J. C. W. (2022). Applications of wireless sensor networks and internet of things frameworks in the industry revolution 4.0: A systematic literature review. *Sensors*, 22(6): 2087.

[21] Abiodun, O. I., Abiodun, E. O., Alawida, M., Alkhawaldeh, R. S., & Arshad, H. (2021). A review on the security of the internet of things: challenges and solutions. *Wireless Personal Communications*, 119: 2603–2637.

[22] Wang, T., Liang, Y., Shen, X., Zheng, X., Mahmood, A., and Sheng, Q. Z. (2023). Edge computing and sensor-cloud: Overview, solutions, and directions. *ACM Computing Surveys*, *55*(13s): 1–37.

[23] Asad Javed, Avleen Malhi, Tuomas Kinnunen, and Kary Främling. (2020). Scalable IoT platform for heterogeneous devices in smart environments. *IEEE Access*, 8:211973–211985,

[24] Munivel, E., and Ajit, G. M. (2010, January). Efficient public key infrastructure implementation in wireless sensor networks. In *2010 International Conference on Wireless Communication and Sensor Computing (ICWCSC)* (pp. 1–6). IEEE.

[25] Goar, V. (2022). 6LoWPAN in wireless sensor network with IoT in 5G technology for network secure routing and energy efficiency. *International Journal on Future Revolution in Computer Science & Communication Engineering*, 8(2): 15–25.

[26] Granjal, J., and Pedroso, A. (2018). An intrusion detection and prevention framework for internet-integrated CoAP WSN. *Security and Communication Networks,* 1: 1753897.

[27] Olenik, S., Lee, H. S., and Güder, F. (2021). The future of near-field communication-based wireless sensing. *Nature Reviews Materials*, 6(4): 286–288.

5 Security and Privacy Issues for Blockchain Scenarios in IoT and WSN-Based Real-time Applications

Talea Hurаysi

5.1 INTRODUCTION

5.1.1 Background

Nowadays, Internet of Things (IoT) is widely used for various applications [1,2]. The growth in telecommunication technologies enforces the users to utilize the bandwidth for machine-based sensing applications. Not only IoT, but the growth of artificial intelligence and machine learning algorithm has also made the system very powerful for IoT applications. In the current scenario of the world, IoT is used for almost all applications. IoT 4.0 is continuously developing for industrial applications needs. There are various challenges to develop IoT-based systems. However, the current scenario and the development of other related technologies made the system very powerful. Therefore, IoT technology is in great demand. Due to the high demand for the IoT network, researchers are working in the different fields of the IoT network. Broadly, the research-based study of IoT networks can be classified into eight different categories [1].

5.1.2 IoT Systems

A typical IoT network consists of the following components:

- Physical layer
- MAC layer
- Network layer (Routing)
- Application layer
- IoT network security mechanism
- Applications
- Energy-efficient bandwidth utilization methods
- Quality-of-service (QoS) and quality-of-experience (QoE) analysis

The above-mentioned field can be further sub-divided into different categories. The section deals with IoT security methods and protocols. As the IoT network is utilized for various applications, high-level security is the basic need of the network. The IoT network is not only designed for private use but also it will be used for commercial as well as public (e-governance) and private

DOI: 10.1201/9781003491910-5

applications. Therefore, the security of the network is a major concern for the developers. The IoT security methods are focused on layer-based processing of the data for the IoT protocol suite. The IoT security protocol analysis is categorized into various layer-based protocols and applications. Threat analysis for the IoT network is also a growing field for researchers and developers for the analysis and development of efficient security protocols. Various threat analyses and the security protocol for the different types of threats are already proposed by researchers. The security threats-based research works can be categorized into two different categories. Few of the researchers are working for the improvement of the existing protocols and others working on the current and future security challenges. In the section, the different threats and the related research are analyzed. The research works based on the security protocols are discussed in Section 5.2. All the major sub-categories of the IoT-based security protocols are discussed in detail in the next section.

Due to the huge demand for the IoT network, the attackers target IoT-based applications more frequently. The section deals with application-specific IoT security protocols and also explores the solution based on blockchain methods. For the deep discussion of the proposed method, first, the discussion will start with the different types of security challenges and existing methods reported to deal with the issue. The typical architecture of the IoT security method is shown in Figure 5.1.

As shown in Figure 5.1, in an IoT system, the sensors sense the required parameter from the field and transmit the data to the network gateway. The sensor network plays an important role in the collection of data. The data collected from the field are many times temporally correlated. The cumulative collection of the data of the same parameter from the different spatial locations are also spatially correlated. The sensor network data is transmitted to the IoT Cloud where the data is processed in the headquarters or monitoring station. The station generates some feedback signal or alert signal based on the analysis.

The feedback signal is transmitted to the controlling station. The controlling station then actuates the related actuators or motors on the field to perform the counter operation. At the front end, the physical devices perform operations, for example, IoT devices, IoT Gateway, Cloud, Server, Monitoring Station, etc. However, at the back-end, the operation can be classified into different other levels. The back-end operation is shown in Figure 5.1. Sensors' data is transmitted to the bus via a sensor network. The cumulative data is operated by a management network. The

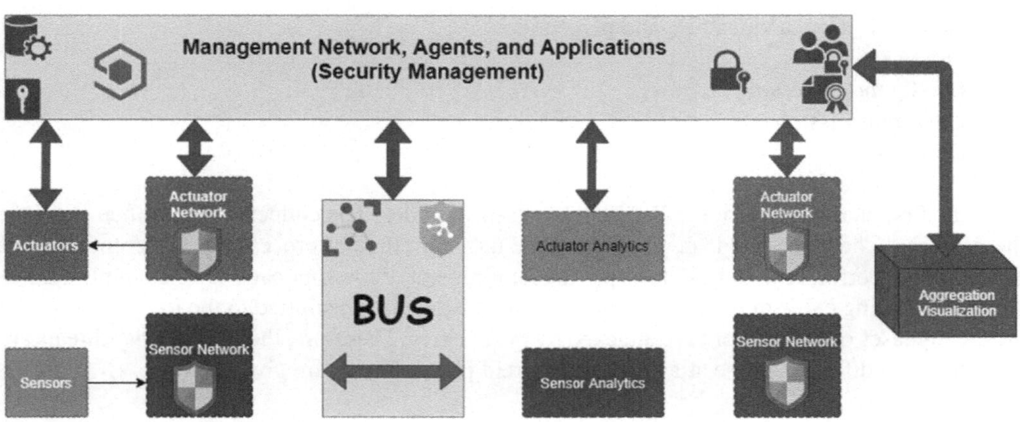

FIGURE 5.1 IoT security architecture components.

management station performs various operations. It uses agents for data logging. It uses the management system for the distribution of data for enterprise architecture. The management system also divides the data into clusters based on the application and parameters. The data is collected from the end device and transmitted to the cloud server. The attacker can attack at any level of the system. The intruder tries to intentionally introduce wrong data to the system to disturb the operation of the monitoring device. For this, the intruder targets the end devices. The malicious device must be identified and isolated from the network. For the secure operation of the end devices, a set of standard security protocols should be used. Sometimes attackers only try to hack the security passwords to enter the network and to get the important data of the network. A malicious device can also target the network by introducing some virus/malware in the system.

5.1.3 IoT Security

Many of the attackers directly target the network by unauthorized access in the network. The researchers have proposed various protocols for network security. Few of the protocols are based on the traditional methods and others are based on newly proposed ideas to efficiently deal with the problem. The network security protocols are very important for the IoT applications as the attacker intentionally jams the whole network. Sometimes, it targets the group of end devices. The next layer is the application layer at the cloud end. The main motive of the attacker is to hack the complete system and try to utilize the system for their own benefit. As the end-user is unaware of with the intention of the hacker, most of the times, hacker harms the end-user as well as the organization. Therefore, application-layer security is also an important challenge for IoT networks.

To manage all the operations and the security of the entire network, security management is used in the IoT network as shown in Figure 5.1. The management system manages the overall security of the entire network. It allows the users for joining the network based on authentication and security. The management system checks the security of the newly joined network devices. It also performs regular security checks for the IoT network layer and also deals with the application layer security. It identifies the malicious node in the network and isolates them. It also identifies the malware/virus in the network and takes the necessary actions. The operation of the different phases of the IoT security architecture is explained below to clearly understand the process of IoT security methods. The operation is divided into five phases:

- Data collection, acquisition, and perception
- Storage
- Intelligent processing
- Data transmission
- Delivery

In the first phase, the data is collected by the sensor nodes. The collected data is then stored in the database. The operation is performed on the data for efficient processing. Different types of operation are performed on the data as per the requirement of the application, for example, aggregation, clustering etc. After intelligent processing, the data is transmitted to the to the server. The different phases of the network are attacked by the hackers. Therefore, the IoT security threats are classified into different phase attacks. The different phase attacks are given below:

1. *Data leakage or breach*: Data leakage is a serious problem in an IoT network. It occurs intentionally or unintentionally. The data is transmitted from one place to another place

and sometimes it transmits from one tenant of the cloud to another tenant of the cloud. Therefore, data leakage can cause a serious threat to the network. For security, the management system uses data leakage prevention (DLP) methods.

2. *Data sovereignty*: For the global uses and enterprise architecture of the IoT network, it is important to use the standard protocol and rules that are agreed by the global community. The countries have their own rules and regulations. The data sovereignty should be followed by the organization for its global use.
3. *Data loss*: Data loss is different from data leakage. The data loss may occur due to hardware and software problems accidentally.
4. *Data authentication*: The intruder can attack any of the devices to introduce forged data in the system. Also, during transmission, the data can be targeted. Therefore, data authenticity assurance is the requirement from the management system to maintain the integrity and the originality of the cloud data. In addition, the data once stored in the server should be protected from tampering.
5. *Attack on availability*: The availability of the server for the client is the primary requirement for the smooth operation of the devices. The distributed denial of service (DDoS) attack is the most common type of overload attack that targets the availability of the intended user. It occurs due to large numbers of distributed attackers.

The attacks can be further classified as per the architecture although standard architecture is not yet defined for IoT applications. However, vendors and organizations have defined their architectures to understand the layerwise operation of the IoT network. The basic IoT architecture consists of four layers: sensing layer, network layer, transportation layer, and application layer. The attacks as per the architecture are discussed in Table 5.1.

Different types of methodologies are proposed to address the above-mentioned attacks and issues. However, centralized approaches are more vulnerable to attacks. The privacy and originality of the data are not much secure in the centralized system as the attacker can target only a

TABLE 5.1
IoT Attacks

Application layer	• Revealing sensitive data • User authentication • Data destruction • Intellectual property
Transport layer	• Denial of service • Distributed denial of service • Cross heterogeneous • Man-in-the-middle
Network Layer	• Routing protocol attack • Address compromise
Sensing Layer/Perception Layer	• External attack • Link-layer attack • Witch attack • HELLO flooding • Wormhole and sewage pool • Selective forwarding • Access control

single system. The single system failure will break down the complete IoT network. To address the issue, researchers have proposed a decentralized approach. The decentralized approach provides better security and privacy of the network. The literature study of the various previously reported works has addressed the issue using blockchain methods. The methods reported by the researchers prove that the blockchain-based methods have enough capability to prevent major IoT attacks. In the section, a blockchain-based security method is proposed for enterprise architecture and organizations. The major objective of the chapter is to develop a blockchain-based model that the vendors can use for the security of the network.

The blockchain can be used as a decentralized methodology for cryptocurrency transactions. The initial cryptocurrency transaction was Bitcoin. However, currently overall more than 700 cryptocurrencies are available for such secure applications, for example, Ethereum and Ripple. The power of the blockchain is that there is no single entity for the transactions. Therefore, the distributed approach of blockchain provides better security as compared to centralized security methods. The blockchain methods have few advantages, but it is also targeted by the hackers. The blockchain participants and related concerns are discussed in the next sub-sections [2,3].

5.1.4 Blockchain-based IoT Security

5.1.4.1 Blockchain Participants and Related Concern

The first participant of the blockchain-based IoT is the blockchain user. End-user security is the major concern for any business organization. The IoT devices directly communicate with the internet via IoT Gateway. Therefore, centralized control does not provide high standard security from hackers. The blockchain-based decentralized method is highly preferred for the privacy of the end-user. The blockchain regulatory is the next important participant of the IoT-based blockchain network. Blockchain developers manage and control the overall network operations and also perform the overall security of the network. The developer should follow the global standard privacy policy and also they should follow the country-wise privacy policy of the IoT network. The certificate authority provides the certificate to operate the heterogeneously approved blockchain. The policy of the certification authority should be transparent and strong. This increases the trust of the users. The most important concern of the users and vendors is trust [2].

5.1.4.2 Blockchain Components

The important blockchain components are described below [3]:

A. *Ledger*: It consists of the current state of global blockchain transactions.
B. *Smart Contract*: Encapsulated code of transactions for the business actions.
C. *Consensus Network*: The group of peers for the set of the data is required for the ledger network.
D. *Membership*: Manages identity, transaction certificates, and other aspects of the certificates as wells as access rights. Write, read, control, data access, and data editing are the different access rights of the network.
E. *Events*: It generates the notification for each new event. It also generates the notification for the new block and the smart contract.
F. *Management*: It controls and generates new blockchain components and blocks and manages the interconnections between the blocks.
G. *System Integration*: It connects and integrates the blocks in a bidirectional manner.

Different types of attacks of blockchain should be described for a better understanding of the challenges of the blockchain for IoT networks. The different types of possible attacks of the blockchain-based IoT network are described in the following subsections [4,5].

5.1.5 Attacks and Solutions

A. *Liveness Attack* [6]: The liveness attack consists of three stages: preparation stage, transaction denial, and blockchain delay. The major target of the attacker is to delay the transaction. In the preparation phase, the attacker tries to gain the advantage to grow the block for the honest player. In the transaction denial phase, the attacker tries to delay the genuine transaction, and in the last phase, it tries to decrease the development rate of the blockchain.
   i: To address the issue, in [7], the author has proposed conflux's consensus protocol. It is a decentralized system and provides fast response in a highly secure manner.
B. *Double Spending Attack* [6,8,9]: In this type of transaction, the attacker duplicates the successful transaction for the same funds. It is impossible to stop the double-spending attack even using blockchain methods.
   Solution [10,11]**:** To address the issue, K. Nicolas et al. proposed a multistage secure pool (MSP) framework. The proposed method provides a pool for authentication. It consists of overall four stages to address the issue: detection, confirmation, forwarding, and broadcast.
C. *51% Vulnerability Attack* [12]: For the mutual trust in a distributed network, the blockchain follows an agreement in a distributed manner. There is a 51 percent vulnerability in an agreement mechanism. The attacker tries to utilize this to control the entire blockchain.
   Solution [13,14]: Sayeed et al. proposed a five-layer security mechanism to overcome the 51 percent attack due to the hash problem. The author has used low-hashing power to analyze 51 percent vulnerability attacks.
D. *Private Key Security Attack* [15,16]: The private key is generated for the user to verify the transactions as well as to access the funds. The private key generates only once. The key is user-specific and so the attacker targets the key to steal cryptocurrency.
   Solution: In [17], the group key approach is used for group authentication to maintain the privacy of the individual user.
E. *Transaction Privacy Leakage*: The attacker can trace the blockchain behavior. It consists of important privacy information. Therefore, the security methods must take corrective measures to secure the IoT network and privacy of the user.
   Solution: In [18], the author has proposed a secure transaction methodology. The proposed method uses multiple key approaches for secure transactions. Many security measures the author have been proposed for secure transactions. Ring signature, homographic crypto security system, and many they have used for the overall security of the network.
F. *Selfish Mining Attack*: This type of attack is initiated by some miners to waste the valid miners' unpaid rewards.
   Solution [7,19,20]: In [19], the author has proposed the true state of the blocks and height to each transaction for the secure transaction and to avoid self-attack.
G. *DAO Attack*: Distributed autonomous organization is one of the important features of the blockchain that provides a distributed control as there is no centralized authority in the blockchain. In this attack, the attacker targets directly to the DAO. In 2016, the attackers have stolen $60 Million from Ethereum's installed smart contract model. This is the largest attack on the Ethereum Consensus model.

Solution [21]: In [21], the author has proposed a scheme and analyzed the method in the Contiki tool. It is a high-efficiency, low-power tool for devices that have limited resources.

H. *BGP Hijacking Attack*: The border gateway protocol (BGP) is used for the routing information. It consists of all the IP information of the IoT network and routes the traffic. The attacker can manipulate the routing information to hijack the blockchain-based IoT network.

   Solution [22]: In [22], the author has proposed a smart contract scheme to supervise resource assignments. It is a tamper-resistant blockchain for BGP protocol.

I. *Sybil Attack*: In this attack, the attacker tries to forge the identity of the system. In peer-to-peer network communication, this type of blockchain attack takes place.

   Solution [23]: In [23], the author has proposed the behavior tracing scheme to trace and track the behavior of the IoT devices that are blocking only the particular user.

5.2 RELATED WORKS

Internet of Things (IoT) is growing exponentially due to the development of telecommunication technologies. The large available bandwidth in 5G and 6G can be utilized for IoT applications. The IoT is majorly used for monitoring applications. The researchers are working in the different fields of IoT for the optimal placement of IoT devices for better coverage and connectivity [24]. However, the most important challenge is to maintain the security of the network. The intrusion attack, vulnerabilities in the network, and security threats are the serious problems of the network system. To protect the system, the protocols should be able to defend the system from the attack and also should be able to detect the intrusion. Similar to the traditional systems, the protocol architecture can be divided into layers as in an open system interconnection (OSI) model and TCP/IP model. Different protocols are used for different layers and therefore protection is required at different layers. In the basic architecture of IoT and wireless sensor network (WSN), the operation is divided into four basic layers as shown in Figure 5.2. The threats are classified into various categories based on layers. The security protocols are classified into different categories to protect the devices from different types of attacks. In this chapter, the challenges are discussed for the various layered protocols. The hackers can attack the network on several levels.

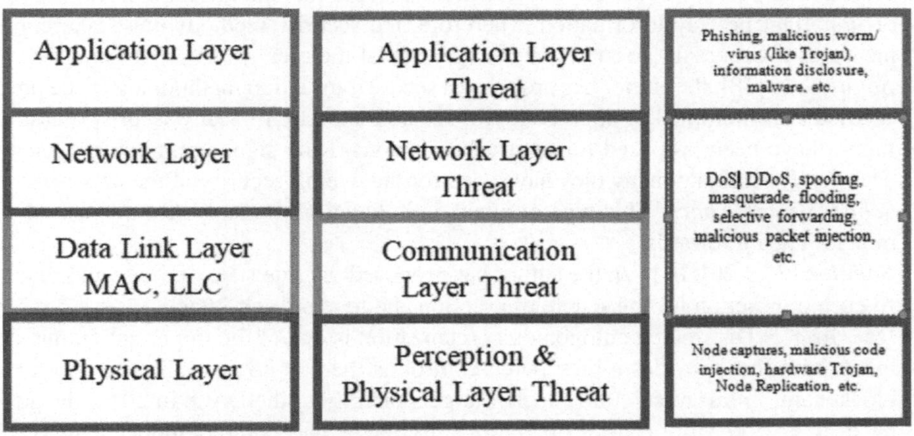

FIGURE 5.2 Layer-wise organization of IoT network devices and classification of threats.

Therefore, the security from the different types of attack can be classified into three major categories: data security, device security, and communication security [25].

The IoT security is important in all respects. The researchers have worked on various attack models. The chapter also concentrated on various trust models and threat models. The researchers have studied various threat models. The blockchain methods are widely used for various purposes. First of all, it is used for secure transactions. However, due to its distributed security approach, researchers are now focused on various secure data transmission. The IoT can be utilized for various applications. The IoT is now used for monitoring application as well as other social and private/public data transmission application. The IoT is widely used for smart grid application, smart shopping application, automatic driving application. The advances in telecommunication industry opens a new door for the IoT. Therefore, in recent years, the demand for IoT has increased due to its wide range of applications and good quality of service (QoS) with 5G. The researchers have proposed a wide range of works for the integration of 5G with IoT. Thus, the application is now utilized for the huge data traffic demand. The railway monitoring application and health monitoring application generate very high data traffic. In the recent developments, researchers have proposed many works for utilization of IoT for railway monitoring application. Due to the huge demand for an IoT-based network, security is the major issue for many of the critical applications.

In this section, the discussion will start with the types of attacks and threats. It will be followed by the requirement of security and the challenges in the designing of security protocols. It will be continue with the classification into different types of security protocols based on the layered architecture. In the end, the literature study will be concluded based on the final findings.

5.2.1 Comparison of Different Types of Security Protocols

The different security protocols for the different applications are discussed in Table 5.2. The name of the journal/conference, the simulation platform, the contribution of the author, parameters, remarks, and findings are discussed in this section. Each of the protocol is discussed briefly in the next section. The contribution of the authors/researchers are categorized in different sections, for example, IoT attacks, IoT threats, different layer threats, proposed solutions etc.

5.2.2 Blockchain Security Methods

Blockchain technology is very popular nowadays for network security. The same can be utilized for the security of the IoT network. In this section, blockchain-based network security algorithms are proposed to enhance the security of the network. Blockchain is a system of recording information in a way that it is nearly impossible for the hacker to attack the system. In [33], the author has proposed the hardware for the client and server devices. The TLS-IM is used at the client end and the TLS-SE is used at the server end. A blockchain-based PSK key is used to devise login. The Wi-Fi System on Chip is used as a radio trans-receiver and the TCP/IP protocol suite is used as a protocol suite for the IoT network analysis.

In [34], the author has proposed an ethereum blockchain-based method to enhance the security of the protocol. The scalability is the major issue of the IoT network. As the user demand is increasing, the challenge of scalability of the network is also increasing. To address the issue, the author has proposed a blockchain-based strong security method that supports the high scalability of the network. The obtained results confirm the suitability of the network for the blockchain application. Similarly, in [36], the author has proposed a blockchain-based method to enhance the security of the protocol. The author has also analyzed the performance of the blockchain-based method and traditional method [36].

TABLE 5.2
Comparative Analysis of Different Security Protocols

SN	Reference and Year	Name of Journal/ Conference	Simulation/ Testbed/ Analytical	Contribution/ Problem address/ objective	Parameters/ Matrix evaluated	Technique/ approach used	Remarks/ Findings
1.	[24]	*IEEE Transactions on Reliability*	Testbed	Testbed framework to analyze the security of heterogeneous network	Scanning, Fingerprint, Data Leakage, Management Access etc.	Author used testbed at end device (Lab-view), and communication layer	The proposed method is effective in determining vulnerabilities
2	[25]	*IEEE Communications Letters*	MATLAB	Harvesting and threat aware security protocol is proposed	IEEE 802.15.4 Standard Parameters	Changes the security configuration based on residual power	The proposed scheme provides high network security with low energy consumption.
3	[26]	*ICECCO* (IEEE)	Testbed	Analysis of perception layer threat	Node capture, malicious code injection, false data injection, replay (freshness) etc.	A multilayer model is used. The insider attack has been tested by introducing wrong data in the perception layer.	Results show that strong protocol also can't protect from the insider attack.
4	[27]	Global Conference on IoT (IEEE)	Testbed & Simulation	Proposed Ethereum Blockchain to protect from insider attack in the perception layer	Edge Computing, Side channels	The insider attack is generated at the perceptional layer and processed for edge computing using Ethereum Blockchain before data being analyzed, processed, and stored.	The results show that the Ethereum Blockchain method is useful significantly to protect the system from perception layer threat.

5	[28]	IFIP Networking (IEEE)	Simulation	A lightweight framework (NLSec) for Network Layer Security is proposed.	NL Attack, Collector, Mitigator	The proposed protocol identifies the compromised nodes and mitigate the attack by isolating the compromised nodes.	The framework is proposed that can efficiently protect the network by simply isolating the compromised IoT Devices.
6	[29]	*IEEE Access*	Modelling	The author analyzed the 5G network layer IoT security issues and existing security protocols.	Generic threats, Virtualization threats, and Multi-Edge Computing Threats	Bio-inspired security framework is analyzed for 5G and IoT applications to ensure high level of security.	The bio-inspired algorithms are more suitable and capable to provide high level of security.
7	[30]	*IEEE: Internet of Things*	Survey	Various attacks are analyzed for the low budget IoT devices that can't support strong security protocols. Different types of radio-trans-receiver and their vulnerabilities are reported	Security attributes, namely integrity, anonymity, confidentiality, privacy, access control, authentication, authorization, resilience, self-organization	A survey has been done on existing IoT threats, and real time threats.	Two open challenges are reported related to the management of the public key and vulnerabilities for network layer protocol.
8	[31]	*IEEE Communication Surveys and Tutorials*	Survey	The paper categorizes the IoT vulnerabilities discussion into various categories in terms of attacks and their counter solutions.	Malicious scripts, Distortion, Selective message forwarding, Phishing, etc.	Various threats, attacks are discussed based on the layered applications and solution is proposed.	It is observed that the same attack causes various vulnerabilities in the IoT paradigm

(*continued*)

TABLE 5.2 (Continued)
Comparative Analysis of Different Security Protocols

SN	Reference and Year	Name of Journal/ Conference	Simulation/ Testbed/ Analytical	Contribution/ Problem address/ objective	Parameters/ Matrix evaluated	Technique/ approach used	Remarks/ Findings
9	[32]	*IEEE: Internet of Things*	Analysis & Discussion	The challenges and requirement of the network is analyzed. SDN based solution is proposed for the various standard IoT applications.	Physical attacks, Data sensitivity, Limitations, Heterogeneity, etc.	The software defined networking approach is proposed for the IoT network security.	ML technology and SDN based technique provides a very strong security protocol to maintain the privacy and integrity of the network.
10	[33]	CCNC (IEEE)	Hardware Model	The client and server hardware device model is proposed with prototype	TCP/IP WiFi SoC	In the proposed network PSK key based security method is proposed. Two hardware devices TLS-IM and TLS-SE are used for the client and server ends	A secured protocol is proposed with enhanced privacy and integrity
11	[34]	CSNet (IEEE)	Simulation	Ethereum Blockchain method is proposed to enhance the IoT network security	Average Standard Deviation	A simple blockchain based authorization solution is proposed for the IoT network	The obtained results confirm the suitability of the proposed method for the IoT application
12	[35]	WF-IoT (IEEE)	Discussion & Analysis	Blockchain based enhanced security protocol is proposed	Smart Contract, Consensus, Cryptography, Shared Ledger	A blockchain based method is proposed for the secure data transmission	Enhances privacy and scalability

In [37], the authors have proposed a permissioned blockchain (Hyperledger Fabric) that have lower latency and lower overhead with respect to ethereum blockchain. The IoT devices are geographically distributed in the field and have limited resources. Therefore, the lightweight security protocol is the basic need of the IoT system. In this paper, author has assumed that the device security is compromised. The proposed approach automatically isolates the compromised device. The blockchain based method can enforce the security policies as long as majority of IoT devices are not compromised. The proposed scheme offers better security with lower latency. Therefore, the proposed scheme is also suitable for event-driven emergency applications and time-constraint applications.

5.3 METHODOLOGY AND IMPLEMENTATION

5.3.1 Aims and Objectives

In this section, a blockchain-enabled IoT security solution will be proposed. The advancement of the telecommunication technologies opens doors for many of the new developing technologies because of high availability of the bandwidth. The IoT-based networks are now widely used for various monitoring as well as data collection applications. However, due to the early stage of the development of IoT, no standard protocol suite or layer model is available. Moreover, many of the service providers are using the existing security protocols for the IoT network deployment and services. Therefore, in the section, we have proposed the blockchain-based security protocol. The blockchain-based method provides better security for IoT applications. To further strengthen the existing method, the weight factor-based trust parameter is used for optimal performance. The trust parameter depends upon three constraints: application, data sensitivity, and latency. To illustrate the features of the proposed blockchain method, a basic process diagram for the formation of the new blocks and the formation of the blockchain is shown in Figure 5.3.

5.3.2 The System Overview and Workflow

The blockchain is formed with the help of blocks. The blocks consist of a group of transactions. The successful transactions form a block. All successful transactions of the block are called settled transactions. The process of formation of a new block is called mining. All the nodes which participated in the mining process (transaction process) in the formation of new blocks are called mining nodes. In the process of formation of the new block, all mining nodes participate in the cryptographic quiz. If all the transactions of the block succeed to solve the quiz, the new block forms are added to the existing chain. The information of the newly formed block is broadcasted to all the mining as well as non-mining nodes.

5.3.3 Core Components

A. *Mining Nodes*: All the nodes which participated in the mining process (transaction process) in the formation of the new block are called mining nodes.
B. *Non-Mining Nodes*: All the nodes which have not participated in the mining process are called non-mining nodes.
C. *Smart Contract*: In the process of the formation of a new block, all the mining nodes participate in the formation of the cryptographic puzzle. After a successful transaction, the amount is transferred to the service provider's wallet and the contract is started between

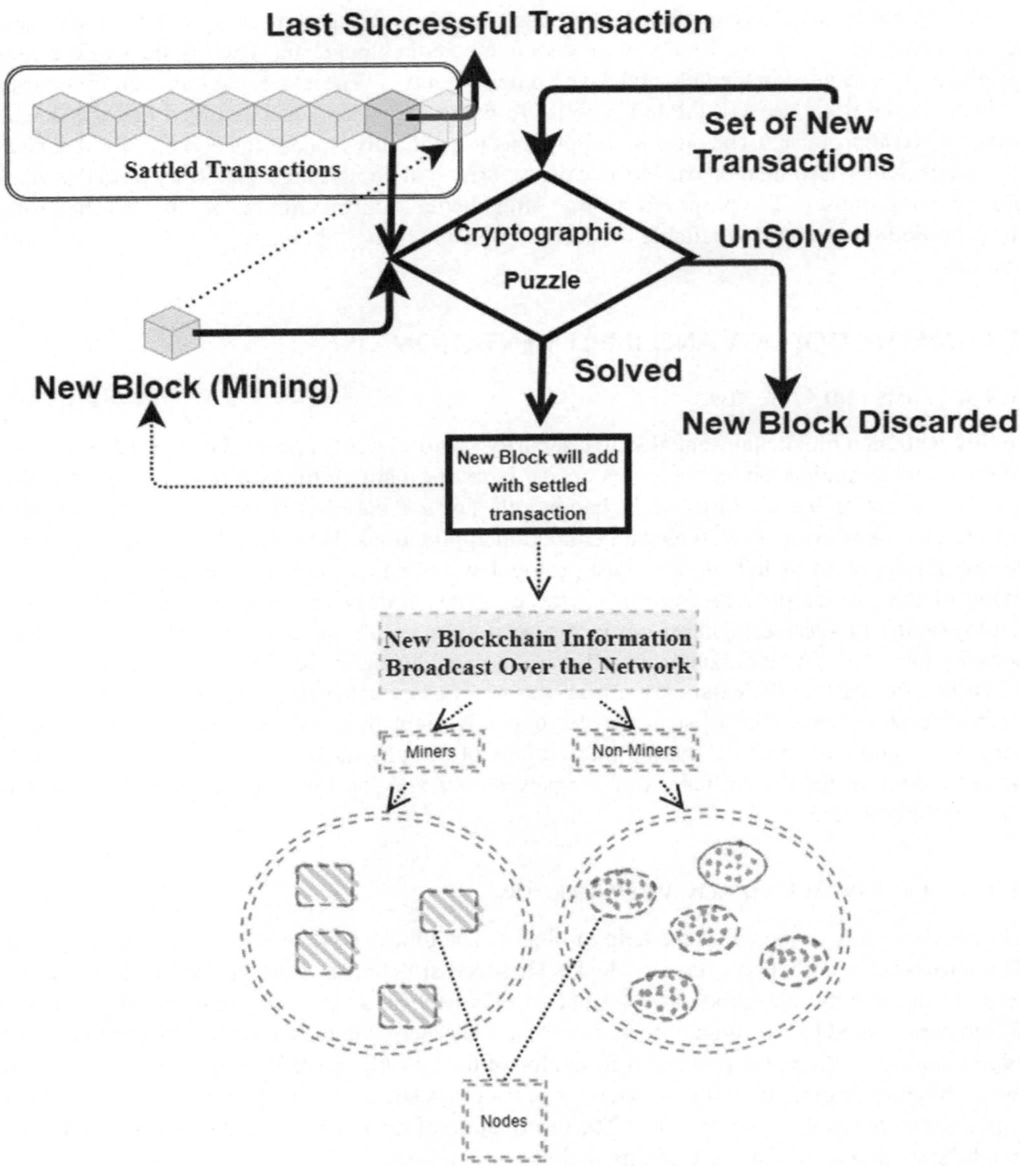

FIGURE 5.3 Process flow model of blockchain.

the client and worker. Once the worker finishes his work and successfully submitted to the client, the client approves the successful submission. Immediately after the approval from the client, the service provider transfers the amount into the worker's wallet. This process is called a smart contract.

The settled transactions are represented as a chain of blocks. The last transaction information plays a key role in the formation of the new block. For the new successful transaction, it is the mandatory condition that the participants (miners) of the mining process (a process of formation of the new block) solve a cryptographic puzzle. The information of the last settled transaction is also used for the cryptographic puzzle. For the successful solution of the cryptographic puzzle, a new block is formed and added to the settled transaction. However, if the puzzle remains unsolved, the new block is discarded. The successful formation of the block is then broadcasted over the network. This information is transmitted to both the miner and non-miner nodes. Miner nodes are those nodes that participate in the formation of the new block [38].

5.3.4 The Proposed Research Methodology

The chapter deals with the below-mentioned research gaps. The contribution and the novelty of the proposed work are explained below:

1 Due to the high load of existing security methods for IoT applications, the service provider's uses low-end security protocols. To overcome the issue, the lightweight blockchain method is proposed for IoT application.
2 The proposed method is developed for the ethereum blockchain called ether cryptocurrency. For ethereum blockchain, solidity language is used.
3 The application-specific blockchain based security protocol is proposed for the IoT application.
4 The applications are classified based on the time-constraint, non-time-constraint applications; low, medium, and high sensitivity of the data.
5 The weight factor has been used for the optimal selection of the block size.
6 The trade-off between security and complexity of the algorithm is managed based on the weight factors for the optimal selection of the block size and the improvement of the throughput.
7 A lightweight blockchain method is proposed for IoT applications. The complexity of the blockchain-based security protocol is reduced based on the selection of the weight factors.
8 The concept of the smart contract is used. The contract in form of a tiny program is remains saved inside the blockchain.
9 The cross-layer efforts are done for the improvement of the throughput. The medium access layer protocol modifications are proposed for efficient performance.

5.3.5 Proposed Methods

The flow diagram for the classification of the proposed methodology is shown Figure 5.3. The first step of the proposed methodology is to classify the application based on the criticality, data sensitivity, and toleration limit of latency. The weight factors w_0, w_1, and w_2 are used for the various classification parameters. The trust parameter is estimated for the selection of the ethereum block size.

Instead of fixed block size, in the chapter, the dynamic block size method is proposed for the selection of the block size. The application-specific block size management method is proposed for the IoT application. After the estimation of the trust parameter, the threshold ethereum block size is estimated in step 2. The threshold value of the ethereum block size is then compared every time during the estimation of the block size in every new transaction.

The trust function T depends upon three priority parameters. The three priority parameters can be denoted by *A* (Application), *D* (Data sensitivity), and *L* (Latency Constant). The trust

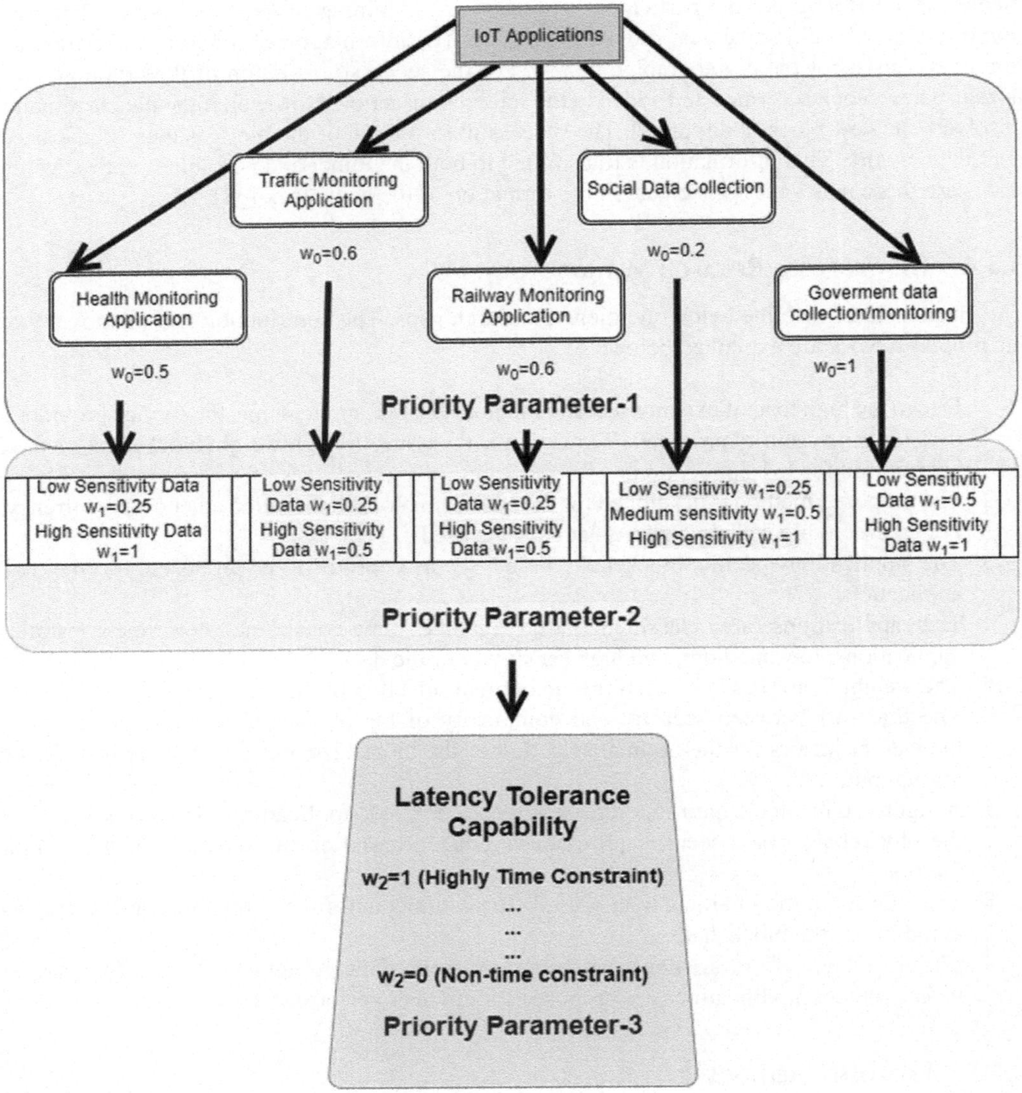

FIGURE 5.4 Step-1 (weight distribution) of the proposed methodology.

function T can be estimated as given below, in which w_1, w_2, and w_3 are weight factors described in Figure 5.4, which can be selected based on the requirement of application.

$$T = Aw_1 + Dw_2 + Lw_3 \tag{5.1}$$

The weight factor can be controlled by the service provider based on previous experiences, machine learning algorithms as well as the cross layer information. For the simplicity of the modeling and analysis, in the chapter, we have analyzed the performance for different possible/relevant values of the weight factors. The parameters *A, D,* and *L* can be controlled by the vendor

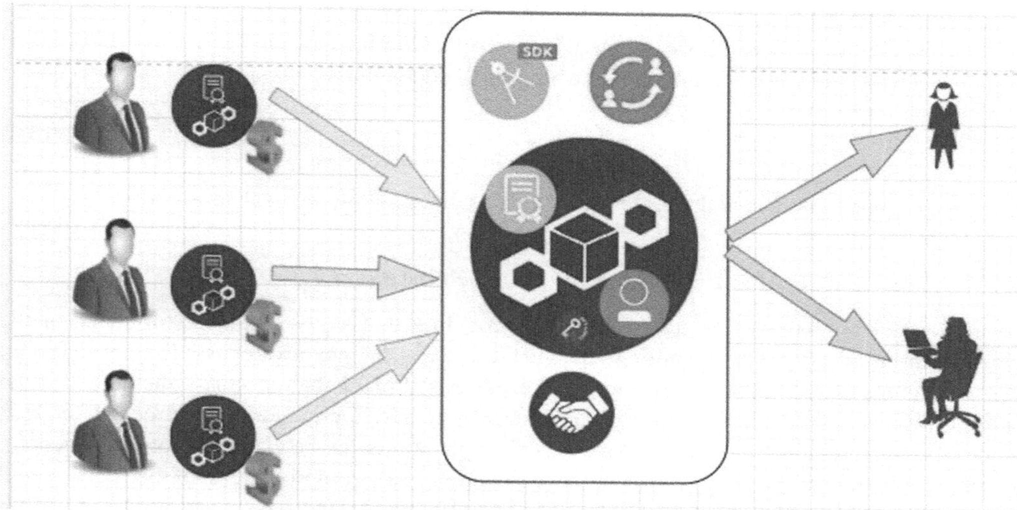

FIGURE 5.5 Smart contract in block chain.

at the time of the manufacturing. Let us assume the maximum block size limit is denoted by B_S. The particular block size limit can be estimated based on the trust function T. The block size for the particular application can be described as $T*B_S$.

During the estimation of the new block, the smart contract method is used between client and server. A third party uses the blockchain method to manage the smart contract. The Ethereum-based blockchain provides two important features in the blockchain method i.e. distributed control and immutable. The immutable feature of the ethereum blockchain improves the trust of the network because once the contract is done; no one can temper or change the terms and conditions of the contract. For the trust parameter, the tiny program is used inside the blockchain. In Step 3, the validation of the smart contract trust parameters is checked for the successful transaction. The smart contract concept between the client and server is shown in the Figure 5.5. The small program is used for the smart contract. In Step 4, the proposed model is checked for the various attacks.

Three attack models are used for the performance analysis of the proposed model:

- Obedient and profit-driven model
- Non-obedient and profit-driven model
- Non-profit-driven model

The three parameters—A_1, A_2, and A_3—play an important role in the calculation of the reward value. The reward value represents the reliability of the security protocol. A higher value of the reward function represents the higher reliability of the result. The reward value α is a function of trust parameter. The value of A_2 and A_3 are the function of A_1. The values of A_1, A_2, and A_3 are defined below in terms of trust parameter.

$$A_1 = k*T \tag{5.2}$$

$$A_2 = (1 - A_1)/(1 + R(m))*R(m) \tag{5.3}$$

where $R = \beta/\gamma$, $0.25 < m < 4$.

β: The new chain will form and new block will add in the new chain.

γ: The new chain will form and new block will add in existing chain.

$$A_3 = 1 - A_1 - A_2 \tag{5.4}$$

The various attack models and threat models will be discussed in the next sub-section.

5.3.6 Discussion on the Background of the Problem

To the best of our knowledge, this is the first modeling that analyzes the performance of the blockchain-based on IoT application, data sensitivity, and latency awareness. However, few of the researchers already reported latency awareness-based blockchain security method. But the optimal utilization of security based on data sensitivity and application requirement is not yet reported in the previous research works. The IoT applications can be classified into very general to very sensitive applications. The sensitive application can't compromise with the security and can also utilize a large part of the resource for good throughput. However, the general application needs high throughput/QoS with low utilization of resources/bandwidth. The general application can compromise with the security as they are less prone to attack by the intruder. In the chapter, we have proposed a security model for the IoT system based on the ethereum blockchain. In the case of the ethereum blockchain, the transactions are grouped in a block. The optimal size of the block size is a mandatory requirement as the larger block size creates more complexity and so that is more secure. However, this also leads to a delay and throughput reduces. Thus, in the chapter, we have proposed the optimal block size as per the application need. For the effective selection of the block size, we have proposed the trust parameter. The trust function is also a sub-function of the three other parameters as reported in the previous sub-section.

5.3.7 Threat Model and Attack Model

The attacks of the different applications are classified into three different categories [39,40]. The attack model is analyzed for performance which is based on the convenience function, *C*. The convenience function for all the three different types of attack models is described below.

5.3.7.1 Obedient and Profit-driven Model

In this attacker model, the attacker tries to gain profit from the communicated data between client and server. The attacker tries to access valuable information of the government agency. In this attack, the attacker tries to only access the important information. To identify the important/critical information, the attacker tries to use the trust parameter as described in the previous subsection [41,42]. The higher the trust parameter signifies more sensitive information. In this work, we have assumed that the trust function is based on three parameters: *A*, *D*, and *L*. The attacker estimated the trust function and based on the trust function, it identifies the sensitive information. The convenience function for the obedient and profit-driven models can be defined as follows:

$$C_1 = E_S \times \mathrm{T} \tag{5.5}$$

Here, $0 \le E_S \le 1$ represents the estimation accuracy of the trust function estimation. Higher value of the convenience parameter *C* causes more chances for the attack.

5.3.7.2 Non-obedient and Profit-driven model

In this attacker model, the attacker tries to gain profit based on the specific application [43]. The proposed attack model is an application-specific attack model. In this model, the attacker tries to identify the sensitive application. The sensitive application can be identified based on parameter A and the corresponding weight factòr w_1. The non-obedient model can be considered as a sub-section of the obedient model. In the non-obedient model, the attacker analyzes only the part of the trust function. The convenience function for the non-obedient model can be defined as follows:

$$C_2 = A * w_1 * E_S \tag{5.6}$$

In this model, the attacker only targets the specific application of their interest. The application sensitivity depends upon the weight factor. The weight factor can be changed and managed by the blockchain management system. However, parameter A is controlled by the service provider. A malfunction client/attacker can try to access the important data of the system by estimating the appropriate value of A and w_1.

5.3.7.3 Non-profit Model

In this model, the attacker doesn't try to get the benefits directly from the attacker. However, the main target of the attacker is to lower down the trust of the client in the system. This type of attacker harms both the service provider as well as to the third party (security management system). This reduces the trust of the client in the current system. For this, the attacker tries to produce more delays in the creation of a new block or new transaction. This extra delay causes timeout and block creation is discarded. In this case, the convenience function only depends upon the latency parameters. The latency also has two parameters: L and w_3. The parameter L is a latency function and only the service provider can change the value. The attacker can attack the service provider for the manipulation of the value and reduce the trust factor. The weight factor w_3 is managed by the blockchain management system. The intruder can also target the blockchain management system to reduce the trust parameter. The convenience function for the non-profit model can be defined as follows:

$$C_3 = L * w_3 * E_S \tag{5.7}$$

The attacker can also target the smart contract inside the blockchain to reduce the trust of the system. The smart contract manipulation sometimes can also be used as a profit model for the malfunctioned client.

5.3.8 Markov Model for the Proposed Solution

In the proposed Markov model, the optimal block size is estimated based on the parameters described above. For the optimal size algorithm, the longest chain is considered a blockchain. The new block mining tries to add to the chain if the size of the newly formed block is lower than the excessive block limit of the corresponding last block of the chain. Each block consists of three important information, that is, distance from the first block (height), the hash value of the preceding parent block, a set of transactions, and a nonce. If the size of the newly formed block is smaller than the existing block limit, an existing chain continues and newly formed block adds to the existing chain. The probability of the occurrence of the event is denoted by α in the Markov chain analysis. If the size of the block is found to be greater than the existing limit, the new chain is formed and the newly formed block either adds to the existing chain or to the newly formed chain with the /state probability of β and γ respectively.

5.3.9 Design

The Markov model is a stochastic analysis model for the estimation of the probability of the allotment of the channel to the corresponding device based on the transition probability of the state and the corresponding action. The transition model is a probability-based stochastic model. The states change as per the probability of the next state. For the application, we have assumed the probabilities of data sensitivity. A five-dimensional Markov model is proposed for the transition analysis of the state space analysis. The proposed method helps to estimate the estimation of the optimal block size based on the application, data sensitivity, and latency parameter. The optimal selection of the excessive block size estimation helps the ethereum blockchain management system in the formation of a more secure blockchain without compromising the QoS parameters. In the proposed method, we have assumed that if the mined block size is lower than the excessive block size it is accepted else the chain is forked into two blockchains.

5.3.10 State Space

The state-space model is a five-dimensional (h_1, h_2, a_1, a_2, k) model for the proposed system. The height of the newly formed block is denoted by the parameters h_1 and h_2 for the two chains. The a_1 and a_2 are chain parameters for the blockchain. The k denotes the number of blocks that is mined to the blockchain before it closes his sticky gates.

5.3.11 Protocol

5.3.11.1 Action

There are two different types of actions that will be performed by the node based on the block size. Based on the data sensitivity and other mentioned parameters, the chain is forked into two chains. If the block size remains lower than the excessive block size, it is remains continued else it is] divided into two chains.

5.3.11.2 State Transition

The system starts with the initial state, (0,0,0,0,0) at the starting of the chain once a new block is mined, its size height increases, and the state changes from (0,0,0,0,0) to (1,0,0,0,0) as given in Eq. 5.8. Again in the formation of the new block, if the block size will be greater than the estimated excessive block size, the chain is forked. The newly formed chain has a state (1,1,0,0,0), else the state remains (2,0,0,0,0) as given in Eq. 5.9 and Eq. 5.10. The Markov chain state diagram is shown in Figure 5.6. Also based on data sensitivity and latency parameter, the value of the weight also changes based on the application. The action value probability a_1 is proportional to w_2, and a_2 is proportional to w_3. Based on the application requirement, every new block changes the state dimensions 3 and 4. The data sensitivity parameter a_1 consist of three states, that is, $1 \le a_1 \le 3$. In this, the states 1, 2, and 3 are showing low, moderate, and high data sensitivity, respectively. Similarly, based on the latency tolerance capability of the node, a new block state will change any value from 1 to 3. The low tolerance value starts with 1 and the high tolerance value consists of 3. The state value lies between $1 \le a_2 \le 3$. If the last block has a state (1,1,0,0,0) and if the newly formed block belongs to chain-2 and has high data sensitivity and moderate tolerance capability

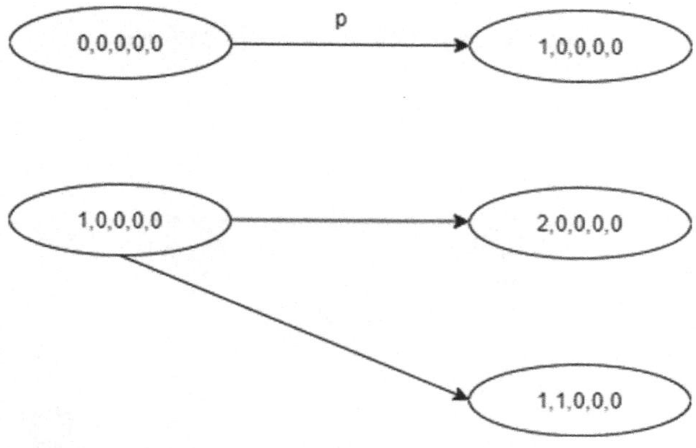

FIGURE 5.6 Markov chain state diagram.

then its state will be (1,2,3,2,0). The last dimension shows the switching state from one block to another block. The value of the k lies between $1 \le k \le 144$.

$$P(1, h_2, a_1, a_2, k| \, 0, h_2, a_1, a_2, k) = p \tag{5.8}$$

$$P(h_1 + 1, h_2, a_1, a_2, k| \, h_1, h_2, a_1, a_2, k) = \alpha \tag{5.9}$$

$$P(h_1, h_2 + 1, a_1, a_2, k| \, h_1, h_2, a_1, a_2, k) = \beta + (1 - \beta)\gamma \tag{5.10}$$

for $1 \le a_1 \le 3$, $1 \le a_2 \le 3$, and $1 \le k \le 144$.

5.3.12 Security Analysis

For the security analysis, the three important parameters are taken in consideration as shown in Figure 5.7. The server provides a service to the client. The blockchain service provider provides a security service to the system. The attackers target the service provider and server. Therefore, in the present model, we have analyzed the security services for different threats.

5.3.13 Trust Assumption

For the analysis, few assumptions have been taken to make it less complex. The trust assumptions are described below:

1 It is assumed that the intruder will try to only attack the system either the service provider or the block management system. The attack on the client is not analyzed in the proposed model.
2 It is assumed that the attacker can only delay the smart contract or block formation but doesn't change the contract conditions. As the ethereum is distributed and immutable.
3 It is assumed that in the proposed method the initial values of the parameters *A, D,* and *L* that are set by the service provider can't be changed.
4 For the performance analysis, it is assumed that the state transition probabilities, that is, a_1 and a_2 are equally probable.

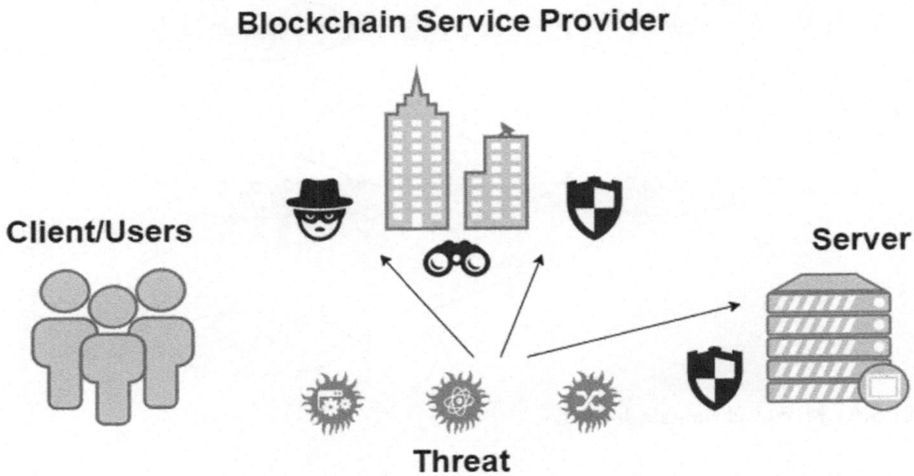

FIGURE 5.7 Threat model for security analysis.

5 The probability of selfish mining is taken 0.5.
6 The above-mentioned assumptions are global assumptions for the complete model and performance analysis. However, the local assumptions are assumed for the performance analysis. The local assumption is described in the performance analysis part of the result section.

5.3.14 Trust Model

Initially, it is assumed that the probability model of the parameters *A, D,* and *L* are optimally taken based on the previous experience. For this, we have analyzed the models and based on the results, we have chosen the fixed optimal value for the complete analysis. The proposed method analyzes the performance based on the global and local parameters related to the proposed model. All the other parameters that are not related to the proposed model are assumed based on the previous literature discussed in Section 5.2. In the proposed model analysis, we have assumed the optimal as much as possible. For the trust model, the following assumptions are made:

- Every node chooses the global excessive block size value without knowing the profit.
- If the block size is discarded due to larger block size, its profit is also discarded.

5.3.15 Implementation

For the implementation of the proposed method, we have used the MATLAB platform. The MATLAB 2021a version is used for the performance analysis of the proposed method. The mathematical modeling toolbox is used for the proposed model. The Markov model equations are analyzed for the optimal values of the convergence. MATLAB's inbuilt nonlinear equation solver methods are used for the implementation and performance analysis of the proposed method.

For the implementation, we have created three different models for three different types of attacks as discussed in Section 5.3. For each model, the three parameters A_1, A_2, and A_3 are analyzed. The initial values of *A*, *D*, and *L* parameters are fixed and are equal for all three parameters. The weight factors are varied for low, medium, and high values. The detailed study of the implementation/result analysis is discussed in Section 5.4.

5.4 RESULT ANALYSIS AND DISCUSSION

The results section of the proposed model is divided into three sections. As already discussed in the previous section, the three incentive model is proposed for well-known attacks. Each incentive model is analyzed for different applications. The weight factors based on the data sensitivity and time constraint are analyzed for the different factors as described below. Each model is analyzed for the two different settings.

5.4.1 Setting 1

Setting 1 is less complex and only determines the reward values for single processing state. In this case, the newly formed blockchain continues as a chain 1. As per this assumption, if the size of the newly mined block will be larger than the maximum, it will form a new chain. In this case, it is assumed that the newly formed block forms block chain 1 (Chain 1), and the existing blockchain continues as a blockchain 2 (Chain 2).

5.4.2 Setting 2

Setting 2 is more complex and determines the reward values for multiple processing states. In this case, it is assumed that the newly formed block forms block chain 2 (Chain 2), and the existing blockchain continues as a blockchain 1 (Chain 1).

The three chain formation factors are taken into consideration. α is the probability that only one chain continues for the complete distributed chain. Let us assume that β is the probability that the larger block size is mined, and the newly mined block continues as chain 1. Similarly, γ is the probability that the newly mined larger block continues in a chain 2. The sum of all the probabilities will be 1, that is, $\alpha+\beta+\gamma=1$. The network is analyzed for the fixed values of α and the different ratios of $\beta:\gamma$. The ratio is varied for 4, 3, 2, 1.5, 1, 2/3, 1/2, 1/3, 1/4. Each application is analyzed for the different values of the ratios and different values of data sensitivity and for time constraint and non-time constraint data traffic applications. The comparative results are shown in Figure 5.8.

The reward of the profit-driven model is lower than the non-profit model. This will save the blockchain network from major sensitive attacks. The reward of the applications changes as per the sensitivity of the applications as shown in the results. The higher the value of the reward represents higher reliability and higher security. The results show the reliability of the network changes as per the application requirement. As shown in Figure 5.8, the obedient and profit-driven model has a lower reward for social media data. This shows that the reliability/security of the blockchain network will be lower for the socially available data application. This is because the attackers are very rarely attacking this type of network. Also, the QoS parameters for such an application will be very good as it is a very lightweight security protocol with low reward is used. The low reward reduces its delay and provides sufficient security without compromising the throughput. On the other hand, government data requires very high security.

The proposed algorithm allows high reliability/reward to the government sector applications. The results for the other models and different attack situations are approximately similar. The replicated results of the two different settings prove that the proposed lightweight blockchain-based security protocol efficiently performs the operation and successfully allots the reward as per the application requirement and data sensitivity. The proposed method is delicately designed

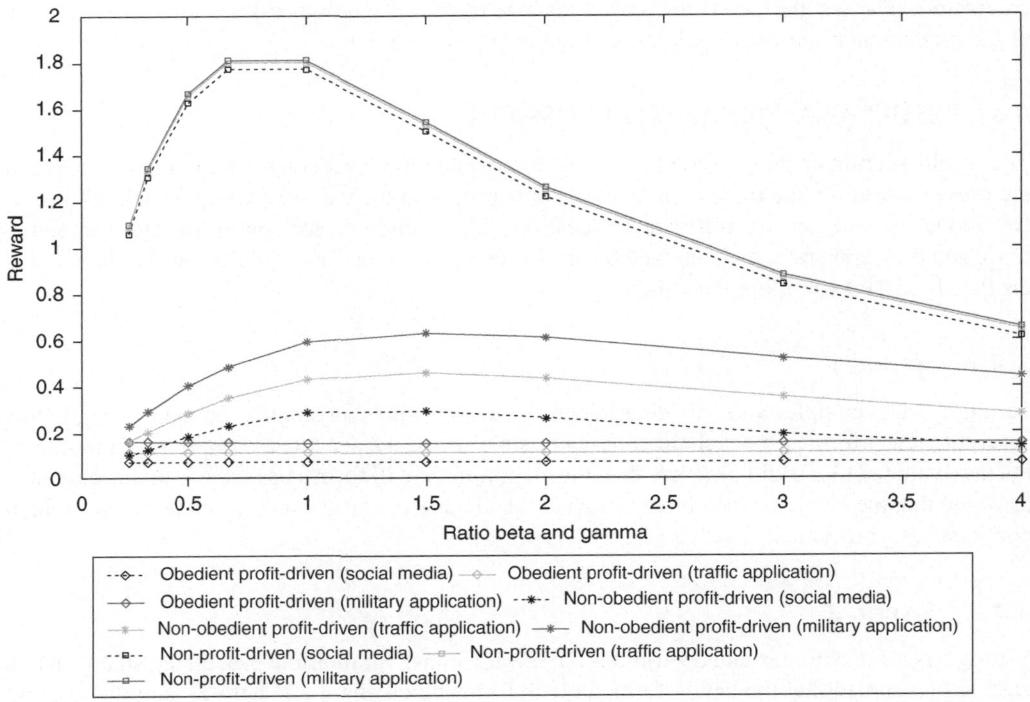

FIGURE 5.8 Comparison of obedient, non-obedient profit-driven and non-profit-driven model.

for IoT applications that can be used for the entire commercial requirement. The comparison of all three models for three different applications is shown in Figure 5.8. The result shows that the reliability is high for military application for all three models. The performance analysis of the proposed method is performed on MATLAB. MDP Toolbox is used for the Markov-based model for the result analysis.

5.5 CONCLUSION

In this chapter, the application-specific blockchain-based security protocol was proposed for the IoT application. The applications are classified based on the time-constraint, non-time-constraint applications: low, medium, and high sensitivity of the data. The weight factor has been used for the optimal selection of the block size. The trade-off between security and complexity of the algorithm is managed based on the weight factors for the optimal selection of the block size and the improvement of the throughput. The proposed protocol is analyzed for the three attack models and for the different applications, data sensitivity, and time constraint as well as non-time constraint applications. The results prove that the proposed method efficiently performs security operations as per the application requirement. The application-specific reward selection fulfills the security requirement of the network without compromising with the QoS parameters.

The proposed method is developed for the ethereum blockchain called ether cryptocurrency. For ethereum blockchain, solidity language is used. The network performance is analyzed for social, health monitoring, railway monitoring, traffic monitoring, and government sector applications. The concept of the smart contract is used. The contract in the form of a tiny program remains saved inside the blockchain.

5.6 FUTURE SCOPE

In future work, the cross-layer efforts will be useful for the improvement of the throughput. The medium access layer protocol modification can be utilized for efficient performance. The physical layer security can be further improved by the efficient detection of malicious nodes. The network can be analyzed for efficient routing protocol for different types of routing attacks. The reliability, reward, and processing time can be measured for cross-layer models. In addition, in this section, the network is analyzed only for the application layer attack model. The work can be extended for other layer attack models. The performance of the security protocol for the network can further be analyzed for the mobility model.

REFERENCES

[1] B. K. Mohanta, "Addressing security and privacy issues of IoT using blockchain technology," *IEEE Internet of Things Journal*, vol. 8, no. 2, pp. pp. 881–888, 2021.

[2] S. Singh, "Blockchain security attacks, challenges, and solutions for the future distributed IoT network," *IEEE Access*, vol. 9, no. 2, pp. 13938–13959, 2021.

[3] C. Miers, "Zerocoin: Anonymous distributed E-Cash from bitcoin," *IEEE Symposium on Security and Privacy*, vol. 3, no. 2, pp. 397–411, 2013.

[4] M. Möser, "Anonymity of bitcoin transactions," Munster Bitcoin Conf. (MBC), vol. 5, no. 2, pp. 1–10, 2013.

[5] "Number of Blockchain Wallet Users Worldwide from November 2011 to January 11, 2021," 2021. www.researchgate.net/figure/Number-of-Blockchain-wallet-users-worldwide_fig1_359218205

[6] A. Kiayias, "On trees, chains and fast transactions in the blockchain," *Int. Conf. Cryptol. Inf. Secur. Latin Amer., in Lecture Notes in Computer Science (LNCS)*, Springer, vol. 11368, no. 2, pp. 327–351, 2019.

[7] K. Nicolas, "Comprehensive overview of selfish mining and double spending attack countermeasures," in *Proc. IEEE 40th Sarnoff Symp*, pp. 1–6, 2019.

[8] M. Rosenfeld, "Analysis of hashrate-based double spending," *arXiv:1402.2009*, 2014.

[9] N. Hajdarbegovic, *Bitcoin Miners Ditch Ghash.io Pool Over Fears of 51, Attack*, New York, NY: CoinDesk, 2014.

[10] A. Begum, "Blockchain attacks, analysis and a model to solve double spending attack," *International Journal of Machine Learning and Computing.*, vol. 10, no. 2, pp. 1–6, 2020.

[11] J. L. Zhao, "Overview of business innovation and research opportunities in blockchain and introduction to the special issue," *Financial Innovations*, vol. 2, no. 1, pp. 1–7, 2016.

[12] L. Chenxin, "A decentralized blockchain with high throughput and fast con_rmation," in *Proc. USENIX Annu. Tech. Conf. (USENIX ATC)*, pp. 515–528, 2020.

[13] L. Odera., "Ethereum classic & IOHK team up to find solutions to prevent 51% attacks on the blockchain," Vols. Available: https://bitcoinexchangeguide.com/ethereumclassic-iohk-team-up-to-_nd-solutions-to-prevent-51-at, 20 Dec 2020.

[14] O. Pal, et al., "Key management for blockchain technology," ICT Express, vol. 7, no. 1, pp. 76–80, 2021. ISSN 2405-9595, https://doi.org/10.1016/j.icte.2019.08.002

[15] B. Bordel, "Trust provision in the Internet of Things using transversal blockchain networks," *Intell. Automat. Soft Comput.*, vol. 25, no. 1, pp. 155–170, 2019.

[16] Y. Sun, "Research on the signal reconstruction of the phased array structural health monitoring based using the basis pursuit algorithm," *Comput., Mater. Continua*, vol. 58, no. 2, pp. 409–420, 2019.

[17] B. Sharma, "Transaction privacy preservations for blockchain technology," in *Proc. Int. Conf. Innov., Comput. Commun.*, Singapore: Springer, pp. 377–393, 2020.

[18] M. Saad, "Countering selfish mining in blockchains," in *Proc. Int. Conf. Comput. Netw. Commun. (ICNC)*, pp. 360–364, 2019.

[19] K. Wang, "A novel double spending attack countermeasure in blockchain," in *Proc. IEEE 10th Annu. Ubiquitous Comput., Electron. Mobile Commun. Conf. (UEMCON)*, pp. 383–388, 2019.

[20] B. Ghaleb, "Addressing the DAO insider attack in RPL's Internet of Things networks," *IEEE Commun. Lett.*, vol. 23, no. 1, pp. 68–71, 2019.

[21] Q. Xing, "POSTER: BGPCoin: A trustworthy blockchain-based resource management solution for BGP security," in *Proc. ACM SIGSAC Conf. Comput. Commun. Secur.*, pp. 2591–2593, 2017.

[22] P. Swathi, "Preventing sybil attack in blockchain using distributed behavior monitoring of miners," in *Proc. 10th Int. Conf. Comput., Commun. Netw. Technol. (ICCCNT)*, pp. 1–6, July 2019.

[23] H. Mayer, "ECDSA security in bitcoin and ethereum: A research survey," *CoinFaabrik* [Online]. Available: www.semanticscholar.org/paper/ECDSA-Security-in-Bitcoin-and-Ethereum%3A-a-ResearchMayer/434a117a2717cdbf78035365d8bab, pp. 1–10, June 2016.

[24] S. Siboni, "Security testbed for internet-of-things devices," *IEEE Trans. Reliability*, vol. 68, no. 1, pp. 23–44, 2019.

[25] B. Mao, "Harvesting and threat aware security configuration strategy for IEEE 802.15.4 based IoT networks," *IEEE Commun. Lett.*, vol. 23, no. 11, pp. 2130–2134, 2019.

[26] Y. M. Ali, "Demonstrating the Effect of Insider Attacks on Perception Layer of Internet of Things (IoT) Systems," 2019.

[27] Y. M. Tukur, "Ethereum Blockchain-Based Solution to Insider Threats on Perception Layer of IoT Systems," 2019.

[28] R. H. Venkatnarayan, "Poster: A Framework to Secure IoT Networks Against Network Layer Attacks," 2019.

[29] K. Saleem, "Bio-inspired network security for 5G-enabled IoT applications," *IEEE Access*, vol. 8, no. 1, pp. 229152–229160, 2020.

[30] F. Meneghello, "IoT: internet of threats? A survey of practical security vulnerabilities in real IoT devices," *IEEE Internet of Things Journal*, vol. 6, no. 5, pp. 8182–8201, 2019.

[31] N. Neshenko, "Demystifying IoT security: an exhaustive survey on IoT vulnerabilities and a first empirical look on internet-scale IoT exploitations," *IEEE Communications Surveys & Tutorials*, vol. 2, no. 3, pp. 2702–2733, 2019.

[32] W. Iqbal, "An in-depth analysis of IoT security requirements, challenges, and their countermeasures via software-defined security," *IEEE Internet of Things Journal*, vol. 7, no. 10, pp. 10250–10276, 2020.

[33] P. Urien, "A new IoT trust model based on TLS-SE and TLS-IM secure elements: A blockchain use case," 2021 IEEE 18th Annual Consumer Communications & Networking Conference (CCNC), vol. 8, no. 1, pp. 1–2, 2021.

[34] A. Fayad, "A Blockchain-based Lightweight Authentication Solution for IoT," 2019.

[35] M. Singh, "Blockchain: A Game Changer for Securing IoT Data," 2018.

[36] J. Kamalakkannan, "IoT System Accomplishment using BlockChain in Validating and Data Security with Cloud," 2020 Fourth International Conference on I-SMAC (IoT in Social, Mobile, Analytics and Cloud) (I-SMAC), pp. 60–64, 2020.

[37] S. Seshadri, "IoTCop: A blockchain-based monitoring framework for detection and isolation of malicious devices in internet-of-things systems," *IEEE Internet of Things Journal*, vol. 8, no. 5, pp. 3346–3359, 2021.

[38] R. Zhang, *On the Necessity of a Prescribed Block Validity Consensus: Analyzing Bitcoin Unlimited Mining Protocol*, ACM, CoNEXT: International Conference On Emerging Networking Experiments And Technologies: New York, NY, 2017.

[39] L. Bahack, Theoretical Bitcoin Attacks with Less Than Half of the Computational Power (draft), 2013.

[40] I. Sirer, *Majority Is Not Enough: Bitcoin Mining is Vulnerable*, Springer 436–454, 2014. https://arxiv.org/abs/1311.0243

[41] A. Gervais, *On the Security and Performance of Proof of Work Blockchains*, Association for Computing Machinery: New York, 2016. https://doi.org/10.1145/2976749.2978341
[42] E. Heilman, *One Weird Trick to Stop Selfish Miners: Fresh Bitcoins, A Solution for the Honest Miner.* In: Böhme, R., Brenner, M., Moore, T., Smith, M. (eds) Financial Cryptography and Data Security. FC 2014. Lecture Notes in Computer Science, vol 8438. Springer, Berlin, Heidelberg, 2014. https://doi.org/10.1007/978-3-662-44774-1_12
[43] A. Kiayias, *Blockchain Mining Games*, pp. 365–382, 2016.

6 Congestion-Aware and Delay-Aware Application-Specific Security Protocol for WSN/IoT

Gaurav Suman, Manoj Tolani, Pankaj Kumar, Arun Balodi, Ambar Bajpai, and Nasser S. Albalawi

6.1 INTRODUCTION

6.1.1 Broad Description and Background

Over time, it is observed that communication has become easy using different devices and modes of communication. If we look back, in the days when someone had to stand in front of a telephone booth waiting for his turn to get a chance to speak to someone on the other side of the wired channel. The time changed, technology evolved and now, with some touch on mobile screen connection is established from any location to the other connected location without wire. Not only between people, but now devices can also communicate between each other intelligently. This is where IoT has grown to be. Technology has evolved and IoT has developed to an extent where multiple devices can communicate with each other and perform important activities. IoT has allowed the user to integrate and communicate between two devices intelligently.

As shown in Figure 6.1, the term "IoT" (Internet of Things) was coined in 1999 by Kevin Ashton, who was the Executive Director of the Auto-ID Center at the Massachusetts Institute of Technology (MIT). The timeline in Figure 6.1 highlights the key developments in the evolution of the Internet of Things over the years [1].

The graph in Figure 6.2 illustrates the transition from conventional devices to IoT devices over the past years. By 2030, it is projected that approximately 75 percent of all devices in use will be IoT-based, leading to a significant increase in data traffic on networks [12].

Together with the advancement in IoT and WSN there are challenges that are being addressed by different researchers in their study.

6.1.2 Existing Challenges of IoT/WSN

The technology underneath the wireless sensor still needs a lot of improvement and development. It is still away from perfection [2]. Energy consumption and maintenance is the major challenge to be handled for IoT devices supported by wireless sensor networks (WSN). The complexity of IoT is heightened by the interaction of various heterogeneous devices operating in diverse environments, which makes the deployment of security mechanisms particularly challenging [3].

DOI: 10.1201/9781003491910-6

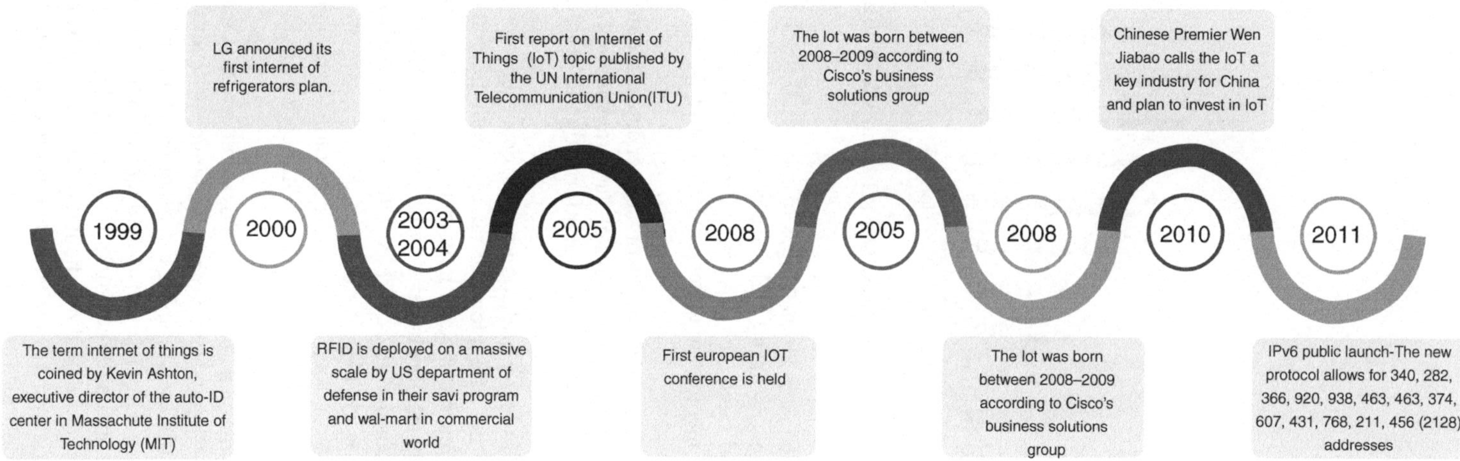

FIGURE 6.1 Developments in the evolution of the Internet of Things over the years.

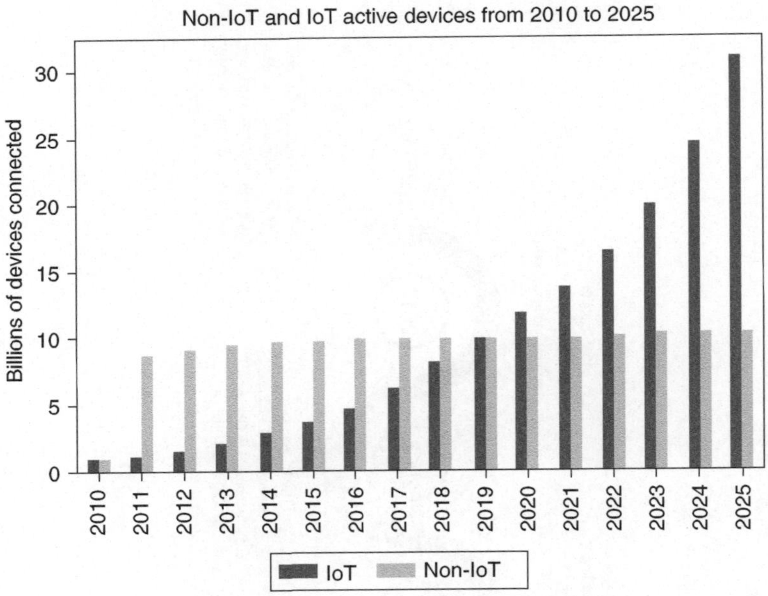

FIGURE 6.2 Development in use of IoT devices vs non-IoT devices from 2010 to 2025.

Kamal et al. [3] have identified several challenges of wireless sensor networks (WSN) in IoT, including real-time management, security and privacy, quality of service (QoS), configuration, availability, data integrity, and confidentiality. Ref. [5] adds scalability, energy efficiency and maintenance to the list. It is imperative to understand them briefly:

i. *Real-time management*: Constant review of the user data is required in resource-controlled sensor networks to minimize the amount of data transmission. This can be achieved by designing a mechanism to monitor that the information to be transmitted is more than the threshold.
ii. *Security and privacy*: In real-world applications, ensuring safety and privacy is a significant challenge. Achieving a high level of safety is both difficult and complex.
iii. *Security*: A security breach can occur if attackers successfully introduce malicious nodes into the network by physically tampering with the WSN. The connection of WSNs to the internet further broadens the attack surface, allowing malicious activities to be carried out from anywhere in the world [4].
iv. *Quality of Services* (QoS): As all real-time applications are highly dependent on timely distributed data, the data must be provided with the threshold timeframe and no delay should be seen in the data transmission.
v. *Configuration*: The addition and deletion of dynamic nodes is inevitable in the real-world application of WSNs. Together with other challenges of security and QoS, sensor nodes need to keep track of new node joining and other detaching nodes [5].
vi. *Data integrity*: Since security is a major challenge in WSN/IoT, data integrity is at stake. If any malicious node enters the network, it will affect the integrity of data. It is essential to maintain the integrity of data throughout the data transmission.
vii. *Confidentiality*: It is attempted to keep the data secure during the transmission by applying data encryptions, but only data encryption does not ensure the confidentiality of data. The

malicious node getting into the network can compromise the secure transmission of data over the network.

viii. *Maintenance*: It is difficult to maintain the power supply, storage and continuous execution of the algorithms throughout the data transmission in WSN.

ix. *Energy efficiency*: WSN must operate on limited power supply and hence it is important that the design of the hardware and software should be optimized to cater the energy challenges.

6.1.3 Security Challenges in IoT/WSN

The IoT/WSN architecture is highly complex, involving billions of sensors and objects that interact not only with each other but also with other entities, including humans and various living or non-living objects. Protecting these interactions is crucial to securing the information exchanged and minimizing the number of incidents that could impact the entire IoT ecosystem [6]. The challenges inherent in WSN/IoT, such as global connectivity and accessibility (allowing access to anyone at any time), create multiple attack vectors [7]. Despite ongoing efforts, creating a secure WSN environment remains a significant challenge and current advancements are still in their early stages. The challenges can be summarized as follows [8]:

(i) *Confidentiality Challenge*:
Keeping communication data and information credentials secure in the most challenging task in IoT security. Several standard encryption functions such as the AES block cipher, Blowfish, and Tripel DES [9] can be used to keep data secure between the interacting parties. The eavesdropping can be executed by the attackers to get the insights into the data. Hence, only performing data encryption is not enough to secure the data for communication.

(ii) *Source Authentication Challenge*:
Source authentication ensures the reliability of data or messages by verifying the origin of the communication. When the source of a message is accurately identified or authenticated, the message is considered reliable. However, attackers can disrupt this process by not only altering packets but also injecting additional false packets during transmission. To achieve data authentication, symmetric and asymmetric mechanisms are employed, where the sending and receiving nodes share secret keys. Despite this, the wireless nature of communication makes it challenging to fully secure data authentication [10].

(iii) *Data Integrity Challenge*:
Data integrity ensures that a message sent from the transmitter remains unchanged and unaltered by the time it is received at the receiver end. Even if the network maintains confidentiality, data integrity can still be compromised if the data is tampered with during transmission [10]. The integrity of the network is at risk in the following scenarios:
   (a) A malicious node within the network injects false or spurious data.
   (b) Unstable conditions in the wireless network lead to data loss during transmission [11].

(iv) *Availability Challenge*:
Availability ensures that the communicating node can utilize the available resources and enquire whether the channel in the network is available for message communications. Availability is the primary requirement for data communication in the network. If the base station fails, it will threaten entire sensor network communication. Hence, to maintain a proper functional and operation wireless sensor network, availability of the network is of prime importance [11].

TABLE 6.1
Security Challenges in Healthcare System

Security Challenges	Description
Impersonation attacks	A delay in the healthcare data storage is caused due to the assaulter's eavesdropping in the wireless sensor networks identity information
Eavesdropping attacks	The assaulter overhears the messages in the wireless node's network and uses the robbed data for evil acts
Data modification	The assaulter can change or modify the patient's information, thereby leading to wrong information to the authorized doctors about the patient. This could lead to wrong medication and leading to death of the patient
Interference	The assaulter can access the transmission channel and introduce delay or loss in sensor data transmission
Message replay attack	The attacker can breach the authentication and authorization and there create a jam in the sensor network, thereby leading to serious consequences. Any delay in medical sensor system could lead to death of patients in case of emergency
Denial of service attack	The attackers may introduce a rapid and continuous message in the system to overload the server's bandwidth, thereby leading to denial of service even to authorized user

Source: [26–28].

6.1.4 Application-Specific Security Challenges

- *Security Challenges in Healthcare Applications*
  - Table 6.1 represents the security threats in health care sensor networks [26–28].

6.1.5 Impact of Congestion and Delay in Secure Data Transmission

Congestion in a network occurs when a node or link is overloaded with data, impacting the network's quality of service. This situation leads to issues such as long data queues, packet loss, connection blockages, poor response times, and reduced throughput [12]. Congestion is an inevitable consequence of the increased traffic and data influx resulting from higher connectivity. In cellular networks, congestion can lead to call drops, unexpectedly interrupting conversations [13].

The effect of congestion in the secure data transmission is described below [17]:

(a) *Packet Loss*:
Packet loss occurs when data packets are successfully transmitted from the source but fail to arrive at the destination. This can result from poor network conditions, or intentional packet drops at a router due to network congestion, as shown in Figure 6.3. If a data packet is not received at the destination within a specified time frame, it is deemed lost. This issue can degrade video quality in online streaming or video conferencing. The study found that increasing the buffer size in a network with multiple communicating nodes reduces packet loss [14].

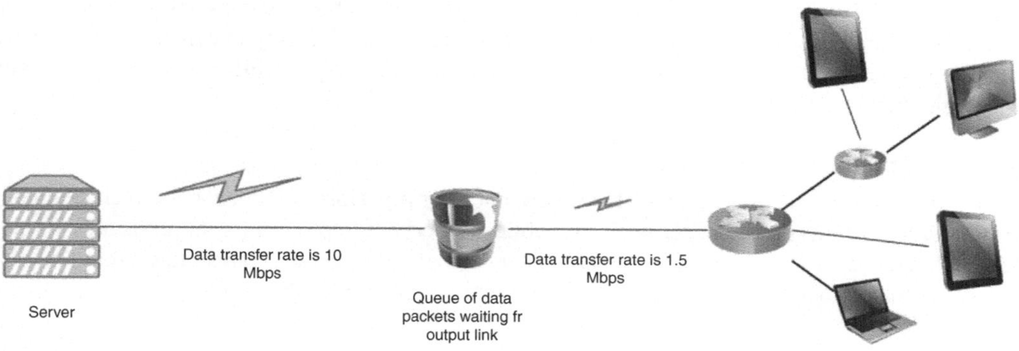

FIGURE 6.3 Network congestion effects.

(b) Jitter
Jitter is defined as variation in the time elapsed between transmission of a data from a transmitter and reception of the data at the receiver. It is a measure of the inconsistency of delay between the packets. This is caused due to several reasons like Inadequate bandwidth, routing issues, network equipment issues, improper queuing, and network interference [15].

(c) *Full Buffer Memory*
The efficiency of the network, to some extent, depends on the buffer as well. Buffers are utilized for traffic regulations mechanism in network devices. Buffers are employed to mitigate packet loss by temporarily storing bursts of data when routers are unable to forward them immediately. This helps manage data flow and reduces the likelihood of packet loss during periods of high network traffic. During congestion, they are useful in keeping the output links fully utilized. Small buffer memory or buffer memory getting filled up leads to congestion in the network [16].

(d) *Loss of Customers*
Due to severe congestion or packet loss in the network, there could be degradation in the number of customers. If the data transmission is jittery or video streaming is lagging, 81 percent of customers tend to abandon the page [18]. This severe delay or congestion in network is one of the major reasons of potential drop in the number of customers.

(e) *Artificial Congestion*
This congestion occurs when the service providers cease to provide the services for routine maintenance or fixing some critical issue in the networks.

(f) *Severe Performance Degradation*
Performance is the key element to network communication. When there is an overload of data or services are running low or reception of data at the destination is delayed, it is said to be a severe performance degradation. Due to the severe performance degradation, the QoS parameters get hit and decrease rapidly [17].

6.2 LITERATURE STUDY

6.2.1 Existing Solution for Security Challenges in IoT/WSN

The security of the communication can be established with efficient and coherent data spoofing resource management, which ensures the security of the network as a whole [19]. Certain security mechanisms will be discussed in this section. Cryptographic methods such as public key cryptography and symmetric key cryptography are discussed in this section. key management protocols, such as key management based on network structure and on the probability of key sharing, are also explained in further sections.

6.2.1.1 Cryptography Methods

Cryptographic methods are essential for secure data transmission over sensor network channels and include various mechanisms such as public key cryptography and symmetric key cryptography. Public key cryptography, which is asymmetric, generally consumes more energy compared to symmetric key cryptography due to the complexity of the underlying mathematical problems [20].

i. Public key cryptography, such as RSA, involves mathematically complex algorithms that often require millions of multiplication operations to complete a single security operation [21]. The efficiency of these algorithms is largely determined by the number of clock cycles needed to perform each multiplication instruction, which impacts the overall performance of microprocessors [22].
ii. Symmetric key cryptography is often favoured in wireless sensor networks due to the computational complexity of public key cryptography. In symmetric key cryptography, a single key is used for both encryption and decryption, which is shared between the communicating parties. One of the main challenges with this approach is securely distributing the shared key between the communicating ends [22].

6.2.1.2 Key Management Protocols

Key management is core area for researchers to ensure the security solutions for data transmission in WSNs. The main goal of key management is to establish the keys securely and reliably among the nodes in the network. The key management protocols need to be light weight as WSNs have computational and power constraints, and hence symmetric cryptography is preferred over public key cryptography as they are computationally intensive [21]. A few important key management protocols are listed below:

(i) Key management based on network structure:
   Key management protocols can be classified as either centralized or distributed, depending on the network structure. In the centralized key management schemes, a single central component is responsible for generating, re-generating, and distributing keys. This central component is known as the key distribution centre (KDC) [21].
   LKHW scheme is an example of centralized key distribution [23].
(ii) Key management on probability of key sharing:
   The probability of key sharing between a pair of sensor nodes holds the base of classification. Key management schemes can be categorized as either deterministic or probabilistic, based on the probability involved in key generation and distribution.
   (a) Deterministic key distribution scheme:
      The localized encryption and authentication protocol (LEAP) is introduced as a key management protocol specifically designed for sensor networks. LEAP's primary goal is to facilitate in-network processing while reducing the security risks associated with a compromised node to its immediate network neighbourhood [24].
      Each node in the network is equipped with four types of keys:
      - Individual key: Shared with the base station

TABLE 6.2
Security Solutions in Healthcare Systems

Security Challenges	Countermeasures
Impersonation attacks	Verification: The data received should be verified in terms of delay or authenticity
Eavesdropping attacks	Encryption: Data encryption mechanism should be introduced to keep data secure
Data modification	Data Security: Security measures should be activated to keep data secure from attackers
Interference	Interference filters: Filters should be introduced to monitor if the data received is already interfered in the communication by some attackers
Message replay attack	Data Freshness: Same message should not be replied again and again many times
Denial of service attack	Authentication: Data access to the authorized and authenticated users is essential for maintaining security and protecting sensitive information

Source: [26–28].

- Pairwise key: Shared with an adjacent sensor node
- Cluster key: Neighbouring nodes are involved
- Group key: All sensor nodes in the network are involved [24]

(b) Probabilistic key distribution scheme:
Eschenauer and Gligor offered a random key pre-distribution scheme for pair-wise key establishment. In this scheme, a key pool is randomly selected from the key space and a key ring. A randomly selected subset from the key pool is stored in each node before deployment. Then, a common key in two key rings of a pair of neighbouring nodes is used for pair-wise key scheme [25].

6.2.2 Existing Solution for Application-Specific Security Challenges

Security Solutions in Healthcare Applications
Table 6.2 shows the existing solution to the security issues in healthcare systems [26–28].

6.3 CONGESTION-AWARE AND DELAY-AWARE SECURITY PROTOCOL

6.3.1 Methodologies to Deal with Security Challenges with Optimal Efficiency

Table 6.3 provides a list of methodologies to deal with security challenges with optimal efficiency. Figure 6.4 represents the order of security mechanisms [10].

6.3.2 Energy-Efficient Possible Solution

Wireless sensor networks (WSNs) are comprised of autonomous devices, small in size, designed to sense, process, and collect data, which is then communicated for further analysis and processing. These networks are cost-effective, easily deployable, and are utilized in various applications such

TABLE 6.3
Methodology/Mechanism of Different Technologies

Reference	Methodology/Mechanism	Idea
[19]	Zigbee	IEEE 802.15.4
[29,30,31]	Multipath and multiphase routing-based stations	Secret sharing in probabilistic approach
[19]	TIK security scheme	Assistance of symmetric cryptography
[32]	BROSK (BROadcast session key negotiation protocol)	Assistance of symmetric cryptography
[33]	TinyPK system	Public Key Cryptography

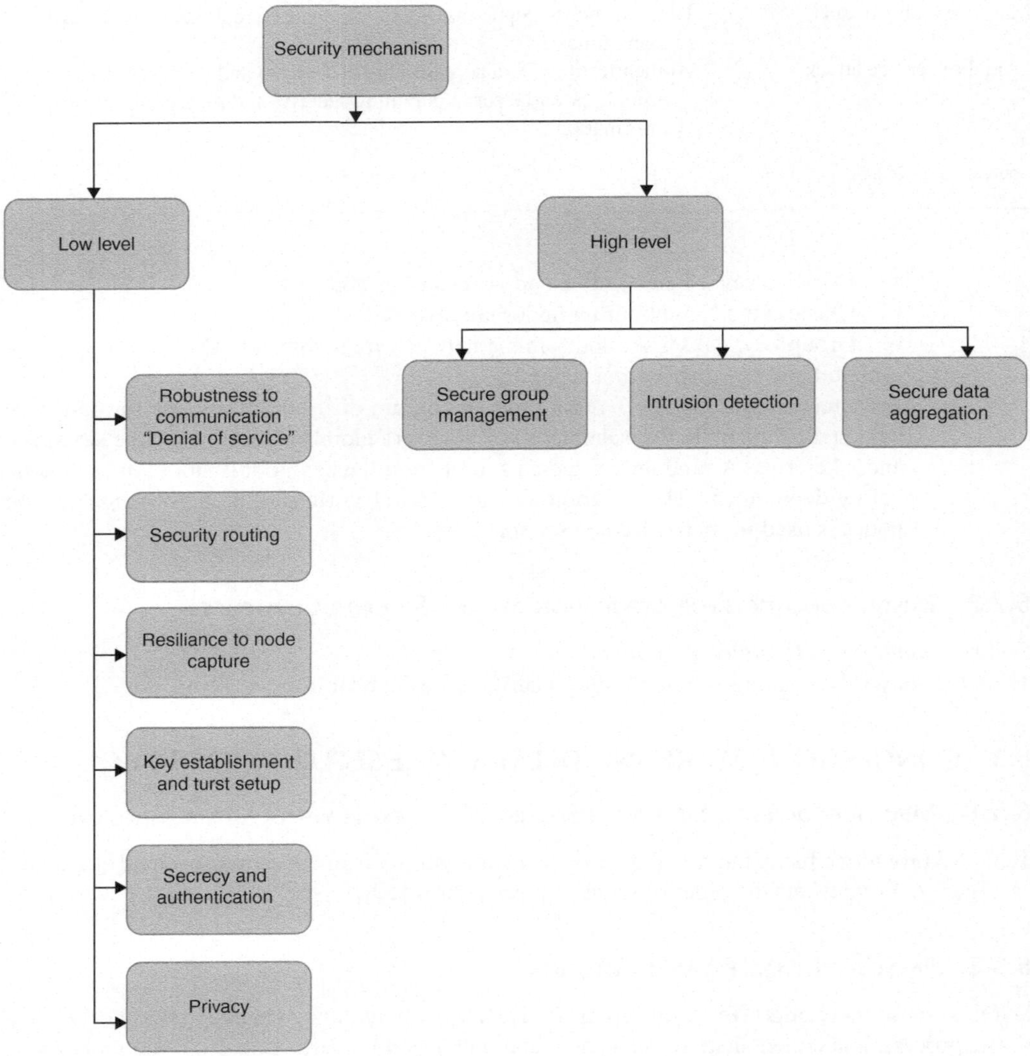

FIGURE 6.4 Security mechanisms.

as battlefield monitoring, pollution detection, health monitoring, building surveillance, security updates, weather forecasting, telemedicine, scientific research, and more. Sensor nodes often operate in harsh and hostile environments and are powered by batteries, making energy consumption minimization crucial for security techniques in WSNs [34].

The survey in [35] covers energy-efficient security architectures and protocols for WSNs. It presents a variety of energy-efficient protocols that can be implemented across different layers of the OSI model, including the physical, data link, network, and middleware layers:

(i) Security in IEEE 802.15.4:
It is one of the first standards which defines low-power wireless sensor networks. These network standard specifications provide several security suits [36,37]. The security suit specifications provide the algorithms and operations that would be required to be enabled based on the security services required in the protocol. The IEEE 802.15.4 standards define eight security suites.

(ii) SPINS
The system comprises two main components: SNEP (secure network encryption protocol) and μTESLA (micro version of timed efficient stream loss-tolerant authentication). SNEP handles confidentiality through encryption, authentication, freshness of data using a message authentication code (MAC) and integrity. μTESLA provides robust security with limited resources, even when the base station and nodes are only loosely time-synchronized [38].

(iii) TinySec
It is designed for implementation in the link layer and is well explained in [39]. It is designed as a less-weight and energy-efficient security package. Integration in any WSN is quite easy. The energy consumption may increase a bit based on the mode and network technology [35].

(iv) LLSP
Ref. [40] discusses a link-layer protocol developed by L. E. Lightfoot et al. that consumes less energy compared to TinySec. To ensure secure data transfer, this protocol proposes using a 4-byte counter for replay protection between the sender and receiver. The feedback shift register (FSR) manages the updating of this counter. Since the counter is synchronized between the sender and receiver, it is no longer necessary to transmit the counter byte within the message data, thereby reducing the data overhead [35].

(v) LEAP/LEAP+:
Localized encryption and authentication protocol (LEAP) is detailed in [41], and LEAP+ is described in [42]. Both are lightweight and energy-efficient security mechanisms for sensor networks (Figure 6.4). LEAP employs four distinct keys for each node: an individual key shared with a base station, a group key shared with all nodes in the network, a cluster key shared with nearby nodes, and a pair key shared with another node in the network. The energy consumption of LEAP depends on the number of nodes in the network [35].

(vi) Security Protocol based on Non-Orthogonal Variable Spreading Factor (NOVSF):
To mitigate the limitations of symmetric cryptography, a code-hopping method utilizing non-orthogonal variable spreading factor (NOVSF) codes is applied to ensure robust security. This cluster-based security protocol, as outlined in [43], incorporates symmetric cryptographic algorithms to strengthen its security framework.

In this technique, each data block is assigned different time slots through permutations in each session, mixing and reordering the data to improve security. Encryption keys are updated over time and across different sessions, ensuring data integrity, freshness, and security. The transmission between nodes and clusters is encrypted with these keys. Notably, this mechanism does not require additional energy for security [35].

(vii) Lightweight Security Protocol (LSec):
The Lightweight Security Protocol utilizes a combination of symmetric and asymmetric encryption methods, providing memory- and energy-efficient solutions by organizing network nodes into clusters. Symmetric encryption is employed for securing data, while asymmetric techniques handle the temporary exchange of secret keys between nodes. This protocol operates at the middleware layer of the communication model, as described in [44].

(viii) The hybrid adaptive security framework (HASF):
This provides security in the network with energy usage lesser than TinySec. HASF is employed in network layer and link layer (MAC) of the OSI model. It uses hybrid adaptive security suite (HASS) similar to IEEE 802.15.4 security suite proposal and is described in [45].

The experiment performed by authors in [45] reflects that HASF performs outstanding compared to HASS based system and TinySec-based Crossbow system in terms of energy usage for providing security. In HASF, all data is divided into *control data*, which is message to manage or control the network operations, and *application data*, which is data related to wireless sensor network services.

6.3.3 Congestion-Aware Possible Solution

Congestion-aware scheduling during the tradition downlink communication has neglected the concept of secrecy among the users/clients. The authors in [46] studied the heterogenous requirement of two users broadcast channel in terms of security and traffic requirements. Most of the works which consider the congestion control, improving the delay and throughput of the network, tend to ignore the secrecy requirement of the clients. The performance of the of the queue having the confidential data can degrade due to network congestion and can easily be exposed to security concerns in the network as shown in Figure 6.3. The authors studied two different broadcast channels with different security and delay requirements and with different decoding schemes and showed that congestion control on the queue holding the confidential message can decrease the average delay per message.

6.3.4 Delay-Aware Possible Solution

In [47], the authors introduced the secured reliable multipath routing protocol (SRMRP), which incorporates distributed trust computation and Carrier Sense Multiple Access with collision intimation within heterogeneous mobile ad hoc networks. Their research focused on two main goals: ensuring secure communication through reference-based trust security mechanisms and achieving reliable communication across these networks. The performance evaluation, including metrics like the number of detected malicious nodes, showed that SRMRP outperformed the existing ad hoc on-demand multipath distance vector (AOMDV) routing protocol.

In [48], the authors presented the secured link quality, delay, and energy aware routing protocol (SLQDEARP), an on-demand unipath routing protocol that builds on features from the ad hoc on-demand distance vector (AODV) protocol. SLQDEARP assesses link quality using signal strength received and selects energy-efficient, low-delay paths to the destination. The node with the best link quality is chosen, and if multiple nodes have similar quality, the one with the lowest energy consumption and delay is preferred. This protocol provides a secure and efficient routing approach based on link quality, energy consumption, and delay awareness.

SLQDEARP incorporates an adaptive node Stability (ANS) mechanism that uses estimated link quality, delay, and energy metrics from neighbouring nodes to inform the routing decision. The most suitable node is selected based on the ANS mechanism, and the packet is routed through that node. Additional ad hoc security algorithms are employed to further secure the transmission process.

6.4 SUMMARY AND CONCLUSION

In today's world, deploying sensor nodes in unattended environments involves significant risks, increasing the network's vulnerability. Wireless sensor networks (WSNs) are now widely used in various fields, including healthcare systems, railways, domestic applications, and countless commercial uses. Given the network's susceptibility, ensuring security in WSNs is paramount.

This chapter begins with a brief introduction to the evolution of the Internet of Things (IoT) over time and its current state. The existing challenges with IoT/WSNs are discussed in the following section, along with security challenges. We also address application-specific security challenges in WSN/IoT, such as those in healthcare systems, and examine the impact of congestion and delay on network security.

Furthermore, existing solutions to the security challenges in IoT/WSNs are reviewed, including application-specific security solutions. Research and methodologies for congestion-aware, delay-aware, and energy-efficient secure data transmission in wireless sensor networks are also shared.

REFERENCES

[1] Madakam, S., Ramaswamy, R., & Tripathi, S. (2015, May 25). *Internet of things (IOT): a literature review. Journal of Computer and Communications*, *3*(5). www.scirp.org/journal/paperinformation?paperid=56616

[2] Zijie, F., Al-Shareeda, M. A., Saare, M. A., Manickam, S., & Karuppayah, S. (2023). Wireless sensor networks in the internet of things: review, techniques, challenges, and future directions. *Indonesian Journal of Electrical Engineering and Computer Science*, *31*(2), 1190–1200.

[3] Gulati, K., Boddu, R. S. K., Kapila, D., Bangare, S. L., Chandnani, N., & Saravanan, G. (2022). A review paper on wireless sensor network techniques in Internet of Things (IoT). *Materials Today: Proceedings*, *51*, 161–165.

[4] Claessens, J. (2008). Trust, security, privacy, and identity perspective. *Panel on Future Internet Service Offer*. www.ijcaonline.org/archives/volume146/number7/25408-201691085/

[5] Naskar, S. (2023, February 23). *Wireless Sensor Networks: Challenges and Solutions*. IntechOpen. www.intechopen.com/chapters/86241

[6] Roman, R., Zhou, J., & Lopez, J. (2013). On the features and challenges of security and privacy in distributed internet of things. *Computer Networks*, *57*(10), 2266–2279.

[7] Han, G., Shu, L., Chan, S., & Hu, J. (2016). Security and privacy in Internet of things: methods, architectures, and solutions. *Security and Communication Networks*, *9*(15), 2641–2642.

[8] Burhanuddin, M. A., Mohammed, A. A. J., Ismail, R., Hameed, M. E., Kareem, A. N., & Basiron, H. (2018). A review on security challenges and features in wireless sensor networks: IoT perspective. *Journal of Telecommunication, Electronic and Computer Engineering (JTEC)*, *10*(1–7), 17–21.

[9] Thakur, J., & Kumar, N. (2011). DES, AES and Blowfish: Symmetric key cryptography algorithms simulation based performance analysis. *International Journal of Emerging Technology and Advanced Engineering*, *1*(2), 6–12.

[10] Padmavathi, D. G., & Shanmugapriya, M. (2009). A survey of attacks, security mechanisms and challenges in wireless sensor networks. *arXiv preprint arXiv:0909.0576*.

[11] Akyildiz, I. F., Su, W., Sankarasubramaniam, Y., & Cayirci, E. (2002). A survey on sensor networks. *IEEE Communications Magazine*, *40*(8), 102–114.

[12] Anitha, P., Vimala, H. S., & Shreyas, J. (2023). Comprehensive review on congestion detection, alleviation, and control for IoT networks. *Journal of Network and Computer Applications*, 103749.

[13] Duraipandian, M. (2020). Long term evolution-self organizing network for minimization of sudden call termination in mobile radio access networks. *Journal of trends in Computer Science and Smart technology (TCSST)*, *2*(02), 89–97.

[14] Saini, P. (2014). Impact of router's buffer size on packet loss due to congestion in TCP. *International Journal of Engineering Research & Technology*, *3*(5), 1053–1055.

[15] Samba, D. (2024, February 15). *What is Jitter in Networking?*. Digital Samba – video conferencing software, webinar software, virtual classroom, video API. www.digitalsamba.com/blog/what-is-jitter-in-networking

[16] Sequeira, L., Fernández-Navajas, J., Saldana, J., Gállego, J. R., & Canales, M. (2014). Describing the access network by means of router buffer modelling: a new methodology. *The Scientific World Journal*, 1, 238682. https://doi.org/10.1155/2014/238682

[17] Sunassee, S., Mungur, A., Armoogum, S., & Pudaruth, S. (2021, April). A comprehensive review on congestion control techniques in networking. In *2021 5th International Conference on Computing Methodologies and Communication (ICCMC)* (pp. 305–312). IEEE.

[18] Datapath.io. (2016, July 12). 'The negative effects of your network congestion problem'. Medium. https://medium.com/@datapath_io/the-negative-effects-of-your-network-congestion-problem-8b7ee5845ebf

[19] Jadhav, R., & Vatsala, V. (2017). Security issues and solutions in wireless sensor networks. *International Journal of Computer Applications*, *162*(2), 14–19.

[20] Chelli, K. (2015, July). Security issues in wireless sensor networks: Attacks and countermeasures. In *Proceedings of the World Congress on Engineering* (Vol. 1, No. 20, pp. 876–3423).

[21] Sen, J. (2010). A survey on wireless sensor network security. *arXiv preprint arXiv:1011.1529*.

[22] Carman, D. W., Kruus, P. S., & Matt, B. J. (2000). Constraints and approaches for distributed sensor network security (final). *DARPA Project report (Cryptographic Technologies Group, Trusted Information System, NAI Labs)*, *1*(1), 1–39.

[23] Di Pietro, R., Mancini, L. V., Law, Y. W., Etalle, S., & Havinga, P. (2003, October). LKHW: A directed diffusion-based secure multicast scheme for wireless sensor networks. In *2003 International Conference on Parallel Processing Workshops, 2003. Proceedings.* (pp. 397–406). IEEE.

[24] Zhu, S., Setia, S., & Jajodia, S. (2003). LEAP: efficient security mechanisms for large-scale distributed sensor networks. *10th ACM Conference on Computer and Communications Security (CCS'03)*. Washington DC, October.

[25] Eschenauer, L., & Gligor, V. D. (2002, November). A key-management scheme for distributed sensor networks. In *Proceedings of the 9th ACM Conference on Computer and Communications Security* (pp. 41–47).

[26] Lupu, T. G. (2009, September). Main types of attacks in wireless sensor networks. In *Proceedings of the 9th WSEAS International Conference on Signal, Speech and Image Processing, and 9th WSEAS International Conference on Multimedia, Internet and Video Technologies* (pp. 180–185).

[27] Meingast, M., Roosta, T., & Sastry, S. (2006, August). Security and privacy issues with health care information technology. In *2006 International Conference of the IEEE Engineering in Medicine and Biology Society* (pp. 5453–5458). IEEE.

[28] Memon, M. H., Memon, M. H., Marium, S. M., & Khan, J. (2019). Security and privacy issues of medical systems in wireless sensor networks: A survey. *Asian Journal for Convergence in Technology (AJCT) ISSN-2350-1146*, *5*(3), 8–12.

[29] Alajmi, N. (2014). Wireless sensor networks attacks and solutions. *arXiv preprint arXiv:1407.6290*.

[30] Hu, F., Ziobro, J., Tillett, J., & Sharma, N. K. (2004). *Secure wireless sensor networks: Problems and solutions*. Rochester Institute of Technology, Rochester, New York.

[31] Jadhav, R., & Vatsala, V. (2017). Security issues and solutions in wireless sensor networks. *International Journal of Computer Applications*, *162*(2), 14–19.

[32] Lai, B., Kim, S., & Verbauwhede, I. (2002, December). Scalable session key construction protocol for wireless sensor networks. In *IEEE Workshop on Large Scale RealTime and Embedded Systems (LARTES)* (Vol. 7).

[33] Ronald Watro, Derrick Kong, Sue-fen Cuti, Charles Gardiner, Charles Lynn and Peter Kruus (2004) "TinyPK: Securing Sensor Networks with Public Key Technology", *Proceedings of the 2nd ACM Workshop on Security of Ad Hoc and Sensor Networks SASN'04*, pp. 59–64, Oct..

[34] Gudivada, R. B., & Hansdah, R. C. (2018, May). Energy efficient secure communication in wireless sensor networks. In *2018 IEEE 32nd International Conference on Advanced Information Networking and Applications (AINA)* (pp. 311–319). IEEE.

[35] Daniluk, K., & Niewiadomska-Szynkiewicz, E. (2012). A survey of energy efficient security architectures and protocols for wireless sensor networks. *Journal of Telecommunications and Information Technology*, 3, 64–72.

[36] Sastry, N., & Wagner, D. (2004, October). Security considerations for IEEE 802.15. 4 networks. In *Proceedings of the 3rd ACM workshop on Wireless security* (pp. 32–42).

[37] Struik, R., & Rason, G. (2002). Security and security architectural recommendations for the IEEE 802.15. 4 Low-Rate WPAN. Certicom Corp.

[38] Perrig, A., Szewczyk, R., Wen, V., Culler, D., & Tygar, J. (2001, July). SPINS: Security protocols for sensor networks. In *Proceedings of the 7th Annual International Conference on Mobile Computing and Networking* (pp. 189–199).

[39] Karlof, C., Sastry, N., & Wagner, D. (2004, November). TinySec: a link layer security architecture for wireless sensor networks. In *Proceedings of the 2nd International Conference on Embedded Networked Sensor Systems* (pp. 162–175).

[40] Lighfoot, L. E., Ren, J., & Li, T. (2007, May). An energy efficient link-layer security protocol for wireless sensor networks. In *2007 IEEE International Conference on Electro/Information Technology* (pp. 233–238). IEEE.

[41] Zhu, S., Setia, S., & Jajodia, S. (2003). LEAP: Efficient security mechanisms for large-scale distributed sensor networks. 10th ACM Conf on Computer and Comm. *Security (CCS'03), Washington DC.*

[42] Zhu, S., Setia, S., & Jajodia, S. (2006). LEAP+ Efficient security mechanisms for large-scale distributed sensor networks. *ACM Transactions on Sensor Networks (TOSN)*, *2*(4), 500–528.

[43] Çam, H., Ozdemir, S., Muthuavinashiappan, D., & Nair, P. (2003, October). Energy efficient security protocol for wireless sensor networks. In *2003 IEEE 58th Vehicular Technology Conference. VTC 2003-Fall (IEEE Cat. No. 03CH37484)* (Vol. 5, pp. 2981–2984). IEEE.

[44] Shaikh, R. A., Lee, S., Khan, M. A., & Song, Y. J. (2006, September). LSec: Lightweight security protocol for distributed wireless sensor network. In *IFIP International Conference on Personal Wireless Communications* (pp. 367–377). Berlin, Heidelberg: Springer Berlin Heidelberg.

[45] Shon, T., Koo, B., Choi, H., & Park, Y. (2009, February). Security architecture for IEEE 802.15. 4-based wireless sensor network. In *2009 4th International Symposium on Wireless Pervasive Computing* (pp. 1–5). IEEE.

[46] Arvanitaki, A., Pappas, N., Carlsson, N., & Mohapatra, P. (2021, June). Secrecy in congestion-aware broadcast channels. In *2021 Wireless Days (WD)* (pp. 1–5). IEEE.

[47] Narasimhan, B., & Vadivel, R. (2012). Secured reliable multipath routing protocol (SRMRP) using trust computation and carrier sense multiple access with collision intimation (CSMA/CI) for heterogeneous IP-based mobile ad-hoc networks. *International Journal of Computer Applications*, *60*(10), 12–16.

[48] Qaed, A. S., & Devi, T. (2013, August). Secured link quality, delay and energy aware routing protocol (SLQDEARP) for mobile ad hoc networks. In *2013 International Conference on Intelligent Interactive Systems and Assistive Technologies* (pp. 15–20). IEEE.

7 Security Concerns of IoT in Health Monitoring Applications

Shipra Upadhyay, Pulkit Singh, Manoj Tolani, Ambar Bajpai, Amit Kumar Pandey and N.P. Yadav

7.1 INTRODUCTION

Repeatedly, the healthcare setting has changed as IoT (Internet of Things) made a breakthrough in health monitoring bringing in a new mode with which diagnostics can take place, preventive healthcare services are offered, and personalized medicine on patient level is prominent. IoT in health monitoring applications includes remote patient monitoring (RPM), chronic disease management, telemedicine and telehealth, smart medical devices, health and wellness tracking, predictive analytics and AI, and elderly care and assisted living and public health surveillance [1]. Finally, IoT in the health monitoring systems is expected to have a vast range of benefits leading to the improvement of healthcare outcomes, the attraction of patients as the prime participants of the treatments programs and the reduction of healthcare expenses through the introduction of the preventive approaches and the health status management as shown in Figure 7.1.

Some of the real-world IoT applications in healthcare are activity recognition, blood sugar monitoring, sleep monitoring, oxygen level monitoring, blood pressure monitoring, stress level monitoring and heart health monitoring. A variety of methods, such as computer vision, active sensor indicators, passive radio frequency identification (RFID), Wi-Fi, and radar, are employed in the healthcare industry for activity recognition. When detecting abnormal activity, conventional activity detection tools often produce misleading results. Support vector machines (SVMs) and dictionaries are two methods of learning that can help with this problem. Applications for activity detection include multiple users activity identification, posture identification, motion abnormality detection, human localization and tracking, detection of falls, and tracking of fitness.

Patients with diabetes may find blood glucose monitoring (BGM) particularly helpful as it offers crucial information for managing the condition [2]. IoT devices can do more than just routine monitoring. They can also monitor patients' meals or suggest healthy eating, provide guidance on following treatment plans, and issue warnings in severe or dangerous situations. Another use for IoT devices is sleep monitoring for patients. Numerous uses include tracking and categorizing the stages of sleep [3], keeping an eye on vital signs while you sleep, and identifying sleep disorders like obstructive sleep disease.

Patients' breathing pattern is a good way for evaluating their well-being. IoT oxygen level monitoring devices include asthma monitoring, medication effects on breathing, and monitoring of newborns for sudden infant death syndrome (SIDS). High blood pressure (BP) is a major

DOI: 10.1201/9781003491910-7

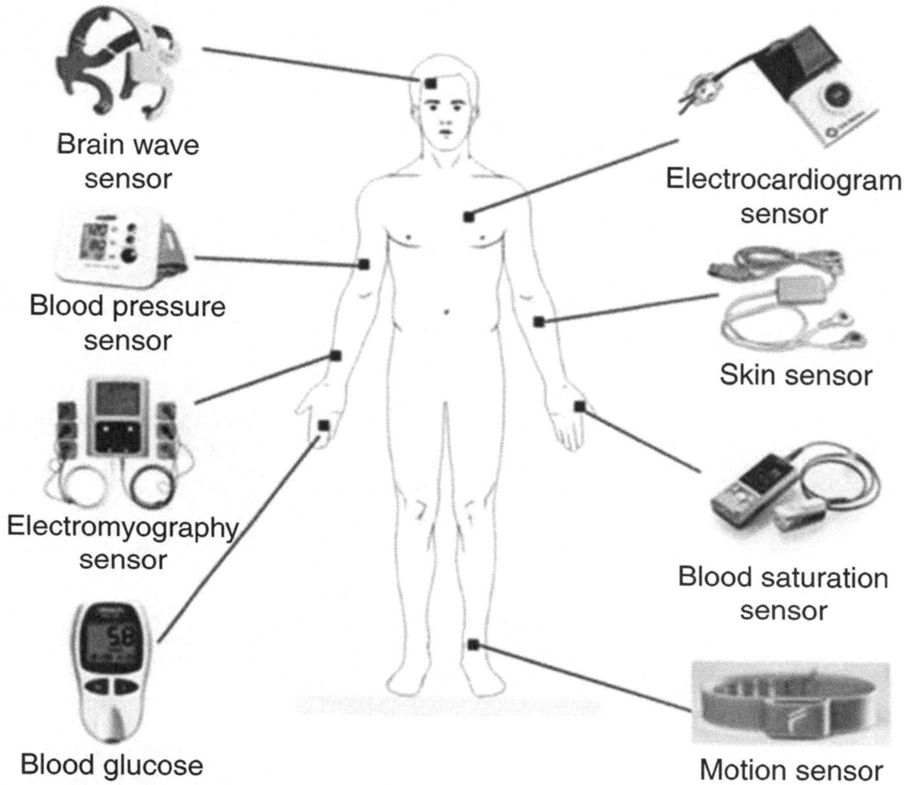

FIGURE 7.1 IoT service utilization in healthcare [1].

health concern for many adults. Addressing it is crucial. There are currently IoT-based high blood pressure detection systems in usage, while certain applications can even regulate processes of decision-making related to hypertension [5]. Similarly for stress level monitoring and intervention, if necessary, various systems have been developed. Some mobile applications offer stress reduction suggestions. Cardiovascular disease accounts for one-third of all deaths worldwide, which leads to major cause of death in the world [6]. Customized and continuous cardiac monitoring, rather than traditional in-hospital monitoring, can reduce cardiovascular disease fatalities and associated costs [7]. Cardiac monitoring devices have come under scrutiny for security and privacy concerns, despite their growing commercial popularity.

On one hand, IoT opens up new horizons for the treatment and prevention of health issues and on the other, raises questions on data privacy, security and the necessity of properly functioning regulatory frameworks for the good use of health data [8,9]. This chapter is organized in such a way that in first section we have presented a brief introduction of IoT in healthcare along with the real-world applications. Section 7.2 discusses the existing literature available on IoT in healthcare. The papers are reviewed based on some inclusion and exclusion criteria. Section 7.3 presents the technologies used in IoT for healthcare applications. Further, the challenges and issues of utilizing IoT in healthcare are discussed and at the end conclusion section provides an overall summary of this chapter.

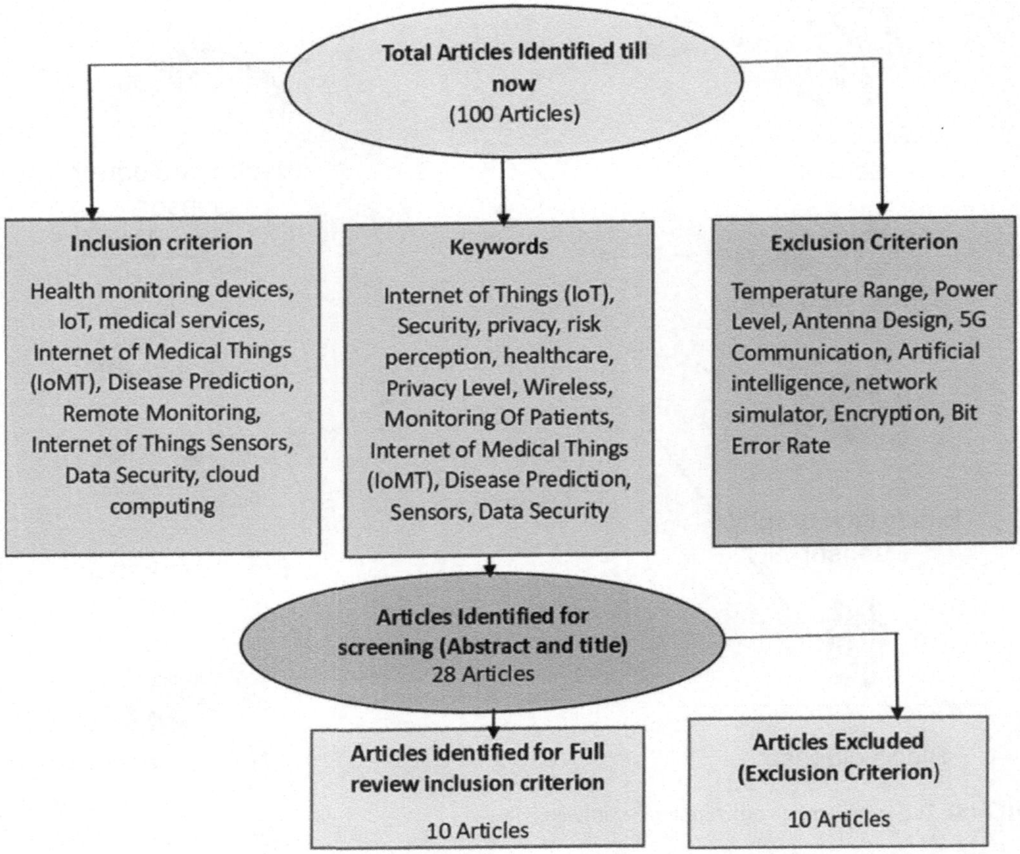

FIGURE 7.2 Screening and identification of the manuscripts.

7.2 LITERATURE STUDY

The literature survey begins with the selection of suitable and relevant articles. The literature review reveals that researchers have reported IoT in healthcare applications in many related works. However, in a few of the conditions, the researchers discovered numerous other issues. We concentrated our screening on security concerns about IoT in health monitoring applications. During the initial search, 100 papers were identified. The keywords are identified, and the articles are filtered in the screening process using the exclusion and inclusion criteria shown in Figure 7.2. For the literature review, we identified closely related manuscripts about the proposed topic. Exclusion and inclusion criteria are also established for the filtration of relevant manuscripts. Figure 7.2 depicts a few of the keywords that were considered for review. After careful consideration, 28 papers were selected for full review in the screening process. Ten papers are chosen from a total of 28 for the comprehensive literature review. Table 7.1 discusses the detailed literature study report.

7.3 TECHNOLOGIES USED IN IOT

Through the use of diverse technology components, IoT-based home health monitoring systems will be able to facilitate proactive, personalized, and continuous tracking of people's health,

TABLE 7.1
Objective, contribution, and conclusion of the works

Objective	Contribution	Conclusion
Investigation of Internet of Things for in-home health monitoring Systems for current advances, challenges and future directions [10]	Illustration of critical components for both implementation and development of the IoT home-based remote monitoring devices; the state of the art on the architecture and main elements of IoT-based home remote monitoring systems have been presented.	This paper outlines the requirements, technological advancements, obstacles, suggestions, and future paths for Internet of Things (IoT)-based in-home health monitoring systems.
Study of chronic disease monitoring using IoT [11]	The tracking and control of chronic health disorders is one of the main applications of IoT. In this paper, a review of several industrial and non-industrial mobile health monitoring systems was done.	This paper considers the integration of innovative IoT technology in healthcare, a mode that focuses on the monitoring of chronic conditions in remote locations. Besides that, varied modes of healthcare monitoring devices are also taken into consideration.
A framework for ECG monitoring for health care applications using IoT with security in data transmission [12]	The paper presents a framework of the IoT-assisted ECG monitoring with secure communication. The strength analysis of ECG signals for the purposes of auto-classification and real-time implementation with the use of sensors, Arduino, Android phones, Bluetooth and cloud servers has been demonstrated.	This article describes an algorithm that determines ECG quality using the ECG signal strength analysis (SSA) techniques. This method is efficient for the evaluation of cardio signals for patients and physical activity. The proposed ECG-SSA performs at the same level as other contemporary methods based on a comparative evaluation based on morphological characteristics, RR duration and both machine learning strategies. ECG SSA decreases the battery energy consumption by transmitting and capturing ECG signals of a quality over the IoT network, which is not further digitized and accepted.
Analysis of a user authentication scheme for IoT in healthcare for security issues [13]	In this paper, authors provides the reader a brief vision of the existing scheme and they first assert that the scheme is not deployable in the proposed format and second they show that it is possible for the attacker to acquire the keys, guess the password, and trace the user, given that the attacker has direct access to the nodes and the doctor's device. Authors offered not just the identification of the problems they addressed, but also the remedies to them generally.	The authors have explained two mistakes in the current plan, which is obstructing it from being carried out in actual. They have as well proposed security enhancements such as extra security mitigation measures to protect the session key disclosure, offline password guessing, and traceability attacks.

(*continued*)

TABLE 7.1 (Continued)
Objective, contribution, and conclusion of the works

Objective	Contribution	Conclusion
A scalable system for IoT and cloud-based healthcare application [14]	The system interface has been created to let patients and doctors share data which they send using the sensors on wearable devices and doctors receive that data in real time.	This article includes several methods to reduce energy consumption, for instance, feeding the sensor data to the cloud-based healthcare system, as well as using Bluetooth version 5.0 and above in smartphones, tablets, and mobile application so as to synchronize data between the sensors and the application.
Development of deep federated learning-based IoT systems for healthcare data analysis [15].	This article describes a deep FL framework that is optimized for the processing of healthcare data obtained from IoT devices to improve visual and textual healthcare data analysis. It provides the system of FL algorithm that will be useful for acquiring local training data process. Also, it features an experiment of skin diseases detection by the proposed routine.	By examining a set of related data, the outcomes illustrate that the DFL algorithms are able to preserve data privacy, while not sharing any, and enhance the IoT decentralized model, which is easy to maintain, guarantee the area under the curve (AUC) at around 97% and minimize the operational costs (OCs) of the service providers.
Preserving transmit security in IoT-powered healthcare systems [16].	This paper outlines a verification mechanism for multi-keyword search through the implementation of a pseudo-random function. The proposed approach settles the challenging data-compression problem in top-k search scenario to prove the correctness of the search in the partial search list. Crafting formal security analysis confirms that proposed scheme provides forward privacy preservation to guarantee privacy in healthcare data.	The scheme to build a trapdoor permutation function and a verifiable forward scheme are described. The proposed solution is successfully solving the dilemma of exactness of the top-K search results in the partial search results case.
Secure data exchange for healthcare IoT using batch verification and privacy Protection [17]	Here, certification free redactable digital signature schemes (RSS) concept is put forth. It also, in a very efficient manner, provides the algorithm supporting the proposed scheme and proves its security using all cryptographic assumptions. The method of proposed introduces validation verification and redaction control techniques, which	The proposed technique is the first of the CLRSS constructions for the health data sharing that protects the privacy in the resource-limited IoT scenes. Batch verification is conducted along with RC, which reduces the number of transmissions and hence improves security through prevention of modifying/editing data by malevolent redactor. To the next computational step, the invention is confirmed as secure with

TABLE 7.1 (Continued)
Objective, contribution, and conclusion of the works

Objective	Contribution	Conclusion
	in consequence also leads to communication bandwidth reduction and the security enhancement of shared data, through preventing bad-faith data modification by the data holder.	ECDL and bilinear t-SDH problematics. One disadvantage of this protocol is that it presupposes the existence of a trusted central server for performing the necessary redaction.
Design challenges and emerging applications of the voice-controlled IoT devices in healthcare [18]	This article provides a review of voice-enabled IoT devices. Besides this, the trends and their special issues in health sector when the devices are in use is discussed in detail.	This brief has presented a review of the recent voice activated IoT devices focusing on healthcare, along with current trends and challenges and some future applications.
Smart context-aware IoT healthcare systems using digital twin [19]	A context-aware healthcare system through the framework of DT is formulated and developed in this paper. The combining of DT with the healthcare sector would be beneficial to the healthcare procedures as it will link patients and healthcare professionals in a smart and comprehensive environment that can scale.	Authors implemented use case entailed five algorithms that yielded the best output accuracy and execution results. From an advanced perspective, the architecture proposed blends DT with the healthcare field to speed up care processes.
Security of healthcare data established by IoT sensor [20]	In this specific article, introduction of the IoT network technology that is used for transmitting the medical data for remote medical care is presented. Further, the data security issues associated with data transmission that is unguarded, such as between smart sensor devices and network routers. Finally, the proposal of encryption of data security at smart sensor devices level is presented.	It has been shown to address security concerns from the very beginning up, eliminating any opportunity for outside parties to exploit the data. It removes any possibility that the data will be interpreted differently before it reaches the cloud by encrypting it as it travels from the sensor device to the cloud and securely forwarding it to the Internet of Things network.

resulting in better health outcomes, lower healthcare costs and enhanced levels of life. The key technologies for IoT-based in-home health monitoring system are given below and as shown in Figure 7.3:

1. *Sensors and Wearables*: Sensors come integrated inside wearable technologies such as smartwatches, fitness bands, or even clothes and monitor different health parameters like heart rate, blood pressure, body temperature, levels of activity, and even sleep patterns. These sensors collect all the data that can be transferred to a central data collection system for examination [21–25].

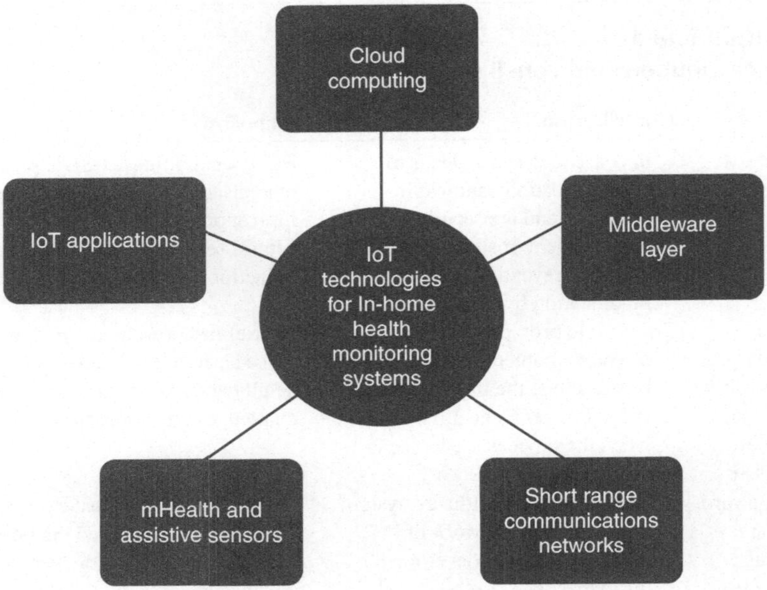

FIGURE 7.3 Key technologies for IoT based in-home health monitoring systems.

2. *Wireless Connectivity*: Home health-monitoring IoT devices usually employ range of wireless communications technologies such as Wi-Fi, Bluetooth, and Zigbee for transmitting data to a central hub or a cloud platform. Such wireless protocols facilitate the smooth communication among devices, hence keeping the data collection and data transmission continuous [26].
3. *Cloud Computing*: Cloud-based data storage and analytics platforms are typically a means for storing and analysing the massive amount of health information that come from the IoT devices. Through cloud computing, scalability, flexibility, and accessibility are now available, easily allowing healthcare providers to get patient information from any place at any time, and thereby advanced analytics that is enhanced by machine learning algorithms [27].
4. *Data Analytics and Machine Learning*: Data analytical tools such as machine learning and artificial intelligence are employed for intelligent processing of health data acquired from IoT devices. Such strategies can be used to determine patterns, trends, anomalies, to predict insights, which can be used for personalized health monitoring, early detection and proactive interventions [28].
5. *Mobile Applications*: The mobile application components are of great importance in home health control systems since they feature user-friendly interface for patients to check their health data, receive alerts and cautions, track their progress, and communicate with the doctors. In most cases, these apps work together using both wearable devices, and cloud platforms ensuring a unified user experience [29].
6. *Security and Privacy Technologies*: Because of the delicacy health data bears, secure and privacy technologies are indispensable to shield the patients' information from intrusion, data breaches and cyberattacks. With regard to the security of the home health monitoring systems, encryption, authentication, access control and secure communication protocols are some of the most important measures implemented [30].

7. *Remote Monitoring and Telemedicine*: Remote monitoring technologies enable healthcare professionals to monitor their patients' health conditions, as well as intervene, all in real time. Telemedicine portals offer online consultations, analysis, and treatment plans which do not require any physical visits, thereby promoting health care accessibility and convenience [31].

7.4 CHALLENGES AND ISSUES IN IOT

The challenges that have to be addressed for secured use of data in health monitoring are as follows:

Data Breaches: IoT devices commonly collect and pass the data that can be classified as personal and health-related, thus evoking an interest from cyberattackers. Data breaching can open a door to unauthorized access to personal information, thereby leading to identity theft, financial fraud and different dishonest actions [32].

Inadequate Authentication and Authorization: Enormous amounts of IoT devices do not possess strong authentication methods and therefore are prone to unauthorized access. Short or weak passwords and simple access controls, as well as some methods of encryption, can be bypassed by an attacker, granting access to the devices and sensitive data [33].

Data Encryption: If the communication occurred in plain text, then intruders are able to intercept data coming from IoT devices and to backend systems. In the absence of properly established encryption methods, the attackers can forcibly listen to the messages and take over crucial data of these messages [34].

Privacy Concerns: IoT devices can provide as such a wide range of data, which includes users, behaviours, preferences, and activities. There is concern about the ways the data is put to work, shared, and stored, and for it being misused in surveillance or profiling people without their consent [35–40].

Device Security: As a matter of fact, most of the IoT devices work with limited computing power and they may lack sufficient security features, which opens the door for attackers to penetrate these devices easily. Vulnerabilities like unencrypted firmware, not patched software and absent secure boot mechanisms can be used for a possible attack to the whole of IoT ecosystem [41–46].

Supply Chain Risks: IoT devices manufacturing involves other supply chain complexity risks due to additional security. Attackers can ever influence hardware or software components during the manufacturing or supply chain causing a compromise of the safety and integrity of the device [47–55].

Interoperability Challenges: IoT ecosystems, often made up of devices that are heterogeneous in origin from different manufacturers with their own protocols and security standard as well is a common feature. Establishing a user-friendly pan-device in a single ecosystem without compromising the security of the system represents a significant challenge, indeed [56,57].

Regulatory Compliance: Together with data protection regulations such as General Data Protection Regulation (GDPR) and Health Insurance Portability and Accountability Act (HIPAA) presents manufacturers and service providers of IoT devices with huge challenges. This issue is potential as devices must cater for regulatory needs such as data privacy, consent management and data security [58].

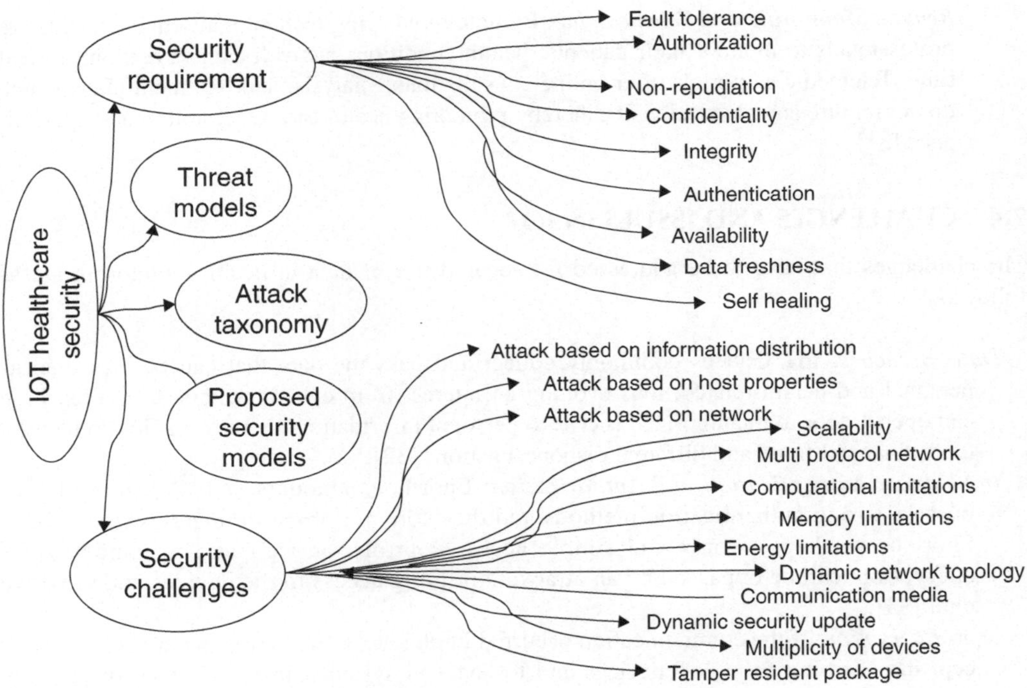

FIGURE 7.4 Challenges for IoT in healthcare [14].

Lifecycle Management: IoT devices still outlive security patches or the update cycle with some devices operating for years without receiving any latest updates. Security management of IoT devices during the whole lifecycle of a device, that is, firmware updates, patch management and end-of-life disposal, is important to decrease cyber risk [59] (Figure 7.4).

7.5 CONCLUSION

Healthcare systems looking towards integrating IoT technologies are the new change-makers of this sector. To begin with, we picked a study of few papers that are published in Internet of Things systems. Next, we discussed few of the technologies used in IoT for healthcare such as such as sensor technology, data analytics, cloud computing and machine learning. These are also the main topics of this discussion. Next, explanation was given on the existing network topologies, architecture and platforms which are employed in IoT for healthcare. We also reviewed, in detail, one of most crucial areas of the IoT healthcare systems—the security aspect. Now we have identified the security requirements that an IoT healthcare system should have and in the common situations when these requirements are difficult to fulfil, then, the topic applications and services came up. Healthcare is one of the areas where IoT is productive to a high extent. As we are discussing this issue, we also provided the respective problems and unsolved issues of IoT in healthcare that still exist. In order to improve the healthcare system, there are scientists all over the world who strive to introduce creatively designed devices, software, and much more. Here, the most fundamental concern is the evaluation of the current state of different contemporary IoT networks with their protocols, architectures, and platforms. This chapter has detailed the research studies in Internet of Things in healthcare covering the security issues and other challenges in person's monitoring and personal health.

REFERENCES

[1] *Mhealth: New Horizon for Health Through Mobile Technologies (Global Observatory for e-Health Services)*, WHO, Geneva, Switzerland, 2011, vol. 3.

[2] S. Kitsiou, G. Paré, M. Jaana, and B. Gerber, "Effectiveness of mHealth interventions for patients with diabetes: An overview of systematic reviews," *PLoS One*, vol. 12, no. 3, Mar. 2017, Art. no. e0173160, doi: 10.1371/journal.pone.0173160.

[3] M. C. Alberto, M. G. Ruano, M. Herrero, A. Jiménez, J. García, and E. Díaz, "Sensory system for the sleep disorders detection in the geriatric population," in *Proc. IEEE 4th Exp. Int. Conf.*, 2017, pp. 329–334.

[4] H.-K. Ra et al., "Asthma guide: An asthma monitoring and advice ecosystem," in *Proc. IEEE Wireless Health (WH)*, Bethesda, MD, Oct. 2016, pp. 1–8.

[5] P. Muntner et al., "Potential U.S. population impact of the 2017 ACC/AHA high blood pressure guideline," *Circulation*, vol. 137, no. 2, pp. 109–118, 2018. [Online]. Available: www.ahajournals.org/doi/abs/10.1161/CIRCULATIONAHA.117.032582

[6] S. Clarke, L. G. Jaimes, and M. A. Labrador, "mStress: A mobile recommender system for just-in-time interventions for stress," in *Proc. 14th IEEE Annu. Consum. Commun. Netw. Conf. (CCNC)*, 2017, pp. 1–5.

[7] S. Hijazi, A. Page, B. Kantarci, and T. Soyata, "Machine learning in cardiac health monitoring and decision support," *Computer*, vol. 49, no. 11, pp. 38–48, Nov. 2016.

[8] A. Froytlog et al., "Ultra-low power wake-up radio for 5G IoT," *IEEE Communications Magazine*, vol. 57, no. 3, pp. 111–117, Mar. 2019.

[9] K. Guk, G. Han, J. Lim, K. Jeong, T. Kang, E. K. Lim, and J. Jung, "Evolution of wearable devices with real-time disease monitoring for personalized healthcare," *Nanomaterials*, vol. 9, no. 6, p. 813, 2019, doi: 10.3390/nano9060813.

[10] N. Y. Philip, J. J. P. C. Rodrigues, H. Wang, S. J. Fong and J. Chen, "Internet of things for in-home health monitoring systems: Current advances, challenges and future directions," *IEEE Journal on Selected Areas in Communications*, vol. 39, no. 2, pp. 300–310, Feb. 2021, doi: 10.1109/JSAC.2020.3042421.

[11] Singh, G. (2019). "IoT for healthcare: system architectures, predictive analytics and future challenges". In: Singh, A., Mohan, A. (eds) *Handbook of Multimedia Information Security: Techniques and Applications*. Springer, Cham. https://doi.org/10.1007/978-3-030-15887-3_36.

[12] M. S. H. Talpur et al., "Illuminating healthcare management: A comprehensive review of IoT-enabled chronic disease monitoring," *IEEE Access*, vol. 12, pp. 48189–48209, 2024, doi: 10.1109/ACCESS.2024.3382011.

[13] S. Wang, X. Zhou, K. Wen, B. Weng and P. Zeng, "Security analysis of a user authentication scheme for IoT-based healthcare," *IEEE Internet of Things Journal*, vol. 10, no. 7, pp. 6527–6530, 1 April1, 2023, doi: 10.1109/JIOT.2022.3228921.

[14] M. M. Islam and Z. A. Bhuiyan, "An integrated scalable framework for cloud and IoT based green healthcare system," *IEEE Access*, vol. 11, pp. 22266–22282, 2023, doi: 10.1109/ACCESS.2023.3250849.

[15] H. Elayan, M. Aloqaily and M. Guizani, "Sustainability of healthcare data analysis IoT-based systems using deep federated learning," *IEEE Internet of Things Journal*, vol. 9, no. 10, pp. 7338–7346, 15 May15, 2022, doi: 10.1109/JIOT.2021.3103635.

[16] K. Wang, C. -M. Chen, Z. Tie, M. Shojafar, S. Kumar and S. Kumari, "Forward privacy preservation in IoT-enabled healthcare systems," *IEEE Transactions on Industrial Informatics*, vol. 18, no. 3, pp. 1991–1999, March 2022, doi: 10.1109/TII.2021.3064691.

[17] F. Zhu, X. Yi, A. Abuadbba, I. Khalil, S. Nepal and X. Huang, "Authenticated data sharing with privacy protection and batch verification for healthcare IoT," *IEEE Transactions on Sustainable Computing*, vol. 8, no. 1, pp. 32–42, 1 Jan.–March 2023, doi: 10.1109/TSUSC.2022.3211298.

[18] P. Spachos, S. Gregori and M. J. Deen, "Voice activated IoT devices for healthcare: design challenges and emerging applications," *IEEE Transactions on Circuits and Systems II: Express Briefs*, vol. 69, no. 7, pp. 3101–3107, July 2022, doi: 10.1109/TCSII.2022.3179680.

[19] H. Elayan, M. Aloqaily and M. Guizani, "Digital twin for intelligent context-aware IoT healthcare systems," *IEEE Internet of Things Journal*, vol. 8, no. 23, pp. 16749–16757, 1 Dec.1, 2021, doi: 10.1109/JIOT.2021.3051158.

[20] K. M. Besher, Z. Subah and M. Z. Ali, "IoT sensor initiated healthcare data security," *IEEE Sensors Journal*, vol. 21, no. 10, pp. 11977–11982, 15 May15, 2021, doi: 10.1109/JSEN.2020.3013634.

[21] M. N. Bhuiyan, M. M. Rahman, M. M. Billah and D. Saha, "Internet of things (IoT): A review of its enabling technologies in healthcare applications, standards protocols, security, and market opportunities," *IEEE Internet of Things Journal*, vol. 8, no. 13, pp. 10474–10498, 1 July1, 2021, doi: 10.1109/JIOT.2021.3062630.

[22] A. Lee and K. Lee, "The Internet of Things (IoT): Applications, investments, and challenges for enterprises," *Business Horizons*, vol. 58, no. 4, pp. 431–440, Jul./Aug. 2015.

[23] The Rise of Remote Patient Monitoring. Accessed: May 2019. [Online]. Available: https://thejournalofmhealth.com/the-rise-of-remote patient-monitoring/

[24] A. L. Bui and G. C. Fonarow, "Home monitoring for heart failure management," *Journal of the American College of Cardiology*, vol. 59, no. 2, pp. 97–104, Jan. 2012, doi: 10.1016/j.jacc.2011.09.044.

[25] F. Bonomi, R. Milito, J. Zhu, and S. Addepalli, "Fog computing and its role in the Internet of Things," in *Proc. 1st Ed. MCC Workshop Mobile Cloud Comput. (MCC)*, Helsinki, Finland, Aug. 2012, pp. 13–16.

[26] H. Hayajneh, G. Almashaqbeh, S. Ullah, and A. V. Vasilakos, "A survey of wireless technologies coexistence in WBAN: Analysis an open research issues," *Wireless Networks*, vol. 20, no. 8, pp. 2165–2199, Nov. 2014.

[27] M. Hassanalieragh et al., "Health monitoring and management using Internet-of-Things (IoT) sensing with cloud-based processing: Opportunities and challenges," in *Proc. IEEE Int. Conf. Services Comput.*, New York, NY, Jun. 2015, pp. 285–292.

[28] A. L. Beam and I. S. Kohane, "Big data and machine learning in health care," *JAMA*, vol. 319, no. 13, pp. 1317–1318, 2018.

[29] C. Pereira and A. Aguiar, "Towards efficient mobile M2M communications: Survey and open challenges," *Sensors*, vol. 14, no. 10, pp. 19582–19608, Oct. 2014.

[30] C. Hennebert and J. D. Santos, "Security protocols and privacy issues into 6LoWPAN stack: A synthesis," *IEEE Internet Things Journal*, vol. 1, no. 5, pp. 384–398, Oct. 2014.

[31] E. Kaimakamis et al., "Experience of using the welcome remote monitoring system on patients with COPD and comorbidities," in *Proc., Int. Conf. Biomed. Health Inform. (ICBHI)*, vol. 66. Singapore: Springer, 2017, pp. 97–102.

[32] M. A. A. da Cruz, J. J. P. C. Rodrigues, J. Al-Muhtadi, V. V. Korotaev, and V. H. C. de Albuquerque, "A reference model for Internet of Things middleware," *IEEE Internet Things Journal*, vol. 5, no. 2, pp. 871–883, Apr. 2018, doi: 10.1109/JIOT.2018.2796561.

[33] S. Kumar, P. Tiwari, and M. Zymbler, "Internet of Things is a revolutionary approach for future technology enhancement: A review," *Journal of Big Data*, vol. 6, no. 1, Dec. 2019, doi: 10.1186/s40537-019-0268-2.

[34] M. Imran, S. Jabbar, N. Chilamkurti, and J. J. P. C. Rodrigues, "Enabling technologies for social Internet of Things," *Future Generation Computing Systems*, vol. 92, pp. 715–717, Mar. 2019, doi:10.1016/j.future.2018.11.018.

[35] Systems and Software Engineering—Systems and Software Quality Requirements and Evaluation (SQuaRE)—System and Software Quality Models, document TR ISO/IEC 25010, 2010. www.iso.org/obp/ui/#iso:std:iso-iec:25010:ed-2:v1:en

[36] G. White, V. Nallur, and S.. Clarke, "Quality of service approaches in IoT: A systematic mapping," *Journal of System Software*, vol. 132, pp. 186–203,Oct. 2017.

[37] *A Guide to GDPR Data Privacy Requirements*. Accessed: Oct. 25, 2020. [Online]. Available: https://gdpr.eu/data-privacy/

[38] F. D. Hudson, P. A. Laplante, and B. Amaba, "Enabling trust and security: TIPPSS for IoT," *IT Prof.*, vol. 20, no. 2, pp. 15–18, Mar. 2018, doi: 10.1109/MITP.2018.021921646.

[39] The HIPAA Privacy Rule. Accessed: Oct. 25, 2020. [Online]. Available: www.hhs.gov/hipaa/for-professionals/privacy/index.html.

[40] P. Carter, G. T. Laurie, and M. Dixon-Woods, "The social licence for research: Why care. data ran into trouble," *Journal of Medical Ethics*, vol. 41, no. 5, pp. 404–409, 2015.

[41] J. Rumbold, "Big data and diabetes: The applications of big data for diabetes care now and in the future," *Diabetic Medicine*, vol. 37, no. 2, pp. 187–193, 2019.

[42] J. Kiljander et al., "Semantic interoperability architecture for pervasive computing and Internet of Things," *IEEE Access*, vol. 2, pp. 856–873, 2014.

[43] K. Park, J. Park, and J. Lee, "An IoT system for remote monitoring of patients at home," *Applied Science*, vol. 7, no. 3, p. 260, Mar. 2017.

[44] S. Tzafestas, "Ethics and law in the Internet of Things world," *Smart Cities*, vol. 1, no. 1, pp. 98–120, Oct. 2018.

[45] C. Seeger, K. Van Laerhoven, and A. Buchmann, "MyHealthAssistant: An event-driven middleware for multiple medical applications on a smartphone-mediated body sensor network," *IEEE Journal of Biomedicine and Health Information*, vol. 19, no. 2, pp. 752–760, Mar. 2015.

[46] R. Zgheib et al., "Semantic middleware architectures for IoT healthcare applications," in *Enhanced Living Environments (Lecture Notes in Computer Science)*, vol. 11369. Cham, Switzerland: Springer, 2019.

[47] M. A. A. da Cruz, J. J. P. C. Rodrigues, A. K. Sangaiah, J. Al-Muhtadi, and V. Korotaev, "Performance evaluation of IoT middleware," *Journal of Network and Computer Applications*, vol. 109, pp. 53–65, May 2018.

[48] T. Chomutare, L. Fernandez-Luque, E. Årsand, and G. Hartvigsen, "Features of mobile diabetes applications: Review of the literature and analysis of current applications compared against evidence-based guidelines," *Journal of Medical Internet Research*, vol. 13, no. 3, p. e65, Sep. 2011.

[49] R. Goffredo, D. Accoto, M. Santonico, G. Pennazza, and E. Guglielmelli, "A smart pill for drug delivery with sensing capabilities," in *Proc. 37th Annu. Int. Conf. IEEE Eng. Med. Biol. Soc. (EMBC)*, Milan, Italy, Aug. 2015, pp. 1361–1364.

[50] T. Antonio, N. Nasiri, and S. De, "Wearable and miniaturized sensor technologies for personalized and preventive medicine," *Advanced Functional Materials*, vol. 27, no. 15, Apr. 2017, Art. no. 1605271, doi:10.1002/adfm.201605271.

[51] M.-V. Moreno and E. Herrera, "Evaluation on phantoms of the feasibility of a smart bra to detect breast cancer in young adults," *Sensors*, vol. 19, no. 24, p. 5491, Dec. 2019.

[52] M. G. Eshghi, Z. Fruhideh, V. M. Alviri, and M. M. Asem, "Electro-chemical biosensors for cancer detection using different biomarkers," in *Proc. IEEE 9th Annu. Comput. Commun. Workshop Conf. (CCWC)*, Las Vegas, NV, USA, Jan. 2019, pp. 0989–0996.

[53] C. Ornetzeder, F. Reiterer, M. B. Christensen, K. Norgaard, G. Freckmann, and L. del Re, "Feasibility of fully closed loop insulin delivery in type 2 diabetes," in *Proc. IEEE Conf. Control Technol. Appl. (CCTA)*, Hong Kong, Aug. 2019, pp. 906–913.

[54] P. Sever and M.-S. Niculescu, "Portable optical coagulation analyser based on real-time image processing algorithm," in *Proc. 11th Int. Symp. Adv. Topics Electr. Eng. (ATEE)*, Bucharest, Romania, Mar. 2019, pp. 1–6.

[55] T. Aledavood, J. Torous, A. M. T. Hoyos, J. A. Naslund, J.-P. Onnela, and M. Keshavan, "Smartphone-based tracking of sleep in depression, anxiety, and psychotic disorders," *Current Psychiatry Reports*, vol. 21, no. 7, Jul. 2019, doi: 10.1007/s11920-019-1043-y.

[56] H. S. Gauvin, J. Mertens, P. Mariën, P. Santens, B. A. Pickut, and R. J. Hartsuiker, "Verbal monitoring in Parkinson's disease: A comparison between internal and external monitoring," *PLoS One*, vol. 12, no. 8, Aug. 2017, Art. no. e0182159, doi: 10.1371/journal.pone.0182159.

[57] J. Jorge Rodrigues Barata, R. Munoz, R. D. De Carvalho Silva, J. J. P. C. Rodrigues, and V. Hugo C. De Albuquerque, "Internet of Things based on electronic and mobile health systems for blood glucose continuous monitoring and management," *IEEE Access*, vol. 7, 2019, pp. 175116–175125.

[58] The New European Interoperability Framework (EIF), 2017. Accessed: Oct. 25, 2020. [Online]. Available: https://ec.europa.eu/isa2/eif_en

[59] Interoperability for IoT Systems—Part 1: Framework, document ISO/IEC 21823 1:2019. [Online]. Available: www.iso.org/standard/71885.html

8 Proactive Security Approaches for IoT in Health Monitoring Applications

Saranga Mohan, Sunita Panda, Ambar Bajpai, and Manoj Tolani

8.1 INTRODUCTION

Healthcare systems across the world are facing hindrances, like aging population, skyrocketing healthcare expenses, and spiking cases of illness. We need to handle this by focusing more on utilizing technology to strengthen healthcare services and to enhance outcomes and by streamlined resource management. One of the milestones in healthcare applications is the merging of Internet of Things (IoT) (Rejeb et al., 2023) and wireless sensor networks (WSN). Latest developments in IoT and WSN have enabled real-time, continuous, and individual healthcare monitoring. IoT encompasses a group of devices that are enabled or connected with sensors, actuators, and connectivity features so that they can gather and share data via the internet. WSN are tiny sensor devices which can capture patients' health data and transmit this information to a central monitoring hub. Adding the features of IoT and WSNs in the healthcare domain (Haghi Kashani et al., 2021) enables remote patient monitoring, anomaly detection, and personalized healthcare support via continuous and non-invasive monitoring. Due to cost-effective methods and better outcomes, WSNs have gained tremendous popularity and acceptance in disparate healthcare facilities, including hospitals and home care although more optimizations need to be done in factors such as such as energy efficiency, data security, and interoperability for better alignment in healthcare. The applications of IoT/WSN technologies in the healthcare domain are vast and diversified and greatly affect the quality of patient care, medical research, and clinical management (Onasanya & Elshakankiri, 2021). These technologies enable remote patient monitoring through wearable sensors and smart devices tracking patient's vitals, adherence to medication, and progression of ailments in real time. Clinical workflows are optimized, and inventory management processes are automated through IoT/WSN systems, allowing for more efficient resource allocation and patient management, leading to greater patient satisfaction. The technologies supported by IoT/WSN facilitate independent aging by monitoring seniors' activities and detecting falls to provide timely assistance, thus allowing for a better quality of life and aging in place. Figure 8.1 shows the WSN/IoT integration in the real-time world. In inference, the areas of application of IoT/WSN solutions in health care are broad and encompass the entire spectrum from preventive care and remote monitoring to acute and chronic illness management; hence, they support the patient-centred and data-driven approach to care delivery.

The characteristics of IoT–WSN in healthcare monitoring represent the specific requirements and challenges associated with healthcare environments, mainly reliability, scalability, security, and interoperability. In this regard, high reliability is required to avoid false-positive and false-negative detection events, which would lead to patient safety risks. For instance, the reliability

DOI: 10.1201/9781003491910-8

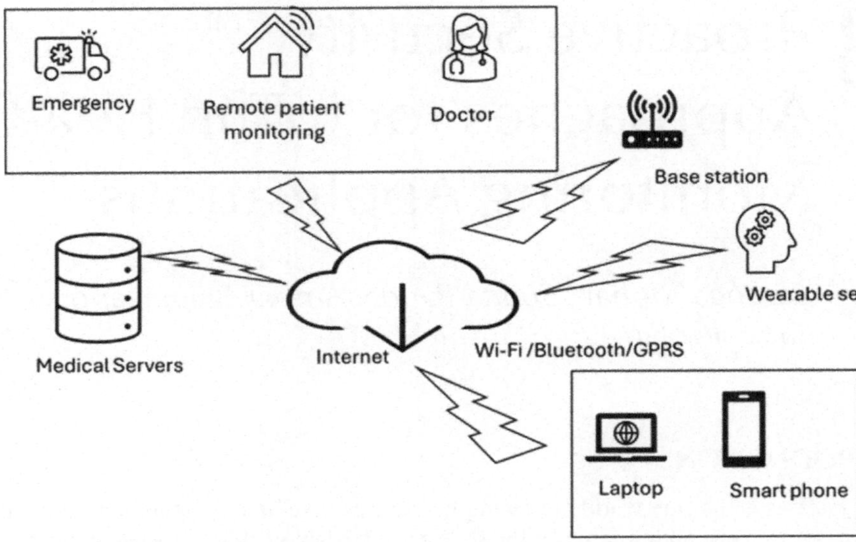

FIGURE 8.1 Real-time integration of WSN and IoT in healthcare domain.

of medical functioning components is very critical; otherwise, a patient would have a probability of being in danger if WSN makes an error. The second concept is interconnected with each other such that the growth of scalability leads to the enhancement of security. Security measures such as data encryption (Chandnani & Khairnar, 2022), access controls, and authentication procedures are crucial for protecting patient privacy and sensitive healthcare information from unauthorized access or breaches. For example, although IoT–WSN currently employs security encryption mechanisms, a patient could die if a hacking occurred since a nurse or doctor does not continuously monitor the patient.

Above all, interoperability standards and protocols ensure that IoT–WSN devices and networks, health systems, and electronic health record platforms can be seamlessly integrated and made interoperable, allowing data exchange and patient care to be continuous and coordinated among disparate systems and providers (Lata et al., 2021). By adhering to these characteristics, IoT–WSN technologies in health monitoring have a sender, which is the healthcare provider; a receiver, which is the patient; and the medium, which is IoT–WSN device or sensor and the message, which represents the transmitted health data to improve patient outcomes while ensuring data privacy, security, and interoperability.

8.2 APPLICATIONS OF IOT/WSN IN HEALTHCARE MONITORING

The use of IoT–WSN in healthcare monitoring has a range of applications from overseeing patients to managing hospital operations. Each application comes with its advantages and challenges. Remote patient monitoring is particularly noteworthy as it enables tracking of signs, medication adherence and disease progression outside traditional medical settings. Wearable devices with IoT–WSN technology allow patients to monitor their health metrics in time and share the data with healthcare providers aiding in the detection of issues, timely interventions, and personalized treatment plans. Additionally, IoT–WSN technologies play a role in improving workflows automating inventory management and optimizing resource allocation, within hospital settings. Smart hospital solutions use IoT–WSN-enabled devices and sensors to track the location of medical assets, monitor patient flow, and streamline operations, ultimately boosting operational efficiency, lowering costs, and increasing patient satisfaction (Ghubaish et al., 2021)

However, there has been a significant security problem raised by the widespread usage of IoT–WSN in the healthcare domain to conserve patient privacy and sensitive healthcare data (Yadav et al., 2021). The exposure of IoT–WSN device data includes insufficient authentication, improper encryption, more prone to malware attacks, and data breaches. To lessen these security threats, healthcare organizations must establish adequate safety precautions such as frequent security audits, intrusion detection systems (Abedini & Al-Anbagi, 2024), access controls, encryption methods, etc. to ensure the confidentiality, integrity, and availability of healthcare data in IoT/WSN-enabled environments.

8.3 BACKGROUND AND RELATED RESEARCH

8.3.1 Relevant Studies in IoT and WSNs Healthcare Applications

The integration of IoT and WSN contributed to a lot of advancements in the healthcare domain, especially for remote real-time patient monitoring, personalized care, and other patient outcomes. This also leads to a lot of security challenges and vulnerabilities that require meticulous checking and scrutiny, especially for patient data privacy and system integrity. Data privacy is the most important parameter in health care applications to ensure confidentiality and protection in preserving the patient sensitive health information from unauthorized access. Authentication methods confirm the identities of individuals and devices that log into healthcare platforms deterring access and protecting against threats, from malicious individuals. Also, encryption techniques can be used to secure data transmission and storage using some unreadable ciphertext and decrypted using appropriate decryption methods. In healthcare networks, access control mechanisms manage user permissions and privileges by limiting entry to information according to roles and credentials. Intrusion detection systems keep a watch on network traffic with system operations swiftly identifying and addressing security threats or unusual activities. This is very important in healthcare applications which leads to the reliability, resilience, and trustworthiness of IoT/WSN enabled ecosystem (Kharroub et al., 2020).

Gunasekaran (2023) proposed a solution called monitored access constraint security (MACS) to address the security concerns in WSN and IoT. By expanding the capabilities of the platform to include WSN nodes, MACS guarantees data privacy by monitoring node interactions and holding nodes accountable, for adjusting data aggregation levels. An assessment that factors in node accountability and information retrieval attributes showcases security protocols, resulting in reduced security breaches and improved performance indicators, like aggregation loss, latency, error rate, throughput, and validation time. Quincozes et al. (2023) presented a machine learning technique for identifying denial of services (DoS) attacks in WSN networks by evaluating both supervised and unsupervised ML techniques on a public WSN data set. This study reveals that supervised learning methods achieved the highest F1 score for detecting attacks in WSN than unsupervised learning techniques highlighting the appropriate selection of ML methods.

A. Ali et al. (2022) introduced a search-enabled blockchain system based on deep learning utilizing homomorphic encryption to boost security and allow users to access patient health records (PHR) stored in a decentralized database securely. By integrating revocation and update strategies, the research seeks to rectify current vulnerabilities in healthcare systems based on blockchain. It encompasses a test using a dataset to exhibit security, privacy and monitoring user behaviour, which spotlights the matching of the above method in comparison to rest of the models. Chawla and Mehra (2023) put forward the quantum-based secure cryptosystem using mutual authentication for healthcare (QSMAH) protocol, leveraging mutual authentication and quantum cryptography to tackle the problems originating from quantum computing model. By using quantum entanglement and teleportation (QET) protocol for transfer of data, this protocol provides an innovative solution to safeguard the data privacy of patient in IoT-enabled healthcare systems. Amer et al. (2023 proposed a method that leverages intelligent surfaces (RISs) to improve the safeguarding of WSNs by diminishing the opportunities of eavesdropping. This method optimizes the secrecy rate by sensor schedule combination, RIS phase shifts and jamming power and showcases the effectiveness of improving security in WSN.

Li et al. (2023) put forward a unique detection scheme adding a deep belief network (DBN) and density-based spatial clustering of applications with noise (DBSCAN) to solve selective forwarding attacks in event-driven networks of WSN. By using the DBN for behaviour feature extraction and analysis, alongside DBSCAN for effective node classification, the scheme gains the best results, ensuring robust data transmission integrity and efficiency in harsh network environments. Abedini and Al-Anbagi (2022) proposed a novel active eavesdroppers detection (AED) system for addressing the challenges that can occur due to the broadcasting feature of wireless channels. By utilizing a unmanned aerial vehicle (UAV)-assisted monitoring system and leveraging Z test algorithm, the proposed model achieves good detection rates and low false-positive rates which help to treat eavesdrops threats in WSN environments. Elsadig (2023) suggested a method to address the denial of service (DoS) attacks by proposing a machine learning method using a decision tree algorithm with Gini feature selection technique which could achieve a good accuracy rate compared to other existing machine learning approaches. Ramasamy et al. (2022) put forward a novel method to address the security challenge and to enhance the data privacy in a reconfigurable wireless sensor network by eliminating duplicate packets using hashing distance computation (HDC) and a power-efficient trust-based routing scheme named cell-by-cell golden sector-based emperor penguin colony technique. A reading-based dual validation (RbDV) is also proposed for intrusion detection by isolating suspicious nodes which ensures data privacy and hence improves the confidentiality and node reconfiguration capabilities.

8.3.2 Securing Healthcare IoT/WSN: Essentials and Risks

Security plays a major role in health monitoring systems because of the nature of the data involved and the potential risks associated with unauthorized access or malicious attacks and its critical to maintain patients' health data. The growing use of IoT technologies like devices, smart sensors and remote monitoring platforms is a wake-up call to implement foolproof security measures. Major implications such as device hacking, theft of personal identities, and data breaches can cause faulty diagnosis, adverse publicity, and legal consequences of both patients and healthcare professionals. Hence it is imminent to implement role-based access control, authentication, and authorization for handling the data.

Below are the excerpts from various studies done on security and healthcare applications. Batista et al. (2021) investigated the security challenges of wearing health-tracking devices and suggested encryption in transit. Similarly, research conducted by Kocher and Kumar (2021) concentrated on enhancing the security in sensor networks for health monitoring applications through machine learning models to detect intrusions. P. Sharma et al. (2022) suggested the benefits of integrating blockchain technology and IoT to address the issues associated with centrally stored medical records in a cloud server. By proposing a framework named an identity-based encryption mechanism, the efficiency and security of the health care data to enhance the data sharing is improved when compared to other schemes.

To obtain secure health surveillance, several challenges with paramount concerns especially safety, accessibility, and authenticity of patient data regardless of technological advancements and security threats are very high. The major security assaults can be eavesdropping, denial of service (DoS) attacks and data manipulation. Many studies have given innovative solutions to these challenges, which include reliable routing protocols, malware detection systems, and encryption strategies devised specially for resource-limited WSN networks. A study by Ayub Khan et al. (2022) proposed a blockchain-based framework called BIoMT to ensure integrity, transparency, and security associated with health-related operations through the adoption of a blockchain hyperledger fabric platform. Leveraging the NuCypher re-encryption method, this framework preserves the individual transaction details and offers a consensus method to alleviate blockchain resource constraints.

Furthermore, the adoption of IoT technology for health surveillance brings many security concerns with secure communication protocols, data encryption and device authentication. Providing complete security and safety is very critical to safeguarding critical patient data and preserving credibility between the user and the provider. Figure 8.2 depicts the security challenges and vulnerabilities for secure healthcare systems. Many studies have been done to develop security measures for IoT health monitoring systems. A study by Sarosh et al. (2022) presented a scalable and adaptive architecture targeted to enhance the security of multimedia data sent via e-healthcare platforms. This model uses 3-D chaotic network systems and pixel diffusion methods to improve security which is ideal to use any AI-based healthcare applications. All these recent advancements in improving security and privacy in the healthcare domain further assist in alleviating the challenges of secure health monitoring.

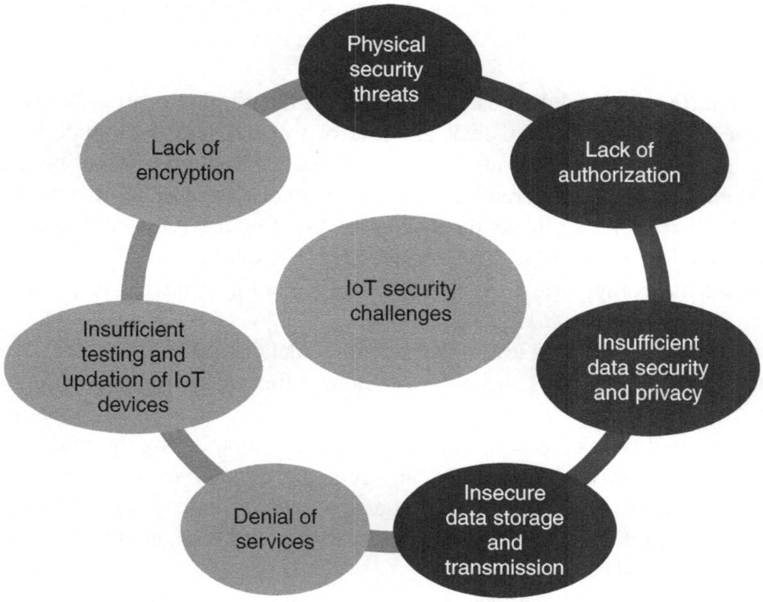

FIGURE 8.2 Security challenges for secure health care systems.

8.4 SECURING IOT/WSN: AUTHENTICATION MECHANISMS, BREACHES, AND ATTACKS

IoT is an expansive group of devices which includes sensors, embedded devices, RFID tags, actuators, and servers. Due to their limitations such as low processing power, limited energy conservation, and less storage capacity, they require specialized protocols and techniques. Health care data are so sensitive such as patients' treatment plans, diagnoses, and prescription drugs and it requires robust security and privacy to safeguard the information (Aslam et al., 2017). Security violations occurring in IoT deployments can lead to a loss in patients' faith, penalties from regulatory compliances and reputational impairment to the healthcare organizations. Hence its very essential to establish secure communication protocols to ensure the privacy, reliability and data legitimacy exchanged between IoT/WSN systems and the health domain. To ensure the quality of the authentication in IoT systems, strict safety and privacy standards must be met to be maintained (El Zouka & Hosni, 2021). Below are some of the essential requirements that must be met on the authentication protocols in an IoT environment.

Reliability: Role-based access control and authorization is imperative to access the private data of a patient.

Authentication: Authentication is required to confirm the identity and its legitimacy.

Untraceability: This ensures that malicious attacks cannot be traced back to the source of data or to the user or sensor node.

Anonymity: This ensures the identity of patients will be safeguarded and this is required for compliance.

Session key establishment: This is imperative for encryption and decryption of ongoing sessions between the user and the server.

8.4.1 Security Breaches in Authentication System

There exists a variety of attacks on authentication protocols in wireless medical sensor networks (WMSN) (Bahache et al., 2022). These are the disparate ways of security threats.

Man-in-the-middle attack: Malicious actors intercept the communication between source and destination and either they will leak the data or impersonate the source to get access to the destination systems (Salem et al., 2022). The adversary pretends to be a mediator and secretly even modifies the interaction messages between the user and the server.

DoS attack: Malicious actor attacks the system by flooding it with user requests and crashing the system making it unavailable for services (M. H. Ali et al., 2022). This attack typically consumes all the computation power and energy making it unable to process any further requests.

Replay attack: Malicious actors leverage intercepted data and use the authentication information in the data to get access to secured systems after eavesdropping on the transmission medium.

Impersonation attack: An adversary can gain access by intercepting the real identity of legitimate parties in communication. This can occur through server, user, or sensor impersonation in IoT settings. In a node capture attack, seizing a node grants the adversary insight into authentication protocols and access to cryptographic keys, enabling them to clone and deploy malicious nodes.

Desynchronization attack: This attack probably occurs on a system which shares confidential data especially secret keys and passwords before the method is completed. Here malicious agent alters the data and corrupts the system. Making wrong entities for operating the system will corrupt the system and result in a desynchronization security threat.

Stolen mobile attack: The attacker decrypts data in stolen mobiles and uses it to access systems.

Privileged insider attack: This will be an insider attack where an authorized person uses data for accessing and leaking sensitive information.

Stolen verifier attack: To reduce the risks, in most authentication schemes that rely on passwords, the authentication server stores the user's password verifier table rather than the actual passwords. In this attack, the adversary steals this table and then can impersonate a user.

Wormhole attack: This happens when malicious agents capture the traffic and tunnel to another adversary who will exploit the system.

Password guessing attack: Here the attacker tries to intercept the user's password. There are two common methods of password guessing: online guessing attacks and offline guessing attacks.

- *Online guessing attack*: The attacker predicts the user's password by interacting with the authentication system. This involves trying various permutations and combinations of passwords.
- *Offline guessing attack*: Attacker obtains the hashed password and use some decryption technique to crack this. Below are some of the major offline guessing attacks.
- *Dictionary attack*: In this method, the attacker uses the known passwords available and tries all combinations to crack it.
- *Brute force attack*: In this method, attacker tries all combinations by guessing the password. This will be time-consuming.
- *Rainbow table attack*: These are regenerated tables designed for cracking cryptographic cyphers. The attacker will feed the encrypted password to this and crack it.

To mitigate this, healthcare industry should institute the following measures:

- *Strong password policies*: mandate users to generate strong complex passwords.
- *Multifactor authentication*: This will be one time code sent to the mobile number after logging in with a password which adds another layer of security.
- *Account lockout*: Implement policies to lockout accounts after certain number of failed attempts.
- *Password encryption*: Enforce encryption at rest and transit for all data exchanges.

8.4.2 Classification of Authentication Schemes in IoT/WSN

Diverse authentication classification techniques were used by researchers to analyse the performance and assign them to a relevant category. Figure 8.3 highlights some of the potential categories used for the classification of authentication schemes.

8.4.2.1 Based on Authentication Schemes

In the healthcare sector, authentication mechanisms are very important in maintaining the integrity and safety of IoT and WSN deployments (Cheng et al., 2023). The three main categories taken into consideration are symmetric key authentication, asymmetric key authentication, and cryptographic-based authentication. Symmetric key authentication leverages a shared secret between source and destination for encryption and decryption while asymmetric encryption

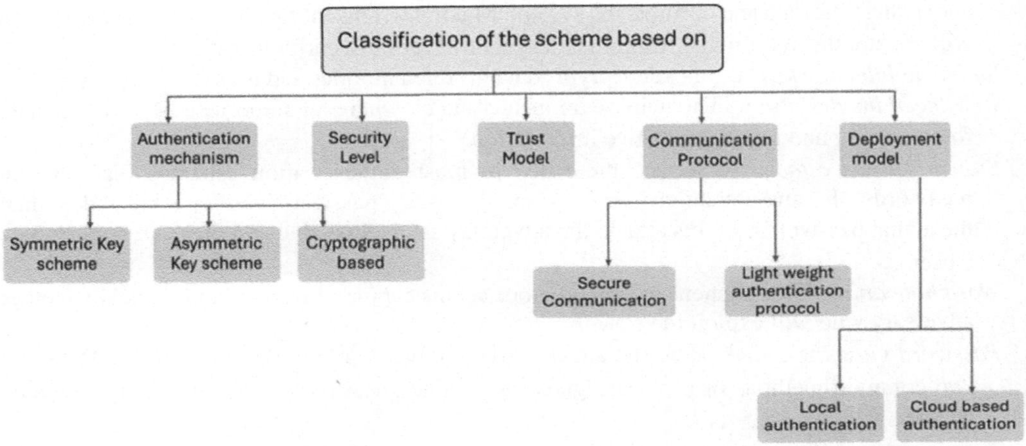

FIGURE 8.3 Classification of authentication schemes.

leverages public and private key for encryption and decryption. Encryption will happen with public key and decryption will happen via private key. The private key is secret and won't be shared. Cryptographic-based authentication (S. Sharma et al., 2021) involves the use of various cryptographic algorithms and ciphering techniques to verify the identity of communicating entities in a networked environment. This authentication method relies on cryptographic algorithms and keys to ensure secure communication and prevent unauthorized access.

8.4.2.2 Based on the Deployment Scenario

Local authentication occurs within the local network or device, typically using lightweight protocols suitable for resource-constrained IoT/WSN devices. Cloud-based authentication is performed through cloud services or centralized authentication servers, offering scalability and centralized management but potentially raising concerns about data privacy and latency.

8.4.2.3 Based on Communication Protocol

- *Secure Communication Protocols*: Authentication schemes integrated with secure communication protocols such as TLS/SSL, IPSec, or DTLS to establish secure channels for data transmission.
- *Lightweight Authentication Protocols*: Designed specifically for resource-constrained IoT/WSN devices, utilizing lightweight cryptographic primitives and protocols to minimize computational overhead and energy consumption.

By categorizing authentication schemes based on these criteria, stakeholders in the healthcare domain can better evaluate and select appropriate authentication mechanisms to ensure the security and integrity of IoT/WSN deployments in healthcare settings.

8.5 CASE STUDY: SAFEGUARDING MEDICAL IOT INFRASTRUCTURE VIA AWS GUARD DUTY

Let's us consider "X" healthcare is a major medical service provider which monitors the vital health data of patients leveraging IoT and AWS. Due to its dependency on IoT and cloud to gather and process this data, it's imperative to secure the data and to be compliant with various standards. "X" Healthcare utilizes AWS services to manage its IoT infrastructure, including AWS IoT Core for device management and AWS GuardDuty (Bedoya et al., 2023) for threat detection. All the data from the remote is sent to AWS for processing and actionable insights.

8.5.1 Use of AWS GuardDuty

Threat Detection: GuardDuty proactively and reactively checks the threads in data transmitted via AWS flow logs and cloud watch logs. GuardDuty identifies insider threats by behaviour patterns of users and checks with role-based access control, helping "X" Healthcare detect and solve unchecked access.

Malicious Access Detection: GuardDuty checks for unauthorized authentications, anomalous API calls, and vague network behaviour that may indicate a malicious IoT device or unchecked access to secret data.

8.5.2 Case Study Implementation

"X" Healthcare deploys AWS GuardDuty across its AWS environment coupled with AWS IoT core. It monitors AWS flow logs, and CloudWatch logs and alerts the security personnel via simple notification service (SNS) in case of emergency. Once the alert is triggered, the security personnel will check the details and block the malicious traffic. Based on the recent alerts and findings the security team of "X" healthcare keeps improving the posture and rectifying any defect in the infrastructure design. Figure 8.4 shows the block diagram implementation of securing AWS IoT network using AWS GuardDuty.

8.5.3 Results

By depending on AWS GuardDuty to protect its medical IoT infrastructure, "X" Healthcare gains the following results:

GuardDuty can provide the count of findings based on the severity of issues identified as shown in Figure 8.5. This can be categorized as high, medium, and low. High-severity alerts should be taken maximum priority. GuardDuty categorizes this alert based on the inbuilt information about the severities.

This also gives the nature of severities such as runtime/new binary executed, runtime/suspicious command as depicted in Figure 8.6. GuardDuty alerts suspicious traffic originating from instances and clusters of application by monitoring the flow logs.

GuardDuty provides the complete summary of all severities and resources as shown in Figure 8.7. This also provides the details of the AWS accounts where these instances belong.

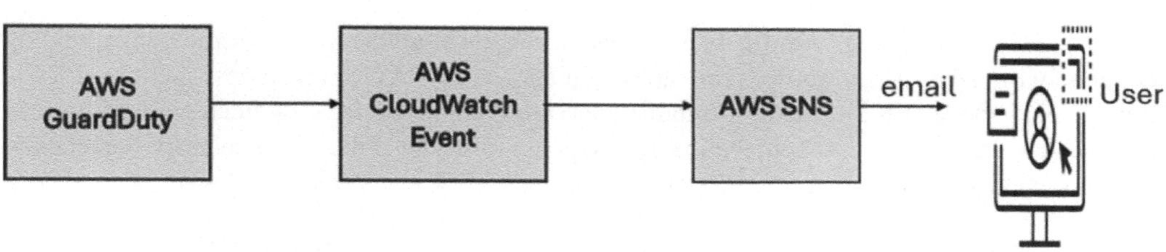

FIGURE 8.4 Securing AWS IoT network using AWS GuardDuty.

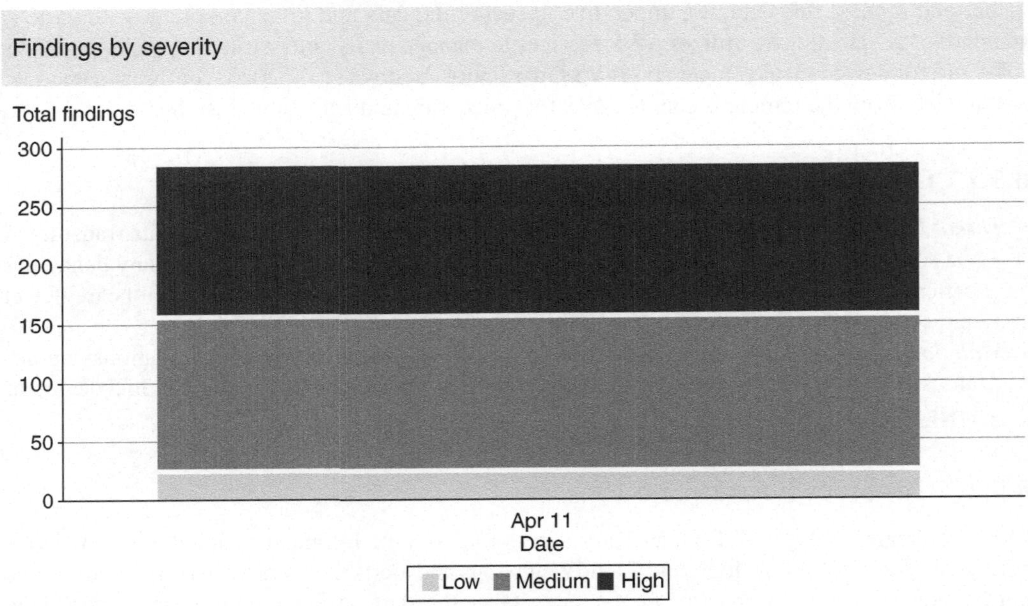

FIGURE 8.5 Severity detection by AWS GuardDuty.

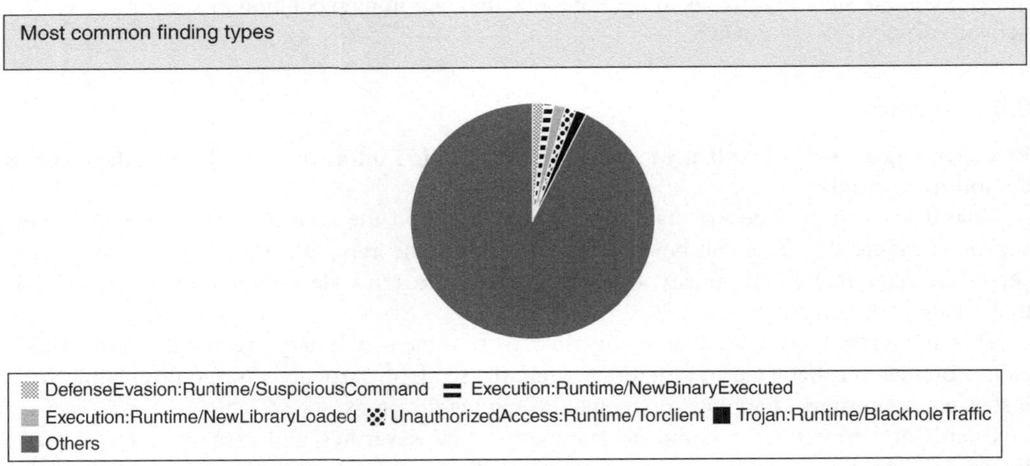

FIGURE 8.6 Severity types of distribution.

Figure 8.8 explains how GuardDuty provides the details of all the instances and corresponding accounts with suspicious traffic. The above image shows AWS resources such as Elastic Kubernetes Service (EKS), Elastic Container Service (ECS) clusters. The healthcare sector can leverage AWS GuardDuty to achieve the below goals to detect threats and security breaches to maintain integrity, reliability and confidence.

- GuardDuty enables real-time visibility and proactive alerting of threats.
- GuardDuty helps "X" Healthcare to be compliant with healthcare global standards.

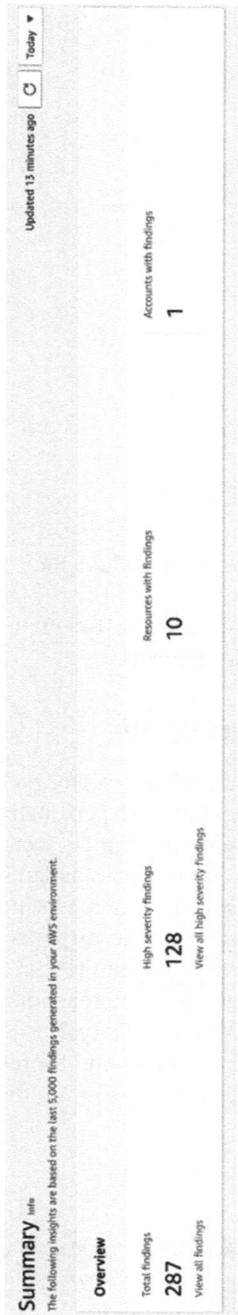

FIGURE 8.7 Summary of severities.

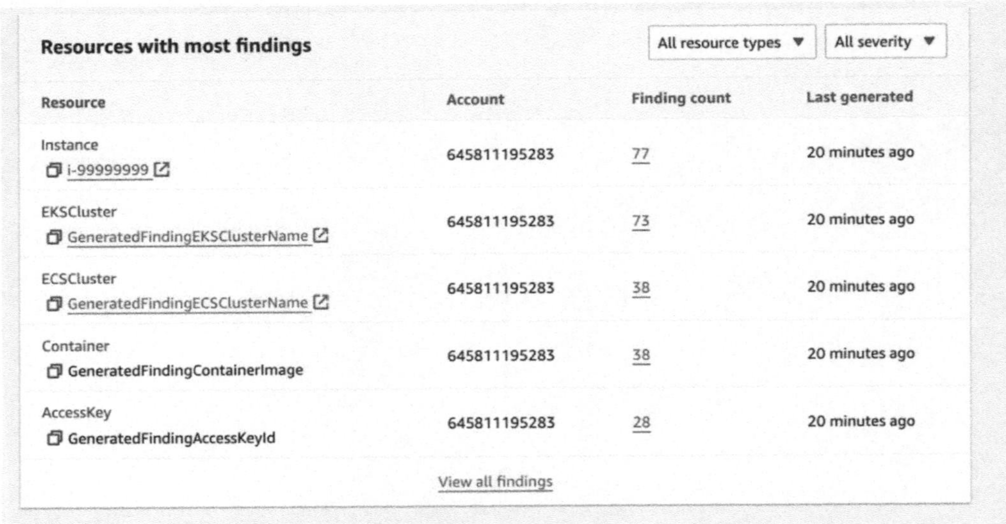

FIGURE 8.8 Instances causing the severity threats.

- "X" Healthcare leverages guard duty and reduce the chances of malicious attacks or data breaches.
- GuardDuty improves operational efficiency by improving security posture and hence reduces cost of demanding security incidents.

8.6 CONCLUSION AND FUTURE SCOPE

The integration of WSN and IoT in the healthcare sector promises an immense amount of real-time data gathering, remote patient tracking, and personalized healthcare services. Malicious threats in the health care industry present challenging scenarios and this must be rectified to maintain the integrity of data and ensure compliance standards. Our chapter covers a wide variety of security approaches for IoT in health care applications which is useful in medical domain. The developing landscape of healthcare industry presents disparate challenges ranging from unauthorized access to data breach. This chapter focuses on the vital significance of mitigating security and privacy concerns in medical applications, comprehending and lessening security threats by adopting innovative technologies like AWS GuardDuty. Hence, it's imminent for the stakeholders to understand these ever-evolving nature of threats and form strategies to rectify and proactively prevent all threats. This can be further enhanced in future by leveraging Machine learning capabilities like anomaly detection.

REFERENCES

Abedini, M., & Al-Anbagi, I. (2022). Active Eavesdroppers Detection System in Multi-hop Wireless Sensor Networks. *Proceedings – IEEE Symposium on Computers and Communications, 2022-June*, 1–6. https://doi.org/10.1109/ISCC55528.2022.9912466

Abedini, M., & Al-Anbagi, I. (2024). Enhanced Active Eavesdroppers Detection System for Multihop WSNs in Tactical IoT Applications. *IEEE Internet of Things Journal*, *11*(4), 6748–6760. https://doi.org/10.1109/JIOT.2023.3313048

Ali, A., Pasha, M. F., Ali, J., Fang, O. H., Masud, M., Jurcut, A. D., & Alzain, M. A. (2022). Deep Learning Based Homomorphic Secure Search-Able Encryption for Keyword Search in Blockchain Healthcare System: A Novel Approach to Cryptography. *Sensors*, *22*(2), 528. https://doi.org/10.3390/s22020528

Ali, M. H., Jaber, M. M., Abd, S. K., Rehman, A., Awan, M. J., Damaševičius, R., & Bahaj, S. A. (2022). Threat Analysis and Distributed Denial of Service (DDoS) Attack Recognition in the Internet of Things (IoT). *Electronics (Switzerland)*, *11*(3). https://doi.org/10.3390/electronics11030494

Amer, A., Abd El-Samie, F. E., Salem, A. A., Shokair, M., & Benaya, A. M. (2023). Secure Transmission in Wireless Sensor Networks via Reconfigurable Intelligent Surface. *Digital Signal Processing: A Review Journal*, *140*, 104083. https://doi.org/10.1016/j.dsp.2023.104083

Aslam, M. U., Derhab, A., Saleem, K., Abbas, H., Orgun, M., Iqbal, W., & Aslam, B. (2017). A Survey of Authentication Schemes in Telecare Medicine Information Systems. *Journal of Medical Systems*, *41*(1). https://doi.org/10.1007/s10916-016-0658-3

Ayub Khan, A., Wagan, A. A., Laghari, A. A., Gilal, A. R., Aziz, I. A., & Talpur, B. A. (2022). BIoMT: A State-of-the-Art Consortium Serverless Network Architecture for Healthcare System Using Blockchain Smart Contracts. *IEEE Access*, *10*(August), 78887–78898. https://doi.org/10.1109/ACCESS.2022.3194195

Bahache, A. N., Chikouche, N., & Mezrag, F. (2022). Authentication Schemes for Healthcare Applications Using Wireless Medical Sensor Networks: A Survey. *SN Computer Science*, *3*(5), 1–25. https://doi.org/10.1007/s42979-022-01300-z

Batista, E., Angels Moncusi, M., López-Aguilar, P., Martínez-Ballesté, A., & Solanas, A. (2021). Sensors for context-aware smart healthcare: A security perspective. *Sensors*, *21*(20), 1–60. https://doi.org/10.3390/s21206886

Bedoya, M., Palacios, S., Diaz-López, D., Nespoli, P., Laverde, E., & Suárez, S. (2023). Securing cloud-based military systems with Security Chaos Engineering and Artificial Intelligence. *ACM International Conference Proceeding Series*. https://doi.org/10.1145/3600160.3605076

Chandnani, N., & Khairnar, C. N. (2022). An analysis of architecture, framework, security and challenging aspects for data aggregation and routing techniques in IoT WSNs. *Theoretical Computer Science*, *929*, 95–113. https://doi.org/10.1016/j.tcs.2022.06.032

Chawla, D., & Mehra, P. S. (2023). QSMAH: A novel quantum-based secure cryptosystem using mutual authentication for healthcare in the internet of things. *Internet of Things (Netherlands)*, *24*(September), 100949. https://doi.org/10.1016/j.iot.2023.100949

Cheng, Y., Liu, Y., Zhang, Z., & Li, Y. (2023). An Asymmetric Encryption-Based Key Distribution Method for Wireless Sensor Networks. *Sensors*, *23*(14). https://doi.org/10.3390/s23146460

El Zouka, H. A., & Hosni, M. M. (2021). Secure IoT Communications for Smart Healthcare Monitoring System. *Internet of Things (Netherlands)*, *13*, 100036. https://doi.org/10.1016/j.iot.2019.01.003

Elsadig, M. A. (2023). Detection of Denial-of-Service Attack in Wireless Sensor Networks: A Lightweight Machine Learning Approach. *IEEE Access*, *11*(August), 83537–83552. https://doi.org/10.1109/ACCESS.2023.3303113

Ghubaish, A., Salman, T., Zolanvari, M., Unal, D., Al-Ali, A., & Jain, R. (2021). Recent Advances in the Internet-of-Medical-Things (IoMT) Systems Security. *IEEE Internet of Things Journal*, *8*(11), 8707–8718. https://doi.org/10.1109/JIOT.2020.3045653

Gunasekaran, A. (2023). Internet of Things-based Wireless Sensor Networks for Monitoring Access Constraint Security Measures in Liable Data Aggregation. *International Journal of Communication Systems*, *36*(17), 1–19. https://doi.org/10.1002/dac.5596; https://onlinelibrary.wiley.com/doi/10.1002/dac.559

Haghi Kashani, M., Madanipour, M., Nikravan, M., Asghari, P., & Mahdipour, E. (2021). A Systematic Review of IoT in Healthcare: Applications, Techniques, and Trends. *Journal of Network and Computer Applications*, *192*(January), 103164. https://doi.org/10.1016/j.jnca.2021.103164

Kharroub, S. K., Abualsaud, K., & Guizani, M. (2020). Medical IoT: A Comprehensive Survey of Different Encryption and Security Techniques. *2020 International Wireless Communications and Mobile Computing, IWCMC 2020*, *0*, 1891–1896. https://doi.org/10.1109/IWCMC48107.2020.9148287

Kocher, G., & Kumar, G. (2021). Machine Learning and Deep Learning Methods for Intrusion Detection Systems: Recent Developments and Challenges. *Soft Computing*, *25*(15), 9731–9763. https://doi.org/10.1007/s00500-021-05893-0

Lata, S., Mehfuz, S., & Urooj, S. (2021). Secure and Reliable WSN for Internet of Things: Challenges and Enabling Technologies. *IEEE Access*, *9*, 161103–161128. https://doi.org/10.1109/ACCESS.2021.3131367

Li, Q., Ma, Y., & Wu, Y. (2023). Utilize DBN and DBSCAN to Detect Selective Forwarding Attacks in Event-driven Wireless Sensors Networks. *Engineering Applications of Artificial Intelligence*, *126*(PD), 107122. https://doi.org/10.1016/j.engappai.2023.107122

Onasanya, A., & Elshakankiri, M. (2021). Smart Integrated IoT Healthcare System for Cancer Care. *Wireless Networks*, *27*(6), 4297–4312. https://doi.org/10.1007/s11276-018-01932-1

Quincozes, S. E., Kazienko, J. F., & Quincozes, V. E. (2023). An Extended Evaluation on Machine Learning Techniques for Denial-of-Service Detection in Wireless Sensor Networks. *Internet of Things (Netherlands)*, *22*(August 2022), 100684. https://doi.org/10.1016/j.iot.2023.100684

Ramasamy, K., Anisi, M. H., & Jindal, A. (2022). E2DA: Energy Efficient Data Aggregation and End-to-End Security in 3D Reconfigurable WSN. *IEEE Transactions on Green Communications and Networking*, *6*(2), 787–798. https://doi.org/10.1109/TGCN.2021.3126786

Rejeb, A., Rejeb, K., Treiblmaier, H., Appolloni, A., Alghamdi, S., Alhasawi, Y., & Iranmanesh, M. (2023). The Internet of Things (IoT) in Healthcare: Taking Stock and Moving Forward. *Internet of Things (Netherlands)*, *22*(February), 100721. https://doi.org/10.1016/j.iot.2023.100721

Salem, O., Alsubhi, K., Shaafi, A., Gheryani, M., Mehaoua, A., & Boutaba, R. (2022). Man-in-the-Middle Attack Mitigation in Internet of Medical Things. *IEEE Transactions on Industrial Informatics*, *18*(3), 2053–2062. https://doi.org/10.1109/TII.2021.3089462

Sarosh, P., Parah, S. A., & Bhat, G. M. (2022). An Efficient Image Encryption Scheme for Healthcare Applications. *Multimedia Tools and Applications*, *81*(5), 7253–7270. https://doi.org/10.1007/s11042-021-11812-0

Sharma, P., Moparthi, N. R., Namasudra, S., Shanmuganathan, V., & Hsu, C. H. (2022). Blockchain-based IoT Architecture to Secure Healthcare System Using Identity-based Encryption. *Expert Systems*, *39*(10), 1–19. https://onlinelibrary.wiley.com/doi/10.1111/exsy.12915

Sharma, S., Kaushik, B., Rahmani, M. K. I., & Ahmed, M. E. (2021). Cryptographic Solution-based Secure Elliptic Curve Cryptography Enabled Radio Frequency Identification Mutual Authentication Protocol for Internet of Vehicles. *IEEE Access*, *9*, 147114–147128. https://doi.org/10.1109/ACCESS.2021.3124209

Yadav, D. K., Mishra, P., Jayanthu, S., & Das, S. K. (2021). Fog-IoT-Based Slope Monitoring (FIoTSM) System with LoRa Communication in Open-Cast Mine. *IEEE Transactions on Instrumentation and Measurement*, *70*, 1–11. https://doi.org/10.1109/TIM.2021.3126018

9 CEIDS

Cost-Effective and Energy-Effective Intrusion Detection System in WSN

Ambika N

9.1 INTRODUCTION

Wireless sensor networks (Akyildiz, Sankarasubramaniam, & Cayirci, 2002; Nagaraj, 2022) are the assembly of tiny devices that collaborate to accomplish the task. These devices sense the environment and provide the same to the pre-defined locations. The assembly is used in many applications including smart homes (Zhang, Song, Wang, & Meng, 2011), military surveillance (Lee, Lee, Song, & Lee, 2009), and habitat monitoring (Mainwaring, Culler, Polastre, Szewczyk, & Anderson, 2002). These devices come together to accomplish the task.

These devices are unsupervised hence they are liable to get compromised. The compromised nodes or adversary can launch different kinds of attacks into the network. Some of the attacks the network has to tackle include denial-of-service (DoS) attacks (Wood & Stankovic, 2002), sinkhole attack (Krontiris, Giannetsos, & Dimitriou, 2008; Le Fessant, Papadimitriou, Viana, Sengul, & Palomar, 2012), Sybil attack (Mian Ahmad Jan, 2015), and wormhole attack (Bendjima & Feham, 2016; Ambika, 2020).

The sensors (Nagaraj, 2021) are tiny devices with low consumption power and liable to different kinds of attacks. Hence the assumptions made about the cluster head to possess unlimited energy and not liable to get compromised can increase the cost of the network setup. The more the number of clusters, the cost will increase. Hence apart from isolating the compromised node (Ambika & Raju, 2014), other limitations have to be considered. The proposed work will focus on these parameters to enable energy-effective and cost-effective working of the sensors.

DoS attack aims to diminish the capacity of the network. Many factors like hardware failures (Thibeault, 2012), software bugs (Li & Regehr, 2010), exhaustion of resources (Vaidyanathan & Trivedi, 1999) and the network conditions can provide the adversary to take over the system. The attack is launched in many ways:

- *Physical layer:* Introducing a jamming attack (Grover, 2014; Babar, 2013) in the network is another way to make the DoS attack successful. If the adversaries are permanently able to jam the routes, the nodes will not be able to transmit the data to the destination or another set of nodes to the other side.
- *Datalink layer*: The collision of packets (Reindl, Nygard, & Du, 2010) may lead to data loss. The packets are requested to be transmitted again by the receiver. The continuous collision leads to exhaustion and hence the DoS attack becomes successful.
- *Network layer*: The attack can drop the packets (Lee, 2014) randomly or on an arbitrary basis leading to a DoS attack. Homing attacks (Zheng, Han, Xu, & Qi, 2010) is one of the attacks

DOI: 10.1201/9781003491910-9

launched by the compromised nodes. In this kind of attack, the passive opponent supervises the traffic to discover critical resources. The attack can misdirect the packets using fabricated route advertisements. Black holes (Al-shurman, Yoo, & Park, 2004) are the attacks launched by the adversary by transmitting zero- cost routes to every other node of the network.

- *Transport layer*: The compromised node can utilize flooding methodology (Braga, de Souza Mota, & Passito, 2010) to drain the resources and delaying the legitimate packets reaching the destination. Desynchronization (Li & Chen, 2003) is another methodology where the adversary replays the forged packets.

The proposed work provides a cost- and energy-effective methodology compared to Jinhui et al. (2018). The detailing of the background used in the proposal is provided in Section 9.2. This is followed by an explanation of various suggestions provided by the authors in Section 9.3. The proposed work is suggested in Section 9.4 followed by simulation in NS2 in Section 9.5. The future scope of the work is discussed in Section 9.6 and the work is concluded in Section 9.7.

9.2 BACKGROUND

The proposal suggests minimizing the DoS attack in the environment. The methodology suggested is cost-effective and energy-effective compared to the previous work. This section describes using different methodologies suggested by the various authors in the work.

The remaining energy (Saha & Chaki, 2012) is calculated using Equations (9.1) and (9.2). In Equation (9.1), E_r is the energy consumed calculated using energy consumed in transmitting or receiving packets E_c, m is the number of bits the message has, amplifier parameter ε_{fs} and distance d:

$$E_r \rightarrow \{(E_c * m + s_{fs} * m * d^2) + (E_c * m)\} \tag{9.1}$$

In Equation (9.2), remaining energy E_{rem} is calculated using the parameters of initial energy E_{init} and energy consumed E_r:

$$E_{rem} \rightarrow E_{init} - E_r \tag{9.2}$$

The distance between two peers (Gunther & Hoene, 2005) can be calculated by sending a packet to the peer and receiving the acknowledgment for the same. The propagation time is estimated. In Equation (9.3), the distance d between two devices is calculated using P_t (the propagation time). d_{im} is the time taken to receive the packets where the transmitter immediately acknowledges and d_l is the time taken to receive the packets after a certain delay.

$$\frac{d \rightarrow (d_{im} - d_l) * P_t}{2} \tag{9.3}$$

9.3 LITERATURE SURVEY

A DoS attack is introduced into the system using different methodologies where the legitimate nodes are hindered to transmit their packets. The following section details many suggestions proposed by various authors to minimize the attack occurrence.

In Jinhui et al. (2018), a suggestion to tackle DoS attack (Kasinathan, 2013; Toledo, 2008) is proposed. The cluster-based approach was adopted in that work. The cluster head is considered to have a large amount of energy and is always in close vicinity with its cluster members. It is capable of handling malicious attacks. The proposed work records the residual energy at different points of time. Using the Pearson correlation coefficient, the power sequence and reference power is analyzed. The node is suspected to be guilty when the linear correlation is weak. The nodes send the information using three tuple-forms to the respective cluster heads. The three parameters include the identity of the node, its position, and energy consumption in the work cycle. The cluster head after receiving the data from its cluster members cross-verifies the same. The identity of the node and its position is verified. If the information is accurate, the cluster head deletes the same. If the information turns to be not accurate, the cluster head triggers an alert. The energy is verified using the prediction formula. The cluster head also calculates the trust value of each node based on the history of the cluster member doings.

Path-based DoS attack is addressed in Deng, Han, & Mishra (2005). The suggested work is lightweight and flexible. The system can easily undergo bootstrapping without any hindrance. The work is scalable to one-way communication against this kind of attack. The system guarantees reliable end-to-end transmission between the source and the destination. The proposed work filters the bogus packets at an earlier stage. The work contains a small overhead to complete the security methodology. The algorithm chooses a parent if the node has multiple parents to transmit its packet. The one-way hash chain is adopted in the work. The adopted methodology aids in minimizing the DoS attack. The sender affixes the hash packet to the data it is transmitting, which is verified by various intermediate nodes. The destination drops the packet if the received packet is not verified. The methodology tolerates packet loss and the node is provided the flexibility to transmit the data at any instance without the need for synchronization.

Using digital signatures in broadcasting aids in authenticating the transmitted messages. The bogus packets can be broadcast affixed with digital signatures by the adversaries. An effective methodology is suggested in Du, Guizani, Xiao, and Chen (2008) to make the broadcasting methodology more secure. The methodology suggests adding a pre-authenticator in the broadcasted packets. The nodes after receiving the packets examine the pre-authenticator followed by an analysis of digital signature. One-way key chain with the sender-id is used in the methodology to secure broadcasting.

The physical layer DoS attack is examined and Muraleedharam and Osadciw (2006) suggest a solution for the same. The nodes in the network do not contain any cluster heads to authenticate them. The four parameters—arbitrary parameter, trail memory, intensity utilized and the intensity with respect to distance—are used in the proposal. The parameters used in the methodology control the performance of the system. The distance between the nodes deployed is calculated using Euclidean distance (Danielsson, 1980). The transmitted packets are initialized and assigned some maximum value. The ant agent's methodology (Ostfeld, 2011) is applied to the packets to move from source to the destination. The transition probability is calculated using the pheromone deposition and tabu list. The link budget is estimated using the Bluetooth protocol (Miller & Bisdikian, 2001). If the packet is not able to reach the destination as estimated, jamming is suspected and appropriate action is initiated.

The Bayesian game formulation is used to isolate illegitimate nodes from the network in Mohi, Movaghar, and Zadeh (2009). The methodology considers the nodes in the network as a two-player game. The cluster head makes the intrusion detection system (IDS) agent (Agah, Das, S. K., & Asadi., 2004; Brutch & Ko, 2003; Jinhui et al., 2018) and the cluster members play the second role. The game has two strategies. The IDS is responsible to identify the members of the clusters as legitimate or not. If the IDS happens to find the member to be illegitimate, it decreases the reputation of the guilty. The guilty are again categorized into two: the cooperative category is where the illegitimate node replays the packets. On confirmation, the illegitimate node loses points and the IDS gains points. If the IDS agent is unable to detect the guilty, it loses points and the illegitimate node gains points. This stage does not cooperate or miss the stage. Even in case of wrong detections, IDS loses points.

The message specific puzzle is suggested in Ning, Liu, and Du (2008) to minimize the DoS attack in the network. The proposal proves to provide security even in the case of the weak authenticator. The authenticator cannot be identified without the non-reusable key. They are used as additional protection. The authentication methodology is independent of the broadcast methodology. The Strawman approach (Opitz & Shavlik, 1995) is used in the work. One-way key chains are generated. The transmitter chooses a random value and generates the hash function continually using the same. This procedure aids in generating the key chain. The sender broadcasts the commitment key to all the nodes before broadcasting the packets. The transmitted message contains the index, message, broadcast authenticator and the weak authenticator. The receiver verifies the packet against the weak authenticator. On mismatch, it discards the packet.

A game-based methodology is suggested in Agah and Das (2007) to minimize the DoS attack in the network. The IDS aid in protecting the system by monitoring the surrounding events. They examine the nodes for any security issues. The interaction between a legitimate and non-legitimate node is analyzed during forwarding of the packets. The nodes are rewarded for their acts. The non-cooperative nodes are punished for their deeds. The points scored to make them eligible for the resources.

Tan, Ostry, Zic, and Jha (2013) address both signature-based and request-based DoS attack. The proposal suggests a mathematical model. The model verifies the number of code updates the promoter has to accept. The count is dependent on the number of nodes deployed in the network. This methodology aids in minimizing the occurrence of DoS attack. The weak authenticator is verified in the received message followed by the digital signature. The committed value used to generate the hash keys are preloaded into the devices. The hash function is generated by the base station utilizing a public function. The keys generated are used for encryption. The length of the keys generated is directly proportional to the program updates or sometimes more than that.

A one-hash chain is proposed in Deng, Hang, and Mishra (2006) to protect the data from path-based DoS attacks. A random number is chosen and the same is applied to the function to generate a sequence of keys. Every node in the network maintains a unique key chain. The base station receives a packet containing the sequence number. The intermediate nodes endorse their verification to the forwarded message. The old chain sequence is discarded after use. The guilty will not be able to generate the chain either will be able to replay the old chain. The methodology takes care of computational cost and tolerates packet losses.

The code is transmitted in the DoS attack environment securely (Hyun, Ning, Liu, & Du, 2008). The paper is an extension of Deluge (Hui & Culler, 2004). The system resists the DoS attack against signature, code distribution, and maintenance packets. The proposal distributes the new code images. The packet transmitted contains hash images and code distribution data items. An immediate authentication of the received packets is provided. The system utilizes a signature to the bootstrap validation procedure. This methodology adapts forward-secrecy.

9.4 PROPOSED WORK

9.4.1 ASSUMPTIONS

- All the nodes are liable to get compromised.
- The base station is a reliable source. It is the responsibility of the base station to embed key credentials into the nodes before deployment.

- The sensors are capable of generating the hash code using the position parameters. The sensors will be able to estimate its position accurately and the neighbor position approximately using the packet round-trip time.

9.4.2 Formation of the Cluster

All the notations are added in Table 9.1. After the deployment the node, self-configure and broadcast hello messages to build the cluster. In the notation (9.4), the node N_i is broadcasting hello message to the network N:

$$N_i \rightarrow Hello\text{: } N \tag{9.4}$$

The nodes within the communication range r reply with an acknowledgment. In the notation (9.5), the node N_j is acknowledging Ack to the broadcast message along with its identification ID_j.

$$N_j \rightarrow \text{Ack ID}_j\text{: } N_i \tag{9.5}$$

The cluster head is chosen based on the trust rating given by the neighboring nodes. In the first round, the cluster head is chosen randomly.

9.4.3 Gathering the Information

The members forward the processed sensed data to the cluster head. They affix the identification, hash code of the position to the message. In Equation (9.6), the cluster member N_i is forwarding its data D_i affixing ID_i and hash code HC_i to the cluster head CH_i.

$$N_i \rightarrow D_i\,\text{ID}_i\,\text{HC}_i\text{:CH}_i \tag{9.6}$$

9.4.4 Role of the Cluster Head

The cluster head is responsible for collecting the data from all the cluster members and forward the same to the next available hop. After the cluster head is chosen, it has to transmit the id's,

TABLE 9.1
Description of the Notations Used in the Proposed Work

Notations	Description
N	Network under study
CH_i	*i*th cluster of the network
N_i	*i*th node of the network
Hello	Hello message
Ack	Acknowledgment
HC_i	Hash code of *i*th node
ID_i	Identity of the *i*th node
r	Communication range/radius
D_i	Data of *i*th node
C	Count of packets

position of itself and other members, and count of packets transmitted by the previous cluster head in the encrypted form. In Equation (9.7), the cluster head CH_i is transmitting identities represented as Σ(ID), positions represented as Σ(P) and count of packets C to the next available hop CH_j:

$$CH_i \rightarrow \Sigma(ID)\ \Sigma(P)\ C\!: CH_j \quad (9.7)$$

9.4.5 Monitoring and Maintaining Information of the Peers

The cluster members monitor each other. They are responsible for providing trust ratings for the other members of the cluster. The energy is estimated for all the peers (Saha & Chaki, 2012). Distance (Gunther & Hoene, 2005) is calculated between two nodes. Table 9.2 provides the details of peer members maintained by the node of the cluster.

- *Cluster head election*: When the cluster head is to be chosen for a session, the nodes are to transmit their remaining energy. This value is cross-verified against the stored value. If the node is advertising false value, its trust rating is decremented by 1.
- *Dropping the packets*: If the cluster head or any other cluster member drops a legitimate packet, the trust rating is decremented by 1.
- *Completing the job cycle*: If the nodes complete their job cycle for the session, the trust rating is increased by 1. The cluster head is responsible for collecting the packets and forwarding the same to the next available hop. The cluster members are responsible for transmitting their sensed packets to the cluster head.
- *Inappropriate data provided by the cluster head:* The cluster head is to affix the estimated distance along with the id's of the cluster members in the encrypted form and dispatch the same to the base station. This data is matched with the hash code affixed with the data received. If there is a mismatch the trust rating is decreased by 1.
- *Affixing the count*: All the cluster heads are to transmit the total count of packets transmitted by the cluster. If the count does not match with the data transmitted, the base station sends an inquiry to the cluster. After receiving the acknowledgment from all the nodes, the base station makes its decision. The guilty's trust rating is decreased by 1.

9.5 SIMULATION

The work is simulated using NS2. Table 9.3 contains the parameters used in the simulation.

TABLE 9.2
List of Details Maintained by the Nodes

Node id	Calculated Position	No. of Packets Transmitted	No. of Packets Received	Estimated Energy Consumed by the Respective Node	Trust Rating
N_i	d_i	T_i	R_i	E_i	TR_i
N_j	d_j	T_j	R_j	E_j	TR_j
....	....	....	....	....	

TABLE 9.3
List of Parameters Used in the Simulation

Parameters Used	Description
Total area of surveillance considered	200m * 200m
Total number of nodes used in the study	44
Number of clusters formed	5 nodes * 6 groups + 7 nodes * 2 groups
Length of location information	64 bits
Length of hash code	16 bits
Length of identification	10 bits
Time of simulation	60ms

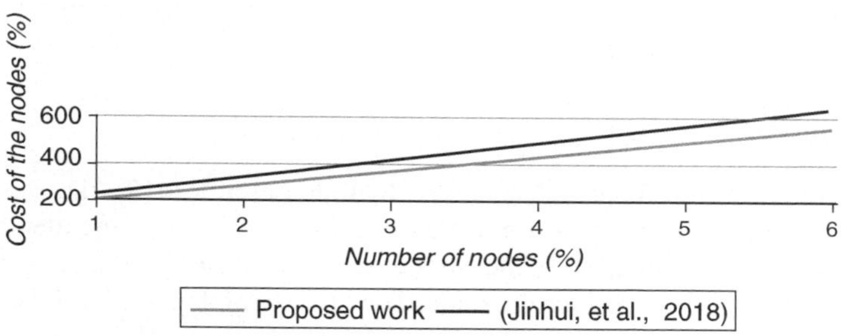

FIGURE 9.1 Comparison of the nodes used in both the work.

9.5.1 Energy Consumption

Energy is one of the limited resources in sensors. Hence the system adopts many methodologies to conserve energy. Some of them are as follows:

- *Cluster-based routing*: This methodology (Dasgupta & Namjoshi, 2003) aids in distributing the work among all the nodes. The cluster head is responsible for aggregating data from all the cluster members and transmits the same to the next available hop. Hence the head requires more amount of energy. In Jinhui et al. (2018), the cluster head is attack-resistant and has a lot of energy. One of the reasons for using sensors in abundant application is because they are cheaply available. The attack-resistant nodes will cost more compared to the regular ones. If the sensors have a lot of battery power, then also they are costly. The cost is 20 percent more compared to the proposal. The same is represented in Figure 9.1.

  As the role of the cluster head is circulated among the members of the cluster, the lifespan of the nodes is increased. The proposed system uses this methodology compared to Jinhui et al. (2018). The rotation of the role also increases security in the network.
- *Multi-hop routing*: The nodes usually consume energy in transmitting or receiving the data. This methodology (Isam & Hussain, n.d.) aids in conserving a large amount of energy.
- *Transmitting large amounts of data*: In Jinhui et al. (2018), the nodes transmit the identity of the node, its position, and energy consumption to the cluster head every time they transmit the packet. In the proposed work, the cluster members transmit only data every

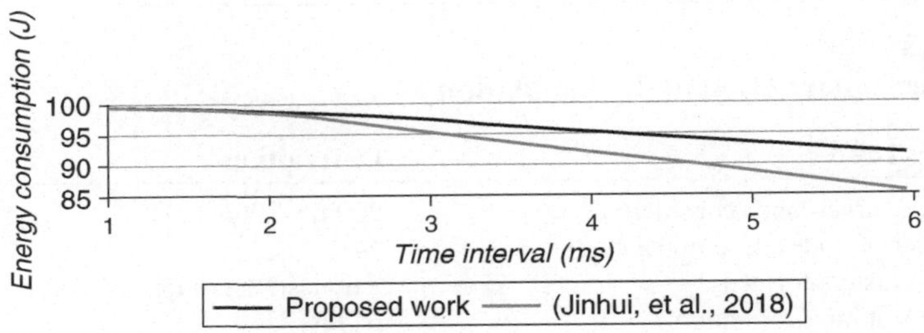

FIGURE 9.2 Comparison of energy consumption.

time. They transmit the hash code of the position only once to the respective cluster head. Hence energy consumption is less by 3.13 percent compared to Jinhui et al. (2018). The same is represented in Figure 9.2.

9.5.2 Security

Security is a priority in these kinds of networks. In Jinhui et al. (2018), the cluster head is the ultimate verifier. The cluster members are to transmit three parameters: the identity of the node, its position, and energy consumption in the work cycle. The cluster head after receiving the data from its cluster members cross-verifies the same. The identity of the node and its position is verified. If the information is accurate, the cluster head deletes the same. If the information turns out to be not accurate, the cluster head triggers an alert. The energy is verified using the prediction formula. The cluster head also calculates the trust value of each node based on the history of the cluster member doings.

In the proposed work, the role of the cluster head is rotated among cluster members. The head is chosen based on the trust rating. The members of the cluster monitor each other and alert in case of any suspicion. The energy and position of the respective node are not transmitted, rather it is calculated by the other member of the cluster and stored in its database. The base station is the final verifier of the position and hence any of the illegitimate nodes can be traced at an earlier stage. Hence the methodology aims at increasing security against DoS attack in addition to reducing cost and energy compared to Jinhui et al. (2018).

9.6 FUTURE SCOPE

The work uses only static nodes. Mobile nodes can be considered, which share some amount of tasks. The advantage of using mobile nodes is the energy consumption will not be an issue to consider. But these nodes are more liable to get compromised. Hence security has to be a matter of concern. The nodes are costly compared to static nodes but can be used reasonably.

9.7 CONCLUSION

Sensors are tiny low-cost devices utilized in innumerable applications. These devices come together to accomplish the task. As these devices are not supervised, they are liable to get compromised. The proposal aids in providing security by decreasing the cost by 20 percent and energy by 3.13 percent compared to the previous contribution. The algorithm is given in Table 9.4. The work is based on cluster-based routing, where the cluster head gathers the readings from the cluster members and forwards them to the next available hop. To minimize DoS attack in the network,

TABLE 9.4
Algorithm Used to Derive Hash Code

Step 1: Choose a random number between 4 and 8
Step 2: Divide the location information into random number of pieces
Step 3: For i=1 to n
    Separate even and odd pieces
Step 4: For i=1 to n (even and odd pieces separately) add the bits
step 5: if the number of bits in each group is less than 16 suffix 0 to the end
step 6: xor the even and odd group bits to obtain hash code

the work has adopted a methodology where the cluster members monitor each other and provide a trust rating for the same. Based on the trust rating and the remaining energy, the cluster head for the next session is chosen. If any of the acts of the nodes happen to violate the trust, an alert is raised. The base station cross-verifies the count of packets and position parameters provided.

REFERENCES

Agah, A., & Das, S. (2007). Preventing DoS attack in wireless sensor network: A repeated game theory approach. *International Journal of Network Security, 5*(2), 145–153.

Agah, A., Das, S. K., Basu, K., & Asadi., M. (2004). Intrusion detection in sensor networks: A non-cooperative game approach. *Third IEEE International Symposium on Network Computing and Applications* (pp. 343–346). Cambridge, MA: IEEE.

Akyildiz, F., I., Su, W., Sankarasubramaniam, Y., & Cayirci, E. (2002). Wireless sensor networks: a survey. *Computer Networks, 38*(4), 393–422.

Al-shurman, M., Yoo, S., & Park, S. (2004). Black hole attack in mobile adhoc network. *42nd Annual Southeast Regional Conference* (pp. 96–97). Huntsville, Alabama: ACM.

Ambika, N., & Raju, G. T. (2014). ECAWSN: eliminating compromised node with the help of auxiliary nodes in wireless sensor network. *International Journal of Security and Networks, 9*(2), 78–84.

Ambika, N. (2020). SYSLOC: Hybrid key generation in sensor network. In Singh, P. K., Bharat, K. B., Paprzycki, M., Kaushal, N. C., & Hong, W-C (eds), *Handbook of Wireless Sensor Networks: Issues and Challenges in Current Scenarios. Advances in Intelligent Systems and Computing* (Vol. 1132, pp. 325–347). Cham: Springer

Babar, S. D. (2013). Jamming attack: Behavioral modelling and analysis. *International Conference on Wireless Communications, Vehicular Technology, Information Theory and Aerospace and Electronic Systems (VITAE)* (pp. 1–5). IEEE.

Bendjima, M., & Feham, M. (2016). Wormhole attack detection in wireless sensor networks. *SAI Computing Conference (SAI), 2016.* London, UK.

Braga, R., de Souza Mota, E., & Passito, A. (2010). Lightweight DDos flooding attack detection using NOX/OpenFlow. *LCN, 10*, 408–415.

Brutch, P., & Ko, C. (2003). Challenges in intrusion detection for ad hoc networks. *IEEE Workshop on Security and Assurance in Ad hoc Networks.* Orlando, FL: IEEE.

Danielsson, P. E. (1980). Euclidean distance mapping. *Computer Graphics and Image Processing, 14*(3), 227–248.

Dasgupta, K. K., & Namjoshi, P. (2003). An efficient clustering-based heuristic for data gathering and aggregation in sensor networks. *2003 IEEE Wireless Communications and Networking, 2003. WCNC 2003.* New Orleans, LA, USA, 2003, pp. 1948–1953 vol. 3, doi: 10.1109/WCNC.2003.1200685.

Deng, J., Han, R., & Mishra, S. (2005). Defending against path-based DoS attacks in wireless sensor networks. *Workshop on Security of Ad Hoc and Sensor Networks.* (pp. 89–96). Alexandria, VA: ACM.

Deng, J., Hang, R., & Mishra, S. (2006). Limiting Dos attacks during multihop data delivery in wireless sensor network. *International Journal of Security and Networks, 1*(3–4), 167–178.

Du, X., Guizani, M., Xiao, Y., & Chen, H. (2008). Defending DoS attacks on broadcast authentication in wireless sensor network. *IEEE International Conference on Communications* (pp. 1653–1657). Beijing, China: IEEE.

Grover, K. L. (2014). Jamming and anti-jamming techniques in wireless networks: A survey. *International Journal of Ad hoc and Ubiquitous Computing*, 197–215.

Gunther, A., & Hoene, C. (2005). Measuring round trip times to determine the distance between WLAN nodes. *International Conference on Research in Networking* (pp. 768–779). Berlin: Springer.

Hui, J., & Culler, D. (2004). The dynamic behavior of data dissemination protocol for network programming at scale. *International Conference on Embedded Networked Sensor Systems* (pp. 81–94). Baltimore, MD: ACM.

Hyun, S., Ning, P., Liu, A., & Du, w. (2008). Seluge: secure and DoS-resistant code dissemination in wireless sensor network. *International Conference on Information Networks* (pp. 445–456). St. Louis, MO: IEEE.

Isam. O, & Hussain. S. (n.d.). An intelligent multi-hop routing for wireless sensor networks. *Proc. IEEE/WIC/ACM International Conference on Web Intelligence and Intelligent Agent Technology Workshops* (pp. 239–242).

Jinhui, X., Yang, T., Feiyue, Y., Leina, P., Juan, X., & Yao, H. (2018). Intrusion detection system for Hybrid DOS attacks using Energy trust in wireless sensor network. *8th International Congress of Information and Communication Technology (ICICT-2018)* (pp. 1188–1195). Elsevier.

Kasinathan, P. P. (2013). Denial-of-Service detection in 6LoWPAN based Internet of Things. *IEEE 9th International Conference on Wireless and Mobile Computing, Networking and Communications (WiMob)* (pp. 600–607). IEEE.

Krontiris, I., Giannetsos, T., & Dimitriou, T. (2008). Launching a sinkhole attack in wireless sensor networks; the intruder side. *IEEE International Conference on Wireless and Mobile Computing, Networking and Communications* (pp. 526–531). IEEE.

Le Fessant, F., Papadimitriou, A., Viana, A. C., Sengul, C., & Palomar, E. (2012). A sinkhole resilient protocol for wireless sensor networks: Performance and security analysis. *Computer Communications, 35*(2), 234–248.

Lee, H. (2014). Greedy data transportation scheme with hard packet deadlines for wireless ad hoc networks. *The Scientific World Journal, 1,* 815123. https://doi.org/10.1155/2014/815123; https://onlinelibrary.wiley.com/doi/abs/10.1155/2014/815123

Lee, S. H., Lee, S., Song, H., & Lee, H. S. (2009). Wireless sensor network design for tactical military applications: Remote largescale environments. *Proc. IEEE conference in Military Communications* (pp. 1–7). IEEE.

Li, P., & Regehr, J. (2010). T-check: bug finding for sensor networks. *9th ACM/IEEE International Conference on Information Processing in Sensor Networks* (pp. 174–185). Stockholm, Sweden: ACM.

Li, X., & Chen, G. (2003). Synchronization and desynchronization of complex dynamical networks: an engineering viewpoint. *IEEE Transactions on Circuits and Systems 1:Fundamental Theory and Applications, 50*(11), 1381–1390.

Mainwaring, A., Culler, D., Polastre, J., Szewczyk, R., & Anderson, J. (2002). Wireless sensor networks for habitat monitoring. *1st ACM international Workshop on Wireless Sensor Networks and Applications* (pp. 88–97). Atlanta, GA: ACM.

Mian Ahmad Jan, P. N. (2015). A Sybil attack detection scheme for a centralized clustering-based hierarchical network. *IEEE Trustcom/BigDataSE/ISPA*, (pp. 1–8). Helsinki, Finland.

Miller, B., & Bisdikian, C. (2001). *Bluetooth Revealed: The Insider's Guide to an Open Specification of Global Wireless Communication.* Prentice Hall.

Mohi, M., Movaghar, A., & Zadeh, P. (2009). A Bayesian game approach for preventing DoS Attack in wireless sensor network. *International Conference on Communications and Mobile Computing. 3*, pp. 507–511. Yunnan, China: IEEE.

Muraleedharam, R., & Osadciw, L. (2006). Jamming attack detection and countermeasures in wireless sensor network using ant system. *Wireless Sensing and Processing, 6248*, 624880G.

Nagaraj, A. (2021). *Introduction to Sensors in IoT and Cloud Computing Applications.* Bentham Science Publishers.

Nagaraj, A. (2022). Adapting blockchain for energy constrained IoT in healthcare environment. In K. Kaushik, S. Tayal, S. Dahiya, & A. O. Salau, *Sustainable and Advanced Applications of Blockchain in Smart Computational Technologies* (p. 103). CRC Press.

Ning, P., Liu, A., & Du, W. (2008). Mitigating Dos attacks against broadcast authentication in wireless sensor network. *ACM Transactions on Sensor Networks, 4*(1), 1.

Opitz, D., & Shavlik, J. (1995). Using heuristic search to expand knowledge-based neural network. *Computational Learning Theory and Natural Learning Systems, 3*, 3–19.

Ostfeld, A. (2011). *Ant colon optimization: methods and applications.* BoD-Books on Demand.

Reindl, P., Nygard, K., & Du, X. (2010). Defending Malicious Collision Attacks in Wireless Sensor Networks. *IEEE/IFIP International Conference on Embedded and Ubiquitous Computing* (pp. 771–776). Hong Kong, China: IEEE.

Saha, S., & Chaki, R. (2012). Weighted energy efficient cluster based routing for wireless sensor network. *IFIP International Conference on Computer Information Systems and Industrial Management* (pp. 361–373). Berlin: Springer.

Tan, H., Ostry, D., Zic, J., & Jha, S. (2013). A confidential and DoS-resistant multi-hop code dissemination Protocol for wireless sensor network. *Computers & Security, 32*, 36–55.

Thibeault, B. K. (2012). Patent No. 8,116,360. Washington, DC: U.S. Patent Office.

Toledo, A. L. (2008). Robust detection of MAC layer denial-of-service attacks in CSMA/CA wireless networks. *IEEE Transactions on Information Forensics and Security*, 347–358.

Vaidyanathan, K., & Trivedi, K. S. (1999). A measurement-based model for estimation of resource exhaustion in operational software systems. *10th International Symposium on Software Reliability Engineering* (pp. 84–93). Boca Raton, FL: IEEE.

Wood, A. D., & Stankovic, J. A. (2002). Denial of service in sensor networks. *Computer, 35*(10), 54–62.

Wormhole Attack Detection in Wireless Sensor Networks. (2016). *SAI Computing Conference 2016* (pp. 1319–1326). London, UK.

Zhang, J., Song, G., Wang, H., & Meng, T. (2011). Design of a wireless sensor network based monitoring system for home automation. *Proc. International Conference on Future Computer Sciences and Applications* (pp. 57–60).

Zheng, L., Han, Z., Xu, M., & Qi, J. (2010). Integrating mobility, multi-homing and security in universal network. *International Conference on E-health Networking Digital Ecosystems and Technologies* (pp. 252–255). Shenzhen, China: IEEE.

10 Mathematics and Queue Discipline

An Approach to Online Examination Data Security

Kala Raja Mohan, Sathish Kumar Kumaravel, R. Narmada Devi, and Regan Murugesan

10.1 INTRODUCTION

In today's digital age, online examinations have emerged as a pivotal component of modern education, offering numerous advantages in terms of accessibility, flexibility, and efficiency. Unlike traditional pen-and-paper exams, online examinations allow students to complete assessments remotely, at their own convenience, and often within a secure digital environment. This shift towards digital assessment methods has been catalysed by technological advancements and the evolving needs of learners and educators alike.

Online examinations play a crucial role in modern education by addressing the diverse needs and preferences of students and educators. They provide a flexible and accessible means of assessment, enabling students to demonstrate their knowledge and skills regardless of geographical location or time constraints. Moreover, online examinations facilitate efficient grading and feedback processes, allowing educators to assess student performance more rapidly and provide timely feedback for improvement.

However, the transition to online examinations also brings forth significant challenges, particularly in ensuring the security and integrity of examination data. The importance of data security in online examinations cannot be overstated, as the confidentiality, integrity, and availability of examination data are paramount for upholding the credibility and fairness of the assessment process. Without robust security measures in place, online examinations are vulnerable to various threats, including unauthorized access, data manipulation, and leakage of sensitive information.

Encryption and decryption play pivotal roles in ensuring the security of examination data in online assessment systems. Encryption involves the transformation of sensitive data into ciphertext using cryptographic algorithms, rendering it unreadable and unintelligible to unauthorized parties. Decryption, on the other hand, is the process of reverting ciphertext back to plaintext using decryption algorithms, thereby enabling authorized access to the data.

In the context of online examinations, encryption is employed to protect examination data during transmission and storage, safeguarding it from interception or unauthorized access. Decryption, on the other hand, allows authorized users, such as exam administrators and proctors, to access and retrieve examination data securely. By incorporating encryption and decryption mechanisms into online examination systems, educational institutions can enhance data security

 DOI: 10.1201/9781003491910-10

and mitigate the risk of security breaches, thereby preserving the integrity and confidentiality of examination data.

In summary, online examinations play a pivotal role in modern education, offering flexibility, accessibility, and efficiency in assessment processes. However, ensuring the security of examination data is essential to uphold the credibility and fairness of the assessment process. Encryption and decryption serve as key mechanisms for protecting examination data and mitigating security threats in online examination systems, thereby enabling educators to leverage the benefits of digital assessment methods while safeguarding the integrity and confidentiality of examination data.

10.2 LITERATURE SURVEY: DATA SECURITY IN ONLINE EXAMINATIONS

Online examinations have become increasingly prevalent in modern education, offering convenience and flexibility for both educators and students. However, ensuring the security and integrity of examination data is paramount to maintaining the credibility and fairness of the assessment process. A comprehensive literature survey reveals various approaches and techniques employed to enhance data security in online examinations.

Ashish Shedge et al. presented a discussion on education system based on online resources in 2024. Basil C.E Oguguo et al. in 2023 proposed a method for improvising the quality of the educational systems through examinations. George F. Fragulis et al. in 2021 made use of software tools in eradicating malpractice in the conduct of examinations. Ivan Trenchev in 2023 applied mathematical techniques in data security. Kala Raja Mohan et al. in 2022 applied hyperbolic tangent function together with Laplace transform in proposing a cryptographic technique. Kerryn Butler-Henderson et al. in 2020 suggested a systematic approach for secured authentication technique in error free conduct of examination.

Mohammad Serajuddin et al. in 2023 proposed methods to apply for data security with internet of things. Kunal S. Pawar et al. in 2018 applied Rasberry PI for the conduct of examination. Muharrem Tuncay Gengoglu in 2020 made use of mathematical models for cyber security. Naqash Azeem Khani et al. in 2016 presented a discussion on internet of things and data security. Nurul Huda Nik Zulkipli et al. in 2021 discussed about the challenges and issues faced in information security. Oguguo et al. in 2023 suggested a method for eradicating malpractices in examination which helps in improvising the standard of education.

Omar Zughoul et al. in 2013 discussed about the security and privacy in the conduct of online examination. Said Ally et al. in 2022 presented a review on online examination using various online softwares. Suresh Rasappan et al. in 2024 presented an encryption technique for image using aboodh transform. S. Vijaya Lakshmi et al. in 2021 performed an analysis on security of information. Temba Saina et al. in 2020 performed a case study at Zambia. Their results have suggested an implementation of online examination. Trung-Hieu Le et al. in 2021 made their case study in the markets of Vietnam. The authors presented a discussion on the uses of internet of their in their study. Vinay Gugueoth et al. in 2023 made use of internet of things for the advancements of online study. Young-Sik Jeong et al. in 2015 presented a study on mathematical models for internet of things.

Based on this study, this chapter proposes a method to secure online examination with the help of queueing models. The various queueing modes are discussed in Section 10.3. The methodology suggested is presented as an algorithm. The method suggested has been verified using the word 'RESULT'. The queueing models have been verified for encryption. Then the validation has been presented with the help of MATLAB. The results, discussion and conclusion are provided.

10.3 QUEUE DISCIPLINE IN DATA SECURITY

Queuing theory finds its application in many fields for optimizing the waiting time. It is helpful for recognizing efficient usage of the server, which benefits the customers. Queues are formed based on the count of the servers, named as single server or multi-server. The queue length depends on the capacity of the system, which can be finite or infinite. Queueing system follows various queue disciplines for their study. This chapter attempts to make use of the queue disciplines in finding a protective way in conducting an online examination. In the realm of data security for online examinations, queue discipline serves as a guiding principle for organizing and prioritizing various security-related tasks. These tasks encompass encryption, decryption, and data validation, each crucial for safeguarding sensitive examination data. By adopting queue discipline principles, such as first-in-first-out (FIFO) or priority-based scheduling, these tasks can be efficiently managed based on their importance and urgency.

10.3.1 Encryption

Encryption stands as the first line of defence, involving the transformation of sensitive examination data into ciphertext through cryptographic algorithms. This process prevents unauthorized access and ensures the confidentiality of the information. In applying queue discipline, encryption tasks are prioritized according to the sensitivity of the data involved. For instance, exam questions, student records, and answer keys might receive higher priority for encryption over less critical data. This helps to code the text message and share it in a non-readable form. It requires a procedure to convert it to manually readable form.

10.3.2 Decryption

Decryption, the counterpart to encryption, involves reverting ciphertext back to plaintext using decryption algorithms. This process enables authorized access to the encrypted data. Queue discipline principles are applied to manage decryption tasks, considering factors such as the arrival of encrypted data and the urgency of accessing specific information for examination purposes. This process helps to convert the coded message to a manually readable form. The reverse process involved in encryption ends up with the decryption process.

10.3.3 Data Validation

Data validation plays a critical role in ensuring the integrity and authenticity of examination data. It involves verifying the validity of the data to detect and prevent tampering or unauthorized modifications. Queue discipline is employed to schedule and prioritize data validation processes. For example, periodic validation checks may occur at regular intervals to maintain the ongoing integrity of examination data. Additionally, validation tasks may be triggered in response to specific events, such as system updates or suspicious activity alerts. Even after providing security, hackers trace the password and misuse the data. There is always necessity to develop the data security method along with the period. Because the data security method then and there gets outdated by hackers.

In most of the data security methods, mathematics plays a vital role. The queue discipline methods are not yet identified by researchers in cryptography. Hence, the method proposed in this chapter fulfills this gap. Queue discipline provides a structured approach to managing security-related tasks in online examination systems. By prioritizing tasks based on their importance and urgency, educational institutions can ensure the confidentiality, integrity, and availability of examination data, thereby upholding the credibility and fairness of the assessment process.

10.3.4 Education System

Education helps to make a person develop his individuality and rise high in career. In ancient years, education was imparted through *gurukulams* (where the students stayed with the master). Here, students learn their education from their guru. The assessment of the study was done by the practical experience they obtain. Then school education system came into existence. Here ranges of classes were fixed based on the age of the students. Blackboard and chalk piece are used as tools in teaching. A set of topics together was framed as syllabus. The syllabus is taught by relevant teachers from the field.

The assessment of the candidates was done by preparing questions based on the syllabus. Then private tutoring classes, distance education, and part-time education were introduced. Private tutoring is undertaken to improve marks, making students get through the exams in a passing grade or more. Distance education was introduced to people who could not afford to attend classes in person. In this process, books are shared related to the study. The candidates prepare themselves and appear for examination. In some cases, classes are also conducted on holidays to make it easy for people going to jobs to attend. In part-time study, officegoers attend classes after their work. Nowadays a lot of self-learning courses are also introduced with the aim of making more people get education. The growth in the education field has also led a wide adoption of technology. Every field has shown its standards of excellence.

10.3.5 Benefits of Education

In ancient times, there were people who excelled in many fields even without academic education. They had the capability to execute the practical knowledge they absorbed through the environment. Nowadays, people have to develop their careers. The educational qualification helps people land jobs in corporate companies. The world of internet has led to developments in each and every field. Without education, survival in jobs has become very difficult. In most of the corporate companies, even after being placed, the resumes need to be updated in the form of additional certificates in some specialized domains and it has become mandatory in some companies. Technology helps to train their kids in their studies. Uneducated people find it difficult to even fill in a challan in the bank.

In early days of education, the teachers were the only source of clearing doubts during study. In this internet era, in addition to teachers, there are many online sources, which provide quality education in many subjects. Virtual study provides an opportunity for students to learn easily. Even kids make use of the facility to clear their doubts without any hurdles. They do not demand elders to help them with their studies. Education does not have a barrier with language. It is made available in all languages. Each language provides its own symbol and explanation for understanding the concepts. There is no age limit for getting education. If there is interest, anyone can learn at any age.

In tune with the current trends, many new courses of study have also been introduced such as textile education, footwear studies, petrochemical studies, fisheries study, leather education, and many more. Education provides an opportunity to find solutions to difficult problems. It provides a path to arrive at an optimal solution to cost-effective scenarios. The education system is expanding in many countries. Technology has played a remarkable role in achieving such changes.

Education does not mean the academic part of study alone. It also includes the moral study required for all living beings. This helps to create harmony among friends, neighbours and people around us. The morality the students learn during their studies helps them live in a peaceful society. It develops helping capacity. It gives confidence to face interviews. It creates a competitive environment among friends, which provides healthy relations in building harmony. It earns respect and brings happiness to educated people wherever they go. People with good education reach high positions with a good pay scale. The happiness received makes the whole family to feel proud. The whole family gets benefited with a single person's education. This gives encouragement for the forthcoming generation to concentrate on education. In some cases, the students get education from their friends in class. This helps to develop harmony among friends. The friendship lasts even after their academic education. This helps to gain self-confidence to build their own livelihood.

Education is the only asset which cannot be stolen by any other person. It grows in multiples when it is shared with others. Apart from academics, many skills such as cooking, drawing, or tailoring can be acquired through online learning. YouTube videos provide opportunities for people to develop their talent. The YouTube channel also provides income for content creators on that platform.

10.3.6 Examination

Each and every person strives hard to present their best selves. Showcasing their talent in their field helps grow in their career. Examination is a process which helps to analyse the knowledge gained during education. It helps to understand the level of understanding of the concept.

Examinations are conducted to assess the level of knowledge acquired in academic studies by a student. This helps to provide ranking to a group of students and to decide on who wins the gold medal. Competitive examinations are conducted to choose the candidates who are eligible for job placement. Examinations are also conducted to provide certificates, awards and many more. These types of exams must be conducted in a malpractice-free environment.

These examinations must be conducted in a proper and right manner. Recently, in a few examinations like National Eligibility cum Entrance Test (NEET) and state-level examinations (SETs), leakage of question papers was reported. Such incidents provides an opportunity for non-eligible candidates to secure good ranking. As a result, deserving candidates may lose their opportunity to achieve good ranks. To provide foolproof security in online examinations, many researchers are working on the problem using the recent advances. These examinations are conducted in two modes: offline and online. The following subsection discusses the two methods of examinations. Till the pandemic period of COVID, most of the examinations were conducted offline only. After that, most of the study courses went online. Examinations were also conducted online. Banking examinations help us to identify suitable person for the job. Examinations like NEET help even poor people to study the medical course if they are truly eligible for it. Examinations conducted nowadays are transparent to candidates, which gives confidence to the appearing candidates. When it was not transparent, the candidates had fears of malpractice to help ineligible candidates get through the examination.

Examinations are conducted in both descriptive mode and multiple choice mode. In competitive examinations like NEET, multiple choice questions method is used. Only if a candidate marks all the correct answers, scoring is given. Some examinations include true or false type of questions also. This helps to increase the difficulty level of the examination. Few scoring systems come with negative marking for wrong answers, which really helps to identify talented people. That in turn helps to bring up truly eligible candidates in the top ranking.

10.3.6.1 Offline Examination

Paper and pen tests are referred as offline examination. Candidates are seated in a hall and printed copies of question papers are provided to them. The answers are written and are used for evaluation. It involves a long procedure in which questions are printed. Hall arrangements are made. Question papers and answer scripts are arranged according to the number of students in each hall. An intimation slip to students is to be pasted in front of halls to make the students know their place of examination.

10.3.6.2 Online Examination

The method of conducting examinations using computers with the help of internet is online examination. This helps to eradicate many faults in the conduct of examination. Copying during the examinations can be avoided in online mode. Particularly while writing multiple choice questions, it becomes easy to share the answers. To overcome this misbehaviour, online examinations provide a solution. Here there is opportunity to shuffle both the questions and answers.

10.3.6.3 Comparison of Online and Offline Examinations

Online examinations require a proper system with internet connection and uninterrupted power supply. The conduct of examinations requires a proper broadcast channel. While offline examinations do not need such commitment. But the practice of copying answers is very less in online examinations compared to offline examinations.

10.3.6.4 Scoring System

Most of the examinations provide marks for scoring. Students and competitive examination aspirants give their full effort in getting a scoring, which gives them good rank. The ranks provide path for many people in getting jobs, medals, awards and many more. Few other examinations use grades to provide results. The grades are provided by fixing a range of marks as per requirement.

10.3.6.5 Ranking System

Based on the scores obtained by the candidates, ranking is provided. When there is a grade system, the grades are accessed based on the cumulative grade point average system obtained by the candidates.

10.3.7 Methodology

In our proposed methodology for enhancing data security in online examinations, we employ queue discipline principles as a foundational framework. This method organizes and prioritizes security-related tasks such as encryption, decryption, and data validation. Through the creation of multiple queues, each representing different types of security tasks with varying priority levels, we ensure a structured approach to task management. Tasks are enqueued into their respective queues based on predefined criteria, such as the sensitivity of the data or the criticality of the task. Subsequently, they are dequeued and processed according to specified queue discipline policies, ensuring that high-priority tasks are addressed promptly while maintaining overall data integrity and security.

Encryption and decryption processes are seamlessly integrated into this framework. Encryption involves transforming sensitive examination data into ciphertext using cryptographic algorithms, while decryption reverses this process to convert ciphertext back to plaintext. Detailed steps involved in encryption and decryption include key generation, algorithm initialization, encryption/decryption execution, and data validation. Furthermore, MATLAB serves as a valuable tool for validating and testing our methodology. It enables simulation and analysis of queue discipline-based encryption and decryption processes, facilitating the assessment of effectiveness and efficiency under various scenarios. Through this integrated approach, we aim to ensure the integrity and confidentiality of examination data in online assessment systems.

In this section, we present the results obtained from implementing our proposed method for enhancing data security in online examinations and discuss its implications and advantages compared to existing methods.

10.3.8 Algorithm

The safety measure of conducting online examinations lies in preventing the question paper from accessed by unknown persons, which may result in unlawful conduct of examination. To safeguard the question paper, data security measures are to be applied. The steps involved in the proposed methodology of safety measures in online examination are given below. The three different queue disciplines used for the methodology are first in first out (FIFO), last in first out (LIFO), and serve in random order (SIRO).

- Form coding table
- Membership function table
- Choose the queue discipline
- Coded text
- Assign membership values
- Graphical display
- Get word from candidate
- Validate and permit for examination

10.3.9 Numerical Illustration

The first process of encryption is to assign numerical values for alphabets. The 26 alphabets are split into two rows and numerical values are assigned to it. The values assigned are presented in Table 10.1.

To each of the alphabet, membership values are assigned. The values are assigned decimal values with a range from 0 to 1. The membership values assigned are presented in Table 10.2. The values are assigned using the relation $(x*10+y)/132$ where x is the number on row heading related to the alphabet and y is the number on column heading related to the same alphabet. This calculation produces a resultant value between 0 and 1. These values are used for the proposed methodology.

TABLE 10.1
Numerical Assignment for Alphabets

	1	2	3	4	5	6	7	8	9	10	11	12	13
1	A	B	C	D	E	F	G	H	I	J	K	L	M
2	N	O	P	Q	R	S	T	U	V	W	X	Y	Z

TABLE 10.2
Membership Values

	1	2	3	4	5	6	7	8	9	10	11	12	13
1	.083	.159	.234	.310	.386	.462	.537	.613	.689	.765	.840	.916	.992
2	.090	.166	.242	.318	.393	.469	.545	.621	.696	.772	.848	.924	1

TABLE 10.3
Sample Coding for FIFO Model

R	E	S	U	L	T
393	386	469	621	916	545

In order to make a clear picture of the process, the word "RESULT" has been chosen. The word is applied to three different models of queueing. For this process, to each of the character the membership values are taken. The methodology adopted is illustrated in the following subsections.

10.3.9.1 FIFO

The first method applied is the FIFO model. As the name indicates, the membership values are taken in the order in which they are appearing. The corresponding membership values are multiplied by 1000 to bring a whole number format. These values obtained are presented in Table 10.3.

The values presented in Table 10.3 are plotted as a graph using Microsoft Excel. This graph obtained is presented in Figure 10.1. *X*-axis labels are provided with serial numbers 1 to 6.

10.3.9.2 LIFO

The second method applied is LIFO model. LIFO means last in first out. Following this procedure, the characters of the word are used in reverse order. The membership values corresponding to the character are multiplied by 1000 and presented as whole numbers in Table 10.4.

The graph obtained from plotting the values in Table 10.4 is presented in Figure 10.2. *X*-axis labels are provided with serial numbers 1–6 irrespective of the order of the characters appearing the word.

10.3.9.3 SIRO

The third method discussed is SIRO model. This model deals with any random order of characters. To illustrate this model, the characters are split as a pair of characters. The pair is shuffled in places for illustration. The rearranged characters are assigned values based on the product of their membership value and 1000. The values obtained are presented in Table 10.5.

Figure 10.3 presents the graph obtained from plotting the values in Table 10.5. In this figure also, *X*-axis labels are provided with serial numbers 1–6 irrespective of the order of the characters appearing the word.

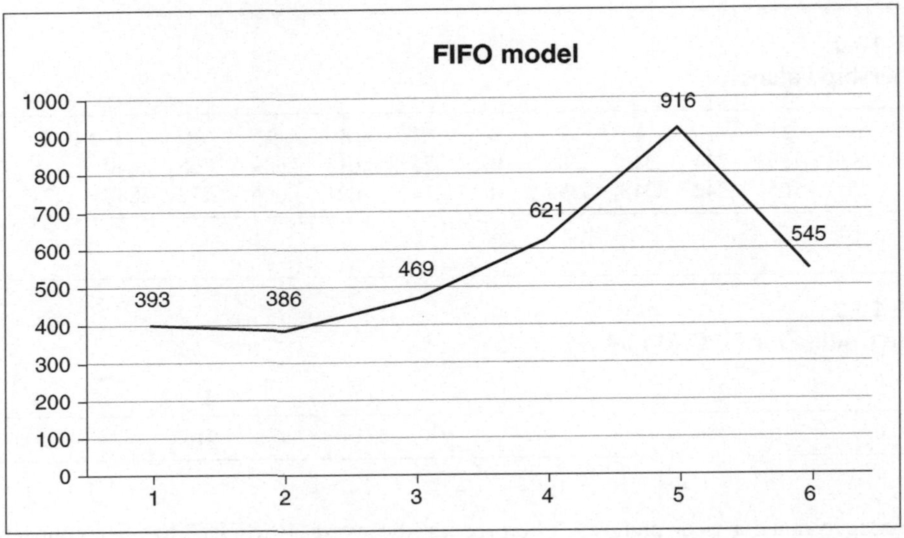

FIGURE 10.1 Manual graph obtained for FIFO model.

TABLE 10.4
Sample Coding for LIFO Model

T	L	U	S	E	R
545	916	621	469	386	393

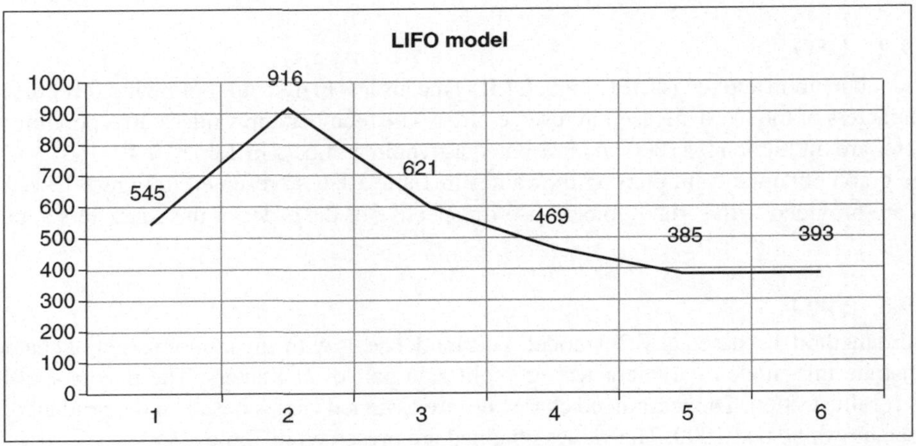

FIGURE 10.2 Manual graph obtained for LIFO model.

TABLE 10.5
Sample Coding for SIRO Model

E	R	U	S	T	L
386	393	621	469	545	916

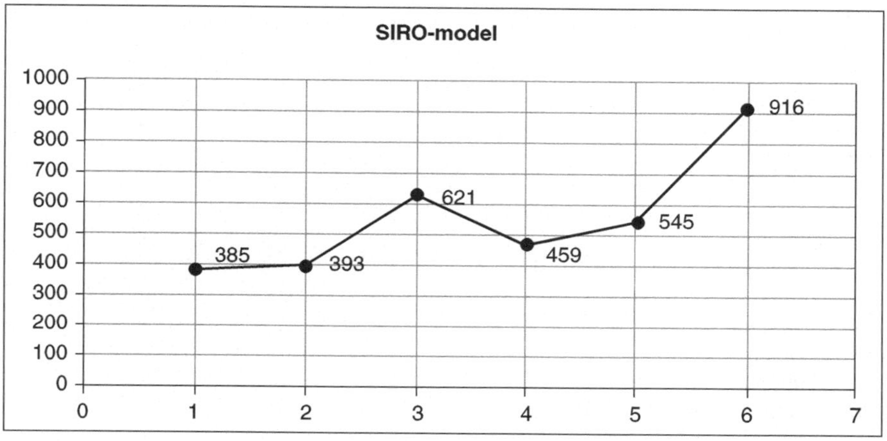

FIGURE 10.3 Manual graph obtained for SIRO model.

10.3.10 Screening of the Candidate

When the candidate tries to login for the examination, the candidate is asked to choose a number between 1 and 3. If the candidate chooses 1, LIFO graph model is shared in screen. For option 2, FIFO graph model is shown on screen. The SIRO model graph is shown for candidate choosing option 3. The candidate inputs the equivalent six-letter word. One the fed in word is correct, the candidate is permitted to attend the examination. This helps to eradicate the unknown person attending the examination. Malpractice can be avoided with this methodology.

10.3.11 MATLAB Coding

MATLAB is a software which helps to bring about solutions for various mathematical problems in an easy manner. It is less time-consuming. Once the coding is created, the data set can be changed and the same coding can be used.

Whenever a work is done, validation of the process using online resources is important because online sources provide a time-consuming error-free validation process. This section describes the coding in MATLAB, which has been done to validate the process proposed. While validating the procedure, it is mandatory to bring about generalization. In the data security procedure, only when the password is autogenerated, the data would be more protective. In order to make the data more secure, the random word generation of alphabets has been used. For an easy understanding of the procedure, a random word consisting of six characters has been taken. The word randomly generated has been applied for all the three queueing models to ensure the data is secured. Each time the coding is run, different random generated words are obtained in a graph format. This graph is to be shared with the candidates for the correct identification of the password. Once they find the correct six-letter word, they can feed them and start their exam. A part of the coding applied to bring about the result has been shown in Table 10.6.

On the successful execution of the coding, the random word obtained for first in first out system of queue is "LEXZL". The graph obtained related to this data is given in Figure 10.4. The

TABLE 10.6
MATLAB Coding

```
n=input('Choose your option from 1 to 3')
if (n==1)
  y=[R E S U L T]
  plot(x, y)
  grid on
  for i = 1:length(x)
  text(x(i), y(i), sprintf('(%d, %d)', x(i), y(i)), ...
    'VerticalAlignment', 'bottom', ...
    'HorizontalAlignment', 'right', ...
    'FontSize', 5, ...
    'Color', 'blue', ...
    'BackgroundColor', 'white');
end

end
if (n==2)
  y=[T L U S E R]
  plot(x, y)
  grid on
  for i = 1:length(x)
  text(x(i), y(i), sprintf('(%d, %d)', x(i), y(i)), ...
    'VerticalAlignment', 'bottom', ...
    'HorizontalAlignment', 'right', ...
    'FontSize', 5, ...
    'Color', 'blue', ...
    'BackgroundColor', 'white');
end
end
if (n==3)
  y=[E R U S T L]
  plot(x, y)
  grid on
  for i = 1:length(x)
  text(x(i), y(i), sprintf('(%d, %d)', x(i), y(i)), ...
    'VerticalAlignment', 'bottom', ...
    'HorizontalAlignment', 'right', ...
    'FontSize', 5, ...
    'Color', 'blue', ...
    'BackgroundColor', 'white');
end
end
```

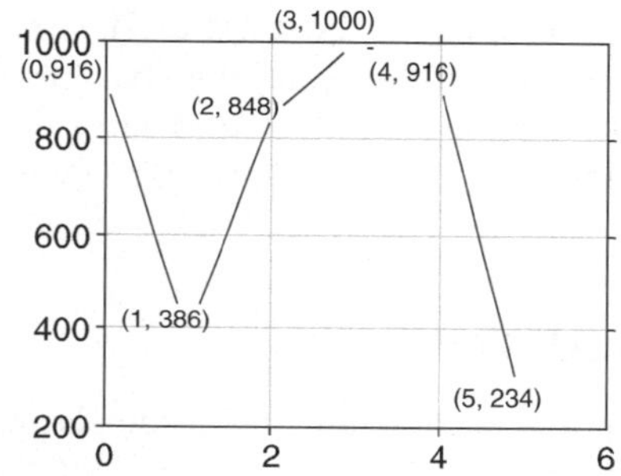

FIGURE 10.4 MATLAB graph obtained for FIFO model.

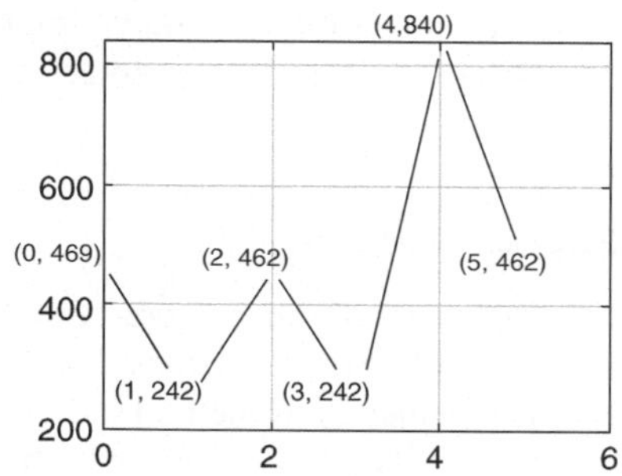

FIGURE 10.5 MATLAB graph obtained for LIFO model.

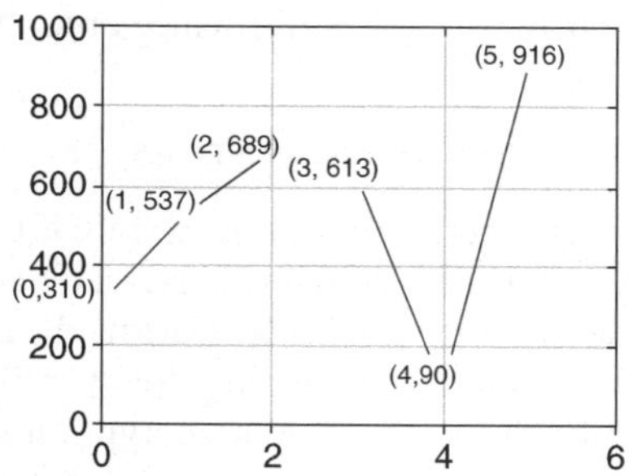

FIGURE 10.6 MATLAB graph obtained for SIRO model.

random word obtained for last in first out model is "FKPFPS", which has been shown as a graph in Figure 10.5. "GDHILN" is the random word obtained for SIRO model whose graph is shown in Figure 10.6.

10.3.12 Comparative Study of Queue Disciplines

The chapter proposed three types of queueing methods. The words are arranged according to FIFO, LIFO and SIRO. The main purpose of the methodology is to secure the data during an online examination. The level of difficulty in identifying the word secures the data more. The FIFO method uses the character of the word as given in the same order. Thus, it is easy to identify. In LIFO method, the characters of the word are just reversed in order, which is not much difficult to understand. But in SIRO model, the characters of the word are shuffled in any order. It is the responsibility of the candidate to identify the order of arrangement of the characters. This involves an additional task in it. This SIRO method serves as a better methodology in data security process.

10.4 RESULTS AND DISCUSSION

The implementation of our proposed method utilizing queue discipline for data security in online examinations has yielded promising results. We observed efficient organization and prioritization of security-related tasks, including encryption, decryption, and data validation, leading to enhanced protection of examination data. By leveraging queue discipline principles, high-priority tasks were addressed promptly, ensuring the integrity and confidentiality of examination data throughout the assessment process. The integration of encryption and decryption processes into the queue discipline framework facilitated seamless data protection, with minimal overhead and complexity.

10.4.1 Comparison with Existing Methods

A comparative analysis with existing methods underscores the effectiveness of our proposed approach in enhancing data security for online examinations. Unlike traditional methods that may lack a structured approach to task management, our method leverages queue discipline principles to streamline security-related processes. By prioritizing tasks based on their importance and urgency, our method ensures timely and efficient handling of security tasks, mitigating the risk of security breaches and unauthorized access to examination data. Furthermore, the seamless integration of encryption and decryption processes into the queue discipline framework enhances data protection without compromising system performance or usability.

10.4.2 Discussion on Implications and Advantages

The use of queue discipline in data security for online examinations offers several implications and advantages. Firstly, it provides a structured and systematic approach to task management, ensuring that security-related tasks are handled in a prioritized and efficient manner. This helps mitigate security risks and vulnerabilities, enhancing the overall integrity and confidentiality of examination data. Additionally, the integration of encryption and decryption processes into the queue discipline framework simplifies data protection mechanisms, making them more accessible and user-friendly for educators and administrators. Furthermore, the scalability and flexibility of queue discipline allow for seamless adaptation to evolving security requirements and changing examination environments, ensuring continued effectiveness and relevance over time.

The utilization of queue discipline in data security for online examinations presents a promising approach to enhancing the integrity and confidentiality of examination data. By prioritizing security-related tasks and seamlessly integrating encryption and decryption processes, our proposed method offers a robust and efficient solution for safeguarding examination data in online assessment systems. Moreover, the implications and advantages of queue discipline underscore its potential to address the evolving challenges and requirements of data security in modern education environments.

10.4.3 Future Direction

This chapter proposes a methodology in which the online examination validates the reliability of the candidate using image decryption procedure. It is also important to secure the question paper also before being processed for examination. The proposed methodology can be used as a tool in securing question paper. Even this method can be applied during question setting procedure. The secrecy can be shared between the question setter, screening officer, technical team for processing online examination and other related people. When others try to open the question paper, it would be hard for them to proceed. This helps to secure question paper from trespassers misusing the question paper.

10.5 CONCLUSION

In conclusion, our research on leveraging queue discipline for enhancing data security in online examinations has yielded significant findings and contributions. Through the implementation of our proposed method, we have demonstrated the effectiveness of organizing and prioritizing security tasks efficiently, including encryption, decryption, and data validation. This structured approach ensures timely handling of high-priority tasks, thereby enhancing the integrity and confidentiality of examination data. The seamless integration of encryption and decryption processes into the queue discipline framework offers a user-friendly solution for safeguarding examination data in online assessment systems. The potential impact of our method on enhancing data security in online examinations is substantial, promising to mitigate security risks and unauthorized access while upholding the credibility and fairness of the assessment process. Suggestions for future research include further refinement of the methodology and exploration of novel approaches to data validation and authentication, aiming to continually improve the effectiveness and reliability of data security measures in online examinations.

REFERENCES

Ashish Shedge, Yash Pethkar, Shreeya Patil, Hira Rakhunde, Tejas Shah, Online Examination System, *International Journal of Research Publication and Reviews*, 5(3), 2664–2670, 2024.

Basil C.E Oguguo, Christopher A. Ocheni, Cybersecurity: a tool for curbing examination breaches and improvement of the quality of large-scale educational assessments, *Information Security Journal: A Global Perspective* 33(4), 359–373, 2023.

George F. Fragulis, Maria Papatsimouli, Lazaros Lazaridis, Ioannis A. Skordas, An online dynamic examination system (ODES) based on open source software tools, *Software Impacts*, 7, 1–5, 2021.

Ivan Trenchev, Willian Dimitrov, Georgi Dimitrov, Tanya Ostrovska and Miglena Trencheva, *Mathematical Approaches Transform Cybersecurity from Protoscience to Science*, 13, 1–18, 2023.

Kala Raja Mohan, Suresh Rasappan and Sathish Kumar Kumaravel, Secured Information Sharing Using Laplace Transform and Hyperbolic Tangent Function, *AIP Conference Proceedings*, 2516, 120003, November 2022.

Kerryn Butler-Henderson, Joseph Crawford, A systematic review of online examinations: A pedagogical innovation for scalable authentication and integrity, *Computers & Education*, 159, 1–12, 2020.

Kunal S. Pawar, Pravin C. Latane, Internet of things (IOT) based advanced online examination using Rasberry PI, *International Journal of Engineering Technologies and Management Research*, 5(5), 26–32, 2018.

Mohammad Serajuddin, Zafrul Hasan, Amjad Khan, Ali Akhtar, Impact of IoT on security and data protection, *Journal of Informatics Education and Research*, 3(2), 2196–2200, 2023.

Muharrem Tuncay Gengoglu, Mathematical modeling in cyber defense, *International Journal of Engineering Science and Application*, 4(4), 165–169, 2020.

Naqash Azeem Khani, Azlan Awang, Samsul Ariffin Bin Abdul Karim, Security in internet of things: A review, *IEEE Access*, 4, 1–22, 2016.

Nurul Huda Nik Zulkipli, Nor Aimuni Md Rashid, Anwar Farhan Zolkeplay, Alya Geogiana Buja, Synthesizing cybersecurity issues and challenges for the elderly, *Turkish Journal of Computer and Mathematics Education*, 12(5), 1775–1781, 2021.

Omar Zughoul, Hajar Mat Jani, Adibah Shuib, Osama Almasri, Privacy and security in online examination systems, *IOSR Journal of Computer Engineering (IOSR-JCE)*, 10(4), 63–70, 2013.

Said Ally, Review of online examination security for the moodle learning management system, *International Journal of Education and Development Using Information and Communication Technology*, 18(1), 107–124, 2022.

Suresh Rasappan, Regan Murugesan, Sathish Kumar Kumaravel, Kala Raja Mohan and Nagadevi Bala Nagaram, Analyzing the efficiency of a new image encryption method based on aboodh transformations, *Baghdad Science Journal*, 1850–1867, May 2024.

S. Vijaya Lakshmi, N. Musrat Sultana, Security analysis and improvements of acess control in the internet of things, *Turkish Journal of Computer and Mathematics Education*, 12(9), 1557–1567, 2021.

Temba Saina, Dr Silumbe M. Richard, Development and implementation of an online examination system: A case study at information and communications University-Zambia, *International Journal of Multi-Disciplinary Research*, 1–32, 2020.

Trung-Hieu Le, Nguyen Thuy Dung, Dinh Tran Ngoc Huy, Nguyen Thi Phuong Thanh, Dinh Tran Ngoc Hien, Nguyen Thi Hang, Internet of things (IoT) uses and applications – solutions in emerging markets and Vietnam, *Turkish Journal of Computer and Mathematics Education*, 12(11), 5546–5550, 2021.

Vinay Gugueoth, Sunitha Safavat, Sachin Shetty, Security of Internet of Things (IoT) using federated learning and deep learning — Recent advancements, issues and prospects, *ScienceDirect*, 9, 941–960, 2023.

Young-Sik Jeong, Mohammad S. Obaidat, Jianhua Ma, and Laurence T. Yang, Advanced mathematics and numerical modeling of IoT, *Journal of Applied Mathematics*, 1–5, 2015.

11 Trust-Based Optimization Routing Algorithm for Wireless Sensor Networks Using Enhanced M-TCAAA Technique

Divyashree Habbanakuppe Balachandra, Puttamadappa Chaluve Gowda, Nandini Prasad Kanakapura Shivaprasad, and Supraja Eduru

11.1 INTRODUCTION

The WSN's sensors are powered by a smaller battery, have less processing power, and insufficient memory for storing data. Because the sensor's battery cannot be replaced or recharged, energy consumption is regarded as the main problem. In order to reduce the energy consumption, a cluster-based routing system is created (Tang et al., 2020). Inter-cluster and intra-cluster communication are the two main categories into which cluster communication is typically divided. The corresponding Cluster Members (CMs) transfer the data directly to the CH during single-hop broadcasting during intra-cluster data transmission (Kansal et al., 2010). Following that, the CH uses a one or numerous bound routing strategy to broadcast the gathered information to the central place. Due to the WSN's open nature and lack of total security against attackers, security is regarded as a critical concern. This is typically related to the environment in which WSN applications operate and the working circumstances of the sensor (Reddy et al., 2021; Divyashree et al., 2023). The lack of security in the sensors' installation makes them vulnerable to malicious attacks. Because the environment is inherently inappropriate and makes it difficult to increase sensor energy, the network must be designed with secure and energy-aware routing.

The generation of networks known as mobile ad-hoc networks often has a vast quantity of inexpensive sensors connected through wireless signals. The aim is to get information from environment using nearby network sensors followed by broadcasting the collected information to the base station. Generally speaking, sensors are capable of mobilizing, detecting, calculating, and transmitting data, among other crucial functions (Prasad et al., 2011). The advantages of the MANETs are lower installation cost, easy deployment, self-configuration capacity and it has the probability of distribution. MANETs are employed in many fields such as intelligent agriculture, environment monitoring, industrial safety, smart home, medicine, education, military and so on. The sensors of the MANETs have inadequate memory for data storage, less computing capability, and lower battery power (Saidi et al., 2020). The leftover energy is considered a primary cause

DOI: 10.1201/9781003491910-11

because battery of sensor is not rechargeable and replaceable. Therefore, a cluster-based routing is developed to minimize the energy consumption.

The following succinctly summarizes the contributions of the research:

- To choose the best safe path and node from the system, artificial algae algorithm is suggested. This study takes into account the artificial algae algorithm (AAA) due to its ability to effectively balance the observation and utilization phases.
- To reduce the energy consumption of the WSN, the K for congregating strategy is combined with artificial algae algorithm positioned SCH selection. In order to achieve dependable network communication, the hostile nodes are evaded during SCH and route selection.
- Artificial algae algorithm is used to maximize the quantity of information gathered by the target node. In addition, the shortest route selection that maximizes efficiency is employed to reduce power usage.

This research study is organized as follows: Section 11.2 provides an overview of the methods utilized for the clustering/routing process and security concerns in WSN. In Section 11.3, the suggested MT-CAAA procedure is described along with a flowchart. Section 11.4 contains the simulation results and a comparison of the MT-CAAA approach. Section 11.5 finally states the conclusions.

11.2 RELATED WORK

The secure cluster-based routing protocol (SCBRP), introduced by Pavani and Rao, enables safe routing and clustering in wireless sensor networks. The SCBRP employed enhanced firefly algorithms to determine the shortest path and compatible particle swarm optimization (PSO) for clustering (Pavani et al., 2019). The input data is encrypted using the advanced encryption standard and RC6 before being broadcast over the network. The trust cost of the node is not known in the interpretation in the path created utilizing firefly techniques. Particle-water wave optimization (P-WWO) was used by Khot and Naik to create a safe route. Combining PSO with water wave optimization resulted in the P-WWO. When choosing the CH to use in the secure data transmission path, PSO-based cellular automata were initially used. In order to choose the transmission path with the least amount of delay and distance, the P-WWO was used (Khot et al., 2022). Although this P-WWO thwarted to analyse the information consignment, it was crucial for an effective analysis. Energy-aware trust and opportunity-based routing with mobile nodes (ETOR-MN) is a research approach that offered as a means of choosing the optimal path across the network (Hajiee et al., 2021). Owing to the large number of control packers required for route identification, the ETOR-MN had a high routing overhead. The grey wolf updated whale optimization (GUWO) was used by Reddy et al. to choose a CH from the network. The GUWO took into account the fitness functions of security, delay, energy, and distance (Reddy et al., 2021). However, the network performance was impacted as a result of the LEACH sending the data to BS directly.

A safe data transmission method utilizing PSO and deterministic finite automata in WSN was presented by Prithi and Sumathi. In order to analyse the node and packet route, learning dynamic deterministic finite automata were built, and the network was dynamically trained. In order to produce energy-efficient communication, the route was further optimized using the PSO (Prithi et al., 2021). However, this effort simply used geographic data to build clusters, which increased energy use. A secure routing protocol based on multiobjective ant-colony optimization (SRPMA) was implemented by Sun et al. for wireless sensor networks (WSNs). The selecting path was carried out deployed on multiple distinct schemes, namely trust worth and power of the node. The trust cost of the junction was assessed in this case using an enhanced D-S evidence theory (Sun et al., 2019). Only secure network routing was taken into consideration when the SRPMA was built. For safe data broadcasting over the WSN, energy consumption, security, increased routing overhead, data transfer across single hops, and improper fitness function computation are further critical difficulties with WSN utilization. More precisely, throughout the conversation, the hostile junction misdirects or loses information.

11.3 PROPOSED METHOD

The artificial algae technique is employed in this work to identify the system's safe paths and the SCH from the clusters. Furthermore, employing M-TCAAA reduces the power utilization of the sensors and extends the life of the WSN. Figure 11.1 displays the M-TCAAA's architecture. The SCH from the clusters and secure routes over the network are discovered using the M-TCAAA. Since the malicious attack causes the packet loss and unneeded power utilization, the proposed M-TCAAA avoids the malicious attacks while broadcasting the data over the MANETs.

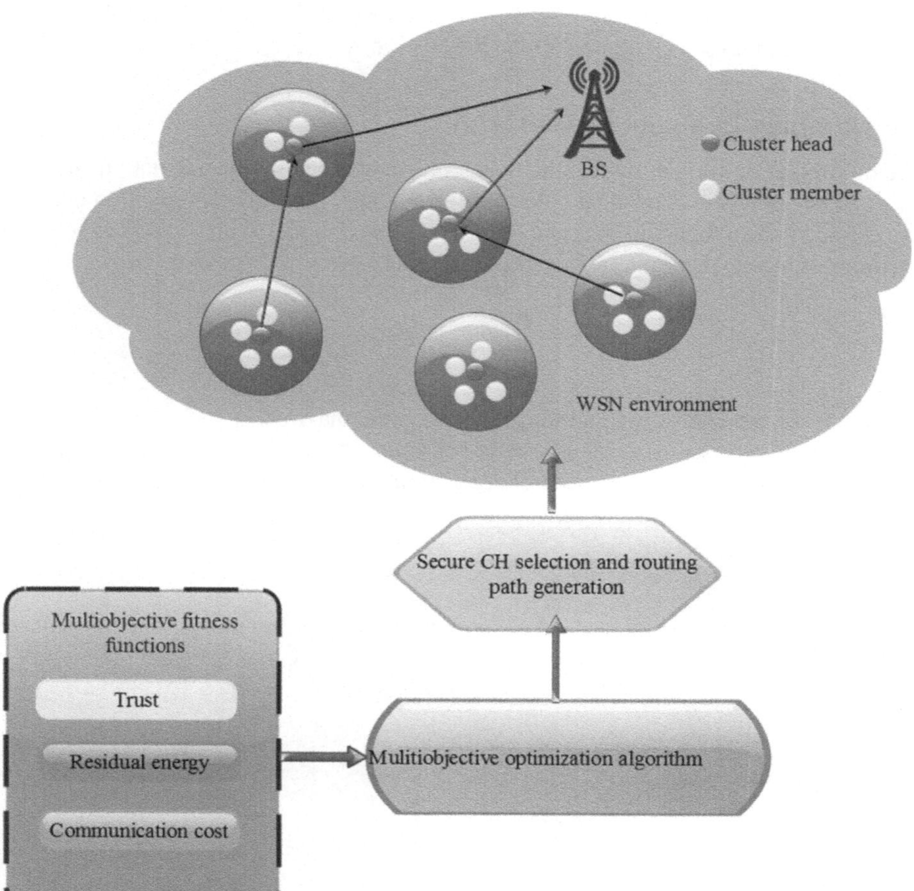

FIGURE 11.1 Design of Artificial algae algorithm.

11.3.1 Clustering Technique

The WSN's nodes are first arbitrarily distributed and then they are clustered utilizing the K-based algorithm. The Euclidian distance between the sensors is the primary determinant of the K-means algorithm. The artificial algae algorithm technique is utilized to identify a safe route and a SCH after the network has been clustered.

11.3.2 Secure Cluster Head Preference

Using the M-TCAAA, the best SCH is chosen from the clusters in order to prevent malicious assaults. The traditional AAA mimics the biological processes of algae in general. The procedure for choosing SCHs is explained in full below.

11.3.3 Initialization for SCH Selection

A collection of applicant nodes must be selected as the SCH. The arbitrary node ID, ranging from 1 till m, is assigned to every algal colony. The entire amount of sensors in the WSN is denoted by M.The i-th algal colony of the M-TCAAA is represented by the symbol D, and its proportion is denoted by the formula $x_i = \left(x_{i,1}, x_{i,2}, \ldots, x_{i,D}\right)$. $x_{i,rc}$, $1 \leq rc \leq D$ is the position of the algal colony, which selects a random sensor among all the WSN's sensors.

11.3.4 Repetitive Technique of M-TCAAA

Algal iteration occurs in three stages: the helical movement phase, the adaptation stage, and the procedure of development. The algal colony will eventually die if its reproduction does not provide the colony with enough nutrients and light. The Monod model, which is utilized to determine the dynamics of the algal community, is displayed in (11.1).

$$\mu = \frac{\mu_{max} S}{K_S + S} \tag{11.1}$$

Here μ and μmax, respectively, stand for growth rate and maximal specific growth; S represents the amount of nutrients or fitness value, and KS represents the constant that indicates the colony's substrate half-saturation. The dimension of algal community at a given interval t+ 1 is displayed in (11.2).

$$G_i^{t+1} = \mu_i^t G_i^{t+1} \tag{11.2}$$

when i varies from 1 to N; y indicates the overall number of communities. The nutrient concentration determines which algal colonies are the smallest and greatest for their function of multiplication; Equations (11.3) and (11.4) illustrate this process.

$$biggest^t = max\left(G_i^t\right) \tag{11.3}$$

$$smallest^t = min\left(G_i^t\right) \tag{11.4}$$

A random algal slot m is chosen among minute set, and Equation (11.5) illustrates the successful multiplication by recreating enormous algal slots:

$$smallest_m^t = biggest_m^t \qquad m = \{1,2,\ldots,D\} \tag{11.5}$$

The artificial algae have a fixed starvation value of 0 at first. In the event of insufficient light reaching the algal cell, the starvation value increases in accordance with time t. The artificial algae are adapted as indicated by (11.7) and has maximum famine cost as indicated by (11.6).

$$starving^t = \max\left(A_i^t\right) \tag{11.6}$$

$$starving^{t+1} = starving^t\left(biggest^t - starving^t\right) \times rand(0,1) \tag{11.7}$$

where the starvation value of the i th algae colony is represented as $Ai\ t$, Moreover, as illustrated in Equations (11.8) to (11.10), the new solution is produced by means of the helical movement:

$$x_{im}^{t+1} = x_{im}^t + \left(x_{jm}^t - x_{im}^t\right)\left(\Delta - \tau^t\left(x_i\right)\right)p \tag{11.8}$$

$$x_{ik}^{t+1} = x_{ik}^t + \left(x_{jk}^t - x_{ik}^t\right)\left(\Delta - \tau^t\left(x_i\right)\right)\cos\alpha \tag{11.9}$$

$$x_{il}^{t+1} = x_{il}^t + \left(x_{jl}^t - x_{il}^t\right)\left(\Delta - \tau^t\left(x_i\right)\right)\sin\beta \tag{11.10}$$

where x_{im}^t, x_{ik}^t and x_{il}^t; the neighbouring algal colony identified by Competition choice is represented by the notation x_j^t; α and β fall within the interval $[0, 2\pi]$; p is within the interval $[-1,1]$; The frictional area on the exterior of the i th algal colony is represented as $\tau^t\left(x_i\right)$.

11.3.5 Derivation of Fitness Function

This part provides an explanation of M-TCAAA's fitness function derivation. For the purpose of selecting safe cluster heads from groups, the M-TCAAA considers multiple fitness metrics. Trust ($fm1$), transmission evaluation ($fm2$), leftover power($fm3$), and degree of node ($fm4$) are the four fitness criteria that are taken into account in M-TCAAA. Equation (11.11) represents fitness function that was discussed in (11.1):

$$S = \delta_1 \times fm_1 + \delta_2 \times fm_2 + \delta_3 \times fm_3 + \delta_4 \times fm_4 \tag{11.11}$$

where the weight parameters assigned to each fitness metric are denoted by $\delta 1 - \delta 4$. The main goal for this SCH selection is seen as the trust mentioned in Equation (11.12). The shortest distance is considered for transmission of data which is indicated in Equation (11.13). The expression for residual energy is displayed in Equation (11.14) as well. The numerous jumps in the cluster head is further defined by the node degree which is expressed in Equation (11.15). The reduced energy usage is attained by using a lower node degree:

$$fm_1 = \frac{Packets\ received_{a,b}}{Packets\ sent_{a,b}} \tag{11.12}$$

$$fm_2 = \frac{d_{avg}^2}{d_0^2} \tag{11.13}$$

$$fm_3 = \sum_{i=1}^{D} E_{SCH_i} \tag{11.14}$$

$$fm_4 = \sum_{i=1}^{D} CM_i \tag{11.15}$$

$ESCHi$ represents the power left over from the i th SCH; and CMi is the total amount of cluster members connected to the i th cluster head. To minimize the sensor power usage, additionally considered is the degree of the node. As a result, the fitness characteristic that was previously mentioned is utilized to select an appropriate SCH. Because rogue nodes cause packet losses across the network, the fitness measures' trust helps to avoid them. The transmission cost is then used to determine which path uses the least amount of energy and is the shortest. The remaining power is used to assess whether or not the node has enough energy to broadcast the data. As consequence, the system's ability to send packets to the BS is increased. In addition, the node degree is considered to reduce the energy consumption of the nodes.

11.3.6 Routing Using M-TCAAA

Using the artificial algae algorithm, the route is discovered following selection of the secure cluster head among the clusters. Figure 11.2 displays the flow diagram entire artificial algae algorithm procedure. To avoid the hostile nodes, the suggested M-TCAAA-based secure CH selection and routing is used. Because the packet bypasses the target nodes and the MANETs minimize energy usage, the packet drops. By lowering the node's power usage, the network lifetime is extended, increasing the quantity of information that can be sent. In order to establish secure, dependable communication in the system, the M-TCAAA, is used. Algorithm 1 provides the pseudo code for the M-TCAAA based SCH selection. Rather than the candidate CH location, the potential pathways are provided as input in M-TCAAA based route finding.

Algorithm 1

- Set the location and ID of algal colonies as potential SCH nodes.
- Determine the initialized solution's fitness (S) using (11.11).
- where time is the simulation time.
- with respect to all populations, do
- Select three of the colony's algal cells at random.
- Develop the fresh answers in light of (21) through (23).
- Transfer one single cell from a large colony to a tiny colony at arbitrarily.
- Employ (11.7) to a large colony to find the most starving colony after the adaption rate control is satisfied.
- Determine the revised solution's fitness using (11.11).
- Use the fitness value (S) to get the ideal SCH.
  If $(Si) < Sbest$, then $(Si) = Si$.
- Retrieves modified strategy as best approach.
- conclude if • conclude for

The flowchart of the entire M-TCAAA approach is presented in the Figure 11.2. Initially, the reference cluster head appeals for the development of a path to all neighbouring CHs that are

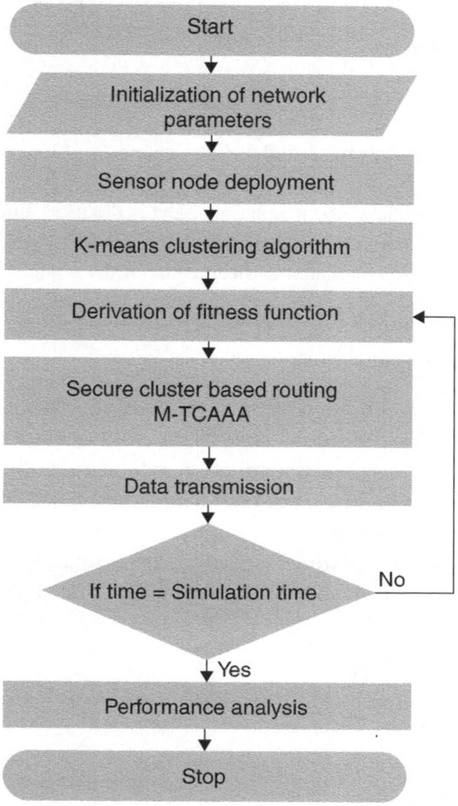

FIGURE 11.2 Flow chart for the entire M-TCAAA technique.

already in the network. Subsequently, the route reply (RREP) communication is sent to the CH that initiated it by the ideal relay node determined by the M-TCAAA. The procedure is continued until the final node, or BS, is reached. When the initial Cluster head receives the RREP notice, a safe route is built in the MANETs.

11.3.7 K-means Clustering algorithm

The goal of K-means clustering, a partitioned clustering approach employing a prototype, is to identify a user-specified number of clusters (k), each of which is denoted by its centroids. First, k is selected in initial centroids, denoting the number of desired clusters, wherein k is a user-specified quantity. The nearest centroid is then allocated to each point, and each group of points allocated to a centroid is referred to as a cluster. Next, each cluster's centroid is altered in accordance with the points allocated to it. The assignment and update procedures are repeated until no point affects the clusters, or equivalently, till the centroids don't move (Revanesh et al., 2020). Figure 11.3 illustrates the network simulation scenario, where sensor nodes are dynamically clustered. The figure highlights the presence of an attack node (in orange) and a sink node (in blue), showing interactions among nodes during data transmission. The varying node sizes indicate transmission ranges, while the timeline at the bottom represents the simulation progression.

Input: k (the number of clusters),
D (a set of lift ratios)
Output: a set of k clusters
Method:
Arbitrarily choose k objects from D as the initial cluster centers;
Repeat:
1. (re)assign each object to the cluster to which the object is the most similar, based on the mean value of the objects in the cluster;
2. Update the cluster means, i.e., calculate the mean value of the objects for each cluster

Until no change;

FIGURE 11.3 K-means clustering algorithm.

Considering data that have Euclidean distance as their closeness measure. The sum of squared errors, or scatter can be utilized, for objective function, which quantifies the quality of a clustering. Stated otherwise, computing the entire sum of the squared errors after calculating the error of each data point, or its Euclidean distance to the nearest centroid. The cluster with the minimum squared error is chosen across two distinct sets of clusters generated by separate K-means runs because it indicates that the centroids of this clustering are a more accurate representation of the points in their cluster.

$$J = \sum_{j=1}^{K} \sum_{i=1}^{n} \| x_i^{(j)} - c_j \|^2 \tag{11.16}$$

where J is objective function
K is number of clusters
N is number of cases
c_j is centroid for cluster j
$x_i^{(j)}$ is case for i
$\| x_i^{(j)} - c_j \|^2$ is the distance function

11.4 RESULT ANALYSIS

The M-TCAAA is implemented and simulated using the network simulator (NS-2.34) on an i5 processor and 6 GB of RAM system. Figure 11.4 uses network animator to show a sample WSN setup for 20 nodes. The simulation parameters used to create the M-TCAAA are shown in Table 11.1.

11.4.1 Energy Consumption

The quantity of vitality used to broadcast and receive data packets via a network is known as energy consumption. Figure 11.5 displays the energy usage comparison between the proposed algorithm and the ETORMN (Hajiee et al., 2021). Figure 11.5 indicates that the M-TCAAA uses very minimal power compared to ETORMN. For example, the energy utilization of the M-TCAAA for 100 nodes is 0.41 J wherein energy consumption of ETOR-MN is 1.94 J. The SCH and secure route selected using the M-TCAAA minimizes the unwanted energy consumption of the nodes, whereas the mobile nodes cause higher energy consumption in ETOR-MN.

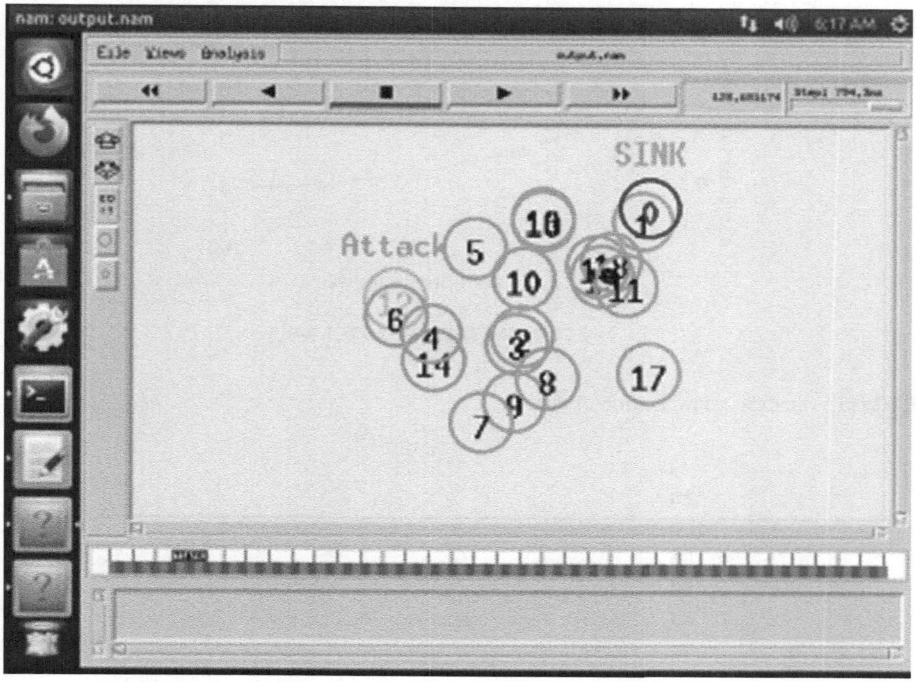

FIGURE 11.4 Simulated network for 20 nodes.

TABLE 11.1
Simulation Parameters

Parameters	Value
Number of nodes	20, 40, 60, 80 and 100
Area	200 × 200 m
Initial energy	5J
Network interface type	Wireless PHY
Mac	IEEE 802.11 DCP
Traffic source	CBR
Propagation model	Two-ray ground reflection
Antenna pattern	Omni antenna

11.4.2 Packet Delivery Ratio

The percentage that separates the amount of messages BS creates and receives is known as PDR. which is expressed in equation (11.17).

$$\text{PDR} = \frac{\text{Amount of received packets at BS}}{\text{Amount of generated packets by source node}} \times 100 \tag{11.17}$$

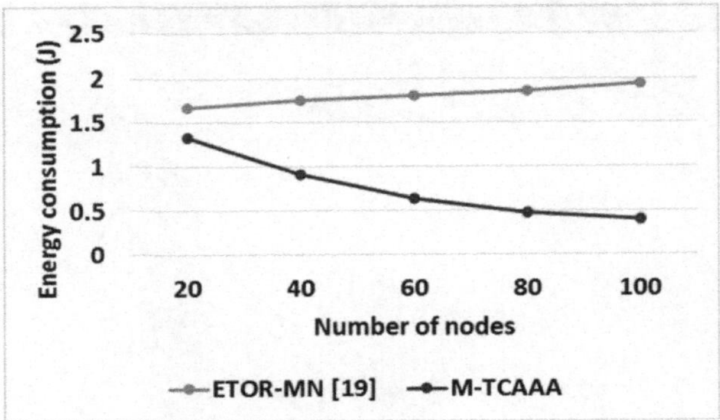

FIGURE 11.5 Analysis of utilization of energy.

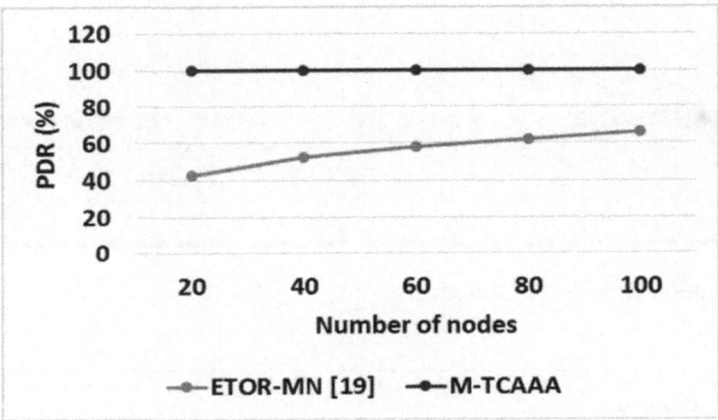

FIGURE 11.6 Analysis of PDR.

The ratio of data generated through base station to data received by base station is known as packet delivery ratio. Figure 11.6 displays the PDR analysis for ETORMN using artificial algae algorithm. As an illustration, the packet delivery ratio of the artificial algae algorithm for 100 nodes is 99.87 percent, while the packet delivery ratio of the ETORMN is 66 percent. The proposed M-TCAAA method achieves higher PDR by avoiding the malicious attacks based on the node's trustworthiness, whereas the link failure that occurs in ETOR-MN results in lesser PDR.

11.4.3 Throughput

Throughput is the amount of packets that the BS accepted effectively at a time T, which is shown in equation (11.18):

$$\text{Throughput} = \frac{\text{Amount of packets successfully received at the BS}}{T} \tag{11.18}$$

The number of messages that are acknowledged at the base station at a given interval is known as throughput (T). Figure 11.7 illustrates a throughput contrast between the artificial algae algorithm

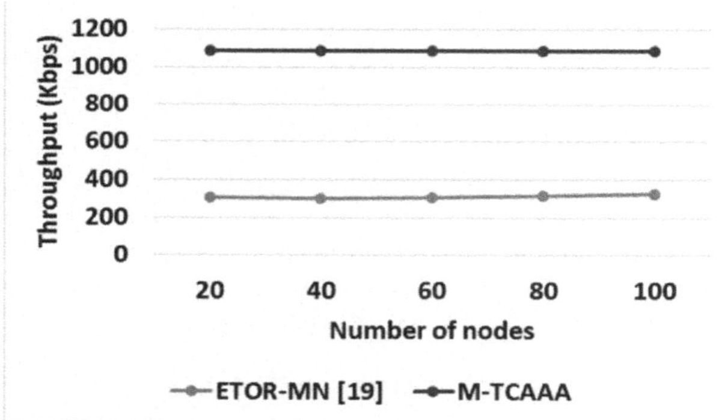

FIGURE 11.7 Analysis of throughput.

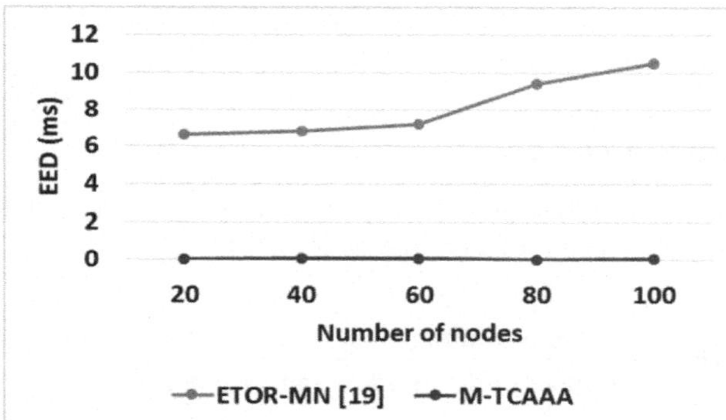

FIGURE 11.8 Analysis of EED.

and ETOR-MN. For example, the efficiency of the M-TCAAA for 100 nodes is 1089.54 Kbps wherein throughput of ETOR-MN is 324.5 Kbps. The malicious nodes avoided by the M-TCAAA improves the amount of data successfully reached base station. Accordingly, throughput of M-TCAAA is increased while transmitting the data packets.

11.4.4 End to End Delay

Overall delay defines the number of duration node required to transfer packets to base station in the system whereas this EED is expressed in Equation (11.19):

$$\text{End to end delay} = \frac{\text{Sum of time taken to transmit packet to receiver}}{\text{Number of packet received by receiver}} \tag{11.19}$$

Total delay specifies how long it takes a node to send data via a network to a base station. Figure 11.8 illustrates an end-to-end delay contrast between the artificial algae algorithm and ETOR-MN. As an illustration, the total delay of ETORMN is 10.5 ms, while the total delay of the artificial algae algorithm for 100 nodes is 0.028 ms. whereas the EED of the ETOR-MN is 10.5 ms. The M-TCAAA achieves lesser EED because of its lesser amount of control packet

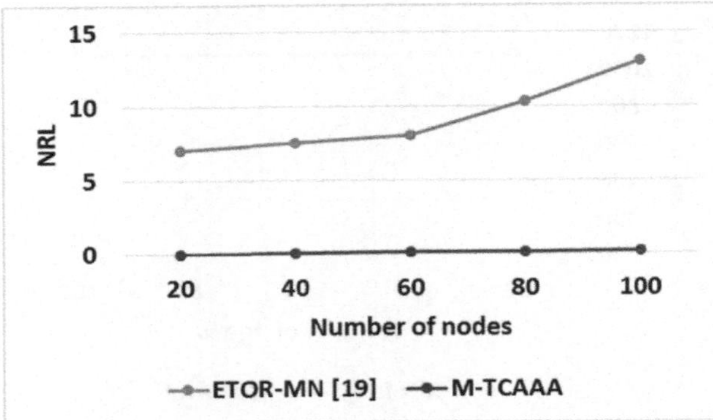

FIGURE 11.9 Analysis of NRL.

utilization and lesser transmission distance. On the other hand, the link failure caused in the ETOR-MN increases the delay while delivering the data.

11.4.5 Normalized Routing Load

NRL is the proportion between the quantity of data packets transmitted and quantity of routing packets transmitted and it is expressed in Equation (11.20):

$$\text{NRL} = \frac{\text{Number of routing packet transmission}}{\text{Number of data packet transmission}} \tag{11.20}$$

The network ratio (NRL) is the ratio of information packets sent over all contrast to information packets sent over the routing packets. Figure 11.9 displays the NRL comparison between the artificial algae algorithm and the ETORMN [12]. For example, the NRL of M-TCAAA for 100 nodes is 0.184 whereas the NRL of ETOR-MN is 13. The M-TCAAA uses lower amount of control packets due to its distinct fitness measures that results in lesser NRL.

11.4.6 Network Lifetime

The duration of the network lifespan is the amount of time that a WSN sensor uses up all of its energy while communicating. Figure 11.10 illustrates an analysis of network lifetime contrast between the artificial algae algorithm and ETOR-MN. The proposed algorithm outlasted the ETOR-MN in terms of network longevity, according to this investigation. This network lifetime gives M-TCAAA achieved greater network lifetime compared to ETOR-MN. For example, the network lifetime of the M-TCAAA for 100 nodes is 781.58 s whereas the network lifetime of the ETOR-MN is 265 s. An unwanted energy utilization done by the area of malicious node is avoided by using the M-TCAAA, Moreover, the route with a lesser transmission distance identified from the M-TCAAA also minimizes the energy consumption. Therefore, the nodes with lesser energy consumption tend to have a higher network lifetime.

Table 11.2 provides the comparative analysis of the M-TCAAA with SCBRP, ETOR-MN, GUWO, SRPMA and MOTAHO, where NA defines the values which are not available in those existing studies.

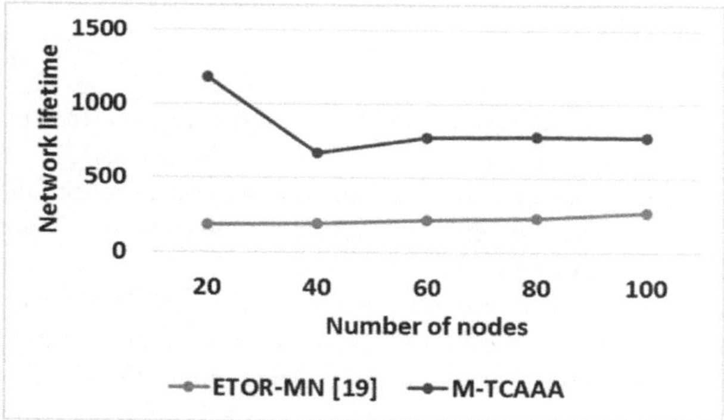

FIGURE 11.10 Analysis of network lifetime.

TABLE 11.2
Comprehensive Examination of M-TCAAA

		Number of Nodes				
Performances	**Methods**	**20**	**40**	**60**	**80**	**100**
Energy consumption (J)	ETOR-MN (Hajiee 2021)	1.67	1.75	1.8	1.86	1.94
	M-TCAAA	1.32	0.91	0.64	0.48	0.41
PDR (%)	ETOR-MN (Hajiee 2021)	43	52.5	58	62	66
	GUWO (Reddy, 2021)	NA	NA	NA	NA	96.12
	M-TCAAA	99.94	99.85	99.87	99.96	99.87
Throughput (kbps)	ETOR-MN (Hajiee, 2021)	305	302	308	317.5	324.5
	GUWO (Reddy, 2021)	NA	NA	NA	NA	242
	M-TCAAA	1089.75	1089.54	1089.54	1090.52	1089.54
EED (ms)	ETOR-MN (Hajiee, 2021)	6.6	6.8	7.2	9.4	10.5
	M-TCAAA	0.014	0.029	0.028	0.022	0.028
NRL	ETOR-MN (Hajiee, 2021)	7	7.5	8	10.3	13
	M-TCAAA	0.017	0.058	0.112	0.124	0.184
Network lifetime (s)	ETOR-MN (M. Hajiee, 2021)	185	193	212	230	265
	M-TCAAA	1177.56	671.56	781.58	782.58	781.58

Here, the nodes are changed to do the distinction. This contrast demonstrates that the M-TCAAA performs greater than SCBRP, ETOR-MN, GUWO, SRPMA and MOTAHO. For example, the PDR of the M-TCAAA for 100 nodes is 99.87 percent, which is much higher than the ETOR-MN, GUWO, SRPMA and MOTAHO. The high number of control packets used during the path revelation increases the routing overhead of the ETOR-MN. Moreover, the direct data transmission of LEACH used in the GUWO raises the packet fall in the system. The distinct fitness metrics employed in route discovery of M-TCAAA helps to minimize the control packets that leads to achieve less NRL. Additionally, the multihop routing accomplished by the M-TCAAA is utilized to enhance the data supply of the MANETs. The malicious nodes that exist in MANETs are avoided based on the trust value considered in the M-TCAAA. Therefore, the proposed M-TCAAA is employed energy utilization and improve PDR of MANETs.

11.4.7 Fitness Parameter Analysis

11.4.7.1 Total Fitness

The graph shows significant fluctuations in total fitness values across different nodes or time steps. In Figure 11.11 high peaks indicate times or nodes where the network is performing optimally, possibly due to efficient data transmission, minimal energy consumption, or high coverage. The low points represent nodes where the network performance is suboptimal, potentially due to high energy consumption, data loss, or network congestion.

In Figure 11.11, the graph represents the total fitness of nodes in MANET. *X*-axis (tnode) represents the index or identifier for each mobile node in the network, ranging from 0 to 100. *Y*-axis (total fitness) shows the total fitness value for each node. Fitness values range from 0 to 50, indicating the relative performance or capability of each node. Each star (*) on the graph represents a mobile node. The line connecting the stars shows the variation in total fitness for consecutive nodes. The pattern is quite erratic, indicating significant variability in fitness values among nodes. The total fitness metric might encompass factors such as battery level, computational capability, signal strength, and connectivity. Nodes with higher fitness are more capable of handling network tasks. Nodes with higher fitness might be preferred for resource-intensive tasks such as routing and data forwarding, to optimize network performance. To prevent overloading high-fitness nodes, load-balancing strategies might be needed, especially if there is a large disparity in fitness values. Managing the workload among nodes with varying fitness levels can help prolong the network's operational lifespan by avoiding rapid depletion of any single node's resources. The graph highlights the dynamic nature of MANETs, where node fitness can vary significantly, possibly due to mobility, energy consumption, or environmental factors. In summary, the graph illustrates the variability in the fitness of nodes within a MANET, emphasizing the need for adaptive strategies to manage network resources and maintain overall performance.

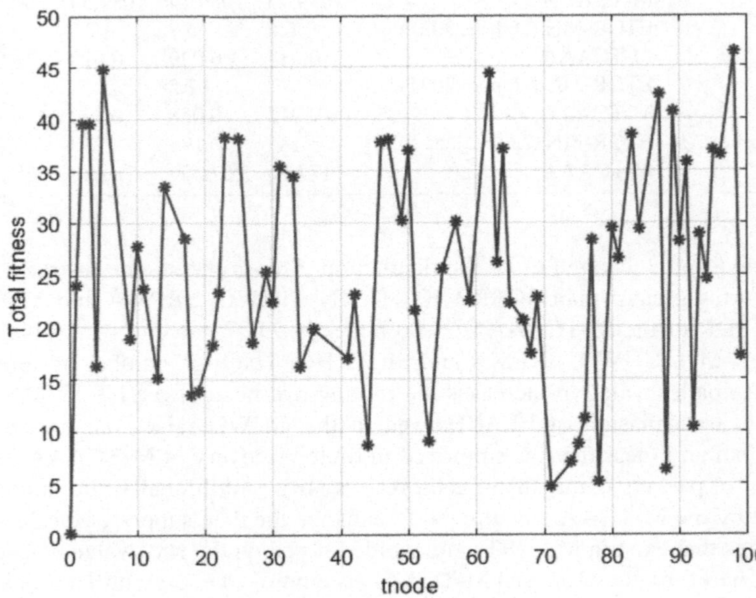

FIGURE 11.11 Total fitness by considering at various instances.

11.4.7.2 Node Degree

Figure 11.12 represents the degree of the nodes, which indicates the number of direct relationships that a node has throughout its network with its peers. The graph shows fluctuations in the node degree values across different time steps or nodes. These high peaks indicate times or nodes where a node has many direct connections, suggesting high connectivity or centrality within the network. The low troughs represent periods or nodes where a node has fewer connections, indicating lower connectivity.

The node degree values do not show a clear trend but vary, indicating the constantly changing topology of MANETs or change their positions. The values tend to fluctuate between 10 and 25, suggesting that most nodes have a moderate number of connections at any given time. The movement of nodes affects their ability to connect with other nodes. High mobility can lead to frequent changes in node degree. Areas with higher node density will have nodes with higher degrees due to more available connections. When nodes shift and the architecture of the network shifts, the node degree will fluctuate accordingly. Physical obstacles and interference can affect connectivity, causing variations in node degree.

The graph provides insight into the dynamic connectivity of nodes within a system. The variations in node degree highlight the constantly changing topology of MANETs, which is influenced by node mobility, density, and environmental factors. Understanding these fluctuations is crucial for optimizing routing protocols, maintaining connectivity, and improving network performance.

Figure 11.12 depicts graph with *X*-axis (tnode) representing specific nodes within the network. Y-axis (energy in joules) represents the energy consumption of the nodes. High Peaks: These peaks might indicate periods or nodes where energy consumption is high, possibly due to increased communication activities, data processing, or transmission power.

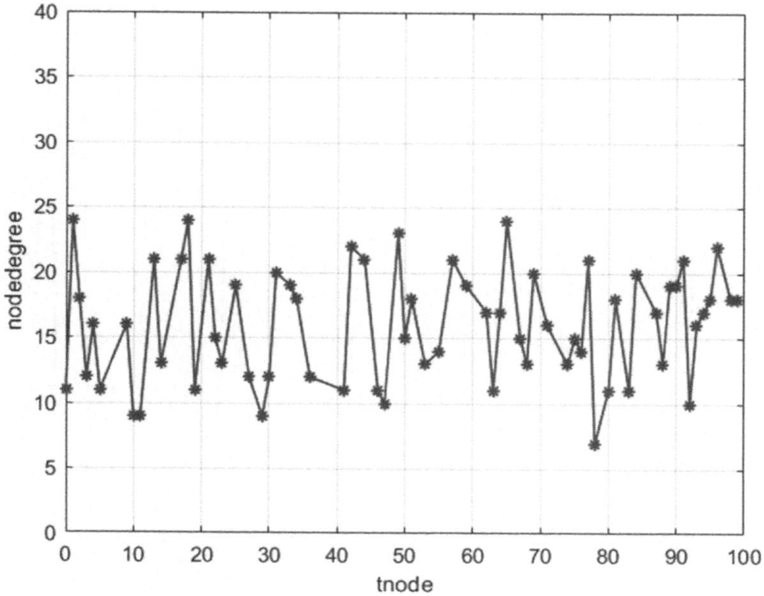

FIGURE 11.12 Analysis of node degree.

11.4.7.3 Residual Energy

The low points represent periods or nodes with lower energy consumption, suggesting idle periods, efficient energy usage, or less communication activity. In Figure 11.13, the energy consumption values fluctuate between approximately 0.9 and 1.5 J, indicating variability in the network's energy usage. There is no clear trend, suggesting that energy consumption is highly dynamic and influenced by various factors such as node activity, mobility, and communication patterns. Frequent movement of nodes can lead to more frequent reconnections and route discoveries, increasing energy consumption. Nodes that handle more data transmissions or relay data for other nodes will consume more energy. Differences in power management strategies and states (e.g., sleep mode, active mode) across nodes can cause variations. External conditions affecting signal strength might require nodes to use more power for communication.

Understanding these fluctuations is crucial for optimizing energy usage, extending the network's operational lifetime and designing energy-efficient protocols. Monitoring and managing energy consumption in MANETs are essential to ensure network sustainability and reliability.

11.4.7.4 Distance to its sink node

Figure 11.14 represents the distance in a mobile ad hoc network (MANET) among nodes and their sinks. *X*-axis (tnode) represents the index or identifier for each mobile node in the network, ranging from 0 to 100. *Y*-axis (distance to its sink in mm) shows the range among every node to its corresponding sink node in millimetres. The distance varies significantly from as low as 0 mm to as high as 1000 mm. Each star (*) on the graph represents a mobile node. The line connecting the stars shows the variation in distance to the sink for consecutive nodes. The pattern is quite erratic, indicating varying distances among nodes. The fluctuating distances illustrate the dynamic nature of MANETs, where nodes frequently change their positions. The variability in

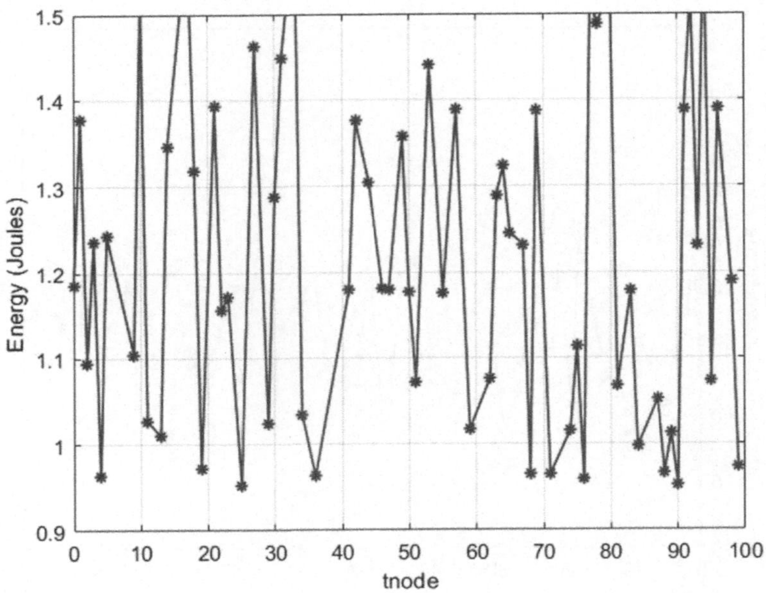

FIGURE 11.13 Analysis of residual energy.

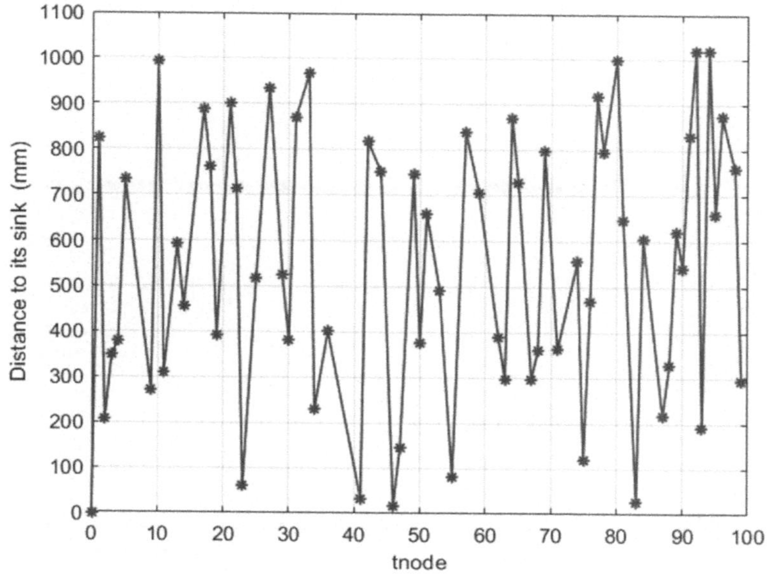

FIGURE 11.14 Analysis of distance to its sink.

distances can complicate routing protocols, as they must adapt to the changing network topology. Nodes that are farther from their sinks might consume more energy due to longer transmission distances, impacting overall network lifetime. The network's performance, including latency and packet delivery ratio, could be affected by the varying distances, as nodes might need to rely on multi-hop communication. The graph highlights the inherent challenges in managing and optimizing communication in system due to the mobility of nodes and consequently fluctuations in distances to their sinks.

11.4.7.5 Trust

Figure 11.15 graph appears to represent the trust levels of nodes in MANET. *X*-axis (tnode) represents the index or identifier for every MN in system, ranging from 0 to 100. *Y*-axis (trust) shows the reliability factor for each node. The trust grades are consistent at 1 for all nodes, indicating uniform trust across the network. Each star (*) on the graph represents a mobile node. The line connecting the stars is essentially a straight line at the trust level of 1, showing no variation in trust among the nodes. The graph indicates that all nodes are equally trusted within the network. This could imply a homogeneous network environment where trust is uniformly distributed, possibly due to identical configurations or a lack of malicious nodes. Uniform trust suggests that the network does not currently face issues with security breaches or unreliable nodes. Each node can be equally relied upon for communication and data forwarding. In MANETs, trust management is crucial to ensure secure and reliable communication. This graph implies that the current trust evaluation mechanism deems all nodes trustworthy. Continuous monitoring is necessary to maintain this uniform trust level, as changes in node behaviour or the introduction of new nodes could impact trust dynamics. In summary, the graph illustrates a scenario in a MANET where all nodes are uniformly trusted, highlighting a stable and secure network environment. This uniform trust level simplifies network management and ensures consistent performance across all nodes.

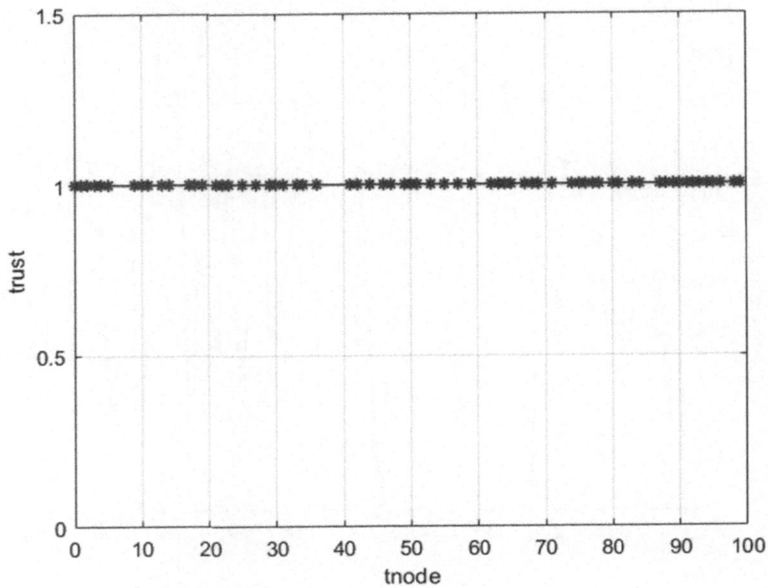

FIGURE 11.15 Analysis of trust.

11.5 CONCLUSION

The issue of increased power utilization brought on by malicious assaults ought to be properly handled to enhance network performance as the WSN nodes have limited battery life. In order to improve network longevity and data delivery under hostile attacks, a safe congregate form routing system is created. The present study employs K implies congregating and artificial algae algorithm form secure cluster head preference techniques to reduce power utilization and enhance protection from malevolent assaults. The data is then transmitted over the network via the secure route that has been chosen by CHs. Node degree, residual energy, communication cost, and trust are among the unique fitness indicators that are used to optimize the M-TCAAA. Thus, by effectively avoiding malicious nodes, the suggested artificial algae algorithm reaches a higher PDR and network lifespan. These outcomes support the M-TCAAA's superior performance over the SRPMA, GUWO, ETOR-MN, MOTAHO, and SCBRP. The packet delivery ratio of the multiobjective trust centric artificial algae algorithm for 100 nodes is 99.87 percent, greater compared to MOTAHO, GUWO, SRPMA, ETORMN, and SRPMA. Eventually, the WSN's performance will need to be enhanced by a unique optimization method.

BIBLIOGRAPHY

Dhiman, S., & Chaudhary, S., "Mobile ad-hoc networks: applications and challenges", *International Journal of Management, IT & Engineering*, vol. 11 issue 5, May 2021.

Divyashree, H.B., Puttamadappa, C., & Nandini Prasad, K.S., "Hybrid optimization algorithm for clustering and routing in WSN," 2022 IEEE 2nd Mysore Sub Section International Conference.

Divyashree, H.B., Puttamadappa, C., & Nandini Prasad, K.S., "Secure cluster-based routing using multi objective-trust centric artificial algae algorithm for wireless sensor network," *International Journal of Electrical and Computer Engineering (IJECE)*, vol. 13, no. 2, pp. 18–28 (2023).

Gopinath, S., Kumar, K. V., Elayaraja, P., Parameswari, A., Balakrishnan, S., & Thiruppathi, M., "SCEER: Secure cluster based efficient energy routing scheme for wireless sensor networks," *Materials Today: Proceedings*, vol. 45, no. 2, pp. 3579–3584, 2021, doi: 10.1016/j.matpr.2020.12.1096.

Hajiee, M., Fartash, M., & Eraghi, N.O., "An energy-aware trust and opportunity-based routing algorithm in wireless sensor networks using multipath routes technique," *Neural Processing Letters*, vol. 53, no. 4, pp. 2829–2852, Aug. 2021, doi: 10.1007/s11063-021-10525-7.

Kalidoss, T., Rajasekaran, L., Kanagasabai, K., Sannasi, G., & Kannan, A., "QoS aware trust-based routing algorithm for wireless sensor networks," *Wireless Personal Communications*, vol. 110, no. 4, pp. 1637–1658, Feb. 2020, doi: 10.1007/s11277-019-06788-y.

Kansal, P., Kansal, D., & Balodi, A. (2010). Comparison of various routing protocol in wireless sensor network. *International Journal of Computer Applications*, vol. 5, no. 11, pp. 0975–8887.

Khot, P.S., and Naik, U.L., "Cellular automata-based optimised routing for secure data transmission in wireless sensor networks," *Journal of Experimental & Theoretical Artificial Intelligence*, vol. 34, no. 3, pp. 431–449, May 2022, doi: 10.1080/0952813X.2021.1882002.

Pavani M., & Rao, P. T., "Adaptive PSO with optimised firefly algorithms for secure cluster-based routing in wireless sensor networks," *IET Wireless Sensor Systems*, vol. 9, no. 5, pp. 274–283, Oct. 2019, doi: 10.1049/iet-wss.2018.5227.

Pramod, M. S., Balodi, A., Pratik, A., Sankalp, G. S., Varshita, B., & Amrit, R. (2023). "Energy-efficient reinforcement learning in wireless sensor networks using 5G for smart cities." In *Applications of 5G and Beyond in Smart Cities* (pp. 63–86). CRC Press.

Prasad, K.S.N., Veerendra, G.R., and Puttamadappa, C.G., "Energy efficient data gathering scheme using cross layer cluster approach for wireless sensor networks," *International Journal on Computer Science and Engineering* (IJCSE), vol. 3, no. 7, pp. 2661–2667, 2011.

Prithi, S., & Sumathi, S., "Automata based hybrid PSO–GWO algorithm for secured energy efficient optimal routing in wireless sensor network," *Wireless Personal Communications*, vol. 117, no. 2, pp. 545–559, Mar. 2021, doi: 10.1007/s11277-020-07882.

Reddy, D.L., Puttamadappa, C.G., & Suresh, H.N.G., "Hybrid optimization algorithm for security aware cluster head selection process to aid hierarchical routing in wireless sensor network," *IET Communications*, vol. 15, no. 12, pp. 1561–1575, Jul. 2021, doi: 10.1049/cmu2.12169.

Revanesh, M., Sridhar, V., & Acken, J.M., "Secure coronas based zone clustering and routing model for distributed wireless sensor networks," *Wireless Personal Communications*, vol. 112, no. 3, pp. 1829–1857, Jun. 2020, doi: 10.1007/s11277-020-07129-0.

Saidi, A., Benahmed, K., & Seddiki, N., "Secure cluster head election algorithm and misbehavior detection approach based on trust management technique for clustered wireless sensor networks," *Ad Hoc Networks*, vol. 106, Sep. 2020, doi: 10.1016/j.adhoc.2020.102215.

Sun, Z., Wei, M., Zhang, Z., & Qu, G. "Secure routing protocol based on multi-objective ant-colony-optimization for wireless sensor networks," *Applied Soft Computing*, vol. 77, pp. 366–375, Apr. 2019, doi: 10.1016/j.asoc.2019.01.034.

Tang, L., Lu, Z., & Fan, B., "Energy efficient and reliable routing algorithm for wireless sensors networks," *Applied Sciences*, vol. 10, no. 5, pp. 1885–1890, Mar. 2020, doi: 10.3390/app10051885.

Thangaramya, K., Kulothungan, K., Gandhi, S. I., Selvi, M., Kumar, S. V. N. S., and Arputharaj, K., "Intelligent fuzzy rule-based approach with outlier detection for secured routing in WSN," *Soft Computing*, vol. 24, no. 21, pp. 16483–16497, Nov. 2020, doi: 10.1007/s00500-020-04955-z.

Tolani, M., Bajpai, A., Balodi, A., Sunny, & Singh, R. K. (2023). "Energy-efficient duty-cycle hybrid medium access control protocol for wireless sensor network." *Wireless Personal Communications*, 131(1), 609–621.

12 Future Scope for Integration of IoT/WSN with Upcoming Wireless Technology

Sampada HK, Rakhi S, Farhana Kausar, Bhaskar MK, Arun Balodi, and Stefano Rinaldi

12.1 INTRODUCTION

Any technology that facilitates communication between devices without requiring physical wires or cables is referred to as wireless technology. It has completely changed the way we engage with our environment, communicate, and obtain information. This includes a variety of communication channels, including satellite communication, Wi-Fi, Bluetooth, near field communication (NFC), and cellular networks (such as 4G and 5G). Rapid advancements in wireless technology are aimed at enhancing speed, range, security, and dependability while opening up new applications and services. Several emerging wireless technologies are expected to shape the future of connectivity. Here are some noteworthy ones:

- 6G: Research and development for the upcoming 6G wireless technology is already under way, as 5G networks continue to be deployed. Anticipated to provide even quicker speeds, reduced latency, and increased capacity, 6G seeks to facilitate cutting-edge applications such as advanced artificial intelligence, immersive virtual reality, and holographic communications.
- Wi-Fi 7 (802.11be): Wi-Fi 7 is expected to significantly improve performance and speed over the current Wi-Fi 6 standard, especially in densely populated areas. It attempts to meet the increasing need for devices and applications with high bandwidth.
- Li-Fi (Light Fidelity): Li-Fi offers potentially faster and more secure wireless communication by transmitting data using light waves rather than radio waves. It uses LED lights as a means of data transmission, making high-speed internet access possible in settings where conventional wireless technologies are constrained.
- Sub-6 GHz and mm Wave: The 5G networks operate in these distinct frequency bands. Wider coverage and improved penetration through obstructions are offered by sub-6 GHz, whereas mm wave offers very high data rates but a shorter range and restricted penetration. Both are essential to achieving 5G's full potential.
- Ultra-Wideband (UWB): Accurate location and fast, low-power data transfer over short distances are made possible by UWB technology. Applications such as asset tracking, secure wireless payments, and indoor navigation are using it more and more.
- Beamforming and massive MIMO: By directing signal transmissions in particular directions or toward particular devices, these technologies increase the capacity and efficiency of wireless networks. They are essential for improving network performance, particularly in congested areas.

DOI: 10.1201/9781003491910-12

- Satellite Internet Constellations: Large constellations of low-Earth orbit (LEO) satellites are being deployed by companies like SpaceX, with its Starlink project, to bring high-speed internet access to underserved areas worldwide. Internet connectivity could be revolutionized by this technology, particularly in remote areas.
- Terahertz Communication: Terahertz frequencies promise very high data rates and a vast amount of bandwidth for wireless communication. For practical implementation, however, obstacles like hardware limitations and signal attenuation must be addressed.

12.2 IOT AND WSN ARCHITECTURE AND INTEGRATION

IoT is a big buzzword out there and each one of us have our own understanding over this. The term "Internet of Things" (IoT) describes a network of real-world items, such as cars, appliances, and other machinery, that are integrated with software, sensors, and network connectivity to enable data collection and sharing. Its runs on a four layered architecture as shown in Figure 12.1. First is data collection from different sensors, data filtering and transmission followed by processing and data applications.

12.2.1 Internet of Things Is Made Possible by a Combination of Technologies

Actuators and sensors:

- Actuators are sensors of pressure, light, motion, temperature, humidity, and other external variables. Actuators are devices that can change their environment physically, such as opening or shutting a valve or turning on a motor. The Internet of Things is built on these devices, which allow machines and other devices to interact with the real world. Automation is possible when sensors and actuators work together to solve issues without requiring human intervention.

Technologies for Connectivity:

- Sensors and actuators on IoT devices cannot transmit data to the cloud unless they are online. Numerous connectivity technologies, including cellular, WiFi, Bluetooth, LoRaWAN, and Zigbee, are used in IoT. *Cloud computing*: The cloud is used to process, store, and analyze the massive amounts of data generated by Internet of Things devices. Cloud computing platforms offer the infrastructure and resources needed to create and execute Internet of Things applications as well as to store and analyze this data.
- *Big Data Analytics*:
  To find patterns and insights in the vast amounts of data generated by Internet of Things devices, organizations need to use advanced analytics tools. Among these tools are machine learning algorithms, data visualization tools, and predictive analytics models.

Security and Privacy:

- The proliferation of Internet of Things deployments has led to an increasing significance of IoT security and privacy. As seen in Figure 12.2, IoT has applications in daily fields. Applications and benefits come with risks as well, such as security concerns because sensitive and private data, such as patient information, can be involved. Since different protocols

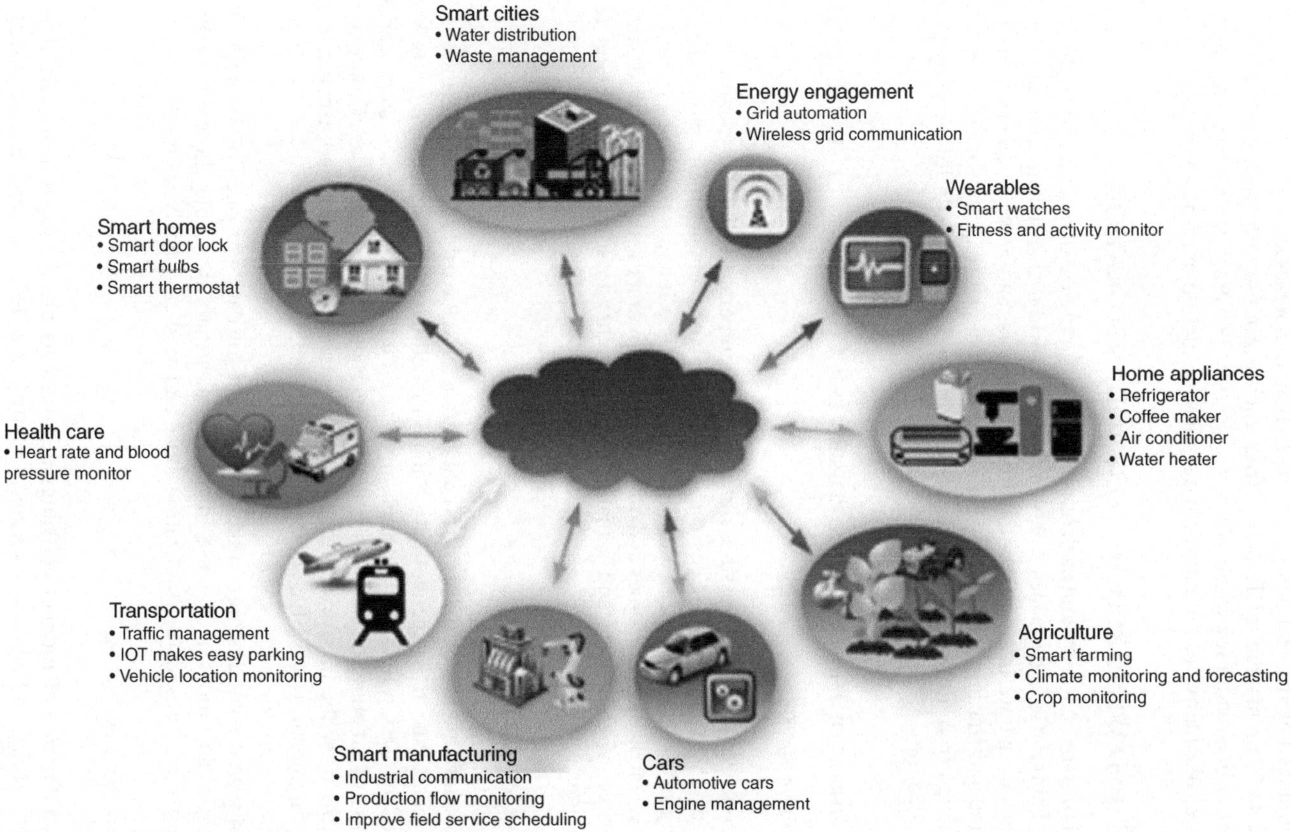

FIGURE 12.1 IoT architecture.

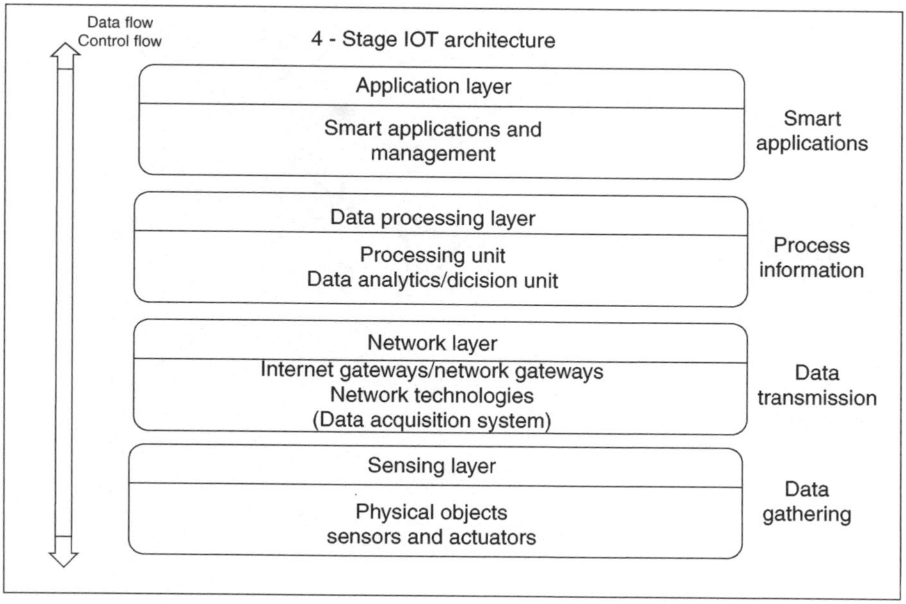

FIGURE 12.2 IoT applications.

are used by different devices, interoperability between them can be difficult. The main obstacles to IoT implementation are data handling, cost, and complexity.

12.2.2 Wireless Sensor Networks Architecture

Sensor, memory, processor, transceiver (transmitter and receiver), and battery are the five main parts of a sensor node. These days, nodes are meant to be compact and affordable. As a result, they have limited resources (usually a smaller battery, less memory, and less processing power). Wireless sensor nodes can only communicate locally, with a limited number of local neighbors, due to the limited transmission power. Therefore, nodes need to work together to complete tasks like sensing, processing signals, computing, routing, localization, security, and so on. WSNs are therefore collaborative networks by nature [1–3]. Usually, only a small number of sink nodes are in charge of data collection, instruction sending, and Internet communication. Figure 12.3 depicts the typical WSN system architecture.

The topology, sink node organization, other nodes, and a comprehensive view of the entire network can all be considered aspects of architecture [3]. The adaptability and autonomy are the crucial factors that need to be taken into account. Because autonomy allows sensors to be placed in physically inaccessible or unattended areas, it means that the least amount of work from base stations or human administrators is needed to keep the sensors functioning. When there is no discernible change in the sensor readings, sensors may lower their duty cycles to save power [4]. Sensor networks function by adjusting to the environmental changes that sensors monitor. Furthermore, the fundamental issue with WSNs is node deployment. The choice of node deployment strategy is made based on applications. The majority of these studies [6–8] make the assumption that the environment is adequately understood and managed. However, sensor deployment cannot be done manually in unfamiliar or hostile environments, such as hazardous urban

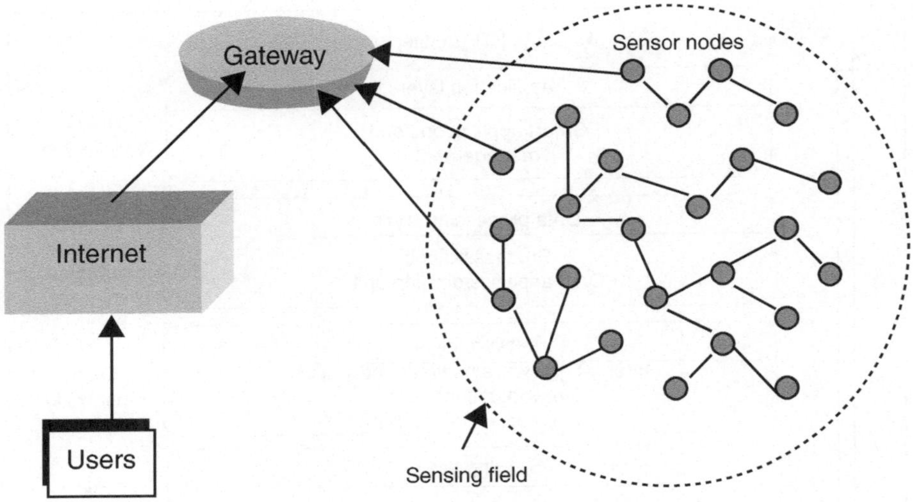

FIGURE 12.3 Wireless sensor network architecture.

areas, remote, harsh fields, and disaster areas. Dispersing sensors via aircraft is one approach that could work. However, because of the wind and other obstructions like trees and buildings, it is impossible to control the precise landing position while using this technique.

12.3 INTEGRATIONS OF IOT-WSN WITH CHALLENGES

The Internet of Things' integration with WSNs opens up a world of applications for use in all facets of life. We are aware that while IoT has a wealth of resources, and WSNs have sensors with constrained memory, processing, and power capacities. The preservation of WSNs' original functions while assisting one another in expanding the application ranges is crucial when integrating them with the Internet of Things.

A few concerns regarding this integration are covered in the section that follows.

The base station is in charge of mapping sensor node data to the corresponding internet protocol and vice versa. Both data from sensor nodes with the format of a unique sensor network protocol and data from the internet with TCP/IP compatibility can be handled by the base station. Additionally, it can communicate via IEEE 802.15.4, a wireless standard, and the MAC layer [5]. The second strategy is known as the "gate-way solution," in which the application layer gateway is a base station. In this case, the base station controls both the WSNs and the lower internet layers. WSNs can retain some degree of individuality using this method, but the table mapping sensor node address to IP address must still be created. At the base station, sensor data collected can only retain its uniqueness up to the TCP/IP layer. Data at the above layer will be handled as common

data. The third option, known as the TCP-IP overlay solution, enables the sensor node to speak with the internet directly through the TCP-IP protocol. By acting as a router, the base station joins the two networks. The node in this method needs to implement the internet's protocol and algorithm. It provides a comprehensive internet and WSN integration. Figure 12.4 makes it abundantly evident that the sensor node needs to have the TCP/IP protocol installed. WSNs can retain their uniqueness in this solution up to the MAC layer, after which there is no distinction between WSN and IoT data.

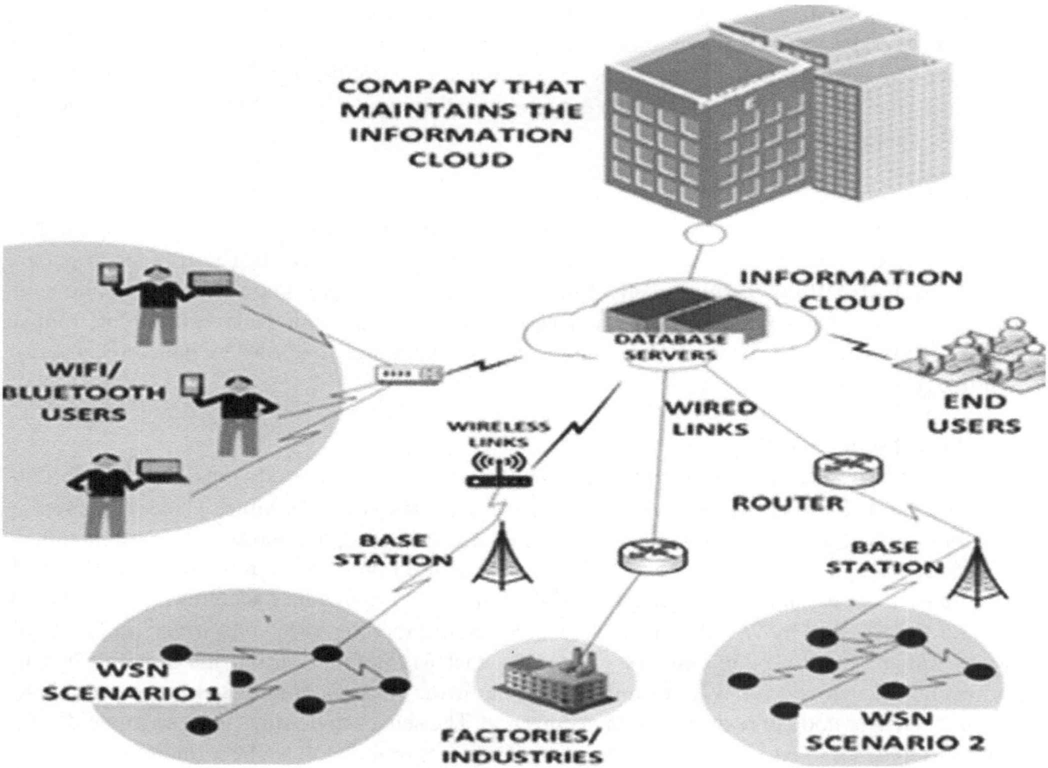

FIGURE 12.4 Integration of IoT-WSN architecture.

12.3.1 Integration Challenges

- **Addressing**

For a front-end proxy solution to work, the base station must be able to facilitate Internet and WSN interoperability. In the latter scenario, the base station serves as an application layer gateway. Both the WSN protocol and the internet protocol must work with it. The sensor node requires direct IP addresses in the third method, where the node can connect to the internet directly. Running a standard internet protocol on a sensor node with limited resources is indeed challenging.

Its protocols are customized based on the particular needs of the application and the surroundings of the event space. Protocols are made to use the least amount of network information necessary to accomplish a task. The reason for this is the node's limited energy and processing capacity. Conversely, the Internet of Things can process data indefinitely and communicate with greater energy efficiency. Since IoT deals with a wider range of applications, its protocol needs to be created in a way that takes into account all of the relevant factors [9]. Care must be taken when integrating application-specific protocols with the general protocol to preserve both interoperability and their inherent functionality [1,10].

- **Data and node accessibility**

Sensory data is WSNs' primary focus. It is dependent upon the sensor node's availability. WSNs have fewer resources overall, particularly power. To lessen the node continuously flips between the active and sleep modes based on power consumption. In the worst case, a node goes dead as a result of excessive power consumption. It suggests that a specific segment of the network is not accessible. The dead node and sleeping node are unable to leave the topology and transmit data. The node's unavailability may prevent the external host from collecting data from the node during the WSNs' internet integration.

- **Mobility**

Another important issue that needs to be carefully addressed is the node's mobility within the sensor network. In numerous applications, the sensor nodes move constantly in order to gather data. Additionally, WSNs include a novel method of data collection known as the mobile sink node. In order to gather the data from the sensor nodes, the sink node follows a predetermined path through the network. Here, the topology is always changing, so it must be handled carefully when integrating with the internet [11].

- **Technical and hardware problems**

Particular uses are intended for wireless sensor networks. The sensor node must supply a certain set of data for as long as feasible while using the fewest resources possible. They conserve the nodes' energy by communicating at a low data rate. Furthermore, the hardware is made to alternate between active and sleep modes. During the integration process, both the protocol that will be used and the application for which it will be used must take this into account. Tiny OS is the operating system used by WSNs. Rather than using multithreading, the event-driven professional programming model is used in Tiny OS. Other OSs, such as LiteOS, Contiki, and 6LoWPAN, had been recently developed for WSNs on the same platform. These operating systems are made to activate the sensor node in response to an occurrence. The sensor node stays in sleep mode during other times in order to conserve energy. Each sensor is integrated with a 64-bit microprocessor or a small 8-bit microcontroller. Their capacity to store data is restricted; RAM typically has a few kilobytes in size.

Security: They are placed in an area that is prone to events, either inside or close to the events. Wireless channel is used to transfer data. Any hostile opponent can use the node to the extent of their evil intent. Here, we focused on the specific area covered by WSNs; however, when we discussed how WSNs and IoT [12] can work together, we opened up the node's global reach. IoT is highly susceptible to outside attack. Integration suggests that the WSNs node is now vulnerable in the same way. From any location in the world, the attacker could pose a threat to the WSNs. Malware downloaded from the internet has the potential to negatively impact WSN performance.

- **Infrastructure and connectivity**

WSNs must be connected to the internet in order to begin the integration process. WSNs can be connected to the internet in three different ways. The base station serves as an interface between the sensor nodes and the internet in the first method, known as the front-end proxy solution. The primary controlling component that can receive data from sensor nodes and transmit control signals to them is the base station. Between the sensor node and the internet, the base station served as an insulator. The ability to implement its algorithms and protocol is granted by the sensor node's total autonomy.

12.4 UPCOMING WIRELESS TECHNOLOGIES TO INTEGRATE IOT-WSN

The integration of IoT and WSN with upcoming wireless technologies holds significant potential to revolutionize various industries and applications. Here's how:

- *AI–ML-based approach* [12–14]: The Internet of Things (IoT) and intelligent heterogeneous wireless devices, such as sensors and actuators, collaborate and exchange data. In today's smart world, these devices not only manage, track, collect data, monitor, and control embedded objects or individual entities, but they also provide a new avenue for utilizing artificial intelligence. Nonetheless, the most popular Internet of Things technology is wireless sensor networks (WSNs). WSN-IoT systems have made it feasible to transmit sensor and control data between satellite and Internet network infrastructures. Artificial intelligence (AI)-enabled intelligent connections between people and objects are at the heart of innovative business and industrial operations. IoT-AI networks will function in both terrestrial and non-terrestrial environments, such as those used by satellites. The automated operation of IoT nodes placed in smart cities can be effectively managed with the use of machine learning (ML) and artificial intelligence (AI) techniques. Smart buildings, smart waste management, smart traffic monitoring, and patient healthcare monitoring are the main Internet of things applications in smart cities. Gateways are typically used to transmit data from small-sized IoT nodes that are based on low-power Bluetooth (IEEE 802.15.1) and wireless sensor networks (WSN) (IEEE 802.15.4) standards to remote locations. The design challenges associated with WSN-IoT, or wireless sensor networks, encompass concerns related to network coverage and connectivity, energy efficiency, bandwidth demands, maximizing network lifetime, communication protocols, and cutting-edge infrastructure. To the best of the author's knowledge, this is the first comprehensive review of the literature on all machine learning techniques related to low power consumption WSN-IoT for smart cities. According to the findings of this special survey article, for smart city applications, supervised learning algorithms have been applied the most frequently (61 percent), followed by unsupervised learning (12 percent) and reinforcement learning (27 percent).
- *Enhanced Connectivity*: Future wireless technologies with lower latency, greater reliability, and higher data rates include 5G, Wi-Fi 7, and 6G. By combining these technologies with IoT and WSN, a wide range of sensors, actuators, and devices can connect seamlessly, allowing for real-time data collection, analysis, and response.
- *Massive IoT Deployment*: With the introduction of technologies like LTE-M (Long-Term Evolution for Machines) and NB-IoT (Narrowband IoT), future wireless standards are made to accommodate large-scale IoT device deployments. This makes it possible for Internet of Things applications to scale across a variety of environments, including smart cities, industrial automation, agriculture, and healthcare.
- *Edge Computing and Processing* [15]:
  By utilizing edge devices' computational power to process data locally, IoT/WSN in conjunction with edge computing capabilities lowers latency and bandwidth consumption. Distributed computing architectures are made possible by emerging wireless technologies, which allow for more effective communication between edge devices and centralized/cloud servers. All computing outside of the cloud can now occur at the network's edge thanks to EC, a computing paradigm that expands on cloud computing and is especially useful for applications requiring real-time data processing. These days, the local network's "Edge" designates the location of sensor nodes and Internet of Things devices. EC processes vast amounts of data produced by edge network users or sensor nodes. Regarding context awareness, on the other hand, context information represents processed raw data, whereas data generated by one sensor node or by several sensor nodes represent unprocessed data. A centralized data processing system called the "cloud" uses enormous amounts of instantly accessible data to function. Edge data centers are specialized data centers that are situated closer to the edge than the cloud. They offer real-time data transmission costs and minimal

latency compared to the centralized cloud, along with faster processing than edge devices. Physical hardware components known as edge devices are used to transfer data between a local network and a central cloud. Traditional edge devices can be anything from firewalls and routers to chips and edge sensors. Sources of data accumulation are sensor nodes. These technologies include chips and edge sensors that can collect, sense, and process data to a certain degree [17, 18].

- *Improved Reliability and Resilience*: Emerging wireless technologies frequently include characteristics that improve network coverage, dependability, and resistance to interference and environmental factors, such as massive MIMO, beamforming, and network slicing. Critical Internet of Things applications like smart grids, driverless cars, and medical monitoring systems will especially benefit from this.
- *Advanced Sensing and Actuation*: IoT and WSN deployments can leverage advanced sensing and actuation capabilities, like LiDAR, radar, and terahertz imaging, through integration with emerging wireless technologies. These innovations improve how IoT devices perceive and interact, opening up new possibilities for more advanced uses in fields like environmental monitoring and smart infrastructure.
- *Security and Privacy*: Robust security mechanisms will be given priority in future wireless standards to safeguard IoT and WSN deployments against cyber threats and unauthorized access. End-to-end encryption, secure bootstrapping, and device authentication are examples of features that improve the security posture of interconnected systems, protecting private information and guaranteeing user privacy [19].
- *Energy Efficiency*: The goal of many emerging wireless technologies is to increase energy efficiency and increase the battery life of sensors and Internet of Things devices. Devices deployed in remote or inaccessible locations can operate longer thanks to reduced energy consumption made possible by low-power communication protocols, energy harvesting strategies, and optimized network protocols.

Overall, the integration of IoT/WSN with upcoming wireless technologies enables the development of innovative solutions that address complex challenges across various domains, including healthcare, transportation, agriculture, smart cities, and industrial automation. By leveraging the capabilities of these advanced wireless networks, organizations can unlock new opportunities for efficiency, productivity, and sustainability.

12.5 CONCLUSION

The WSN and IoT integration opens up a wide range of opportunities in practically every area of life. Although the integration appears fascinating at first, there are hidden difficulties involved. Sensor nodes in WSNs have relatively little hardware and software resources. The operating system of the sensor node operates very differently from the internet node and has a very small processing capacity. Sensor node hardware is engineered to minimize energy consumption and automatically switch to active mode in response to events. IoT, on the other hand, is not constrained by hardware compatibility or processing power.

The layered functions of IoT and WSNs in the integration must be optimized for interoperability. Furthermore, in order to combat online security threats, WSNs nodes must be updated. WSNs must improve their capacity overall for faithful integration, and IoT must modify its layered operation to make it compatible with WSNs. Figure 12.5 shows the various research trends in integrating IoT–WSN. IoT gadgets and WSNs integrate with ease. Wireless network protocols are changing and low-power options like LoRaWAN are outperforming Wi-Fi because

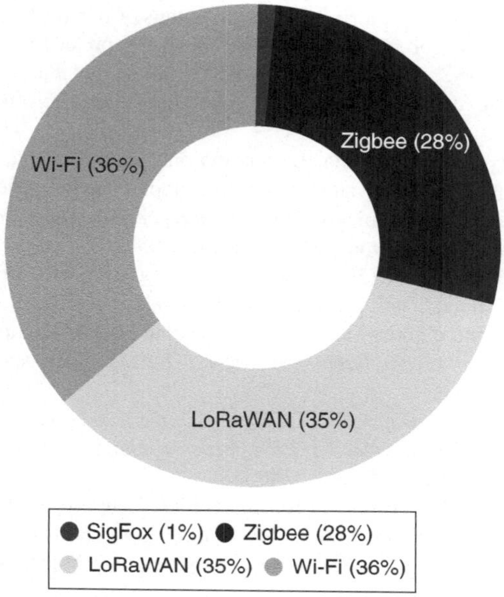

FIGURE 12.5 Research contribution distribution in IoT-WSN with various wireless technologies.

of their effectiveness, network coverage, and in areas low power needs. Furthermore, SigFox continues to be a topic of interest for IoT research in agricultural systems because it uses narrowband technology and provides wide coverage with fewer base stations. As Figure 12.5 illustrates, although its usage has remained at 1% since 2019, SigFox and LoRaWAN are not interchangeable due to their different levels of flexibility. LoRaWAN is more appropriate for certain agricultural setups that need more control or distinct coverage patterns because of its increased flexibility.

REFERENCES

[1] R. Dhiman and J. Thakur (2023). "Evolution of WSN into WSN-IoT: A study on its architecture and integration challenges." In: Gupta, D., Khanna, A., Hassanien, A.E., Anand, S., Jaiswal, A. (eds) International Conference on Innovative Computing and Communications. *Lecture Notes in Networks and Systems*, vol 492. Springer, Singapore. https://doi.org/10.1007/978-981-19-3679-1_14

[2] R. Sharma, S. Prakash and P. Roy, "Methodology, applications, and challenges of WSN-IoT," *2020 International Conference on Electrical and Electronics Engineering (ICE3)*, Gorakhpur, India, 2020, pp. 502–507, doi: 10.1109/ICE348803.2020.9122891.

[3] V. R. Pathmudi, N. Khatri, S. Kumar, A. S. H. Abdul-Qawy and A. K. Vyas, "A systematic review of IoT technologies and their constituents for smart and sustainable agriculture applications", *Sci. Afr.*, vol. 19, Mar. 2023.

[4] N. Alam, "Opportunity assessment and feasibility study of IoT-based smart farming in Bangladesh for meeting sustainable development goals". In *The Fourth Industrial Revolution and Beyond*, Cham, Switzerland: Springer, pp. 723–736, 2023.

[5] S. Basnet, A. Wood, E. Röös, T. Jansson, I. Fetzer and L. Gordon, "Organic agriculture in a low-emission world: Exploring combined measures to deliver sustainable food system in Sweden", *Sustainability Sci.*, vol. 18, no. 1, pp. 501–519, 2023.

[6] H. Allioui and Y. Mourdi, "Exploring the full potentials of IoT for better financial growth and stability: A comprehensive survey", *Sensors*, vol. 23, no. 19, pp. 8015, Sep. 2023.

[7] T. Anees, Q. Habib, A. S. Al-Shamayleh, W. Khalil, M. A. Obaidat and A. Akhunzada, "The integration of WoT and edge computing: Issues and challenges", *Sustainability*, vol. 15, no. 7, pp. 5983, Mar. 2023.

[8] A. Bhola, S. Srivastava, A. Noonia, B. Sharma and S. K. Narang, "A status quo of machine learning algorithms in smart agricultural systems employing IoT-based WSN: Trends challenges and futuristic competences". In *Machine Intelligence Big Data Analytics and IoT in Image Processing: Practical Applications*, Wiley, pp. 177–195, 2023.

[9] K. Shrivastav and R.B. Battula (2023). "WSN-IoT integration with artificial intelligence: research opportunities and challenges". In: Yadav, R.P., Nanda, S.J., Rana, P.S., and Lim, M.H. (eds) Proceedings of the International Conference on Paradigms of Computing, Communication and Data Sciences. *Algorithms for Intelligent Systems*, Springer, Singapore. https://doi.org/10.1007/978-981-19-8742-7_31.

[10] M. AlSelek, J. M. Alcaraz-Calero and Q. Wang, "Dynamic AI-IoT: enabling updatable AI models in ultralow-power 5G IoT devices," *IEEE Internet of Things Journal*, vol. 11, no. 8, pp. 14192–14205, 2024, doi: 10.1109/JIOT.2023.3340858.

[11] P. Raja (2022). "ML in WSN using IoT for smart cities: A survey." In: Mukherjee, S., Muppalaneni, N.B., Bhattacharya, S., Pradhan, A.K. (eds). *Intelligent Systems for Social Good. Advanced Technologies and Societal Change*. Springer, Singapore. https://doi.org/10.1007/978-981-19-0770-8_1.

[12] H. Sharma, A. Haque, and F. Blaabjerg. "Machine learning in wireless sensor networks for smart cities: A survey." *Electronics* 10, 1012, 2021. https://doi.org/10.3390/electronics10091012.

[13] A.A. Al-Saedi, V. Boeva, E. Casalicchio, & P. Exner. "Context-aware edge-based AI models for wireless sensor networks—an overview." *Sensors* 22, 5544, 2022. https://doi.org/10.3390/s22155544.

[14] M. N. Mowla, N. Mowla, A. F. M. S. Shah, K. M. Rabie and T. Shongwe, "Internet of things and wireless sensor networks for smart agriculture applications: A survey," *IEEE Access*, 11, 145813–145852, 2023, doi: 10.1109/ACCESS.2023.3346299.

[15] M. Merenda, C. Porcaro, and D. Iero, "Edge machine learning for AI-enabled IOT devices: A review." *Sensors* 20, 2533, 2020.

[16] P. Kansal, D. Kansal, Compression of various routing protocols in wireless sensor network, *A Balodi International Journal of Computer Applications*, *5*(11), 0975–8887.

[17] M. Tolani, A. Bajpai, A. Balodi, Sunny, and R.K. Singh, "Energy-efficient duty-cycle hybrid medium access control protocol for wireless sensor network", *Wireless Personal Communications Wireless Personal Communications Wireless Personal Communications* 131 (1), 609–621.

[18] M.S. Pramod, A. Balodi, A. Pratik, G.S. Sankalp, B. Varshita, and R. Amrit, "Energy-efficient reinforcement learning in wireless sensor networks using 5G for smart cities", *Advanced Sensor Systems for Robotics and Autonomous Vehicles,* CRC Press.

[19] M. Tolani, A.A. Ajasa, A. Balodi, A. Bajpai, and Y. AlZaharani, "Advanced sensor systems for robotics and autonomous vehicles", *Sunny Artificial Intelligence for Robotics and Autonomous Systems Applications,* Cham: Springer International Publishing.

13 Securing the Future

Navigating Privacy Challenges in Real-time IoT and WSN Applications

Pooja Dehankar and Susanta Das

13.1 INTRODUCTION

The introduction of wireless networking technologies has brought about significant changes in all aspects of our daily life. IoT is one of the technologies that will develop the fastest in the future. The integration of IoT allows for the connection of numerous devices in the real world, significantly changing our way of life. As a result, communications are becoming more and more important everywhere and at all times, but notably in areas with a lot of activity. The integration and communication of intelligent devices is one way to think about the Internet of Things. The Internet of Things' supremacy creates new technologies and applications. A range of transceivers, microcontroller devices, and protocols are frequently used in home appliances, security cameras, and environmental monitoring sensors, among other types of sensors and actuators, to exchange sensor and control data (Cho et al., 2018).

IoT is basically a network of many interconnected objects, or nodes, that may communicate and share information to carry out common tasks. Objects include people, cars, animals, doors, items in the home, cell phones, and everything else you may imagine. Each and every object has a sensor attached to it so that it may interact with its environment. By linking devices from the public, commercial, industrial, and personal sectors, IoT enables the sorting, analysis, and storing of information. In the areas of healthcare, energy generation, and distribution, it is extensively utilized. "A global infrastructure for the information society, enabling advanced services by interconnecting (physical and virtual) things based on existing and evolving interoperable information and communication technologies" is how the International Telecommunication Union (ITU) defines the IoT (Leloglu, 2017).

Researchers have been paying close attention to IoT in the past few years. It is defined as an ever-changing, ubiquitous network of intelligent objects that can be uniquely identified by means of interoperable, scalable, and standardized communication protocols (Li et al., 2015).

Real and virtual objects have characteristics and identities in the Internet of Things that enable them to interact with information networks. IoT is a network of physical objects that are globally connected and integrated with networking, communication, sensing, and processing technologies. With the use of this technology, things can communicate with one another and their environment. IoT networks are composed of large heterogeneous wireless devices that compete for limited resources such as spectrum, electricity, processing power, and other resources. These entities are required to manage a rise in traffic demands while complying with many quality of service (QoS) requirements concerning bandwidth, latency, reliability, and feedback loops. RFID technology is the backbone of the Internet of Things and is used in many real-world applications

DOI: 10.1201/9781003491910-13

such as supply chain visibility, pharmaceutical manufacturing, library systems, access control, inventory monitoring, and race timing (Xu, 2011).

The objects to be connected to the Internet have a wide range of characteristics. This covers both extremely small, stationary devices (like RFIDs) and very large, moving devices (like autos). This kind of unpredictability breeds complexity, making the usage of elaborate middleware necessary to mask it and promote transparency. In particular, devices are being connected to the Internet via wireless sensor networks (WSNs) through a gateway that connects the WSN to the Internet. Sensed data (temperature, motion, pressure, fire detection, voltage/current, etc.) is gathered by WSNs and sent to the gateway via a one-way communication protocol, which sets them apart from other types of networks (Khalil et al., 2014).

A small-scale network of sensor nodes used to perceive, record, and process data relating to a specific application, such a focused phenomenon, is known as a wireless sensor network (WSN) (Rawat et al., 2014).

These resource-hungry nodes are hence highly dependent on data capacity, computation, storage, battery management, and accessible bandwidth. These nodes, which are often set in a particular way and left alone in a remote area that is inaccessible to humans, are used to track and record information. Since messages are delivered via electromagnetic waves over all or a portion of the communication channel, the term "wireless" has evolved to refer to these types of communications in a broad and inclusive sense (Chen et al., 2017).

The term "Internet of Things" typically describes a body of research and innovation that allows users of the Internet to interact with the physical world (Sicari et al., 2016).

There are two fundamental ideas, nevertheless, on what the IoT is and what technological innovations should be considered as a result. However, there are many additional technologies that are connected to the IoT, including RFID, low-range wireless, real-time localization, and network sensors. This viewpoint states that the primary characteristic of the IoT is the usage of pervasive sensor communications, which makes devices functional. However, additional study suggests that the definition of "thing" should go beyond physical things to include theoretical and virtual features, especially those pertaining to services. Considering this, the current endeavor seeks to reduce this difference and will integrate these unique features (Miorandi et al., 2012).

13.2 PRIVACY CHALLENGES IN REAL-TIME IOT AND WSN

When it comes to wireless sensor networks and healthcare applications, privacy is one of the main issues. Health-related data are inherently private. There are several causes of privacy problems. Personal beliefs, the social and cultural context, and other general public and private factors could be the cause. Transmitting patient data over wireless media can seriously jeopardize an individual's privacy. There is a chance that there will be a public backlash that breeds mistrust and prevents technology from being used for the many worthwhile uses where it might provide enormous benefits if the privacy issues are not openly and rationally discussed (Al Ameen et al., 2012).

Since the modern Internet is being used more and more to enable interactions between humans, machines, and robots in any combination, it stands to reason that the vast number of IoT devices and this high degree of heterogeneity will increase the security concerns connected with it. In particular, standard privacy protection techniques and security countermeasures cannot be directly applied to IoT technologies due to their low computing capacity; additionally, scale issues arise due to the vast number of connected devices. The right security, privacy, and trust models need to be designed for the context of IoT applications in order to achieve complete user acceptability (Miorandi et al., 2012; Weber, 2010; Feng & Fu, 2010; Roman et al., 2013; Anderson & Rainie, 2014).

In order to prevent unauthorized users from accessing the system, authentication and authorization processes must be in place in addition to providing data anonymity, confidentiality, and integrity. However, data security and the privacy of users' personal information must be ensured because devices may handle sensitive data (such user habits). Finally, trust is a critical issue since the IoT environment consists of a variety of devices that must process and handle data in line with user desires and rights. It should be mentioned that in order for IoT infrastructures to survive both expected and unexpected changes in the target environment, they must have the capacity to adapt and self-heal. Security and privacy concerns must to be addressed with extreme flexibility (Bandyopadhyay et al., 2011; Chaqfeh & Mohamed, 2012).

Embedded security needs to be included in the devices themselves in order to offer dynamic prevention, detection, diagnosis, isolation, and countermeasures against successful breaches, in addition to standard security solutions (Babar et al., 2011).

IoT has greatly helped users; however, there are also disadvantages. The primary issues are privacy risks and cybersecurity, according to the experts and security specialists on the list. Because of these two, public and private entities are faced with a huge challenge. Frequent, widely reported cybersecurity attacks have exposed the shortcomings of IoT technologies. This risk arises from the fact that content that is unreliable and anonymous can be accessed through the interconnected networks of the Internet of Things, which calls for the creation of novel security measures (Tawalbeh & Tawalbeh, 2017).

A poorly protected or connected item has the potential to significantly impact global Internet security and resilience because of the interconnection of IoT devices. This conduct is just a result of the challenges brought about by the ubiquitous deployment of identical IoT devices. This suggests that both IoT users and developers have a need to ensure they are not threatening other users or the Internet itself, in addition to the reality that some gadgets are capable of mechanically attaching themselves to one another. Today's IoT problems call for cooperation in order to develop a workable and effective solution (Alaba et al., 2017).

Recent advancements in networking, handheld computing, and sensor technology are bringing Mark Weiser's vision of omnipresent and serene computing closer to reality. As a result, smart environments are now a hot topic for research in this discipline. By definition, intelligent settings leverage intricate configurations of small dispersed sensor and processing nodes to identify people and offer customized services during interactions and data exchanges with the surroundings. In these kinds of situations, customers are very demanding solutions that offer security, privacy, and reliability. In cryptography, "security" refers to the techniques employed to safeguard essential data and communication channels. Privacy thus encompasses trust and risk considerations in user interactions (Nixon et al., 2004).

The phrase "security" encompasses a multitude of discrete meanings. It primarily concerns the basic provision of security services, including confidentiality, integrity, authorization, availability, non-repudiation, and authentication. To provide these security services, a variety of cryptographic approaches are available, such as hash functions, block ciphers, and signature algorithms. Keeping track of the cryptographic keys required for each of these processes requires a robust key management system. However, security for the IoT must take into account not only the essential security services but also how the system as a whole applies them and how the security features function (Heer et al., 2011).

Embedded devices are increasingly being incorporated into personal and business infrastructures, ranging from residential to aerospace applications. When these embedded devices connect over the air, it can be challenging to protect applications from malicious intent while maintaining the security and privacy of entities and data. Moreover, the security design criteria for embedded systems differ from those for traditional security design due to their constrained resources and vulnerability to adversaries. Attackers are able to replay, intercept, or change communications transmitted back and forth between two entities while they are communicating over open channels. Depending on the needs of the application, security elements including data confidentiality, integrity, authentication, and availability can be enabled; however, the requirements vary from application to application. Data confidentiality keeps sensitive information safe from unauthorized access. Data integrity ensures that the information hasn't been altered without authorization. By implementing entity authentication, it is ensured that the data is provided and received by reliable organizations. Another essential security characteristic is the availability of the expected services. Short-term app unresponsiveness can be catastrophic for mission-critical apps, put patient lives at risk for medical professionals, and not be customer-centric for traditional apps. Applications need to be set up with the appropriate intrusion detection and prevention systems to ward against potential attackers who might try to prevent legitimate users from utilizing their services (Das, 2015).

IoT entails joining devices together so they may talk to one other and share data. Ensuring customer privacy and safeguarding user data are critical in IoT scenarios. The important subjects of data management, security, collecting, and sharing are currently under discussion. It's crucial to consider IoT administration, object profile protection, and securing data and resource access. These considerations are made possible through the integration of identity management and authentication techniques. Identity management techniques are used to uniquely identify items in the environment, while authentication techniques are used to ensure and validate the identity establishment amongst objects in the IoT environment. IoT environments are mysterious. Thus, in this uncomfortable setting, trust is essential for object-to-object communication. Building safe connections in the uncharted territory of the IoT requires trust. The two viewpoints on trust in IoT are trust between communicating IoT gadgets and trust between users. IoT devices have different shapes, differing capacities for memory, and are limited by the processing power available to them. The aforementioned gadgets are susceptible to hacking. For this reason, security defenses against attacks and countermeasures should be available (Abomhara & Køien, 2014).

Preventing cyberattacks sometimes necessitates striking a balance between security and availability, since integrity and confidentiality are the primary goals of protection for traditional corporate IT systems. In the event of a cyberattack, for instance, the compromised IT systems are often turned off for a while before being restarted. However, since availability is a fundamental need, this strategy is not relevant to Cyber-physical systems security (CPPS). Further differences arise from the long life of industrial production systems, the strict real-time requirements of CPPS, and their constrained energy, memory, and compute resources. Other considerations include the detection of counterfeit components and the protection of configuration and design data. Privacy is becoming a more crucial factor to take into account as CPPS become more networked and their acquired data may be examined utilizing Big Data techniques (Miorandi et al., 2012; Kumar & Patel, 2014).

The IoT's evolving features, technologies, and interaction methods have given rise to specific privacy and security concerns. One of the concerns with IoT privacy and security is the potential to connect an identifier, such as an address, to an individual and associated data. By providing identifying information to companies outside of the user's domain, assigning an identity to a particular context in this case threatens an individual's privacy and increases the opportunity for cyberattacks. IoT-related privacy and security issues also include localization and tracking. The threat in this case relates to determining and recording the individual's movements throughout space and time. Many people may consider this to be a privacy infringement if the data is misused or if they have no choice over the sharing of their location information, even if it is already possible to localize and monitor using a variety of ways, such as internet traffic and mobile phone Global Positioning System (GPS) position. Because of this, the IoT faces challenges in keeping awareness of tracking and control over the location data (Rose et al., 2015).

The hardest thing to do when it comes to IoT security is to keep communication data and information private. Several common encryption features, such as shared secret keys and popular encryption algorithms like triple Data Encryption Standard (DES), Blowfish, and the Advanced Encryption Standard (AES)block cipher, can be utilized to protect data privacy between the communicating parties (Thakur & Kumar, 2011).

However, data and information privacy cannot be fully protected by employing data encryption alone as a security technique. The attacker can easily do a traffic analysis of the encrypted data that was intercepted, revealing sensitive information about it. Confidentiality problems are worse when a hostile node breaches one of the communication's endpoints, possibly releasing important data and information. Using a group-shared key, the rogue node can also successfully penetrate the radio frequency range of other sensor nodes, giving it the ability to intercept and decode confidential information in the connection. Adversaries in conventional sensor networks may add more bogus packets to their attacks in addition to changing the communication packets (Padmavathi & Shanmugapriya, 2009).

Because WSNs share a wireless communication medium and are used in unsupervised environments, ensuring data authenticity is a challenging task. Source authentication can be accomplished by symmetric or asymmetric methods, where the sending and receiving nodes share secret keys to confirm the identity of the resource (Shi & Perrig, 2004).

It is necessary to allow sensor nodes to distinguish between maliciously inserted or spoofing packets and authentic packets. Practically speaking, most applications require data authentication. For example, attackers are clearly incentivized to target sensor nodes by introducing malicious data reports or false routing information in military and safety-critical applications. Therefore, civilian applications—which are expected to be comparatively non-adversarial environments—remain susceptible in the absence of data authentication. Data authentication does not solve the problem of node compromise because a hacked node can still authenticate into the network by collecting the secret keys from the legitimate nodes, even while it stops malevolent attackers from fabricating or maliciously injecting packets into WSNs (Burhanuddin et al., 2018).

13.3 SECURITY MEASURES FOR REAL-TIME IOT AND WSN

Over commercially accessible virtual private network (VPN) services, an encrypted overlay network is developed to increase the privacy of IoT users, especially those using smart home systems (Schurgot et al., 2015).

To enhance and control security-related operations at the sensor level in the IoT, the authors proposed utilizing physical unclonable functions (PUFs) based on hardware. The IoT will have more security because to the usage of PUFs, low-level security features on the devices, and the creation of cryptography software for specialized jobs like verification (Xu et al., 2014).

According to the authors, this is a non-trivial task because of the architecture's complexity in respect to the trust attestation systems. These methods, which might be hardware- or software-based, necessitate large power consumption and extra costs (such PUFs or control flow integrity verification), are not suitable for general IoT application. In the near future, software- and hardware-based remote attestation methodologies for IoT trust establishment could be combined to create some intermediate hybrid solutions that are appropriate for the requirements and capabilities of the things themselves. To make sure that these hybrid systems for the Internet of

Things can operate in scaled contexts, resist denial-of-service attacks, and repel malicious verification conditions, testing and validation are essential (Abera et al., 2016).

In addition to the constrained resources of end devices and lossy communication connections, new and developing networking and communications technologies as RPL, 6LoWPAN, TSCH, MQTT, CoAP, and others make it challenging to provide security in the IoT.

It's crucial to consider the effects of using these technologies—one or more at once—while exercising prudence, keeping in mind IoT network and device limitations (Butun et al., 2019).

The approved web standard for the IoT is currently constrained application protocol (CoAP). Unlike traditional wireless sensor networks, Internet-connected smart device installations require security. According to CoAP, the Datagram TLS (DTLS) protocol has to be the primary secure communication mechanism. For cloud-based apps and resource-constrained IoT devices, the authors create secure CoAP with DTLS protection. The three CoAP security modalities—raw-public key, certificate-based, and pre-shared key—are evaluated by the authors in a real cloud-connected IoT setup. The authors improve a DTLS solution for devices with low resources by combining certificate-based asymmetric encryption with raw-public key integration, and they give secure CoAP capability to SicsthSense, an IoT cloud platform. With limited resources, the author's work attempts to facilitate end-to-end secure communication supporting all three CoAP security types between cloud back-ends and resource-constrained smart devices on both the client and server sides. Open source and Berkeley Software Distribution (BSD) licenses are used to create all of the standard-based protocols that comprise SecureSense's End-to-End (E2E) secure communication architecture for the IoT. The use of open source and open licenses, along with the SecureSense evaluation benchmarks, will enable future Internet of Things product and service providers to assure vendor compatibility and account for security overhead while employing all established protocols (Raza et al., 2017).

13.4 PRIVACY-ENHANCING TECHNOLOGIES

Sensing device custodians are worried that the procedure used to gather the samples of data and the data itself may disclose private information. For instance, when exchanging sensor data, the information supplied may disclose details about the context of a device. Additionally, custodians may not want to reveal information about themselves via sensor data, such as sound, picture, and accelerometer data. Moreover, individuals who aren't custodians or the main targets of the sensing system may unintentionally have their privacy compromised—a "second-hand smoke" effect of people-centric sensing systems (Campbell et al., 2008).

Blockchain is described as a distributed data structure, database, or system by some researchers, but as a decentralized network by others (Bonneau et al., 2015; Kosba et al., 2016; Lewenberg et al., 2015; Ølnes, 2016; Zhao et al., 2016). Blockchain technology originally enabled the digital currency BitCoin (Nian & Chuen, 2015). After its initial application, blockchain technology has been developed and studied in a number of other contexts.

As per González (2015), smart contracts have the ability to utilize blockchain technology in order to expedite and streamline transactions across numerous users. An argument for the potential benefits of blockchain technology in the manufacturing supply chain was presented by Abeyratne and Monfared (2016). They claimed that by facilitating transparency and traceability, the inherent features of blockchain technology increase confidence in any exchange of data, goods, and money. Blockchain has also been referred to as a "trust-free" technology in recent years, and Beck (2016) state that it is anticipated to form the basis of the current sharing economy, which is mostly powered by platforms.

Greiner and Wang (2015) introduced the concept of trust-free systems, which automatically use blockchain capabilities to build an immutable, universally recognized, and publicly accessible record of past transactions, hence eliminating trust difficulties in peer-to-peer systems. The entire system is keeping an eye on this record. As per Rachel Botsman (2017), the distribution of trust via blockchain technology is poised to revolutionize the way individuals establish trust with each other.

Data privacy regulations are a group of legal frameworks designed to regulate the collection, use, storage, and disclosure of an individual's personal data. These regulations are, at their core, a response to the increasing threats associated with living in the digital age, when pervasive technology use has allowed others to access and utilize personal data in ways never previously conceivable. These laws are essential because they define the rights of individuals, the obligations of data controllers and processors, and the processes for enforcement and redress that they establish (Aljeraisy et al., 2021; Gstrein & Beaulieu, 2022; Politou et al., 2022).

In the current digital era, data has turned into a valuable commodity that promotes innovation, increases economic growth, and enhances user experiences. However, the increased usage of data has also increased the likelihood of abuse, unauthorized access, and privacy concerns. Given this, it is impossible to overstate the significance of data privacy. It preserves people's right to privacy, lessens the chance of identity theft, and guards against unwanted access to personal data. Strict data privacy laws also encourage individuals to feel comfortable utilizing online services by fostering a sense of confidence in digital ecosystems (Ahmed, et. al., 2022, Hai, et. al., 2021, Walton & Nayak, 2021).

13.5 CONCLUSION

As sensor network applications expand, consequences will arise. We have tried to address social issues in this chapter, including security and privacy. In this chapter, the causes and consequences of these two issues have been examined. The necessary expansion and development will face formidable obstacles in the near future. Manufacturers, academic institutions, and governmental organizations need to work together effectively in order to overcome these obstacles and guarantee a smooth deployment. The public should be made aware of the benefits and implications as well, to aid in their preparation. Legislation pertaining to cyberspace and current health regulations, for example, must be formalized and put into effect.

For this chapter, a comprehensive and methodical review of the literature was conducted in order to analyze key aspects of smart IoT ecosystems, such as security and privacy. Most IoT setups focus on security issues to address the challenges presented by physical devices, like lightweight, adaptable, and dynamic key management techniques. Concerning security, confidentiality, privacy, dependability, and trust, the concept of IoT poses new challenges. The primary issues are that a large number of devices do not follow the necessary specifications and are not secured by firewalls or other techniques. Wireless channels can attack them with ease. Through theft and analysis, attackers might be able to obtain such devices and access their crucial data. Combining data from several sources is the other major issue since users and data suppliers are never guaranteed security. It is necessary for users of data from IoT devices to have access to a safe platform for sharing information. The concept that people will trust technology if it is safe is supported by the various important privacy and security challenges. If not, employing it won't be possible and might even endanger the patient's life. Key sharing, cryptography, and pseudonyms are the most widely utilized security and privacy mechanisms; ZigBee and 802.15.4 both make use of the latter two. WSN security and privacy are set up in a secure cell where some decoding is necessary before data is transmitted. Reliability is a vital need for WSNs to be used in protecting critical infrastructure. However, other factors affecting the system's dependability are energy consumption, radio connectivity, and security.

REFERENCES

Abera, T., Asokan, N., Davi, L., Koushanfar, F., Paverd, A., Sadeghi, A.R. and Tsudik, G., 2016, June. Things, trouble, trust: On building trust in IoT systems. In *Proceedings of the 53rd Annual Design Automation Conference* (pp. 1–6).

Abeyratne, S.A. and Monfared, R.P., 2016. Blockchain ready manufacturing supply chain using distributed ledger. *International Journal of Research in Engineering and Technology*, *5*(9), pp.1–10.

Abomhara, M. and Køien, G.M., 2014. May. Security and privacy in the Internet of Things: Current status and open issues. In *2014 International Conference on Privacy and Security in Mobile Systems (PRISMS)* (pp. 1–8). IEEE.

Ahmed, Z., Ahmad, M., Murshed, M., Vaseer, A.I. and Kirikkaleli, D., 2022. The trade-off between energy consumption, economic growth, militarization, and CO 2 emissions: does the treadmill of destruction exist in the modern world?. *Environmental Science and Pollution Research*, pp. 1–14.

Al Ameen, M., Liu, J. and Kwak, K., 2012. Security and privacy issues in wireless sensor networks for healthcare applications. *Journal of Medical Systems*, *36*, pp. 93–101.

Alaba, F.A., Othman, M., Hashem, I.A.T. and Alotaibi, F., 2017. Internet of Things security: A survey. *Journal of Network and Computer Applications*, *88*, pp. 10–28.

Aljeraisy, A., Barati, M., Rana, O., & Perera, C. (2021). Privacy laws and privacy by design schemes for the internet of things: A developer's perspective. *ACM Computing Surveys* (Csur), *54*(5), 1–38.

Anderson, J. and Rainie, L., (2014). The Internet of things will thrive by 2025.

Babar, S., Stango, A., Prasad, N., Sen, J. and Prasad, R., 2011, February. Proposed embedded security framework for internet of things (IoT). In *2011 2nd International Conference on Wireless Communication, Vehicular Technology, Information Theory and Aerospace & Electronic Systems Technology (Wireless VITAE)* (pp. 1–5). IEEE.

Bandyopadhyay, S., Sengupta, M., Maiti, S. and Dutta, S., 2011, June. A survey of middleware for internet of things. In *International Conference on Computer Networks and Communications* (pp. 288–296). Berlin: Springer.

Beck, R., Czepluch, J.S., Lollike, N. and Malone, S., 2016. Blockchain–the gateway to trust-free cryptographic transactions. In *Twenty-Fourth European Conference on Information Systems (ECIS), Istanbul, Turkey, 2016* (pp. 1–14). Berlin: Springer.

Böhme, R., Christin, N., Edelman, B., & Moore, T. (2015). Bitcoin: Economics, technology, and governance. *Journal of Economic Perspectives*, 29(2), 213–238.

Bonneau, J., Miller, A., Clark, J., Narayanan, A., Kroll, J.A. and Felten, E.W., 2015, May. Sok: Research perspectives and challenges for bitcoin and cryptocurrencies. In *2015 IEEE Symposium on Security and Privacy* (pp. 104–121). IEEE.

Botsman, R., 2017. *Who Can You Trust?: How Technology Brought Us Together—and Why It Could Drive Us Apart*. London: Penguin UK.

Burhanuddin, M.A., Mohammed, A.A.J., Ismail, R., Hameed, M.E., Kareem, A.N. and Basiron, H., 2018. A review on security challenges and features in wireless sensor networks: IoT perspective. *Journal of Telecommunication, Electronic and Computer Engineering (JTEC)*, *10*(1–7), pp.17–21.

Butun, I., Österberg, P. and Song, H., 2019. Security of the Internet of Things: Vulnerabilities, attacks, and countermeasures. *IEEE Communications Surveys & Tutorials*, *22*(1), pp. 616–644.

Campbell, A.T., Eisenman, S.B., Lane, N.D., Miluzzo, E., Peterson, R.A., Lu, H., Zheng, X., Musolesi, M., Fodor, K. and Ahn, G.S., 2008. The rise of people-centric sensing. *IEEE Internet Computing*, *12*(4), pp. 12–21.

Chaqfeh, M.A. and Mohamed, N., 2012, May. Challenges in middleware solutions for the internet of things. In *2012 International Conference on Collaboration Technologies and Systems (CTS)* (pp. 21–26). IEEE.

Chen, D.B., Zhang, N.L., Zhang, M.G., Wang, Z.H. and Zhang, Y., 2017, May. Study on remote monitoring system of crossing and spanning tangent tower. In *IOP Conference Series: Materials Science and Engineering* (Vol. 199, No. 1, p. 012038). London: IOP Publishing.

Cho, Y., Kim, M. and Woo, S., 2018, February. Energy efficient IoT based on wireless sensor networks. In *2018 20th International Conference on Advanced Communication Technology (ICACT)* (pp. 294–299). IEEE.

Das, M.L., 2015. Privacy and security challenges in internet of things. In *Distributed Computing and Internet Technology: 11th International Conference, ICDCIT 2015, Bhubaneswar, India, February 5–8, 2015. Proceedings 11* (pp. 33–48). Berlin: Springer International Publishing.

Feng, H. and Fu, W., 2010, October. Study of recent development about privacy and security of the internet of things. In *2010 International Conference on Web Information Systems and Mining* (Vol. 2, pp. 91–95). IEEE USA.

González, A., Ramos, J., De Paz, J.F. and Corchado, J.M., 2015. Obtaining relevant genes by analysis of expression arrays with a multi-agent system. In *9th International Conference on Practical Applications of Computational Biology and Bioinformatics* (pp. 137–146). Berlin: Springer.

Greiner, M. and Wang, H., 2015. Trust-free systems-a new research and design direction to handle trust-issues in P2P systems: the case of Bitcoin.

Gstrein, O.J., & Beaulieu, A. (2022). How to protect privacy in a datafied society? A presentation of multiple legal and conceptual approaches. *Philosophy & Technology*, 35(1), 3.

Hai, T.N., Van, Q.N., & Thi Tuyet, M.N. (2021). Digital transformation: Opportunities and challenges for leaders in the emerging countries in response to COVID-19 pandemic. *Emerging Science Journal*, 5(1), pp. 21–36.

Heer, T., Garcia-Morchon, O., Hummen, R., Keoh, S.L., Kumar, S.S. and Wehrle, K., 2011. Security Challenges in the IP-based Internet of Things. *Wireless Personal Communications*, 61, pp. 527–542.

Khalil, N., Abid, M.R., Benhaddou, D. and Gerndt, M., 2014, April. Wireless sensors networks for Internet of Things. In *2014 IEEE Ninth International Conference on Intelligent Sensors, Sensor Networks and Information Processing (ISSNIP)* (pp. 1–6). IEEE.

Kosba, A., Miller, A., Shi, E., Wen, Z. and Papamanthou, C., 2016, May. Hawk: The blockchain model of cryptography and privacy-preserving smart contracts. In *2016 IEEE Symposium on Security and Privacy (SP)* (pp. 839–858). IEEE.

Kumar, J.S. and Patel, D.R., 2014. A survey on internet of things: Security and privacy issues. *International Journal of Computer Applications*, *90*(11), pp. 20–26.

Leloglu, E., 2017. A review of security concerns in Internet of Things. *Journal of Computer and Communications*, *5*(01), p.121.

Lewenberg, Y., Sompolinsky, Y. and Zohar, A., 2015. Inclusive block chain protocols. In *Financial Cryptography and Data Security: 19th International Conference, FC 2015, San Juan, Puerto Rico, January 26–30, 2015, Revised Selected Papers 19* (pp. 528–547). Berlin: Springer.

Li, S., Xu, L.D. and Zhao, S., 2015. The internet of things: a survey. *Information systems frontiers*, *17*, pp. 243–259.

Miorandi, D., Sicari, S., De Pellegrini, F. and Chlamtac, I., 2012. Internet of things: Vision, applications and research challenges. *Ad Hoc Networks*, *10*(7), pp. 1497–1516.

Nian, L.P. and Chuen, D.L.K., 2015. Introduction to bitcoin. In *Handbook of Digital Currency* (pp. 5–30). Academic Press.

Nixon, P.A., Wagealla, W., English, C. and Terzis, S., 2004. Security, privacy and trust issues in smart environments. *Smart Environments: Technologies, Protocols, and Applications*, pp. 249–270, Wiley Online Library.

Ølnes, S., 2016. Beyond bitcoin enabling smart government using blockchain technology. In *Electronic Government: 15th IFIP WG 8.5 International Conference, EGOV 2016, Guimarães, Portugal, September 5-8, 2016, Proceedings 15* (pp. 253–264). Berlin: Springer.

Padmavathi, D.G. and Shanmugapriya, M., 2009. A survey of attacks, security mechanisms and challenges in wireless sensor networks. *arXiv preprint arXiv:0909.0576.*

Politou, E., Alepis, E., Virvou, M., Patsakis, C., Politou, E., Alepis, E., Virvou, M. and Patsakis, C., 2022. Privacy in ubiquitous mobile computing. *Privacy and Data Protection Challenges in the Distributed Era*, pp.93–131, Springer.

Rawat, P., Singh, K.D., Chaouchi, H. and Bonnin, J.M., 2014. Wireless sensor networks: a survey on recent developments and potential synergies. *The Journal of Supercomputing*, *68*, pp.1–48.

Raza, S., Helgason, T., Papadimitratos, P. and Voigt, T., 2017. SecureSense: End-to-end secure communication architecture for the cloud-connected Internet of Things. *Future Generation Computer Systems*, *77*, pp.40–51.

Roman, R., Zhou, J. and Lopez, J., 2013. On the features and challenges of security and privacy in distributed internet of things. *Computer Networks*, *57*(10), pp.2266–2279.

Rose, K., Eldridge, S. and Chapin, L., 2015. The internet of things: An overview. *The internet society (ISOC)*, *80*(15), pp.1–53.

Schurgot, M.R., Shinberg, D.A. and Greenwald, L.G., 2015, June. Experiments with security and privacy in IoT networks. In *2015 IEEE 16th International Symposium on a World of Wireless, Mobile and Multimedia Networks (WoWMoM)* (pp. 1–6). IEEE.

Shi, E. and Perrig, A., 2004. Designing secure sensor networks. *IEEE Wireless Communications*, *11*(6), pp. 38–43.

Sicari, S., Cappiello, C., De Pellegrini, F., Miorandi, D. and Coen-Porisini, A., 2016. A security-and quality-aware system architecture for Internet of Things. *Information Systems Frontiers*, *18*, pp. 665–677.

Tawalbeh, L.A.A. and Tawalbeh, H., 2017. Lightweight crypto and security. *Security and Privacy in Cyber—Physical Systems: Foundations, Principles and Applications*, pp. 243–261.

Thakur, J. and Kumar, N., 2011. DES, AES and Blowfish: Symmetric key cryptography algorithms simulation based performance analysis. *International Journal of Emerging Technology and Advanced Engineering*, *1*(2), pp. 6–12.

Walton, N. and Nayak, B.S., 2021. Rethinking of Marxist perspectives on big data, artificial intelligence (AI) and capitalist economic development. *Technological Forecasting and Social Change*, *166*, p. 120576.

Weber, R.H., 2010. Internet of Things–New security and privacy challenges. *Computer law & security review*, *26*(1), pp. 23–30.

Xu, L.D., 2011. Information architecture for supply chain quality management. *International Journal of Production Research*, *49*(1), pp. 183–198.

Xu, T., Wendt, J.B. and Potkonjak, M., 2014, November. Security of IoT systems: Design challenges and opportunities. In *2014 IEEE/ACM International Conference on Computer-Aided Design (ICCAD)* (pp. 417–423). IEEE.

Zhao, J.L., Fan, S. and Yan, J., 2016. Overview of business innovations and research opportunities in blockchain and introduction to the special issue. *Financial Innovation*, *2*, pp.1–7.

Index

B

C

D

E

F

G

H

I

K

L

M

N

O

P

Q

R

S